THE COLORADO DELTA

THE COLORADO DELTA

BY
GODFREY SYKES *Glenton*

Research Associate

Carnegie Institution of Washington

PUBLISHED JOINTLY BY

CARNEGIE INSTITUTION OF WASHINGTON

AND THE

AMERICAN GEOGRAPHICAL SOCIETY OF NEW YORK

1937

CARNEGIE INSTITUTION OF WASHINGTON
PUBLICATION No. 460

LORD BALTIMORE PRESS, Baltimore
PHOENIX ENGRAVING CO., New York
A. HOEN & CO., Baltimore

FOREWORD

Few detailed studies of great deltas have yet been made despite the importance of such investigations in biological and geological history. In North America only the deltas of the Fraser River in British Columbia and, seventy-five years ago, of the Mississippi have been the subject of monographic treatment. To this insufficient fund of knowledge the present study forms an important addition. It is based on personal observation extending over a period of forty-five years and provides a uniform and continuous survey of the rapid changes that have taken place in this area during that time.

Such a survey is all the more important because the Colorado River is unique among the major delta-forming rivers of the world in that it has alternately discharged its waters into land-locked basins and the sea. The well-known displacement of this nature that took place about thirty years ago, when the river's outlet was diverted from the Gulf of California to the Salton Sink, forms part of the discussion in the present volume. Among rivers discharging into tidal seas it is also unique as regards the effect of the tides on the sediments deposited at its mouth, owing to the exceptionally long and narrow shape of the Gulf and the consequent extreme tidal range at its head—more than three times that at the outlet of the Tigris-Euphrates, its nearest analogue, into the Persian Gulf.

The recent completion of Boulder Dam has inaugurated a new régime for the down-stream section of the Colorado. The violent fluctuations in water volume, both annual and seasonal, which are caused by the varied climatic environments from which the waters of the source streams and other tributaries are derived, will cease in the lower river. The delta, therefore, now enters a period of relative fixity. Channel changes will be very slight in the future. The vegetation will enter upon a cycle of development and an associational history that must of necessity be markedly different from that which it would have experienced had the river been allowed to flow naturally. The present is hence an opportune time to set forth what we know of the river's habits in the past.

My acquaintance with the delta region dates from 1902, when, as member of the staff of the New York Botanical Garden extending my earlier field work in the deserts of Arizona and Sonora and acting as advisor to the Carnegie Institution in the question of establishing a desert botanical laboratory, I visited the area under the guidance of Mr. Godfrey Sykes, of whose familiarity with the valley of the lower Colorado since 1890 I was well aware. Additional explorations were made with Mr. Sykes in 1904 and 1905, and since 1906, with the extension of the organization of the Desert Laboratory, which had been established at

Tucson, Arizona, in 1903, and the inclusion of Mr. Sykes and myself in its personnel, he and I have been closely associated in the physiographic and botanical study of the region. The botanical results are mainly laid down in *Carnegie Institution Publication No. 193,* published in 1914. With the present volume, which is based in part on special studies undertaken by Mr. Sykes under joint sponsorship with the American Geographical Society of New York from 1929 to 1934, the Carnegie Institution presents the physiographic results of its study of the Colorado delta.

D. T. MacDougal

ACKNOWLEDGMENTS

To Dr. John C. Merriam, president of the Carnegie Institution of Washington, the author wishes to express his grateful appreciation of the opportunity to bring to published fruition the results presented in this volume. For supporting interest in his studies for many years, of which the foreword is additional evidence, he is indebted to Dr. MacDougal, director of plant physiology at the Desert Laboratory during the years the author was privileged to be associated with him at that institution. To the companions of his early wanderings in the delta he has attempted to pay tribute in the body of the text (p. 37). Invaluable help in the compilation of factual data and through access to their files of maps and records has been rendered the author by his friend, Mr. H. M. Rouse, chief engineer, stationed in Calexico, of the Colorado River Land Company, and by the officials of the Imperial Irrigation District, with headquarters in Imperial, California.

In editing the volume the American Geographical Society of New York has likewise had the assistance of a number of individuals and institutions; to all of them grateful acknowledgment is hereby made. Professor F. B. Kniffen of Louisiana State University, whose papers on the natural and cultural landscapes of the Colorado Delta constitute one of the leading discussions of this area by a professional geographer, was good enough to read the whole book in proof and made comments from which the final work has benefited. In addition Chapters IX, X, and XI were submitted to Professor John B. Leighly of the Department of Geography of the University of California in Berkeley, who has specialized in stream dynamics. Certain of his observations are indicated in footnotes. Professor Frank Adams of the University of California and Miss M. A. Schnurr of the Bureau of Reclamation, respectively consulting engineer and secretary of the American section of the International Water Commission, United States and Mexico, furnished reports and maps of that commission. Information on the present status of railroads in the delta was kindly supplied by Mr. J. H. Dyer, vice-president in charge of operations, of the Southern Pacific Company, San Francisco.

CONTENTS

LIST OF ILLUSTRATIONS

LIST OF ILLUSTRATIONS

INTRODUCTION

The great canyons carved through many hundreds of miles of an elevated plateau region by the waters of the Colorado River have, because of their magnitude and impressive grandeur, captured the popular imagination, taken rank as one of the best known scenic features of the continent, and brought the name of the river itself into prominence throughout the world. Although not so spectacular as the visible result of the long-continued subtractive process by which the canyons have been excavated, the opposite phenomena, attendant on the disposal of the enormous volume of material removed from the vast voids themselves, are perhaps equally impressive and interesting to the geologist and physiographer.

Aside from the formidableness of the quantity of detrital matter now in evidence in the great deltaic areas about the mouth of the river, several factors have contributed towards making the manner and progress of its deposition and dispersal matters of scientific significance and importance.

The investigation into the bearing of several of these factors upon the process of dispersal and into other causes, contributing to the extent and progress of that dispersal as recorded in the following pages, covers a period of forty-five years of personal observation and traces the development of the lower river, firstly, through the concluding phase of a protracted static or stable period, and then through a great lateral swing or diversion towards the western and still unfilled portion of the area available for dispersal, to, finally, an approximate reversion, by a series of intermittent movements, to its former course down the eastern margin of the delta.

During the earlier years of the study, and notwithstanding a period of some former years of navigation and commercial activity upon the lower river, the region as a whole was still in the condition of an unexplored wilderness, practically unchanged by any form of human enterprise.

In the second period—that of the great westerly diversion of the river waters—the engineering operations incidental to the opening to settlement, as well as the earlier development, of the extensive irrigable areas of Imperial Valley precipitated the probably already inevitable break.

The third phase, which is still in progress, has been one of reclamation activity in certain sections of the delta within Mexican territory and of construction of protective levees; and the excavation of canals and diversion channels has at times accelerated and at others impeded natural channel movements and developments and the deposition of the burden of silt.

Scope of the Study

The results of the study and investigation of the region and its problems as herein presented can be summarized under the following headings:

(1) A brief historical record of early exploration and travel, with special reference to such expeditions as have left available maps, notes, or other data of scientific value or interest.

(2) An account of the development, progress, and ultimate cessation of navigation and associated commercial enterprise upon the lower river within the confines of the delta as presented in contemporary journals and official records and obtained during the earlier years of the investigation through numerous personal contacts with those who had actively participated in the river traffic and in other early commercial enterprises in the region.

(3) A digest and interpretation of the notes taken and of the facts and physiographic developments observed by the writer during the course of the study, from its inception in 1891 to the present time (1935).

(4) A description, based upon personal observation and information gained from officials of development companies operating in the delta and from articles in technical journals, of the various works and undertakings designed for the purposes of control, protection, or diversion which have influenced the movements of the river or the distribution of detrital matter during the present century.

Phases of the investigation which have developed into special studies fall under the following headings:

(a) The origin and physical characteristics of the detrital load carried by the river.

(b) The manner in which the detritus is carried to the delta.

(c) The effect of vegetation, evaporation, and other influencing factors upon the distribution and deposition of the detrital material.

This study has also embraced a consideration of the great tides of the Gulf of California and of the effect of tidal action upon the development of the subaqueous extension of the delta body and upon the floodplains surrounding the estuary.

Features which contribute materially to the complexity and interest of the problems presented by the Colorado Delta are

(1) The excessive variations, both annual and seasonal, in the volume of discharge of the Colorado, with two well-marked, although frequently irregular, periods of maximum flow during the year.

(2) The originally circumscribed and obstructed area available for deposition, into which the river has been forced to deliver its enormous load of detrital material.

(3) The inclusion within this area of a zone of faulting and seismic instability, and the strong probability that the whole region is still undergoing active diastrophic change and isostatic readjustment.

(4) The great tides and strong tidal currents of the Gulf of California, which attain their maximum intensity at the mouth of the river.

GENERAL CHARACTERISTICS OF THE AREA EMBRACED IN THIS STUDY

The Colorado Delta, as brought under consideration in the following studies, is an area of approximately 3,325 square miles, of which the predominant surface constituent is the detrital matter transported there by the waters of the Colorado (Pl. I). It is situated between 31° 3′ and 33° 45′ N. and 114° 25′ and 116° 18′ W., and, though somewhat irregular in outline, it takes the general form of a widely extended letter T with a broad short stem. The full spread of the two arms of the figure is nearly 200 miles, and its height, in a direction perpendicular to this major dimension, approximately 70 miles.

The " stem " constitutes the receiving bay and contains, almost axially, the crest of the flattened deltaic semi-cone and the present termination of the true channel of the Colorado. The right-hand, or northwesterly, arm of the T extends, with generally downward grades, to a level of about minus 275 feet in the bottom of the Salton depression, rising thence again approximately to sea level at the extremity of the arm (here known as the Coachella Valley) and the limit of the alluvial area. The left-hand, or southeasterly, arm is very irregular in outline and tripartite in form, extending down both shores of the Gulf of California and embracing another basin (the Macuata, or Laguna Salada, Basin) which also drops to slightly below sea level at its deepest point. Although physiographically a true portion of the deltaic area, this *bolsón,* or interior basin, is partially separated from it by the long " peninsula " formed by the Cocopa Mountains, by the volcanic outlier of the Cerro Prieto, and by their common encircling fringe of *bajadas,* or piedmont slopes.

Situated as is this great alluvial area of the delta amidst the gravels, sands, and *pedregales,* or stone pavements, of a typically desert region, its marginal line is at nearly all points quite clearly discernible. In sectors where the alluvial surface is subject to inundation and is covered by vegetation, the transition to the surrounding arid area is generally remarkably abrupt and very conspicuous. In others, in which the alluvial soil is strongly impregnated with alkaline substances deterrent to plant growth, the scanty xerophytic vegetation of the desert, venturing almost to the edge of the salt-laden soil, marks the marginal line with almost equal plainness.

The southeastern, eastern, and northeastern margins of the entire area are further accentuated by an almost continuous low terrace, or escarpment, exhibiting a generally wind-eroded face of gravel or coarse sand and marking the edge of the encircling mesa or sand-dune areas. The continuity of this rim is much broken around the northern, northwestern, and western margins by mountain salients, imperceptible bajada slopes, and other interruptive features, but it appears again in the southwest and continues, with some minor interruptions, by broad sand washes to the shore of the Gulf and the limit of the river-derived material in that direction.

While the region thus outlined constitutes the entire visible or subaerial portion of the area of deposition, there is strong presumptive evidence—supported by marine soundings, examination of bottom material from the Gulf, and a consideration of the tectonic frame in which the entire region is set—that the subaqueous portion of the accumulated detrital matter derived from the Colorado is much more extensive and that it extends as a gradually thinning prism or wedge at least as far as Cape San Lucas at the southern end of the peninsula of Lower California.

Within the area thus roughly delimited the Colorado River has delivered, during the period occupied by this study, a mass of detrital material substantially in excess of 6,500,000,000 tons, at rates varying from a few tons a day to more than a thousand tons per second.

The collection and interpretation of data concerning the amount, physical properties, and other characteristics of this material and concerning the sources from which it has been derived and the manner of its delivery, dispersal, and deposition within the deltaic area form the central theme of the technical portions of the present study.

PART I

HISTORY OF EXPLORATION
AND NAVIGATION

CHAPTER I

HISTORY OF EXPLORATION (1539-1858)

Francisco de Ulloa, 1539

Our earliest historical knowledge of any portion of the great region dominated by the Colorado River and its tributary streams begins in a fragmentary way within fifty years of the first landing by Columbus upon the shores of the Western Hemisphere, when, on September 27, 1539, Francisco de Ulloa, a captain and adventurer in the service of Cortés, found himself embayed at the head of the " Vermilion Sea " and surrounded by the shoals and muddy waters of the estuary. His visit was a brief one, as the object of his voyage of exploration was to examine the coast line towards the northwest, but both he and Francisco Preciado, who accompanied him, have left us records [1] of their discoveries and experiences which show, to those familiar with the delta, that they are those of actual observers.

The height of the tides and violence of the tidal currents impressed both, and the descriptions of the great expanse of muddy flats beyond which were distant mountains " the bases of which we could not see for the earth's curvature," and of the violence of the tides which caused " the sea to run with so great a rage into the land that it was a thing to be marvelled at, and with a like fury it turned back again with the ebb," would apply equally well today in this region of mirages, vast distances, muddy desolation, and tidal commotion.

Ulloa " took possession " of the region he so briefly visited and named it the " Ancón de San Andrés y Mar Bermejo " " because it is that color and we arrived there on the day of San Andrés."

The term *ancón,* as applied to the observed local conditions, has given rise to some speculation, but there seems to be a strong probability that it is intended to signify just such conditions as they found to exist at the time of their visit—the breaking in, or temporary flowing of water across the land—for Preciado states in his account of the voyage as recorded by Hakluyt : " The following day, the Captain and Pilot went up to the ship's top and saw all the land full of sand in a great round compass, and joining itself with the other shore, and it was so low that whereas we were a league from the same we could not well discern it and it seemed that there was an inlet of certain lakes whereby

---

[1] Specific references to the accounts of exploration cited in this chapter will be found in the bibliography at the end of volume, in the section " History of Exploration " under the explorer's name.

2

the sea went in and out." This is fully descriptive of the conditions observable at the river mouth today at times of the spring tides, and it appears that Ulloa's visit coincided with such a period.

They do not appear to have entered the river, although the map which is believed by Wagner [2] to illustrate their voyage up and down the Gulf shows two well-defined channels entering the sea. The map in question, which is a portion of the well-known Cabot planisphere in the Bibliothèque Nationale in Paris, shows little detail other than the coastline but seems to indicate that the two outlets to the river were slightly convergent in their courses as they approached the sea.

Ulloa discovered no evidence whatever of human occupation of the region, and, in fact, he remarks that in following the coast from " El Puerto de los Puertos " (identified with the present harbor of Guaymas) " We did not see a person or sign of any; I do not believe that such a land can be inhabited."

Hernando de Alarcón, 1540

Within a year of the time of Ulloa's visit, another Spanish explorer, Hernando de Alarcón, in the employ and under the instructions of Don Antonio de Mendoza, Viceroy of New Spain and political rival of Cortés, also reached the mouth of the river and, on August 26, 1540, began to work his way up it with two heavy ship's boats. The great tides and violent currents at the entrance were again found to be serious obstacles to navigation, but, having successfully overcome them, Alarcón ascended the river for a distance which he estimated at 85 leagues. The account of this memorable journey, translated from the explorers' original journals and dispatches, has been published many times, notably in the pages of Hakluyt, and is well known. It is interesting in its bearing upon the physiographic history of the delta, from the fact that it gives us definite information that a well-defined open channel to tidewater existed at that time, which was apparently found and ascended without any especial difficulty after the tidal hazards had been overcome.

Ulloa's " Ancón," on the other hand, left the question somewhat open to doubt, and neither he nor Preciado seem to have recognized any very definite connection between the troubled tidal waters in which they found themselves involved and the great river which they assumed was near at hand.

The chart which purports to illustrate the geographical discoveries of Alarcón bears the name of Domingo del Castillo (Fig. 1) and is to be found in Lorenzana's " Historia de Nueva España " (Mexico, 1770). According to this chart the main entrance to the river was the easterly

[2] Henry R. Wagner: Spanish Voyages to the Northwest Coast of America in the Sixteenth Century, San Francisco, 1929, Pl. 4, facing p. 298.

one, and there is no indication of islands or definite shoals blocking the mouth of the estuary, as do today Montague and Gore Islands with their associated sand and mud banks.

Melchior Díaz, 1540

Somewhat later in the autumn of 1540, Melchior Díaz, also a subordinate of Mendoza's, left the frontier settlement of Corazones with a small body of horsemen, for the purpose of carrying on some further exploration towards the northwest and of getting and keeping in touch with the Alarcón expedition. He traveled up beyond the head of the Gulf on its eastern side, and, reaching the banks of the river, he found a cached letter from Alarcón, announcing that he, with his boats, had already passed up stream. Díaz pushed on, still on the left bank of the river with which he was in contact; failed to find or hear further of Alarcón; crossed the river on rafts in spite of some opposition by the aborigines; and began his homeward journey down the right-hand, or western, bank. He was fatally wounded shortly afterwards, apparently somewhere down the western margin of the delta, and his companions, after again crossing to the Sonoran shore, made their way back to the outlying Spanish settlements.

Little local information is to be gathered from the brief account of the journey extant, except a mention of "burning sands" and other volcanic activity which was encountered somewhere to the west of the river. A group of hot springs and an associated area of heated ground which lies at the eastern base of Cerro Prieto may have attracted their attention. A homeward course passing close to these boiling mud-pots and skirting the edge of the dense vegetation of the lower ground would be the obvious one to have been followed by horsemen encumbered, as they appear to have been, by sheep and other domestic animals. No mention is made of the method whereby they succeeded in crossing the lower river or estuary when traveling homeward, but it is probable that they forded it or swam their stock somewhere near the head of tidewater and at a period of low tide.

Results of These Three Journeys

The geographical value of the accounts of these three pioneer expeditions to the head of the Gulf and lower river, fragmentary though they may be, is greatly enhanced by the perspective of nearly four hundred years which is given us of a region subject to rapid and extensive change.

The general topographical features appear to have been very similar to those of some of the more recent phases in the development of the delta. The river entered the Gulf directly by means of at least one channel passable for heavy ship's boats, and, as the contemporary maps seem to indicate, down the eastern margin of the more indefinite region of shoals, invasions of the flood tide, and uncharted openings which constituted the main part of the delta area. Tidal action was very pronounced and the tidal range great, and we are led to suppose that the river was fordable, or passable by some primitive method, by a cavalry troop at some point far down in the delta.

Despite the vigor with which these adventurers from New Spain had pushed forward into this new region the high hopes of discovering rich centers of population and opportunities for profitable intercourse or conquest were quickly abandoned with a realization that a few more tribes of naked savages were its only inhabitants. Navigation had been found to be hazardous, and the approach by land difficult and slow, and so further interest in northwestern exploration died out, and the reports of discovery in this direction were forgotten, as new fields for enterprise absorbed the exploratory energy of these restless frontiersmen.

So complete was the subsequent oblivion that the very fact that the Gulf was a *cul de sac* was soon lost sight of, and the entire region became involved, after a few decades, in that supreme and long continued mystery of Pacific geography, the Strait of Anian and Island of California myth.[3] Charts and maps were drawn and published during the following century and a half, which reflected various contemporary geographical theories concerning this forgotten corner of the western coast line of the continent but which give us no clue as to changes or developments taking place in the Colorado delta.

The latest map which seems to give evidence of having been directly inspired by the discoveries of Ulloa and Alarcón, with perhaps some additional local knowledge obtained during the intervening half century, was the one of New Granada and California by Wytfliet, published in 1597 (Fig. 2). As conceived and depicted by him, the head of the " Vermilion Sea " terminates in an extensive area of shoal, an island has appeared close to the " Cabo de + [Cruz] " of the Castillo chart at the eastern entrance to the estuary, and the great river which gives access to the " Seven Cities " of contemporary desire, but which bears no name on the map, is the most easterly one of the three entering the sea.

Although the Hondius conception of fourteen years later [4] also contains detail attributable to the recorded discoveries of seventy years before, its author has plainly been influenced by the growing Anian belief of his time and indicates a further extensive strait opening, or bay, to the northwest.

[3] Godfrey Sykes: The Isles of California, *Bull. Amer. Geogr. Soc.*, Vol. 47, 1915, pp. 745-761.
[4] The Hondius map of 1611 is reproduced in Sykes, *op. cit.*, p. 749.

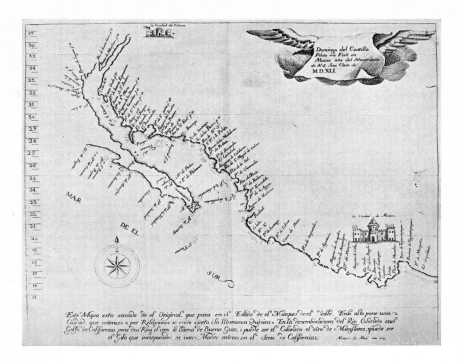

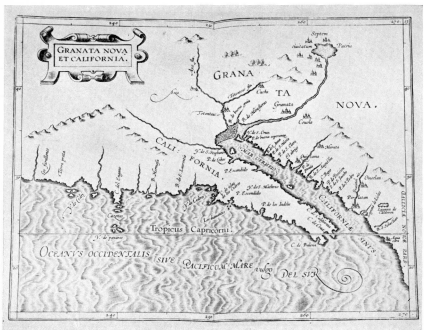

Fig. 1—Domingo del Castillo's map of the Gulf of California, which probably embodies the discoveries of the Alarcón expedition of 1540. As the inscriptions state, the map was copied in Mexico City in 1541 from the original in the possession of Cortés. It was engraved and published in Mexico City, 1770, in " Historia de Nueva-España escrita por su esclarecido conquistador Hernan Cortés, aumentada . . . . por . . . . Don Francisco Antonio Lorenzana," Mexico, 1770.

Fig. 2—Wytfliet's map of New Granada and California, 1597, showing the Gulf of California in more stylized form. It reflects the results of the Ulloa and Alarcón expeditions and probably of later voyages also, such as that of Vizcaíno in 1596. From " Descriptionis Ptolemaicae Augmentum, sive Occidentis Notitia," by Cornelius Wytfliet, Louvain, 1597. (Figs. 1 and 2 from the copies in the library of the American Geographical Society.)

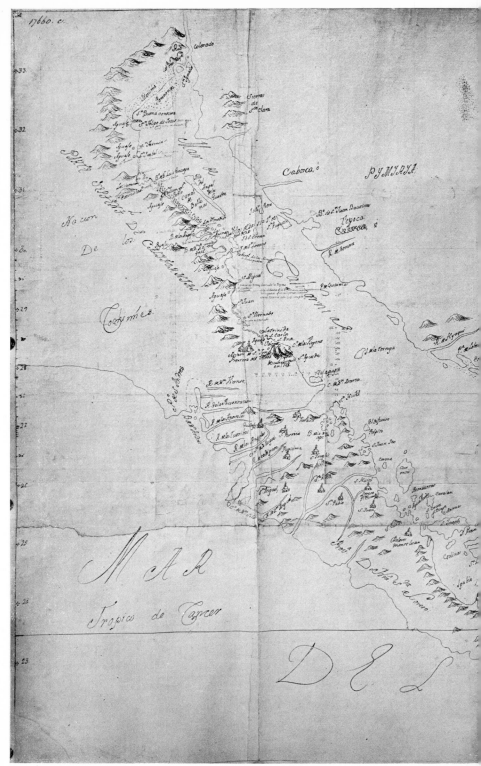

Fig. 3 (in two parts)—Manuscript map of the Gulf of California embodying, in the upper half of t
Gulf, the results of Father Consag's journey of 1746. The title reads: "Seno de Californias y su cos
oriental nuevamente descubierta y registrada desde el Cavo de las Vyrgenes hasta su termino que es el R
Colorado, por el Padre Fernando Consag de la Comp.ª de Jesus, Misionero de Californias, año de 1746

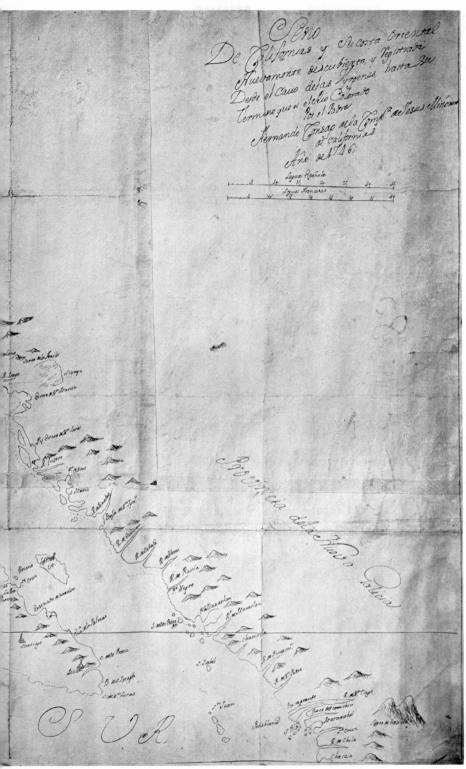

Seno
De Californias y su costa oriental
Nuevamente descubierta y registrada
Desde el Cauo delas Virgenes hasta su
Termino que es el rio Colorado
Por el Padre
Hernando Consag dela Comp.a de Jesus Misionero
de californias
Año de 1746

Leguas Españolas

Leguas Francesas

Provincia dela Nueva Galicia

S U R

om a MS. copy in the British Museum, Addington MSS. No. 17660.) The engraved map accompanying
account of Father Consag's journey published in Madrid in 1757 (see bibliography) is practically the
valent of this manuscript map north of the horizontal crease in latitude $27\frac{1}{2}°$, to which part, strictly, its
is alone applicable. The titles of the two maps, manuscript and engraved, are practically identical.

Fig. 4—Enlargement of the head of the Gulf on the preceding map. Some of the less legible inscriptions at the uppermost end read: on the three mountains at the mouth of the river, *los tres reyes;* on the marsh and mud-flats indicated by stippling, *marisma* and *pantanos;* following the name San Felipe de Jesus, *desde aqui esta* (?) *la barra* (*marea?*) *al oriente;* and following the name Santa Isabel farther south, *hasta* (?) *aqui llegan los placeres de perlas* (thus far extend the pearl grounds). The word *aguaje* affixed to small circular symbols along the western shore of the Gulf denotes wells or water holes. On the original map lines of sight on distant features are visible radiating from the southeastern end of Isla del Angel de la Guarda.

FATHER KINO, 1701-1702

Credit has been given, and quite justly so, to Father Eusebio Kino for finally exploding the misconception concerning California, by means of two journeys which he made into the delta in 1701 and 1702. Although these expeditions were detailed minutely in his diary, and his geographical discoveries recorded in his well-known map, the information he gives us about the actual physiographic condition of the delta is impressionistic rather than precise. He crossed the river in 1701 at an unidentified point some 25 or 30 miles below the Colorado-Gila junction and proceeded for a distance of three leagues in a westerly direction through fertile bottom lands, abundantly cultivated by the Indians. He re-crossed the river the following day and returned to his base camp at the junction. In March, 1702, he was again upon the banks of the lower Colorado and traveled down to tidewater upon the eastern side. The party was prevented from crossing the river again upon this occasion by the soft muddy ground, due either to tidal overflow or to recent floods from the river. Although the misconception concerning the insularity of California was at last removed by these two journeys into the delta, it is difficult to piece together the records of daily travel upon the unknown background of local conditions at that time.

FATHER CONSAG, 1746

A further period of more than forty years was to elapse before we are again able to see the region through the eyes and by means of the cartographic ability of a competent observer, the occasion and the man being a journey in small dugout canoes made by Father Ferdinand Konšćak, or Consag, up the western shore of the Gulf, through the estuary, and for some distance into the delta, in 1746.

A certain manuscript map (Fig. 3) now in the British Museum (Addington MSS. No. 17660), which purports to be Consag's personal delineation of the voyage, gives some interesting detail about the head of the Gulf and for some little distance inland (Fig. 4). An island appears in the fairway at the mouth of the river to which the name " San Ignacio " is given, and this, and other features of the estuary, are described in the explorer's diary, as translated by Monsignor M. D. Krmpotic. The account is realistic and furnishes some valuable geographical detail.

The following quotation begins when the canoes left San Felipe Point and were approaching the mouth of the river (pp. 75-79):

. . . . from north point of San Phelipe we had sight of another cape on this side, which appeared to form a large bay, but it was no more than appearance, there being no such bay, the point of the hill lying within the mouth of the river Colorado up the country.[5] . . . .

---

[5] An outlying spur of the Sierra de las Pintas, which gives this impression.—AUTHOR'S NOTE.

From this corner the shore is entirely level, marshy in several parts at spring tides, and in hard weather overflowed. All the way from San Phelipe to the river Colorado there is neither bay nor watering place.

10th [of July, 1746]. We made little progress this day, a strong northeast wind blowing down the shore, which was contrary to us. The points in that part running northeast and north-northeast form the strait closing here. At noon we got ashore with great difficulty, the water being shallow and a great sea running along this coast, which is extremely barren. The serrania or ridge of mountains is three or four leagues distant from the sea, and in some parts more. At night we came to a better shore, though with a high sea. The bottom here was found to be mixed with mud.

11th. Made but little way, and came to some red marshes, whence we concluded we were near the mouth of river Colorado or red river. We however continued our course till the evening, having endeavored to land in several places, but to no purpose; the fens not only hindered the boats from coming ashore, but likewise would not bear those who endeavored to cross them. Under this difficulty we came to an anchor facing an island, which forms a creek at the end of the strait in the form of a bow. The water even here differs from that of the sea, being of such a malignant quality as to carry off the skin whenever it touches, and all were wet with it except myself, and were accordingly afflicted with very painful inflammations in the most sensitive parts of the body, and which continued till the end of the expedition. . . . .

12th. Had a hard gale at south which separated the canoes. One endeavored several times, but without effect, to weather by taking the point of the fen, at which the island mentioned yesterday terminates. This canoe was very near foundering, the sea running very high; another canoe was [forced] to throw the greatest part of her lading overboard; but the other two, though the lading and people were wet, had the good fortune after weathering the cape to find a safe shore, being now beyond the fens.

13th. The canoe which had put ashore on the other coast, after making away the greatest part of the night, betwixt seven and eight in the morning arrived at San Bonaventura, where the lading was taken out and exposed to the air, and canoe grounded. Some people from the others came in search of her but were hindered by a creek.   *   *   *   *

18th. Went up the entrance of the river Colorado, and within it lies the before mentioned island, which is triangular, and divides the stream into two arms: one in California running northward, and the other of the opposite side running northwest. The people went ashore in the island, and found themselves betwixt two rapid currents, one of the river's ebb, and the other in the sea was flowing in with no less impetuosity, [so] that they had a very narrow escape but lost only some of their lading. The canoes removed to the coast of California as more secure, where in the night time they saw fires, but in the day time not one of the Indians showed himself.

19th. Continued the discovery of the river, but the currents here became so rapid that the canoes could not stem it with rowing, and they were obliged to have recourse to towing, by which they made a little headway; but as one canoe could not be towed for want of ropes it altered its course and steered for the other side, which was one of three islands discovered by our people on this occasion. On the 18th, they saw the first, which divides the river into two parts; the second, like the first, lies in the river's bed and faces it at a little distance; the third lies on the side of the other two, the river, dividing itself on the side of this lateral island towards the other shore, forms an arm, but so small that at a low water it is almost dry. This side of California, lying low, is overflowed by [the] Colorado so that all along to the foot of the mountains one sees pieces of trees, weeds and the like left there by its waters. Our people also saw here a kind of threshing floors, where the natives thresh a kind of seed like wheat but small as any [anise] seed.

20th. The canoes continued grounded, and the flood was attended with such rapidity and at the same time a very high sea that the canoe which had parted from the others was in greatest danger, and the smallest, which was now coming in, immediately made for it in order to save the people. . . . .

* * * *

23rd and 24th. During these days, though we endeavored to go forward, the wind and the current obliged us always to put back to the place whence we had come. This was an elbow near a great well [?] running eastward. The canoes were not able to make way. They who had been sent on the survey reported that the river took its course along the serrania on the side of California.

25th. The survey of the gulf or sea of California being carried to its utmost limit, we steered not directly to the harbor from whence we had sailed, but to take a view of some harbors, which, by reason of circumstance, had been omitted in our coming. Fifteen men traveled some way by land, took an exact account [i. e. made a survey] of the situation and course of the creek at the point of the fens, and it stands delineated in the map.

First let it be observed that in this [description of the] journey we have taken no notice of the latitude, this being exactly set down in the map of this survey.

Although there are a number of obscure points in this account of Father Consag's voyage of exploration, owing perhaps as much to difficulties of translation by one not familiar with local conditions as to ambiguities or omissions in the original narrative, it gives us valuable glimpses of the conditions in a portion of the delta and of the phase of development of the estuary and tidal channels existing at that time, such as are not at present available from any other source.

LIEUTENANT HARDY, 1826

A further period of almost exactly eighty years elapsed before Lieutenant R. W. H. Hardy, a British naval officer, reached the mouth of the Colorado from Guaymas in a small schooner named the *Bruja*. Although, as he confesses in his journal of the voyage, he was without chronometer, sextant, or even a nautical almanac, he had a chart of the Gulf and west coast of North America, published by Arrowsmith, of London, by means of which he found his way to the head of the Gulf. The Arrowsmith chart shows the junction of the Colorado and Gila Rivers as taking place at the head of a funnel-shaped estuary, approximately in latitude 32° 43′ N., the Colorado coming in from the north and the Gila from the east-northeast. This conception, derived perhaps from erroneous information obtained from pearl-divers, had crept into the supposed geography of the head of the Gulf after Consag's reconnaissance and was a source of much confusion to Hardy.

The *Bruja* reached the mouth of the river on July 20, 1826, and Hardy was astonished and somewhat disconcerted, as each previous navigator of the head of the Gulf had been, by the range and violence of the tides. He anchored in two fathoms of water, at what he judged to be about the last of the ebb, but grounded during the night and found

only two feet alongside before daylight. He describes the Californian
shore as being low, flat, and covered with drift, and the river mouth as
having three channels, divided by two low islands.

Taking advantage of the flood tide and a fair wind, he ran up the
estuary for a few miles, until the trend of the channel forced him to
beat round an obstructing point. The *Bruja* lost her way while going
about, was carried stern on into the bank, and broke her rudder. This
having been repaired, great difficulty was experienced in shipping it on
account of the rapidity of the tidal currents. Hardy remarks paren-
thetically, " But in the Rio Colorado there is no such thing as slack
water " (p. 329).

The period of the spring tides having now passed, the *Bruja* was
left aground while still in a disabled condition, through the neap tides,
and Hardy took the opportunity of doing some charting and exploring.
He found the eastern channel at the head of the estuary to be shallow
and, as he judged, of little importance. He therefore continued his
examination of the more promising western one by the use of his boat.
He found that this also shoaled about six miles above the junction, at
what he estimated to be latitude 32° 12' N. His longitude, which is
greatly in error in all his work about the river mouth, was put at
114° 24' W. Being surrounded by Indians whom he strongly suspected
of hostile intentions, he kept the *Bruja,* which continued aground for
eight days, in a state of armed readiness, and only allowed a few of
the Indians aboard at a time.

The large-scale plan of the estuary (Fig. 5) which appears in Hardy's
volume is probably fairly representative of conditions there at the time
of his visit, for, although he was obliged to rely upon his compass for
his bearings and upon dead reckoning and estimation for his distances,
he was a trained and practical navigator, and he had plenty of opportunity
during his enforced stay of twenty-six days within the mouth of the
river to check and verify his work.

The plan of the estuary, although it may be substantially correct, leaves
us in doubt as to the condition and alignment of the river through the
delta area. We have, however, corroborative evidence that a continuous
and practicable channel existed at about that time from the Colorado-
Gila junction, at about its present location in latitude 32° 45' N., to
tidewater.

JAMES PATTIE, 1827

Early in December, 1827, James O. Pattie and a party of trappers
who had spent some months in the Gila valley, began a journey down
the Colorado from the junction of the two streams, with the intention
of disposing of their peltry at the Spanish settlements which they
assumed existed somewhere in the delta. They built eight dugout

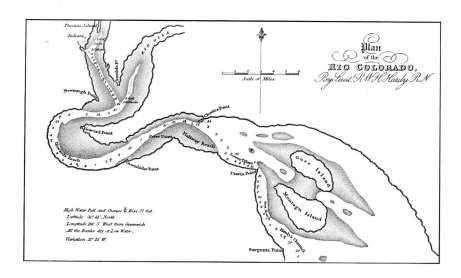

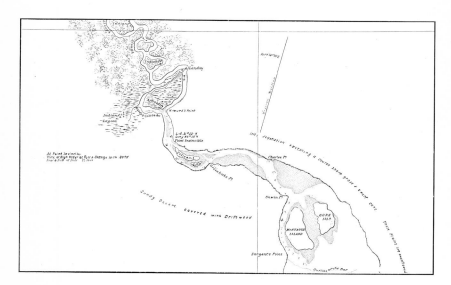

Fig. 5—Lieutenant Hardy's chart of the estuary of the Colorado River in 1826. (Reduced to 1 : 550,000 from map in his "Travels in the Interior of Mexico," London, 1829.)

Fig. 6—Lieutenant Derby's chart of the estuary in 1851. (Reduced section, 1 : 750,000, from map in his official report, 1852, cited in the bibliography.)

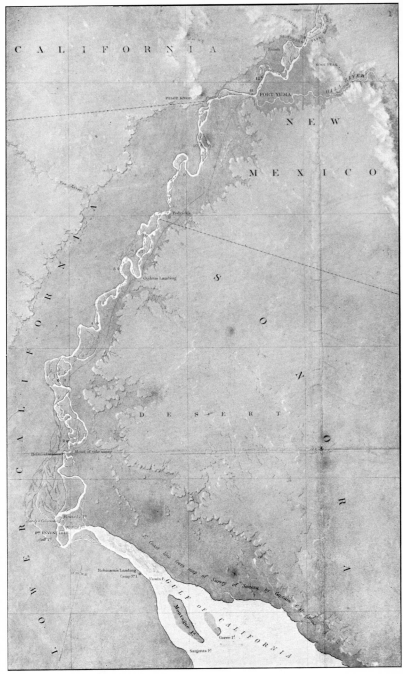

FIG. 7—Lieutenant Ives's map of the lower Colorado and estuary in 1858. (Reduced to 1:770,000 from map in his official report, 1861, cited in the bibliography.)

canoes, which were lashed in pairs, catamaran fashion, and the party continued to trap beaver as they floated down stream.

Pattie's personal narrative of his western wanderings was edited by Timothy Flint in 1831, shortly after his return to civilization, and it was re-edited by Dr. R. G. Thwaites in 1905.

The portion relating to the journey down the lower Colorado will bear partial quotation for the light it casts upon river conditions at that time (1831 edition, pp. 141-143, 150-151):

We started on the 9th, floating with the current, which bore us downward at the rate of four miles an hour. . . . We floated about 30 miles, and in the evening encamped in the midst of signs of beavers. We set 40 traps, and in the morning of the 10th caught 36 beavers, an excellent night's hunt. . . . The river, below its junction with the Helay [Gila], is from 2[00] to 300 yards wide, with high banks, that have dilapidated by falling in. Its course is west, and its timber chiefly cottonwood, which in the bottoms is lofty and thick set. The bottoms are from six to ten miles wide. The soil is black and mixed with sand, though the bottoms are subject to inundation in the flush waters of June. . . . .

We continued to float slowly downwards, trapping beavers on our way almost as fast as we could wish. We sometimes brought in 60 in a morning. The river at this point is remarkably circuitous, and has a great number of islands, on which we took beavers. Such was the rapid increase of our furs that our present crafts in a few days were insufficient to carry them, and we were compelled to stop and make another canoe. We had advanced then 60 and 70 miles from the point where we built the other canoes. We found the timber larger, and not so thick. . . . .

After a period of very successful trapping and some affairs with the Indians, the party found itself at a point which Pattie judged to be about 100 miles from the Colorado-Gila junction, where the river seemed to run upon a high ridge, from which, in their boats, they could see for a great distance across flats covered with mesquite and other low and scrubby trees. The land was found to be exceedingly marshy. This appearance, of a much extended view and a sense of being upon an elevation, is very noticeable in the Colorado delta as one emerges from the densely wooded region, in which the banks in the winter season are generally high and steep, into the comparatively open country in which they have dropped almost to the level of the water, and Pattie's description indicates quite clearly about where they were in their relation to tidewater and to the permanent geographical features of the lower delta region, and therefore helps toward an understanding of what the river alignment was at that time.

They were now within the influence of the tides and were much astonished and disconcerted at finding first a total cessation of the current and then a greatly augmented velocity.

"We floated on, having had a beautiful evening's run, and did not come to land until late; we then pitched our camp on a low point of land, unconscious, from our inexperience of the fact, that the water would return, and run up stream again." They were aroused by a rushing noise which they thought was an approaching rain and wind storm, but which proved to be the tidal bore. " Our camp was inundated from the river. We, landsmen from the interior, and unaccustomed to such movements of the water, stood contemplating with astonishment the rush of the tide coming in from the sea, in conflict with the current of the river. At the point of conflict rose a high ridge of water, over which came the sea current, combing down like water over a milldam."

The party continued their journey down towards the river mouth until the rough water which they encountered in the estuary convinced them that their makeshift craft were wholly unsuitable for a sea voyage. They, therefore, began to work their way back up stream, using the flood tides as far as they would serve, and then by means of rowing and towing. A sudden rise in the river and a current which they found themselves unable to stem obliged them in the end to abandon their canoes, cache their peltry, and strike out for the Spanish settlements on the west coast.

This overland journey proved to be both arduous and hazardous, from scarcity of water and heavy and difficult country, but the narrative still gives some indication of where they were and, therefore, of the alignment of the river. They were apparently well above tidal influence when they abandoned their canoes, for the water was fresh ; they were within one and a half day's travel, through heavy brush, of open country bordering the Cocopa Mountains, which can probably be most reasonably identified as the Volcano Lake area (Fig. 28), and they could also sight some portion of the main Peninsular Range, which had snow upon it. Such a view is possible across the low ranges or ridges which connect the two higher portions of the Cocopas.

Men encumbered as the members of this party were, and in poor condition for foot travel, as Pattie states was the case, would be unlikely to accomplish more than three or four miles of actual distance through the heavy vegetation which is so characteristic of this portion of the delta within the time given, so that it is a fair inference that the channel down which they had trapped and up which they had attempted to return was at least well over towards the western margin of the area between the Sonoran mesa escarpment and the bajadas of the Cocopas. Furthermore, as beaver had been found to be so plentiful and well established in the waters in which they had been able to trap on their downward voyage, the alignment of that portion of the river must also have been essentially the same for some considerable period.

The available evidence seems to indicate, therefore, that the main channel between the junction with the Gila and the Gulf swung far over towards the possible western limits of its meandering for a period of many years, at least inclusive of the observations of Consag, Hardy, and also, inferentially, of the expedition of the Pattie party.

LIEUTENANT DERBY, 1850-1851

Acting under instructions from Colonel Hooker, Assistant Adjutant General of the Third Division, U. S. Army, Lieutenant G. H. Derby of the Topographical Engineers reached the mouth of the Colorado on December 24, 1850, in the U. S. transport schooner *Invincible,* of 120 tons, for the purpose of making a reconnaissance survey of the head of the Gulf and of as much of the lower river as he might find it to be practicable to examine.

His instructions were detailed and explicit. " You will fix by observations and deductions as far as possible all of the points about the head of the Gulf of California important to the navigation of the Colorado. You will record the soundings when they may have been procured, especially at the entrance of the river and in its course upward. You will ascertain as far as practicable the rise and fall of the tide, and the time of high water at the full and change of the moon at the mouth of the river. Likewise record the character and topography of the country at the head of the gulf and the river, as far as falls within your observation, and make a sketch of all the coast and shores in that neighborhood ; and procure all such other information as may be of use to the service and the public generally."

Derby was equipped with the necessary instruments for establishing his positions and had an assistant with him whose function it was to make the necessary observations. An important object of the expedition was to establish a sea connection with, and deliver rations and other supplies to, the military post which had already been built upon a small isolated hill almost directly opposite the mouth of the Gila. Major S. P. Heintzelman had been placed in command of the small garrison quartered there, and supplies had hitherto been brought overland from San Diego. It had been found to be very costly, and in fact almost impracticable, to fulfil the needs of the post by means of freighting across the mountains and desert, and so it was hoped to open up the river route through Mexican territory for both military needs and for the convenience of the emigrant trains which were already crowding the overland routes to California.

The British chart by Imray, which Derby states that he used in his navigation of the Gulf, is based entirely upon Hardy's map for detail about the mouth of the river ; and he also had in his possession a copy of Hardy's book.

The *Invincible* was worked into the estuary through the western channel, which Derby sounded and charted. Rounding Unwin Point (Fig. 6) and crossing over to the northeast shore, he found that the channel continued on that side for a distance of about six miles and then bore off to the southwest towards Hardy's " Greenhithe Point " (Fig. 5), much as Hardy had found it twenty-five years previously.

The similarity between the two surveys ended here, however, as Hardy's continuous and definite main channel around the bight which he had named Howards Reach was encroached upon by shoals and two new islands, and another, partially developed minor channel appeared close to the northern shore. Farther up still the two surveys became quite irreconcilable and, granting that both were substantially correct at the times at which they were made, indicate that in the intervening quarter of a century some of the extensive changes had taken place which have since been discovered to be so common in the vicinity of the junction of the Colorado and the Hardy.

Derby soon found that it was impracticable, in the existing state of the river, to work the *Invincible* as far up as Hardy had taken the *Bruja*. Her draft was lightened to 7 feet, but inadequate ground-tackle and the poor holding ground to be found in the tidal channels of the estuary caused her to drag her anchors and drift ashore or on to shoals upon several occasions. The " bore " was experienced on January 2, 1851, and is described in the log as follows: " At 12 h. 35 m. flood came up in a ' bore ' with a wall about four feet high, velocity five miles per hour by log; raised anchor and succeeded in beating up about three-quarters of a mile, when we anchored." In endeavoring to carry out the instructions that had been given him, he then continued his survey with a boat, and discovered that the western channel, which Hardy had managed to ascend for several miles with his vessel, was now nothing more than a " slough without current."

Hearing nothing from Major Heintzelman, commanding the post at the mouth of the Gila, he at length determined to proceed up stream with his longboat in order to establish communication with him and at the same time continue his survey of the river channel. His own recon-naissance work terminated, however, some twenty-seven miles above his vessel, when he met the major coming down the river in a light boat with a party of five men. As this party had made a rapid meander survey of the channel as they had come down stream, Derby did not consider it necessary to continue his own work any farther, and he returned to the *Invincible* and shortly afterwards left the mouth of the river on his homeward voyage. The results of the Heintzelman survey were incorporated in Derby's map and published with his report.

Major Heintzelman, 1851

Major Heintzelman's account of his trip is embodied in a letter to Major Emory, which was published in the *San Francisco Daily Herald* of October 22, 1851.

Dear Major:

An Indian brought me a letter from Lieut. Derby, informing me that the U. S. transport schooner *Invincible* was at anchor in the Colorado 30 miles above the mouth. . . . I left our camp at the junction [Colorado-Gila], in a surf boat, with five men, on the 12th of January, and met the ship's boat on the morning of the 14th, 27 miles from the vessel. . . . They having started four hours earlier from her than I did from camp, you may judge the difficulty in ascending the river: they turned back and in five hours we were all on board.

From the junction to Fort Defiance [close to the Pilot Knob elbow of the river] the river is from 200 to 250 yards wide; below it varies from ½ mile to 1¼ mile between the banks—generally less than a mile. . . . At the low stage the water seldom covers more than half this space, and frequently not 200 yards, the channel crossing and recrossing the bed in the most capricious manner; the whole width being filled with shifting sand. . . . There are but few snags. . . . Below the junction, at the lowest stage, I found nowhere in the channel less than four feet; but it is narrow and crooked and the water rapid. . . . . The tide rises from 12 to 15 feet [evidently at the point at which the vessel lay] and flows with great velocity; there is no slack water at the end of the ebb, and the spring tide comes in with a wave two or three feet high, breaking and foaming, and in four hours ebbs again.

The river bottom is several miles wide and covered with willow, cottonwood, and mesquite, with the usual underwood and grass. . . . . The highest water is in June and July and the banks generally overflowed. . . . . This year, owing to little rain and snow west of the dividing ridges between the Rio Grande and the Colorado and its tributaries, the annual rise will not be so great as usual by several feet.

The *Invincible* landed a few stores for us at Howard's Point and I had them waggoned to the Post. . . . . The road is about 75 miles and the sand deep, with some grass and plenty of water.[6]

The desert touches the river at Ogden's Landing. . . . . The sketch [map of the river] from the junction to the figure "93" a few miles above the point called by Lieut. Derby "Heintzelman's Point" is from my notes, the lower part from Lieut. Derby's. . . . . My reconnaissance is necessarily very imperfect, as I had also to steer the boat. . . . . The whole distance from the junction to the mouth is about 150 miles. . . . . The junction is an important point—a military post there can be supplied by the river, either by anchoring a store ship in the mouth and running a small stern-wheel steamer, not drawing more than 2½ to 3 feet of water; or, in June and July, when a boat drawing 6 or 8 feet can ascend without difficulty. The road across the desert is entirely too expensive.

Taken in conjunction with Lieutenant Derby's survey and map of the estuary, this description and channel meander of Major Heintzelman's gives a clear picture of the condition and alignment of the main channel of the river at that time.

The general trend from Pilot Knob to the head of tidewater, was substantially the same as that shown in the Ives map of seven years later, but the region about the Colorado-Hardy junction, which Hardy, Derby, and afterwards Ives, all examined closely and surveyed in detail, was undergoing rapid and extensive change. The western entrance to the estuary—that between the Lower Californian shore and Montague Island—was the deepest and most favorable for navigation, and the tidal channels from Montague Island to Greenhithe Point (of both Hardy and Derby) were much the same as Hardy had found them.

---

[6] This route, which was afterwards developed into the only practicable land route between the mouth of the Gila and the sea, followed the edge of the Sonoran Mesa as far south as the salient afterwards occupied by the headquarters of the Colonia Lerdo, but from that point to its termination at tidewater was rather indefinite, dependent upon the stage of the river and condition of the tidal flats.—AUTHOR'S NOTE.

LIEUTENANT IVES, 1857-1858

The establishment of the military post at the Colorado-Gila junction, the increasing tide of emigrant trains crossing the river at that point, and the development of some mining activity in the lower Colorado valley and surrounding hills were collectively the cause of opening a military and trade route to the outside world through the delta region during the early 1850's, in preference to the more direct but practically slower and more expensive and uncertain one across the Californian mountains and deserts.

Navigation of the river had been developed in a rather haphazard way in response to these several calls upon it during the earlier years of the 1850-1860 decade, as will appear in a subsequent chapter; but the need began to be felt of more precise and detailed information about the region in which the commercial activity was taking place.

As a result of many requests and some political pressure from the interests then engaged in the rapidly increasing transportation business, Lieutenant Joseph C. Ives, of the Corps of Topographical Engineers, was directed by the Secretary of War in the summer of 1857 to organize an expedition, under the direction of the Office of Explorations and Surveys, for the purpose of ascertaining how far and to what extent the Colorado River was available for steamboat traffic, and for charting and mapping the approaches, channels, and the surrounding regions along its course. The work upon the river was to be done, as far as practicable, during the low-water season in order to observe the minimum conditions of discharge and depth.

In organizing the plans for the work it was found that no steamer was available locally for carrying on the exploration, and Lieutenant Ives therefore ordered an iron-hulled, shallow-draft, stern-wheeled boat from a firm of shipbuilders in Philadelphia. She was about 50 feet in length, 14 feet beam, and 3½ in depth amidships, and was designed and built in sections, for ease of transportation. Disassembled, she was shipped to San Francisco by way of the then recently constructed Panama Railroad and ultimately reached the mouth of the Colorado on the schooner *Monterey* at the end of November, 1857.

The river was entered by means of the channel between Montague and Gore Islands, as the western one used by Derby seven years previously was found to have shoaled and become impassable at the low-water stage. A heavy bore was encountered the night after the *Monterey* was anchored in the estuary, and the tidal movement was found to be so violent that it was determined to take advantage of the approaching period of the spring tides to float her at high water into a small slough or creek (at a point which was then, and subsequently, known as Robinson's Landing), unload the hull and machinery of Lieutenant Ives's little steamer on to the surrounding mud, and refloat her at the next spring tide.

This plan was successfully carried out, and in the meanwhile the work of reassembling the steamer was pushed forward with all possible speed. The *Monterey* was released from her muddy cradle on December 14 and discharged the rest of her cargo, chiefly military supplies for the post, while anchored again in the stream, and shortly afterwards left on her homeward voyage.

Shipbuilding operations were completed by December 30, and the little vessel, now christened *Explorer,* was successfully launched the same night. It had been found necessary to make some changes in her as the rebuilding proceeded. As she was so shallow amidships, and without a deck, it was feared that the heavy boiler with which she had been equipped by her designers would soon cause her to buckle and break her back, as a result of the constant grounding which was anticipated in working her way up the uncharted river. The rather clumsy expedient was therefore adopted of bolting two heavy timbers lengthwise, beneath her bottom, to stiffen her hull. These, of course, added greatly to the difficulty of handling her in shoal water and swift current and seem to have been the source of much later trouble. Another defect which had been discovered when her engines had been put into place was that the slots cut into her transom in order to admit the connecting-rods which actuated her wheel were entirely too deep and would have caused her to fill when under way. It was found necessary, therefore, to block up her engines several inches higher and to fit iron patches over the lower ends of the slots.[7]

The journey up the river was commenced on the last day of 1857 and nearly terminated in disaster before the head of the estuary was reached. A sudden squall and a short choppy sea almost caused the open and heavily built boat to founder. The narrow river above was reached next day and the work of mapping it was begun. The river was found to be at an extremely low stage and much trouble was experienced with grounding on bars. Fort Yuma was reached by Ives on January 7, 1858, he having left the boat fifty miles below and come in overland. The *Explorer* arrived on the 9th and at once began her preparations for continuing the survey up stream from that point.

The topographic and hydrographic work accomplished in the delta had, therefore, been completed within a period of about ten days, and, although it had been confined to the main navigable channel and its closely associated sloughs and backwaters, it was even so admittedly incomplete in many respects. In the hydrographic report which is appended to the general account of the exploration, Lieutenant Ives states that much of the information contained in it was obtained from the steamboat captains and pilots who had already had several years' experience upon the river.

[7] It was the discovery of these two patches, still riveted to the remains of the transom of an iron hull which was found almost buried in the eastern part of the delta in 1931, which made certain its identity as Ives's *Explorer*. See also pp. 90-92 and **Fig. 11.**

This report is lucid and concise and may be usefully quoted from as furnishing a composite picture of what was known about the delta at that time (Part 2: Hydrographic Report, pp. 8-9).

Abreast of Ship Rock [Hardy's Clarence Island] I found between seventeen and eighteen fathoms. Lieutenant Derby states that in 1850 he found the depth in the same locality twenty fathoms. The bottom being remarkably flat and uniform, it would appear from this that the Gulf towards its head is rapidly filling up.

Beyond the rock the shores on both sides come in sight, and the Gulf narrows until it is only four or five miles in breadth. The water gradually shoals to two and a half or three fathoms and becomes red and turbid. The bottom is a soft ooze, feeling like grease to the fingers. Two islands, Montague and Gore Islands, and a bar twelve or fifteen miles wide, obstruct the mouth of the river. In the channels across the bar there are only ten feet of water. In the channel of the river, above the bar, as far as the head of tide water, the depth varies from twelve or fifteen to thirty-five feet. . . . .

It is about one hundred and fifty miles by the river from the head of the Gulf to Fort Yuma, though only half that distance in a direct line. Concerning no particular locality can any special information be given that would be of value to the navigator. The shifting of the channel, the banks, the islands, and the bars is so continual and so rapid that a detailed description, derived from the experiences of one trip, would be found incorrect, not only during the subsequent year, but perhaps in the course of a week, or even a day. A few facts of a general character can alone be stated.

The width of this portion of the river varies from one-eighth to half a mile. The course is exceedingly tortuous. The depth in the channel is from eight to twenty feet, but bars are frequently encountered where there are not more than two feet of water. The current, during the low stage of the river, which is from October till the early part of May, has an average velocity of two and a half miles an hour. In some of the bends it is perhaps a mile an hour swifter. The period of highest water is in the early part of July, when the velocity is increased to five or six miles. The average height is then ten feet greater than during the summer months, but the depth is not in all places proportionally increased. New bars at once form when the river begins to rise, and the obstructions to navigation, though not so numerous, are still encountered.

No rocks are met with below Fort Yuma. The bed of the river is composed of quicksand and soft clay. The bars are yielding, and any agitation upon their surface causes them speedily to wash away.

The above description, although it was primarily hydrographic and compiled chiefly from data furnished by the river men, contains practically all that was known at that time concerning the entire delta region. This great area, bounded by a sandy desert upon the east and distant ranges of mountains upon the west, contained merely, as far as any precise geographical knowledge went, a stretch of tortuous and uncertain river, which must be approached and entered through violent tidal turmoil, running through an indefinite region of swamps and jungles. Even the fact that a great portion of the low ground which, as was beginning to be surmised, was susceptible to flooding by the river lay much below sea level was only beginning to be understood and apppreciated.

The map published with the Ives report (Fig. 7) shows only the main navigable channel and the closely associated backwaters and sloughs as observed during the rapid upward voyage from tidewater to Fort Yuma. A shaded margin, roughly parallel to the river and about 8 miles to the west, marks the edge of the low land in that direction. No intervening detail is shown. Although obviously incomplete, this map was generally accepted during the ensuing thirty years as representing the entire drainage system of the delta and was used as the basis of many other published maps embracing the region.

CHAPTER II

NAVIGATION ON THE LOWER RIVER (1852-1876)

Although the establishment of a military post at the head of the delta had been primarily a matter of military expediency and the development of transport facilities upon the lower river a matter of military necessity, it was soon realized by California merchants and other business interests that virgin fields for commercial enterprise could likewise be reached through this gateway. California newspapers were eager to report the various developments incidental to the establishment of the river service, and it is almost solely in the pages of these contemporary journals that any record of the earlier phases of the distinctive form of navigation which the regional conditions necessitated has been preserved.

BEGINNING OF COMMERCIAL NAVIGATION

As recorded in the *San Diego Herald* under date of February 3, 1852, commercial navigation of the Colorado may be considered to have originated with the clearing of the United States transport schooner *Sierra Nevada* for the head of the Gulf and the mouth of the Colorado on January 17, 1852. The voyage was undertaken " to ascend if practicable to the mouth of the Gila. Should this be found impossible, her cargo will be carried up in flatboats provided for that purpose. A large military post will be established permanently at the junction of the Gila and Colorado, on the western side, and a ferry established, completing the connection through from Santa Fe and affording protection to the numerous bodies of emigrants by that route."

On April 3, 1852, the following news item appears in the same paper : " The *Sierra Nevada* arrived at the mouth of the Colorado on February 17. It took nine days to assemble the flatboats. The boatmen on their first trip up the river were very unfortunate. One boat was swamped— boat and cargo entirely lost. The contractors have experienced very great and unexpected difficulties on the river. Major Heintzelman's command uses up supplies about as fast as they can be delivered, and it is not expected that full delivery of supplies will be completed before the first of July."

An official report issued on April 17 says : " The schooner transport *Sierra Nevada* is moored in the Colorado at a point 70 miles from Camp Yuma. A thorough examination of the river has been made, and all parties are satisfied that it can be safely navigated with small steamers such as are used on the Ohio, which will make it possible to supply a line of posts on the Gila."

The Gila River still formed the boundary between United States and Mexican territory, as the Gadsden Purchase agreement had not yet been signed. Besides that occupied by the military camp upon the Californian side the only other high ground near the Colorado-Gila junction—that which has since formed a part of the townsite of Yuma—was also within the Mexican area. Commercial development was afterwards centered upon and about the three isolated hills and the edge of a sandy mesa of which this solid ground consisted, as also was the civilian settlement.

Supplying the Military Post

The task of supplying even the needs of the military post was soon found to be quite a serious one, because of the difficulties encountered in the navigation of the river, and in June, 1852, a contract was entered into by the military authorities, as reported in the *San Diego Herald* of June 28, with " a party in Benicia, to deliver supplies to Camp Yuma *via* the Gulf and river, at $120.00 per ton for the first cargo and $50.00 per ton for all that may be needed thereafter during the balance of the year."

This transaction was the initial step taken towards the organization of the Colorado Steam Navigation Company, and the contractors were Messrs. Hartshorn, Wilcox, and Johnson.

Continuing the quotation: " The contractors design taking a steam-tug down with them from San Francisco to tow their lighters up the Colorado, which is said to be navigable, for vessels drawing five feet, to within a few miles of the post even at the lowest stages of the river."

In the development of these amended plans the United States transport schooner *Capacity,* which arrived at the head of the Gulf early in the winter of 1852-1853, had on board, in sections, the small shallow-draft, side-wheel steamer *Uncle Sam,* designed for work on the river. She was 65 feet in length, 14 to 16 feet in beam (the various accounts of her dimensions do not agree on this point), with a depth of hull of $3\frac{1}{2}$ feet amidships, and she was planned to work on a $2\frac{1}{2}$ foot draft. Her boiler was a 20 horsepower locomotive type, and she proved to have displacement enough to be capable of supporting 25 tons of freight on a draft of 22 inches. She proved to be very deficient in power, and was doubtless greatly handicapped by the fact that her pilot and crew were entirely unfamiliar with the problems and difficulties to be encountered in handling a power vessel on the Colorado, and so, notwithstanding the low-water season and easy river conditions at the time of her maiden voyage, she was unable to deliver her freight at the post, even with a partial cargo.

The uncertain channels and shifting bars in the great bend of the river above Pilot Knob were always difficult to navigate, especially during periods of low water, and they appear to have constituted an insuperable obstacle to this lightly powered boat, for she is reported never to have succeeded in getting farther up stream than the Pilot Knob landing. The first solid ground on the western bank was reached at that point by boats coming up from the Gulf, and a practicable wagon road existed between there and the post at most stages of the river.

The *Uncle Sam* was moored at the Pilot Knob landing during the following summer, and was being cleared out in order to make some changes in her power equipment, when she was accidentally allowed to fill and sink, through the removal of a bilge plug. Her hull was never recovered.

Navigation Before the Civil War

The next steamer to be put into service was the *General Jessup*. She was also a side-wheeler, but larger and more powerful than the *Uncle Sam*. Her dimensions were: length, 104 feet; beam, 17 feet, and, over the paddle-boxes, 27 feet. She was powered with a 70 horsepower engine and was designed to handle a load of 60 tons on a two-foot draft. Her maiden voyage from the mouth of the river was made on a 16-inch draft, with a load of 37 tons. She reached Camp Yuma early in February, 1854, this being the first successful and complete voyage by a powered vessel to the mouth of the Gila and head of the delta. A boiler explosion took place aboard her on August 20 of the same year, when she was moored at Ogden's Landing on the Sonoran side of the river, killing her engineer and wounding two other men. She was repaired, however, and again placed in service before the end of the year.

River traffic was by this time increasing very rapidly, as, in addition to the military needs of the river posts, there were to be satisfied the requirements of the emigrants who were crossing in great numbers at the mouth of the Gila and had to depend largely upon the post and the sutler's store for their supplies. The owners of the navigation company therefore placed another steamer in service. She was a stern-wheeled boat—a type far better suited for handling in the narrow bends of the lower Colorado—somewhat larger than the *General Jessup* and very heavily engined. Her hull was framed in a San Francisco yard, and she was assembled and engined at the mouth of the river. She was christened *Colorado* and was afterwards identified as *Colorado No. 1* to distinguish her from a later boat to which the same name was given. She made her first upward voyage to Camp Yuma in May, 1854.

The next steamer to navigate the river was the small iron stern-wheel surveying boat *Explorer* (Fig. 8), with which Lieutenant Ives made his examination of the Colorado in the winter of 1857-1858, as related in the preceding chapter. She was sold out of the government service to private owners after her one and only voyage upstream to the mouth of

FIG. 8—The *Explorer*, the vessel of the Ives expedition, which was assembled in the estuary. (From the frontispiece in Ives's report.)

FIG. 9—The *Cochan*, a stern-wheel steamer of the Colorado Steam Navigation Company, rebuilt at Yuma in 1893 from the *Gila* (launched in 1868), typical of the steamers handling the trade of the lower Colorado River in the last third of the nineteenth century.

Fig. 10—The remains of the hull of the *Explorer*, discovered in 1930 in an open flat surrounded by thickets in the old meander zone of the Colorado, near the abandoned Ockerson Levee in about 32°20′S. (See Pl. I and pp. 90-92.)

Fig. 11—Detail of the hull of the *Explorer* showing the iron patch covering the slot in the starboard side of the vessel's transom that made positive the identification of the hull. (See pp. 21 and 91.)

the canyons less than six months after she was launched from the slough at Robinson's Landing. She did very little work under private ownership (see below, pp. 91-92), and she had proved herself to be unwieldy and hard to handle, with the two massive wooden bilge-keels with which Ives had equipped her beneath her bottom.

Business was very prosperous upon the river during the years immediately preceding the Civil War, and several additions were made to the fleet of steamers and barges owned by the Colorado Steam Navigation Company. Another stern-wheeler, the *Cocopah,* the hull of which was also framed in a San Francisco yard, was built and launched in a slough on the northern shore of the estuary, and she was shortly followed by the *Colorado No. 2,* which was built upon the river bank opposite Camp Yuma.

ESTABLISHMENT OF SHIPYARD ON THE ESTUARY

The rough usage to which these pioneer boats were subjected was exceedingly hard upon hulls and superstructures. They were constantly being worked over bars in making crossings, and butts were started and planking torn loose by the heavy impacts against banks, shoals, and occasional snags. The consequence was that hulls were condemned, rebuilt, or re-engined, and boilers and engines were placed in new boats as the strenuous service made such changes necessary. Names of obsolete or condemned boats were transferred to new ones under very lax rules of registration in ways which make their identification at the present time exceedingly difficult.

A small, but usefully equipped shipyard, with storage and supply warehouses, was established some distance up a deep and convenient slough, named Shipyard Slough, near the Sonoran shore anchorage. By building levees round the area used, excavating a tidal basin for repair work on hulls, and by doing some channel clearing and straightening, this shipyard was gradually developed into an almost indispensable feature of the river trade. It also became the ultimate resting place of most of the worn-out and superannuated river craft. The great tidal range made the beaching of old steamers and barges a simple matter, when they were condemned and broken up, and it also facilitated the operation of the tidal basin as a dry dock when required. Puerta Isabel was the name given to this collective enterprise. Most of the actual building of new steamer and barge hulls was, however, carried out upon launching ways constructed on the river bank opposite Camp Yuma, at the foot of the main street of the infant settlement which in time developed into the town of Yuma, but which was at first known as Colorado City.

Navigation During and After the Civil War

The outbreak of the Civil War and the withdrawal of Federal troops from the frontier and river posts, with the substitution of the California Volunteers as garrisons, made heavy calls upon the navigation company, but, notwithstanding the general national disorganization due to war conditions, the river fleet was maintained at a high point of efficiency and in successful competition with the more directly routed overland freight traffic from the Pacific Coast.

River traffic was further expanded during the early sixties by the development of some upstream business to fill the needs of various small mining communities and other settlements. The most important feature, however, was still the handling of the incoming freight between the mouth of the river and Yuma, and the storage and distribution of government and commercial supplies at and from that point.

Early in 1867 the active fleet of the Colorado Steam Navigation Company consisted of the *Colorado* of 70 tons, the *Cocopah* of 100 tons, and the *Mojave* of 70 tons. All were stern-wheelers. There were also three barges of about 100 tons each.

As the bulk of the freight handled between the Gulf and Yuma was " upstream " there were frequently empty or lightly loaded barges to be taken downward to the mouth of the river to receive fresh cargoes. These were usually worked down in flat-boat manner, with sweeps and by the occasional use of warps and kedge anchors or grapnels, by Indian or half-breed crews. On upward trips, if barges were required, they were towed by the steamers, but occasionally, and especially at times of high water and difficult navigation, the steamers alone made the round voyage, freight being carried as a deck load.

Two stern-wheel steamers, the *Esmeralda* and the *Nina Tilden,* were brought round Cape San Lucas from San Francisco, in or about 1867, together with two large barges, the *White Fawn* and the *Black Crook,* and the flotilla was placed in the river trade by their owners, organized under the name of the Pacific and Colorado Navigation Company. The *Esmeralda,* although powerful and fast, proved to be of too deep draft for profitable working on the Colorado, and the line was soon absorbed by the original company, the Colorado Steam Navigation Company. The *Nina Tilden* continued in service under her new ownership for several years, but was eventually capsized and lost at the mouth of the river, being carried away from her moorings by an exceptionally heavy bore. The *Esmeralda* was beached at the shipyard, and her hull was afterwards used as a warehouse.

The last steamer to be built and put into service by the Colorado Steam Navigation Company was the *Gila,* which proved to be very successful and exceptionally fast. She became well known in later years for some remarkably quick trips, both up and down stream, and had the reputation of being the easiest boat to handle under all conditions of the river.

Duration of Voyage and Freight Rates from San Francisco

The company's flotilla, as then constituted, represented the highwater mark of commercial and navigational activity on the Colorado, and the era of prosperity continued through the late sixties and more than half through the following decade, while the Southern Pacific Railroad was slowly approaching the river from the Pacific Coast. The voyage from San Francisco to Yuma, including the time consumed in making the transfer of freight and passengers from the sea-going to the river steamers at the head of the Gulf, was scheduled at from twelve to fourteen days. The time depended somewhat upon the season and the state of the river. Passengers were frequently carried upstream upon the barges, in tow by the steamers; and fares were fixed at $60.00 for the cabin passage or $40.00 for steerage, for the complete voyage.

Inclusive time when the sea voyage was made under sail was of course more uncertain, the brig *Josephine,* for instance, while under charter for the sea-going link of the combined service having taken forty-two days in the late summer of 1869 to make the passage from San Francisco to the river mouth.

Freight consigned to river points originated, in nearly all cases, in San Francisco or San Diego and was brought around Cape San Lucas and up to the mouth of the river in chartered vessels. In the earlier days of the trade these were sailing vessels, generally schooners or brigs, of from 400 to 600 tons burden. Attempts were made in some of the earlier voyages to bring them up to or beyond the head of tidewater, either by sailing or by working the tides by kedging or warping. It was almost impossible to find safe storage ground ashore for the incoming freight on account of the great tidal range and the general insecurity of the low and impermanent banks of the estuary. As soon, therefore, as the development of the trade warranted it and the equipment and facilities of the company made it possible, the sea-going craft upon arrival were anchored or moored wherever adequate shelter could be found in the estuary, and cargo was handled over their sides either into lighters or directly on to the decks or into the holds of the waiting river steamers. Comparatively secure berths for such transfer could generally be found either in the main northeastern channel, near the Sonoran shore and under the lee of Montague Island, or above Unwin's Point and near the Lower Californian shore of the estuary.

Steamers were afterwards used in the sea service, and, as the volume of trade increased and warehousing facilities were established in old steamer-hulls at the shipyard, these made regular and scheduled trips.

Current freight rates from San Francisco to various river points were quoted by a commercial observer in 1867-1868 as follows:[1] San Francisco to Yuma (per ton), $47.50; to La Paz (small mining town above Yuma), $57.50; to Fort Mojave, $77.50. Ore, as return freight to San Francisco, $15.00 per ton.

PROBLEMS AND TECHNIQUE OF NAVIGATION ON THE COLORADO

Successful steamboating upon the Colorado, at least within range of the tides and through the uncertain channels of the delta, was far more a matter of personal skill and resourcefulness of the pilots than of any strict adherence to the rules of orthodox navigation. It was the generally expressed opinion of the river men who conducted this traffic from the Gulf to Yuma that experience gained upon other navigable streams gave the master of a boat but slight advantage in operating upon the lower river.

The first hazard to navigation upon entering the river mouth was the great and devastating tides which sweep the estuary. These always developed heavy and quickly reversing currents, with the added complication of the bore (Fig. 14) at the times of the spring tides. Some of the smaller sea-going craft were grounded in convenient sloughs while discharging was carried on through a neap-tidal period. This saved much risk of dragging anchors and parted moorings out in the channel. Holding ground was poor on account of the soft and shifting bottom, and fixed moorings were generally impracticable for the same reason.

In the earlier phases of the service it was customary to work the incoming vessels up as far as possible in order to discharge cargo, but after the Puerta Isabel storage facilities were available they seldom went above Philips Point. No use was ever made of sea-going tugs, although the river steamers themselves sometimes assisted in working sailing craft in and out of the river mouth. Taking all the facts into consideration, it is improbable that in any other river service in the world has it been necessary to operate with such light steamers as the conditions upon the Colorado demanded, against equal hazards of open sea and violent tides.

When the difficulties of the estuary had been overcome by upward-bound steamers and tows, the region of indefinite channels and obstructive shoals about the mouth of the Hardy River was the next impediment to navigation. It was customary to cross these troublesome flats towards the last of the flood tide, when there was depth enough over the shoals to give easy entrance to the river channel proper and while the slack water might still be made use of to the head of tidal influence.

When the Colorado-Hardy junction was passed river conditions were usually more favorable. The channel was more stable, the banks being

[1] W. A. Bell: New Tracks in North America, London, 1869.

Fig. 12—The steamer *Cochan* and the barge *Silas J. Lewis* moored to the river bank at the Yuma custom house, 1905.

Fig. 13—The *Silas J. Lewis* converted into and doing service as an improvised suction dredge at the Imperial Canal heading in 1913.

Fig. 14—The *Retta*, one of the smaller and later boats navigating the lower Colorado, encountering a tidal bore in the estuary about in 1905. (See also Fig. 19.)

covered with coarse grass or tules, which resisted erosion and gave more permanence to the bends. As the zone of willow and cottonwood was reached the banks became higher and the ground somewhat firmer.

There was one recognized and convenient landing on the edge of the eastern mesa, some twenty-five miles to the south of the Colorado-Gila junction. This was known as Ogden's Landing, and it was connected by a practicable dry-ground road with the ferry crossing at Camp Yuma. The only permanently dry and solid ground upon the entire western, or right, bank of the river between Camp Yuma and the mouth was the toe of the Pilot Knob massif, five or six miles below the post. Some very bad and uncertain river stretches were usually encountered between the two landings, and passengers frequently used Ogden's Landing as a point of debarkation.

Yuma was made a port of entry in 1867, and thereafter clearances had to be taken out by steamers and barges going down river to receive cargo, and manifests were required for all incoming freight, although, as practically everything imported was of domestic origin, no duties had to be paid. Mexico was always lenient in its attitude towards the trade and never established a custom house at the mouth of the river or at any other point south of the boundary, simply ignoring, as far as official action of any kind was concerned, all goods passing through her territory and all movements therein of vessels under United States registry.

As no systematic logs or records of channel changes appear ever to have been kept by the masters and pilots of the steamers engaged in the river trade and as no permanent channel marks were ever established, little can now be learned except indirectly concerning actual physiographic conditions in the lower river during this interesting navigational period. It is obvious, however, that in an unmarked and rapidly changing channel situated in a practically unknown region, and upon a river which was subject to great and oftentimes sudden rises, any particular voyage might reasonably be anticipated to develop into an adventure or an exploration rather than into a mere commercial undertaking. It is not surprising, therefore, to learn of steamers and barges, especially when dropping down stream, occasionally blundering or being helplessly carried into openings in the always treacherous western bank in times of high water, and having funnels, pilot-houses, hog-posts, or other superstructures wrecked or carried away by falling or leaning trees, in swift narrow channels, before they could be brought under control or could work their way back into known parts of the main river.

It was found to be possible, with some of the larger and more powerful steamers which were used in the service, to accomplish the distance between the estuary and Camp Yuma within a single working day, either up-stream or down, if the stage of the river and condition of the channel were favorable. Under unfavorable conditions two weeks or more were often required for the single trip. No attempt was ever made to move boats upon the river by artificial light.

During periods of high river a certain amount of water was always escaping to the westward in the upper part of the delta, re-uniting with the main stream at the mouth of the Hardy; and it was, therefore, lost for navigational purposes in the intermediate reaches. At times this leakage became quite serious and caused much trouble to the pilots in working through the sections below the diversion. It was amidst such surroundings that the skillful pilot was at his best and ability to " read the river " most essential.

The barge, or barges, in tow were nearly always astern, far enough from the wheel to be free of the backwash, although necessarily shortened up at times in making the frequent short and awkward bends. The tow was occasionally cast off while the steamer " backed-up " to an obstructing bar, to dig its way across by the use of the wheel. The wheel was also frequently used to throw water under the tow when it took the ground. Kedging or warping by means of trees and stumps ashore was at times necessary in making bends and crossings with a strong beam wind, as the barges generally exposed a high freeboard on a shallow draft and readily drifted to leeward. " Sounding " in difficult river stretches was usually done by an Indian stationed at the bow, by means of a long peeled willow pole which he alternately thrust down to the bottom and pulled up again in sight of the pilot.

Snags were never very much of a menace or impediment to navigation. The heavier pine, cedar, or mountain-oak trunks which come down stream from the upper basins of the river system at every period of high water, are generally smoothed and waterworn into mere floating fragments by their long journey through the canyons and do not lodge readily. The lower basins furnish very little vegetal debris of any size, and the willow and cottonwood saplings which grow so profusely upon certain portions of the floodplains are light and decay quickly.

Vessels Employed in the River and Sea Service

The key service through the delta lasted for less than twenty-five years and terminated as soon as it became possible to deliver freight at Yuma by rail from the Pacific coast. The " upstream " business from this supply point gradually languished as the small mining camps in the river valley and adjacent hills were abandoned or developed other lines of communication with the outside world and steamers were broken up as their usefulness ended. No complete and authentic list of those engaged in the service appears to be available, although the following, based upon information furnished in 1893 by Captain J. A. Mellen, one of the most famous of the old river pilots and commanders, is believed to be substantially correct.

NAME OF STEAMER	WHERE BUILT	APPROXIMATE DATE
Uncle Sam	San Francisco	1851
General Jessup	San Francisco	1853
Colorado (No. 1)	Estuary	1854
Explorer (Lieut. Ives)	Estuary	1858
Cocopah (No. 1)	Estuary	1858
Colorado (No. 2)	Yuma	1868 (?)
Cocopah (No. 2)	Yuma	1865
Mojave (No. 1)	Yuma	1866
Mojave (No. 2)	Rebuilt from Mojave (No. 1)	Date not ascertained
Esmeralda } Nina Tilden }	Colorado Pacific Line	Arrived from San Francisco 1867
Gila	Yuma	1868
Cochan (see Figs. 9 and 12)	Rebuilt from Gila, at Yuma	1893

Later boats working in restricted service on the river were the following:

Searchlight	Searchlight, St. Vallier, and Retta made occasional trips to
St. Vallier	the mouth of the river as long as the old navigable channel
Electra	continued to be passable, with supplies to certain mining
Retta (see Fig. 14)	camps in Lower California. Cochan and Searchlight were also used in engineering services incidental to closing the breach into the Imperial Valley and to the development of the Yuma project.

The following barges were used in the river trade at various times:

Barges Nos. 1, 2, and 3.................Colorado Steam Navigation Co.
Black Crook, White Fawn..............Colorado Pacific Line
Silas J. Lewis (see Fig. 12)............Various owners. (Ultimately converted into improvised suction-dredge (see Fig. 13), in service of California Development Co.)

The following vessels were engaged at various times in the sea service, in connection with the river traffic:

Bruja	Sloop	(Hardy, 1827)
Invincible	Top-sail schooner	(Derby, 1850)
Monterey	Schooner	(Ives, 1857, and subsequent voyages)
Capacity	Schooner	1852
Sierra Nevada	Schooner	1852
General Patterson	Schooner	1853, 1854 (lost in estuary); several voyages

Clara Bell	Barque	
Laura	Brig	
Josephine	Brig	
Victoria	Sailing barge, converted into auxiliary steam-schooner, lost in estuary on maiden voyage, 1867	
Santa Cruz	Steamer	1859
Uncle Sam	Sea-going steamer	1859
Centennial	Steamer	
Newbern	Steamer	1870-1876

End of River Navigation

Profitable transportation business between the sea and Yuma ceased in 1877, when the Southern Pacific track reached the Colorado. In order to avoid possible disastrous competition between the two services, the railroad company quickly acquired the rights, property, and good will of the river company, retaining the boats for such up-river business as might continue to be profitable. The shipyard at Puerta Isabel was dismantled early in 1878.

Since the diversion of the river in 1909, no practicable navigable channel even for the smallest craft has existed through the delta.

Through communication above Yuma was also severed in 1909 by the construction of the Laguna diversion weir by the U. S. Reclamation Service. The periodical erection of temporary diversion weirs at the intake of the Imperial Canal in extreme southern California has left the bed of the international section of the river dry for longer or shorter intervals, according to the stages of the river and the water requirements of the Imperial Valley. This barrier is placed across the channel under a permit from the U. S. War Department.

The erection of Boulder Dam has been declared in a famous decision of the Supreme Court of the United States to be primarily for the improvement of the Colorado as a navigable river, and so it may be presumed that the construction of the impounding and diversion dam at the mouth of Bill Williams Fork will have a further beneficial effect upon navigation, the passing of which, with its many picturesque features and marked influence upon local prosperity, many of the older residents of the river valley and surrounding region still deplore.

PART II
PHYSIOGRAPHIC HISTORY

CHAPTER III

THE PERIOD OF RELATIVE STABILITY (1890-1900)

By the beginning of the last decade of the nineteenth century the delta south of the international boundary had once more become almost a *terra incognita*. River traffic had ceased entirely, and a few semi-nomadic family groups of Cocopa Indians, who ranged from the *bajadas* of the Cocopa Mountains to the banks of the Colorado, were practically the only inhabitants of the region.

The shipyard which had been developed and maintained by the Colorado Steam Navigation Company at Shipyard Slough on the Sonoran shore had been abandoned, the stores and equipment removed to Yuma, and the crews withdrawn. The two remaining river steamers rarely made trips down stream, and then only for the purpose of obtaining soft-wood fuel for their boilers from the abundant willow and cotton-wood thickets. Knowledge of the lower river and of the extensive regions subject to tidal influences and overflow was rapidly slipping away, and channel changes in both the river and estuary were generally unnoticed and unrecorded.

Several small ranches were operated, principally upon the more stable Sonoran side of the river, and a few hundred head of stock—cattle and horses—were run upon the more accessible parts of the bottom lands; but agriculture generally, and also such development schemes as had originated during the steamboat days, had been allowed to lapse. The Colonia Lerdo which had been planned near the southwesternmost projection of the Sonoran mesa as one of the more ambitious of such schemes was occupied by a family of Mexicans engaged in stock raising, and the tule lands about the head of tidewater were overrun by numbers of hogs, the wild descendants of some domesticated swine that had been brought into the region years before as a commercial enterprise; and these were hunted at times by parties from north of the border.

RUNNING SURVEY FROM YUMA TO THE GULF

Under these circumstances it was realized that important geographical information might be obtained by journeys of observation and exploration in this little visited region, and the writer [1] hence undertook to visit the area whenever occasion offered. His first voyage for this purpose was made from Yuma to the Gulf of California in the winter of 1890-1891.

---

[1] Most of these earlier journeys were undertaken in partnership with companions whose names and whereabouts are no longer known to the writer. They are not forgotten, however, and he here wishes to pay tribute to their cooperation and good fellowship.

It was determined upon this initial passage down the river to make a rapid, although reasonably accurate, running survey of the navigable channel in order to compare the then existing alignment with the only available chart covering the region through Mexican territory, namely Chart No. 619 of the U. S. Hydrographic Office, which was based on Ives's survey of 1858, supplemented by the *Narragansett* reconnaissance of 1873.

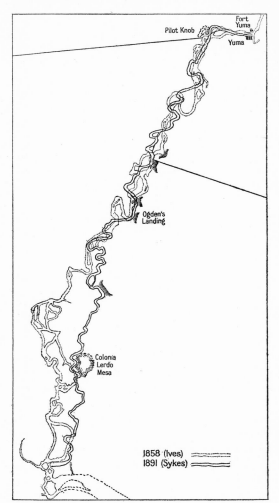

It was quickly discovered that the channel then under observation bore little resemblance to the Ives traverse (Fig. 15) ; so the work was extended to cover a portion of the lower Hardy, the tidal channels in the estuary, and the entrances to the river at the times of both high and low water. The western shore of the Gulf was also followed and examined, both from the sea and shore, as far south as San Felipe Point.

Changes in channel alignment appeared to have been most extensive along the lower portion of the river, from the Colonia Lerdo to the estuary, in the estuary itself, and especially about the junction of the Colorado and Hardy. The

Fig. 15—Map of comparative courses of main Colorado channel between Yuma and the estuary according to Ives's map of 1858 (see Fig. 7) and the writer's running survey of 1891. Scale 1: 750,000.

notes and other data obtained upon this initial voyage were therefore placed before steamer captains and others who had possessed intimate knowledge of the navigable channels a few years previously, and the extent of the change which had taken place was confirmed.

OVERFLOW OF RIVER TOWARD SALTON SINK, 1891

No discharge measurements of the Colorado were taken at Yuma in 1891, nor in fact until eleven years later, but gauge readings had been made by the Southern Pacific Railroad Company at their bridge crossing since 1878,[2] and these indicated that, following upon the years of rather moderate discharge, the summer flood of 1890 had peaked up slightly above the average and that the river had remained somewhat above the mean summer level for almost two months. The gauge height at the beginning of the year (1891) and during January had hovered between 17 and 18 feet, with a slight final tendency to rise. Precipitation during the latter part of the winter had been unusually heavy throughout the Southwest, and swollen streams had been responsible for several disasters, notably for the failure of the Walnut Grove dam on the Hassayampa River in central Arizona, with the resultant loss of many lives and much property. As the Yuma gauging station was situated below the mouth of the Gila the inflow of water from this source was also recorded.

A violent flood from the Gila itself, and from its various tributaries then or recently in flood, entered the Colorado early in February, carrying out the frail levees which had been designed to protect Yuma from such back-door invasions, virtually wrecked the then existing town, and raised the Colorado level at the gauging station to the unprecedented height of 33.5 feet. Passing downwards into the delta, it overtopped the banks for a distance of many miles, opening breaches at several vulnerable points along the western bank into the heads of the drainage systems of the Alamo and Paredones (Fig. 28).

A great volume of water passed through these openings, which remained partially open as the river level fell, and the result was a steady although gradually decreasing flow through the cleared channels during the spring and early summer of 1891.

Much of this water found its way through the Paredones into Volcano Lake and so ultimately into the Gulf through the Hardy, but the greater portion, diverted by vegetation and secondary fans and other obstructions left by previous floodings, passed on towards the northwest through the plexus of sloughs and interlacing channels which then connected the Paredones, the Alamo, and the more westerly distributary known as New River. Extensive sheet flooding also took place down the slopes towards the north and west.

The region was practically uninhabited at that time and the ramifications of its drainage but little understood, so that, when water in apparently great volume began to appear to the southward of the Southern

---

[2] A graph showing daily gauge heights, 1878-1915, and one showing daily discharge in second-feet, 1902-1915, of the Colorado River at Yuma are published in *U. S. Geol. Survey Water-Supply Paper 395*, 1916, Pls. 23 and 24. Discharge figures for subsequent years through 1934 will be found in the publications listed in *Water-Supply Paper 764*, 1936, p. 9, column 9.

4

Pacific Railroad fully 70 miles northwest of Yuma, much speculation took place as to its origin.

Boat Journeys Toward Salton Sink, 1891

It was determined to attempt to solve the riddle. The writer hence left the river in mid-March, 1891, in a small light boat through an opening which was shortly found to connect with the Alamo drainage system and which appeared to offer a feasible route towards the northwest.

Passage through the tortuous channels afforded few opportunities for obtaining satisfactory cross-bearings or for taking other means for establishing positions, and so the intention of mapping the course of the water had to be abandoned. In the inundated and heavily brushed region afterwards encountered it was even more difficult to maintain a sense of distance or direction. The boat was at length abandoned, after a strenuous and somewhat hazardous voyage, on a soft and muddy flat, at a point which was probably a few miles to the northwest of the present town of Holtville. From here the smoke of the Southern Pacific trains could be seen far to the north, and the journey was finished on foot to the little railroad siding of Volcano.

Although the attempt to map the course of the flood water had been unsuccessful, it was felt that at least some information of value had been gained by actually following it from the point at which it escaped from the river to the bed of the Salton Sink. So far as is known, this voyage was the first one to be successfully accomplished from the Colorado to the basin.

Other expeditions, seeking for a solution of the origin of the water and information as to the extent of the inundation, were organized during the spring and summer of 1891, notably one led by H. W. Patton, under the auspices of the *San Francisco Examiner*. The party left the river on July 9, shortly after the crest of the rather moderate summer flood had passed, and made a landing at Salton five days later. By this time the water had opened somewhat more definite channels through the inundated region, and the lake which had formed in the lower part of the depression had filled to a firmer shore line. An account of this journey was written by Mr. B. A. Cecil-Stephens and published in the *Bulletin of the American Geographical Society* for September 1891.[3] W. Convers and Charles Thiesen also worked boats through the Alamo channel during the same season.

Stability of River and Changes in Estuary, 1891-1893

Predictions were freely made in Yuma during the summer and autumn, by persons claiming to have late and intimate knowledge of the

[3] Vol. 23, 1891, pp. 367-377; reference on pp. 374-375.

Fig. 16—On one of the river journeys of the writer in the 1890's: running out a towline preparatory to working the boat up the edge of a bar.

Fig. 17—Boat moored to edge of mud bank in slack water. Banks as shown are typical of a falling river.

state and prospective developments of the lower river, that it would thenceforth abandon its channel and continue to flow into the Salton basin. Another journey for the investigation of conditions between Yuma and the Gulf was therefore undertaken by the writer during the succeeding winter, 1891-1892. The western banks of the river were at that time carefully observed, but it was seen that no material changes, other than some realignments of the channel such as always occur during high-water periods, had taken place during the intervening months. There was every evidence that the sudden and extremely high flood of the previous winter had opened the breaches which were still to be seen in places along the right bank of the river but that these had been abandoned as the water fell and the old channels became once more competent to pass the flow. Much drift and wreckage was piled in some of these openings, some of it plainly representing the destruction in and about Yuma, and all of it striking evidence to the violence of the flood.

Continuing the journey down stream and noting various changes in bends, cut-offs, and shoals, great alterations were seen to have taken place about the mouth of the Hardy River and in the upper part of the estuary. The Hardy had cut through into the main river from the concave side of a bend some distance above its former debouchure, and a great expanse of tidal flats now occupied the former site. In the estuary a long, narrow, lenticular-shaped island, which had only been separated from the southwestern shore by a narrow channel during the previous winter, was now divided from it by a wide and deep low-water passage through which there was much tidal movement. Other islets had appeared or disappeared as erosion had taken place along the shores, and the wide channel along the Sonoran shore and to the east and northeast of Montague and Gore Islands was again clearly the main entrance to the river, as shown in U. S. Hydrographic Office Chart No. 619, although during the previous winter most of the tidal water, both at the flood and ebb tides, was clearly passing to the westward of Montague Island and around Unwin's Point.

The return journey up to Yuma was made early in 1892, against a rising river and with some difficulty. Water was passing in some volume through nearly all cut-offs and backwaters, and the main channel was almost bank-full, although upon reaching Yuma it was found that the gauge height of the river was only about 20 feet. The condition was doubtless due to the lessened capacity of the channel through partial and temporary silting by the heavy load of detrital material which had entered the river from the Gila during the flood of the previous winter.

The channels between Yuma and the sea were again traversed and examined later in the spring of the same year (1892), the voyage being extended as far south as the San Luis group of islets, close to the Lower California shore of the Gulf in latitude 30° N. The downward and return journeys were, however, both accomplished before the main spring rise took place in the river, and no material changes were noticed in channel alignment, although it was evident that much scouring and clearing of the bed had taken place, allowing the current to pass more freely and lessening the complexities of navigation. In the estuary much cutting had taken place along the northeast shore, with deepening of the channels upon that side, but exit from and entrance to the river were both made through the channel to the southwest of Montague Island.

In the late summer of 1893 another voyage was made by the writer from the Mojave Valley to the sea and back again to Yuma, during the height of the summer flood, which was recorded at the Yuma gauging station at slightly above 25 feet. The sloughs and backwaters along both sides of the lower river were examined for navigable openings or the efflux of any large volume of water, without anything more being discovered than a gentle transriparian flow along certain stretches at the crest of the flood, the larger openings made in 1891 having now sealed themselves and become unrecognizable.

It thus became evident that at that time the lower river was in a fairly stable condition, occupying a meander zone which was in places several miles in width, from which farther wandering was generally restricted by higher margins or dense growths of vegetation, except during periods of very exceptional high water.

Changes Observed in 1893-1894

An interesting series of occurrences was noted in making a later trip upstream from the mouth of the river to Yuma during the same year (1893). The passage from Yuma, with the boats and facilities then available, consumed anywhere from seven to ten days, the boat having to be towed almost the entire distance by manpower. A rapid rise in the river took place during the night of October 1-2, soon after the upstream journey had begun, and the water, from its color, was recognized as having come from the Gila. The following morning, upon resuming the work of towing the boat, thousands of dead fish were noticed in the shallow back-waters, and many more were observed, plainly in distress, swimming close to the surface. The river began to fall again in a few hours, and it was then seen that literally hundreds of tons of dead fish were piled upon all the bars and shoals, showing that some wholesale poisoning had taken place. Decay began to set in very quickly in the masses of exposed bodies, and the river water, the only available supply, became quite undrinkable from the floating oil and animal refuse as the result of several exceptionally warm days.

It was not until October 5-6, when another rise took place, that tolerable potable water was again obtained. The water in this instance, being from the Colorado, quickly freshened the stream and carried the putrifying masses of fish towards the sea.

It was learned later, upon reaching Yuma, that a defectively built diversion dam on the Gila in the vicinity of Gila Bend, which had been constructed principally of tarred pine plank and creosoted paper, had been swept away during a sudden freshet, allowing the strongly impregnated water behind the dam to escape, with the effect of killing a very large percentage of the fish between that point and tidewater, a river distance of about 400 miles.

Further changes were observed to have taken place about the mouth of the Hardy, the junction with the Colorado now being made through some rather indefinite channels across a tidal flat instead of through deeply cut openings as seen in the two previous years. The lower part of this open expanse, where the junction had existed in the winter of 1890-1891, was again being cut into by the main channel of the estuary. Later observations have shown that changes of this description have constantly taken place at the junction of the two waterways, where the tidal scour, the fluctuating amounts of water passing through them, and the paucity of vegetative cover or binder upon the readily eroded banks all combine to make such readjustments possible and to bring them about.

The years 1894, 1895, and 1896, were entirely normal ones as regards Colorado River discharge, except for a short sharp freshet in the beginning of 1895, which again brought some water into the Salton basin, although not in any great volume.

Two journeys for the investigation of conditions along the lower river were made between Yuma and the sea in 1894, and the Hardy was followed up beyond the base of the Sierra Mayor to the apparent head of tidal influence. Volcano Lake was not reached at that time, but reports were received from reliable informants that at its highest seasonal stage during the summer it covered an area of some 12 to 15 square miles.

CONTEMPORARY STATUS OF KNOWLEDGE OF CENTRAL DELTA REGION

The *bajada* slopes of the Cocopa Mountains, the adjacent lowlands, and the western portion of the great basin region farther to the north were at that time beginning to attract cattlemen, who were establishing camps at various points, but the central region of the delta was still practically unoccupied and unknown. The Cocopa Indians alone had any detailed knowledge of its intricate system of waterways and flood channels or of the extent of the occasional inundations. Under the expert guidance of one of these men a journey was made, during the summer high-water season (1894), through the long tortuous series of channels which were later shown collectively upon the maps as Boat Slough (Fig. 18), between a backwater of the river almost opposite the

Colonia Lerdo mesa and a small channel which joined the Hardy a few miles below the Sierra Mayor. This connecting slough, which cut across the line of river discharge and paludal drainage as its exists at present, has since disappeared or survives as portions of other systems.

No maps or comprehensive surveys had been made in the delta at that time, except some preliminary work to establish the boundaries of certain grants and concessions and a reconnaissance survey which had

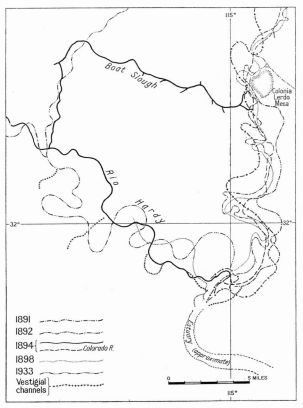

FIG. 18—Sketch map of Boat Slough and Río Hardy in 1894, in relation to various alignments of the lower Colorado from 1891 to 1933. Scale 1: 300,000.

been carried along the western bank of the Colorado and through the Alamo system of channels to the margin of the Salton depression in 1892 and 1893, on behalf of the Colorado River Irrigation Company. The project contingent upon this work had, however, been allowed to lapse, and the survey itself was merely a marginal one so far as the geography of the delta was concerned. Surveying parties working under the United States and Mexican Boundary Commission relocated the terminal points of the Arizona-Sonora and California-Lower California sections of the international boundary line and made two detailed surveys of the intervening stretch of river in 1893 and 1894, the latter portion of the work being carried out in March, 1893, and February and March, 1894, by United States and Mexican parties respectively. The work of these expeditions was not carried beyond the limitations imposed by the treaty and agreement between the two Governments, and so the surveys were not extended down stream towards the Gulf.

Below the termination of the Arizona-Sonora line, and extending into and embracing the estuary, the running surveys of the navigable channels made by the writer in the interests of this investigation, with the cooperation of his brother and two associates, still constituted the only available data for estimating changes in alignment or for making seasonal or annual comparisons of river volume or navigable conditions. Although no pretensions to great accuracy were made in mapping the minutiae of the channels, it was found in practice that the notes so obtained were sufficiently precise for all practical purposes.

Evidences of Approaching Limit of Silt-Carrying Capacity of River

The winter and spring months of 1897-1898 were again devoted to work upon the lower river and estuary, camps being maintained for more than a month at various points below the mouth of the Hardy for the purpose of observing the tidal intervals and range and the development and varying phases of the tidal currents. The main navigable channel below the mouth of the Hardy was found at this time to follow close to the concave side of a deep bight in the Californian shore, then to make a diagonal crossing, somewhat obstructed by shoals, over to the Sonoran shore, but shortly thereafter to cross back again to the Californian side, which it followed almost to the point designated as Robinson's Landing on the earlier maps. It then made a final clear crossing to the Sonoran shore, which was reached just below the old Philips Point beacon, which was at that time still in place, and followed down towards the bar.

The western channel, between Montague Island and the Californian shore, had again shoaled and was obstructed and practically impassable even with very light draft, at any stage lower than about half-tide.

On April 28, 1898, a heavy southwesterly gale was experienced whilst in temporary camp upon the Sonoran shore, where it was washed by the rain channel. The incoming tide was strongly deflected against the high clay bank under which the boats of the expedition were moored, placing them in some peril. The rapidity with which such a shore will disintegrate under the combined attack of a heavy current and violent wave action is almost incredible. It was found that the shoreline in the vicinity of the boats was receding at a rate of more than two feet a minute, in spite of the fact that it stood fully ten feet above the half-tide level and had a depth of water alongside of about two fathoms. So heavy was the scour that an examination of the foreshore at the succeeding low-water stage showed that practically all the eroded material had already disappeared.

The estuary was quite thoroughly examined at this time, and the impression was gained that it was in general shallower, with less definite banks and more obstructive shoals, than had been observed three years previously.

There appeared to be two possible explanations for this condition: either that it was merely a temporary one and the effect perhaps of a protracted series of such storms as had just been experienced, or, and more probably, that it was to be understood as a continuing, rather than a transitory, state and the effect of an overloading of the estuary by an excess of detrital matter from the river.

Subsequent events have practically proved that this was the correct hypothesis and that the final years of the nineteenth and the first five years of the twentieth century marked the culmination of a phase in the geomorphic development of the delta during which the river channel above the head of tidewater was gradually reaching the limit of its carrying capacity for suspended and saltatory material, prior to the inevitable serious breaching of one or both banks and the initiation of the phase of deposition and development of top-set beds throughout the delta in place of a continued rapid advance of the fore-set and bottom-set beds such as was then in progress.

CHAPTER IV

THE DECADE OF THE GREAT DIVERSION (1900-1910)

The opening decade of the twentieth century ultimately developed into the most important one in the recent history of the delta and especially of the Salton depression, although during its first quinquennium there was little apparent change in the river. The bed of the channel was undoubtedly steadily rising, and the building up of local accumulations of sedimentary matter became obvious from the increasing tendency of the river to enter and develop cut-offs and break across its banks at each period of high water.

Attempts were being made at this time to develop rating-curves based upon the gauge readings at Yuma and in accordance with the accepted practice of the U. S. Geological Survey,[1] in order to work out reliable discharge data for the lower Colorado River. The plan was abandoned, however, owing to the great and generally rapid fluctuations in depth which were found to exist there in consequence of the loose and shifting nature of the river bed. The trouble is increased locally by the close proximity of the mouth of the Gila, with its widely varying volume of discharge and percentage of suspended matter. Beginning in 1902, current-meter observations were therefore made, first at intervals of three or four days, and these have since been maintained and gradually developed into the complete and accurate system employed at the present time.

During the earlier part of the period under discussion, however, reliance had to be placed entirely upon exploration and visual observation in estimating the trend of channel changes and developments, and expeditions were organized from time to time with this end in view.

CONDITION OF LOWER RIVER AND ESTUARY IN 1901-1902

A protracted and profitable expedition covering the lower river and estuary was carried out by the writer during the winter and early spring months of 1901-1902, during a period of unusually low river. The gauge readings at Yuma, as obtained upon returning there, had varied between 17.5 and 18.5 feet, corresponding perhaps to a discharge of from 2,500 to 3,500 second feet. This followed a low river during the previous autumn, with a minimum reading of 16.8 feet in September. Conditions might, therefore, be considered as representative of normal low water

---

[1] See: Methods of Stream Measurement, *U. S. Geol. Survey Water-Supply Paper 56*, 1901. This was later expanded into: Hydrographic Manual of the United States Geological Survey, *Water-Supply Paper 94*, 1904. Other numbers in the same series dealing with methods of stream measurement are Nos. 375E, 375F and, with their accuracy, Nos. 64, 95, 400D. On the measurement of silt-laden streams see No. 400C.

and channel stability, and observation confirmed this hypothesis. The channels remained unaltered in general alignment; bars, shoals, and crossings changed very little from week to week; and bank-cutting in bends appeared to be reduced to a minimum, although local shoaling, due to deposition of suspended matter in the slackened current, was causing diversions here and there into minor cut-offs. The eastern bank appeared to be particularly subject to attack at this time, in contradistinction to the more general tendency to escape towards the west which had been observed during several of the previous years. The change was attributed at the time to the fact that local shoalings and breaking up of the channel had plainly occurred at several points immediately below these major diversions to the west, carrying the current over to the other shore and towards available openings upon that side. This is plainly one of the processes by which an aggrading stream maintains its general direction across open lowlands, supplementing the more obvious process of attacking its banks alternately through a scouring action along concave shores and a deposition of the overburden of detrital matter immediately below, with subsequent short-cutting across the deepened bends.

During the course of the downward voyage a breakaway channel to the east was encountered and entered on March 10, 1902, through a swiftly flowing shoot, almost at right angles to the general course of the river at that point, which was quite representative of this tendency. The passage through this channel is thus described in the field notes: " Entering a well-defined opening in the eastern bank some three miles below the last-observed, although now dry, breach on the western side, the water was found, for the first two or three miles, to be passing very swiftly through a dense thicket of willow trees. It was evidently flowing in part through rather deeply depressed areas, from the appearance of the surrounding trees, which seemed to be standing in eight or ten feet of water. As their roots were loosened they whipped and thrashed in the swift current, placing the boat at times in considerable danger, as the passage between the trees was so narrow and tortuous that it was difficult to handle or control it. Following through what appeared to be a series of submerged lagoons or backwaters, margined or obstructed by occasional large poplars or cottonwoods, the main sweep of the water carried us past a deserted Mexican cattle-ranch. Then an area of *carrizo* (cane, *Calamagrostis gigantea*) was encountered, and soon afterwards the main river channel was re-entered at a point which was estimated to be about 15 river miles below the point of divergence. The re-entry was made over a series of miniature rapids and falls, the drop being estimated as about 3 feet in a distance of 100 feet. The distance through the cut was estimated as about 7 miles."

Several more small cut-offs and diversion channels were seen and examined upon the eastern side of the main river before reaching the head of tidewater. Some water was found to be passing into a series of small channels which were known to connect with Santa Clara Slough, which, heading near the main river channel a short distance above the Colonia Lerdo had at times of high water generally carried a certain amount of the overflow directly to the head of the Gulf.

Further changes were found to have taken place about the mouth of the Hardy, through which very little river water was passing. This made the actual junction of the two waterways very indefinite and difficult to identify at periods of low tide.

FORMATION OF A TIDAL BORE

A camp was maintained for ten days upon the Sonoran shore, almost abreast of Montague Island, in order to observe the "birth" and development of the bore (Fig. 19). The observations were made on two occasions when the absence of wind and stage of the tidal period made conditions almost ideal. The phenomenon was described in the field notes as follows: " The birth of the bore is a curious sight as witnessed from a favorable point on shore. Following on the long period of ebb, one sees small uneasy wavelets forming in the slackening current, and these gradually develop into patches of broken water, moving to and fro without any apparent purpose or method. Gradually, out of the gathering uneasiness, a gentle stationary roller is formed in the channel and at right angles to the current. It quickly extends, until in a few minutes it stretches from shore to shore. As it becomes more pronounced and steep-fronted from the gathering pressure behind it, the front edge forms into a comber and it begins to move up-stream, quickly increasing in size and speed as it goes and being followed by a further series of rollers and a rapid rise in the water level."

The height of the breaking edge of the front wave was estimated, upon the occasion of this detailed observation, at from $2\frac{1}{2}$ to 3 feet in mid-channel, about a mile above the region of genesis.

There, concentrated upon itself by irregularities in the shoreline or constrictions in the channel, it would swell up to 6 or 7 feet, with a broken tumbling front and much turmoil and confusion. The roar of the rushing and falling water is very striking and almost awe-inspiring when heard from a stranded boat in the face of a night-time bore. This predicament was experienced upon one occasion, in a small boat, but fortunately with a rather moderate bore and no damage other than partial swamping.

The rapidity of the rise in water level after the passage of the first breaking wave and the following rollers is remarkable and seems to take place with a surging movement. An observation made by means of some previously driven and calibrated stakes on the face of a precipitous hard clay bank, during one of the same series of spring tides, showed a vertical movement of approximately 10 feet within a period of five minutes. This measurement was made, however, at a selected point at which a rapid rise had previously been observed, and may represent the combined effect of several extreme conditions.

The Boat Slough, connecting the lower Colorado with the Hardy, which had been examined in 1894 was again passed through in a westerly direction. No material changes either in the channel or volume of flow at corresponding stages of river and tide were noticed (see Fig. 18 for map of 1894 stage).

The upward journey to Yuma was made in April (1902), while the river was still at a low stage, and the entire flow was then found to be passing through the new eastern channel which had been examined on the way down. The small rapids at the lower end had already been cut out, the local drop having evidently been distributed in the general gradient. A definite but shallow channel had appeared in the section through the *carrizo* brakes, with bars showing in places at sides or center. In the upper portion many more trees had loosened and had either been carried away or had lodged in mid-stream and formed the nuclei of accumulations of drift piles or shoals. This scavenging process had increased the width of the waterway and eliminated many of the abrupt turns, but the current was found to be still swift, and some difficulty was experienced in working the boat up through it.

During the upward voyage to Yuma in April the river still remained at or about the 18-foot stage. The summer rise of that year was very moderate, both in volume and duration, scarcely reaching 24 feet and falling off again very rapidly during July.

Another down-stream journey was made in September (1902) in order to observe the seasonal developments. No appreciable amount of water had escaped to the westward, and the channel appeared to have been scoured out and somewhat cleared and straightened as the result of the very moderate flood conditions and the absence of a high silt-content during the initial rise. The flow into Santa Clara Slough had ceased although the river was at approximately the same height at Yuma, but probably with a somewhat greater volume of discharge, owing to changed channel conditions, during the period of this autumnal expedition than it had been during the spring.

THE ESTUARY IN 1902

No material changes were observed in the estuary. The journey was continued to Montague Island, and a camp was maintained there for several days, and the island and the adjacent Gore Island were thoroughly examined. Both are entirely alluvial and are frequently sub-

merged at periods of high tide and river. They are added to and sub-
tracted from, and the long and extensive fore-set beds and shoals into
which they almost insensibly merge at their southern extremities are
washed and deflected from side to side by transient changes in wind
and tide.

Where subjected to the direct erosive action of the river and tidal
currents the shore line is generally a hard and tenacious clay bluff from
15 to 20 feet high, as seen at periods of low water, while at high tide
a semi-submerged fringe of salt grass is all that is visible.

A broad shallow depression was found to cross Montague Island from
east to west about a mile below its northern headland, dividing it into
two separate islands above the half-tidal level. Quantities of recent
drift matter, principally young willow and poplar trees which had
stranded along the sides of this hollow, were thought to represent the
uprooted trees from the Noche Bueno cut. The deposit was of interest
as an illustration of the manner in which drift may be carried to sea
or distributed about the tidal flats (Fig. 20) or islands at the river mouth.
From the fact that so much material of one kind, and identified with
reasonable certainty as coming from one source, should be found deposited practically in a body, it appeared probable that tidal action in the
estuary was the collecting and segregating agency. Some investigation
followed, in development of this theory, and several small " rafts " of
drift matter—wood refuse, brush, tules, and the like—which were found
stranded upon the flats about the mouth of the Hardy, were followed
down the estuary upon the first of the ebb tide at the " pre-spring " tidal
period and were found to maintain their identity as units to the river
mouth.

Beginnings of Irrigation Canal System, 1901-1902

The upward journey to Yuma was again uneventful, but upon
approaching Pilot Knob it was noticed that a new entrance had been
cut into the canal which had been excavated during the previous year
close and parallel to the western bank of the river, for a distance of
about 3 miles below the Pilot Knob bluff. The operations then in
progress in this immediate vicinity were destined to have a profound
influence upon the future development of the delta and the extensive
valley areas to the northwest.

Settlers were already beginning to occupy the region henceforth to
be known as the Imperial Valley, and reconnaissance surveys were being
carried out by various development interests in the western part of the
delta. Cattlemen were pushing their herds on to such feed as could be
found along the slopes of the Cocopa Mountains and the banks of the
Hardy, and the channel of the Alamo was being cleared, straightened,
and diked where necessary, to serve as a main feeder for the canal
system which was being rapidly developed to the northwest. The central

and lower portions of the delta, and the still navigable channel of the
river, remained practically untraveled and unknown, and the intricate
system of feeder, distribution, and overflow channels existing between
the western bank of the river and the Cocopa Mountains was still an
unsolved riddle.

Overflow Conditions in Summer of 1903

The river remained at a low stage during the first three months of
1903 but thereafter began to rise steadily and quite rapidly, reaching
a summer peak of nearly 28 feet on the gauge and a discharge figure
of nearly 73,000 second-feet in June at Yuma. This was higher than
any previous stage recorded since the great winter flood of 1891.

A downstream journey was undertaken in the latter part of July, with
the river discharge still at about 50,000 second-feet although gradually
falling, in order to observe conditions along the western banks. It was
found that a good deal of over-bank flow had taken place in the region
which was known to be within the drainage influence of the Paredones
and the Río Abejas, although without having caused any definite breaking of the banks. It was not possible, therefore, to work a boat into
either of these channels, and unfortunately no other effective means of
exploring the region in this direction were at hand.

Water was found to have overtopped banks and escaped towards
the eastern margin of the delta in many places south of the international
boundary, filling lagoons and backwaters. All surplus upon this side
of the river above the influence of the Santa Clara drainage was
returned to the main channel by the salients of the Sonoran mesa.

Upon reaching Colonia Lerdo it was found that a series of severe
earthquake shocks had occurred there in February (1903), throwing
down and wrecking several of the massively built adobe buildings of the
hamlet, breaking trees, fissuring the ground, and causing other damage
and much consternation.

As the whole region is subject to frequent seismic disturbance [2] the
shocks may have been widespread but have escaped notice in the areas
of soft alluvium and scanty settlement. The little group of buildings
that were damaged were the only ones located upon unquestionably solid
ground in the lower delta at that time, and would undoubtedly be subjected to the full amplitude of vibration.

There was evidence that unusual flood conditions had recently existed
along the Hardy, and a definite channel across the tidal flats and shoals
again connected it with the Colorado channel. A stream of considerable
volume, estimated at about 1,000 second-feet, was found to be issuing
from it at dead low water. This was doubtless overflow water which

---

[2] F. B. Kniffen (The Natural Landscape of the Colorado Delta, *Univ. of California Publs. in
Geogr.*, Vol. 5, No. 4, p. 100 and map) extends the San Jacinto fault southeast to pass along
the eastern front of the Colonia Lerdo mesa and thence the western front of the Sonoran Mesa.

had escaped to the westward through the Paredones and Río Abejas during the previous weeks.

The journey was continued to Montague Island, and the return pull up stream to Yuma was accomplished without much trouble or incident. The general impression gained upon the upward trip, which was accomplished as usual by towing from the banks or edges of bars or shoals and therefore from a favorable situation for examining the channel in detail, was that shoaling and the breaking up of the river in the more open reaches were again taking place very rapidly.

Silt and Botanical Investigations of 1903-1904

An important series of investigations covering the character and quantity of suspended matter in the Colorado water and the seasonal fluctuations of the detrital burden in the Colorado and Gila were begun at Yuma in September, 1903, and continued until the end of August, 1904, the work being done jointly by the U. S. Geological Survey and the Agricultural Experiment Station of the University of Arizona. The data obtained as a result of this work [3] have been accepted as the basis of nearly all subsequent studies, although the investigation was admittedly incomplete, both in scope and duration.

During January and February of 1904 the writer participated in an expedition through the delta and as far as San Felipe, which was sponsored by the New York Botanical Garden. In addition to the hydrological and geographical work accomplished, Dr. D. T. MacDougal, at that time Assistant Director of the botanical garden, was able to make a comprehensive botanical reconnaissance of the region and obtain a valuable series of photographs. Professor R. H. Forbes, who had charge of the silt investigations mentioned above, was also a member of the expedition down to Colonia Lerdo, leaving it at that point and completing his tour of inspection of the delta region by returning overland on horseback to the infant settlement of Mexicali, under the guidance of a Mexican cowman who had some knowledge of the route through the intervening thickets.

The river remained at a very low stage during the time the expedition was in the field, the discharge, as measured at the newly reorganized Yuma station, standing at about 4,500 second-feet until March 1, rising to about 9,000 second-feet by the 15th, and then rapidly falling again to about 6,000. In spite of this prevailing low water the current was found to be vigorously attacking the escarpment of the Sonoran Mesa (Figs. 21, 23) around a great bend a mile or more in length. Upon the initiative of Professor Forbes a line of stout stakes was driven into the undisturbed surface of the mesa, at an approximate distance of 15 feet from the

[3] R. H. Forbes: The River Irrigation Waters of Arizona, *Arizona Agric. Exper. Sta. Bull. 44,* Tucson, 1902; *idem,* Irrigating Sediments and Their Effects upon Crops, *ibid.,* No. 53, 1906.

edge and at intervals of 100 yards. The intention was to measure their position relatively to the eroding face of the escarpment when the next downstream expedition would be made. As events proved, however, the estimate of erosion at this time and place was entirely too small, for the whole line had disappeared before the following winter, when the mesa edge was again examined.

Much change had, as was anticipated, taken place in the Colorado-Hardy junction region, some difficulty being experienced in even discovering the mouth of the tributary stream. The estuary had also greatly changed within a few months, the channel now making a bold sweep down the Sonoran shore for a distance of several miles, a well-defined branch channel then cutting across towards Unwin's Point and again allowing exit from and entrance to the river at any stage of the tide by means of the channel between Montague Island and the Californian shore. This western channel was in fact used by the expedition both in leaving and re-entering the estuary.

The botanical reconnaissance was continued down to San Felipe Point and Bay, embracing the arid slopes and foothills to the westward. Tidal observations, especially upon current velocities and reversals, were made in the estuary and entrance channels. The upward journey to Yuma was upon this occasion made overland from Colonia Lerdo, the boat used by the expedition being worked up stream from the head of tidewater by a crew of Cocopa Indians.

FLOOD CONDITIONS DURING FURTHER BOTANICAL EXPEDITION, 1905

Another expedition, undertaken for the purpose of extending the area covered by the botanical reconnaissance of the previous year to include the valley of the Colorado from the vicinity of Needles and to embrace the western margin of the delta, was sponsored by the New York Botanical Garden in the early spring of 1905. Dr. MacDougal again took charge of this phase of the investigation, and, after he had made his examination from Needles to Yuma, the main expedition to cover the delta region was organized at that point. Mr. E. A. Goldman, of the U. S. Biological Survey, joined the party for the purpose of making collections of mammals, birds, and reptiles, in the hitherto unworked regions to the west of the lower Colorado.

The combined party left Yuma on March 26, river conditions being found to be radically different from those encountered during the previous season. The discharge at Yuma of the combined Colorado-Gila flow had exceeded 82,000 second-feet in February, rising to over 110,000 second-feet by the time the expedition cast off.

Although it was scarcely realized at the time, the end of the long era of peaceful meandering of the Colorado down the eastern margin of the delta had already arrived and the series of great sweeps towards the west had begun.

FIG. 19—A small tidal bore coming up the estuary of the Colorado River, 1904. (See also Fig. 14.)

FIG. 20—Flood-plain on the southwestern side of the estuary, showing driftwood and "pie-crust" surface.

FIG. 21—Impingement of the Colorado River on the escarpment of the Sonoran Mesa about 17 miles south-southwest of the western end of the Arizona-Sonora boundary (the bluff half-way between Ogden's Landing and Colonia Lerdo Mesa on Fig. 15): view looking northwards (upstream) in 1904.

FIG. 22—Salt Slough (Rillito Salado on Pl. 1) in February, 1904, which forms a part of the Santa Clara system of channels draining the Colorado River in the extreme southeast.

FIG. 23—Contact of the Colorado River with the Sonoran Mesa: view in 1904 from about the same point as Figure 21, looking southwards (downstream).

FIG. 24—Approximately the same view in 1925 as Figure 23: abandoned channel of the river, with silted-up and overgrown bed, abutting on weathered edge of the mesa.

Fig. 25—Río Hardy and overflow channels as seen from the lower slopes of the Sierra del Mayor, the foot of which appears in the lower right (see also Figs. 54 and 57 below, *Carnegie Instn. Publ. No. 99*, Pl. 30, and *Memoirs Natl. Acad. Sci.*, Vol. 16, No. 1, Pl. 23, Fig. 2). View at the flood season in April, 1905. Toward the right the waters eventually flowed around the range and drained into the Macuata Basin.

Fig. 26—Same area as in Figure 25, in the dry season in February, 1907.

Fig. 27—San Felipe Point, marking the extreme southern end of the Colorado Delta, where the Sierra de San Felipe, an isolated volcanic outlier of the Peninsular Range of Lower California impinges obliquely on the western shore of the Gulf of California.

The whole region between Pilot Knob and the head of tidewater was now practically under water, with but three possible landing places accessible to the navigable channel at which dry ground might be found. These were the three exposures of the escarpment of the Sonoran Mesa which were touched by the river south of the international boundary. At the second one, the great sweep into the gravel tableland which had been examined the previous year, search was made for the line of stakes which had been set by Professor Forbes for the purpose of measuring erosion. All had disappeared, and a rough estimate, based upon other range marks and conspicuous objects, seemed to indicate that during the intervening months not only 15 feet but approximately 50 yards of solid cliff had been washed towards the sea. This had taken place although the highest discharge during the previous summer had hardly exceeded 50,000 second-feet. The wastage at the time of the second observation was found to be very rapid, volumes of the dry material continuously sliding and rolling down into the rapid current at some point along the great arc, with clouds of ascending dust. It was an impressive illustration of the erosive power of a great river under favorable conditions.

Having passed the third point at which the escarpment was touched, even semi-solid ground was not again found until well down within the sphere of tidal influence and at periods of low tide. Estimates of channel changes, at points other than the Sonoran Mesa exposures, had been impracticable during the voyage down stream, most of the country upon both sides of the river being flooded and the banks generally indistinguishable, the boats merely being kept within the influence of the main sweep of the current and in the general direction of the sea.

The conditions encountered during this haphazard voyaging through a drowned wilderness developed a keen appreciation of the problems in navigation that had been faced under similar circumstances by the pilots of the lightly powered, although often heavily burdened, river steamers in earlier years.

Some difficulty was again experienced in locating the mouth of the Hardy amidst the tidal and flood-water channels which obscured its junction with the Colorado. It was, however, at last entered on the flood tide, and progress westward was made for a few miles during slack high water. A strong outward current, which gave some indication of the amount of flood water then pouring across the delta, was soon encountered, and it was found that this had to be stemmed through flooded areas until the solid toe of the Cocopa Mountains was reached at Sierra Mayor. Making progress by towing from banks or the edges of shoals was in this case quite impossible, as no solid ground was anywhere visible, and the chief reliance had to be placed upon rowing. A powerful Cocopa Indian, thoroughly familiar with the region, had been engaged at Colonia Lerdo, and he materially assisted as motive power and was able to direct the expedition through backwaters and cut-offs which he recognized amidst the partially submerged brush and tules. A small skiff, engined with a minute single-cylinder inboard motor, constituted one unit of the equipment, its principal use in this region being to explore for solid ground for camping and collecting purposes amidst the surrounding expanses of mud and shallow water.

The prevailing conditions proved to be almost ideal for biological collecting, as practically all animal life is at such times driven by the rising water to isolated spots of higher ground, and these, when found, could be examined in detail.

A heavy flow was noticed as taking place, although merely as a general surface movement and without any especial channel concentration which could be identified, round the southern extremity of the Cocopa Mountains and undoubtedly working towards the Macuata Basin upon the western side of the range (Fig. 25).

A landing was at length made upon the solid "toe" of the Sierra Mayor, which constitutes the semi-isolated southerly extension of the Cocopa massif. This being a favorable location for geographical, botanical, and biological work, a camp was established and maintained there for a period of ten days. During that time the main peak of the Sierra Mayor was climbed (April 10, 1905), plane-table work being done from the summit and from several other favorable locations upon both slopes. Much botanical and biological collecting, photography, and general investigation of the surrounding conditions was carried on, and the tidal movements and fluctuations in the flood level were observed.

The journey was then continued and the investigations extended into the Volcano Lake area and its associated plexus of channels. Much Colorado water was entering the lake through the Paredones system at the time the examination was made (April 16), the discharge at Yuma having peaked up to about 95,000 second-feet in mid April. The water area under this condition was estimated at from 100 to 150 square miles, with the shore lines very indefinite. This would represent about the maximum development of the lake at that time, as overflow was found to be taking place freely into the Pescadero and Hardy drainage systems.

It had been hoped that the journey might be continued by boat through the New River channel into the Imperial and Salton basin, into which much Colorado water was known to be passing at the time by means of sheet flooding, and through a very intricate system of sloughs connecting the Paredones and Alamo, but upon approaching the divide which it was realized would delimit the southward and northward flows, the water in the channel gradually failed and the attempt had to be given up. In the end horse transportation was arranged for through the kind cooperation of the owner of a border ranch, and the expedition disbanded at Calexico.

Changes Brought About by the Great Diversion of 1905-1907

Three of the voyages outlined above may be considered as having been made during distinctive, but typical, stages of the river, the winter voyage of 1901-1902 representing a minimum, the 1904 voyage a low mean, and the 1905 journey down stream a maximum condition.

This was the last time the old navigable channel was ever descended by boat in the prosecution of the investigation, and, indeed, its practicable navigation had already definitely ceased except at the highest stages of the river, through the diversion of such a large proportion of the water into the Alamo.

The cause and effect of this loss of water and its influence upon the lower river during the following five years will be briefly outlined here, although the subject will be more fully dealt with in Chapter X.

Certain limitations as to available fall, and therefore as to the capacity of the canal heading which had been cut in the river bank at Pilot Knob in order to supply water to the irrigation developments then being initiated in the great basin to the northwest, had made it necessary to cut successive openings for the purpose of augmenting the flow. These openings were made as circumstances demonstrated their advisability in order to cope with the ever-increasing demands of settlers for water. Being deemed to be temporary expedients only, and also owing to certain international complications, they were left unprotected against flood damage. The year 1905 was an exceptional one for disastrous floods, as stated above, and the consequence was that the entire flow of the river was found to be passing through the most vulnerable opening and directly away from the established main channel, as the summer flood subsided. This condition continued, with only two brief intervals of partial reversion, until February, 1907, when the great crevasse was successfully and permanently closed.

Heavy floods had occurred in November, 1905, and June, 1906, and had caused a certain quantity of water to enter and flow down the practically abandoned channel, but the net result upon each occasion had been a further silting of the bed and lessening of the carrying capacity.

The summer flood of 1907 was a rather severe one, the discharge reaching about 115,000 second-feet at the end of June. It became apparent while it was in progress that the greater portion of the water was again escaping over the western bank within a few miles of the point at which the great break had occurred and that the old channel was becoming incompetent to carry more than a very limited flow.

Vegetation was seen to be playing an important part in bringing about this changed capacity. Heavy growth of seedling willows had invaded the higher parts of the shoals and bars in the river bed, as the result of the practical cessation of flow during the two preceding years, and, on the other hand, the absence of the usual summer flood conditions had caused a marked decrease in the protective growth of vegetation which normally limits marginal erosion.

Without any definite breaching of the banks, and more in the form of a uniform transriparian flow, the water which was raised above the bank level by the lessened carrying capacity of the channel found a ready means of escape across the comparatively unobstructed falling ground into the drainage system of the Paredones, and so ultimately into the Hardy and tidewater. This trend was impeded by building a levee later in 1907 south of the Paredones (C. D. Co. Levee on Fig. 28 and Pl. I).

The year 1908 was characterized by very moderate discharge, the summer peak barely exceeding 60,000 second-feet, and that for a very brief period, and, although much water escaped towards the west, a gentle current still passed through the old navigable channel and added to the steadily accumulating deposit of silt upon its bed.

It became apparent as the summer flood receded that the trend of the westerly escaping water was now definitely towards the head of the Abejas, a rather indefinite confluent of the Pescadero and a connecting link with the Volcano Lake plexus of minor channels.

Although some recessive cuttings had taken place in the heads of certain feeders of the Abejas during 1908, it was not until 1909 that a clear channel was opened through to the Colorado, during the great summer flood. This peaked up to approximately 150,000 second-feet and inundated practically the whole delta area between the Paredones and the Hardy. When the flood subsided it was found that the entire river was passing through a broad opening in the western bank almost immediately opposite the termination of the Arizona-Sonora boundary line and was holding its course and identity as a single outlet for a distance of about 15 miles in a direction slightly south of west. This brought the water out upon the broad flood plain margining the eastern shore of Volcano Lake, covered at that time with a heavy growth of willow. Deposition began to take place immediately and heavily, with the formation of a rapidly growing delta fan, which began to invade the bed of the lake and push across the flood plain and wooded sections towards the southwest, wholly submerging and obliterating the pre-existing system of waterways.

From the beginning of this tendency it was realized that deposition in this region would constitute a grave menace to the basin areas to the north and northwest, inasmuch as it was taking place upon the crest of the flattened cone or low ridge which formed the rim of the great depression and the dividing zone between north-flowing and south-flowing water. To oppose this frequently recurring hazard was destined to form the heaviest responsibility of those engaged in Imperial Valley development during the next twelve years.

Expedition to Salton Sea, 1906-1907

With the virtual closing of the old river channel in 1905, further expeditions to and from the Gulf by that route became impracticable, and, as the center of physiographic interest had now definitely shifted to the Salton basin and the extreme western portion of the delta area, the investigations were continued in that direction. A brief reconnaissance of the western end of the area then being rapidly invaded by the rising waters of the Salton " Sea " was made by the writer in May, 1906.

This was the first expedition made on behalf of the Carnegie Institution of Washington, which hereafter was to assume the direction of the investigation, through the newly organized Desert Laboratory, under the immediate leadership of Dr. D. T. MacDougal.

The participation of Dr. W. P. Blake was fortunately secured in this initial study of the basin region, and he was able to point out various features of interest in connection with his important discovery of 53 years previously that it contained an extensive area much below sea level (see pp. 108-109). This discovery had been the basis for all subsequent schemes for the development of the region by water from the Colorado.

At the time at which this preliminary examination of the Salton area was made the water in the lake was rising at an average rate of about 4 inches a day and had already reached a depth of approximately 50 feet in the deepest part of the depression, with a surface level of minus 240 feet.

In spite of the rapidity of advance across the nearly level floor of the basin which such a daily increase in depth implied, it was observed that a marginal zone of thoroughly saturated soil, which in places exceeded 100 yards in width, preceded the advancing edge of the water. The high degree of capillarity thus indicated in the surface layers of the alluvium was assumed to imply that extensive arrangement of the material by eolian action had taken place since the original deposition.

Upon the slightly steeper piedmont slopes which were also embraced in this brief reconnaissance a miniature cut-bank was formed by wave action, with the usual sorting of material invaded by the rising water, according to the size and density of the dislodged fragments. Scores of more or less clearly defined terraces upon the slopes above marked temporary stabilizations of level or periods of increased wave action at former fillings of the basin.

A great quantity of floating pumice, the rounded fragments ranging from the size of a pea to that of a watermelon, was being carried towards the shore line by the wind and slight current, forming, in association with much organic debris, an almost continuous floating fringe which acted as a damper on the wave action.

Extensive field work was carried out in the early part of 1907, the entire shore line of the lake being examined at the time at which it reached its maximum height, which was generally accepted, upon check-ing up with established bench-marks, as having been minus 197 feet (Fig. 62, p. 118). In addition to the botanical and ecological work ac-complished by the party, collections of mammals (chiefly small rodents) and birds were made.

The southwestern margin of the lake had at that stage advanced beyond the valley-floor alluvium at many points and was invading the lower sands and gravels of the piedmont slopes of the ranges to the westward, even, in one observed case, reaching the broken limestone capping of some low buried ridges. In general, the presence of sandy or gravelly material in the valley at this level clearly implies lateral invasion through atmospheric or hydrologic agency, by material from the sur-rounding mountains, and such an implication seemed to be adequate to account for nearly all the measures that were examined upon this occa-sion, with the water level of the lake available to establish a clearly defined horizon for estimating low slopes.

" Creep " or sheet-flooding has undoubtedly been responsible for much of the movement, although the Carrizo-San Felipe drainage basin has been the source of most of the stream-transported material in this sector, and the " old beach " line which margins the embayment through which the combined creek enters the lower portion of the basin has been at least the proximate source of most of that which has been due to eolian activity.

This conspicuous sand invasion takes the form of a rather loosely grouped series of dunes, mostly of characteristic crescent form, many of which at the time of this expedition were either wholly or partially submerged. The extension of this accumulation of sand across the valley floor had been found to form a partial barrier to the flood water from the river in 1891, but it was passed through by one of the parties which made the voyage in from the Colorado in that year.

EXAMINATION OF MACUATA BASIN

Upon completing the circuit and examination of the lake at the high-water stage the expedition moved down to the international boundary and reorganized for an examination of the Macuata Basin to the west of the Cocopa Mountains, concerning which practically no scientific information was available at that time. The reorganized expedition was placed upon a land-travel basis—team transportation, with all of the minor side trips on foot—and the plan worked admirably over such a terrain.

The basin was found to be some 50 miles in length, from its northern extremity, at which point it was entered, to the southerly tip of the Cocopa Mountains, where the broad flat " vestibule " connecting it with the great tidal and submersible flats of the lower Colorado and

Hardy may be considered to begin. Its width was estimated at about 10 miles, which later and more precise information has shown to be substantially correct.

The journey was made down the eastern margin, skirting or at times passing over some of the low salients of the Cocopa foothills. The basin was found to contain very little water and was evidently at a relatively low stage, to judge from the windrow of dead fish several miles in length which lay at some distance from the shore. The lowest part of the depression, which lies at its northern end and close to the eastern edge, is now known to be slightly below mean sea level, but the aneroids carried by the party were not sufficiently accurate or closely enough calibrated to make any precise estimation of elevation of any value. It was realized, however, that this part of the journey was made very close to sea level.

Difficulty in estimating the width of the valley floor from base lines laid out while traveling down the eastern side was due to the fact that the piedmont slopes upon the opposite side are very flat and indefinite, and their extent and width can only be detected by an actual inspection of the soil texture or vegetation at close range.

Large, and almost continuous areas of sand dunes were seen to margin the other edge of the alluvium, and a few relatively scattered areas of less extent were found upon the eastern side.

Small springs were visited at two points while making the journey along the valley, and their positions were roughly noted. Another exposure of water, greater in volume than either of those seen, and reputed to be unfailing, was said to exist upon the opposite side of the valley in a position which would probably have worked out at about latitude 32° 10′ N., longitude indefinite. This spring, however, was not seen. One of those visited was found to have a temperature of approximately 120° F. and to contain algae and numbers of small species of rainwater fish, specimens of which were secured and afterwards identified as hitherto undescribed.[4]

The level alluvial valley floor was found to narrow to a width of less than two miles at about latitude 32° 7′ N., to be bordered by sand dunes and ridges upon both sides, and to contain a deeply eroded central channel or chain of connected depressions known locally as Las Barrancas.

The existence of these deeply excavated waterways was hard to account for with the inadequate means at hand for detecting slight changes in elevation in the valley floor, which appeared to be practically level. This problem has not yet been entirely cleared up in view of the extremely slight gradient which is now known to exist between the banks of the Hardy and the farthest extremity of the valley—a difference

[4] D. T. MacDougal: The Desert Basins of the Colorado Delta, *Bull. Amer. Geogr. Soc.*, Vol. 39, 1907, pp. 705-729; reference on pp. 716-729.

of less than 10 feet in a distance of approximately 70 miles as traveled by the water, or an average gradient of 0.14 foot to the mile. The explanation seems to lie in wave momentum in the body of water which is propelled violently along the *thalweg* of the depression at the time of each coincidence of high water in the Hardy channel with exceptionally high tide, which is in effect another manifestation of the force which causes the bore to ascend the estuary and the Hardy.

Pools of slightly brackish water were found to exist in different parts of the *barrancas* at the time of the examination, although there was no evidence of recent flow. The basin was known to have received a large quantity of overflow water during the early part of the 1905-1906 winter, and 1905 had been an exceptionally wet year throughout the delta region, the total precipitation having exceeded 11 inches as measured at Calexico; but the bulk of the 1906 flood and practically the entire 1906-1907 winter discharge of the Colorado had been diverted into the Salton basin. The conditions found in the *barrancas* would therefore appear to have been about normal for a low-water period.

The expedition rounded the southern end of the Cocopa Mountains on February 22 (1907), having reached and camped at Coyote Wells the previous day.

Return Journey, 1907

The return journey to the border, at Calexico, was made along the eastern side of the Cocopa Mountains, paralleling the route of two years previously along the Hardy. Sights were taken, and some plane-table work again done, from several points upon the mountain side which had been made use of upon that occasion.

The delta surface, as viewed from these vantage points, was seen to present practically the same appearance as it had done at normal low-water seasons before the diversion into the Salton basin had taken place. Bends of the old navigable channel, once more containing water, could be seen glistening over against the Sonoran Mesa. Volcano Lake was about normal in size and appearance, and the numerous channels, sloughs, and lagoons, which had been overflowing, and had appeared so prominently at the high-water period of the previous visit, were now dry and inconspicuous.

This was, nevertheless, the last opportunity which was ever to be available to see the delta in its familiar pre-diversion aspect.

Menace of Increasing Westward Flooding

During the concluding years of this momentous decade the river continued to flow through its recently developed Abejas diversion channel at low-water stages, but it inundated practically the whole western portion of the delta, from the fast disappearing Volcano Lake southwards to the Hardy, at times of flood. The summer rise of 1909 attained a maximum of nearly 150,000 second-feet at the end of June, and this was followed by another freshet of more than 90,000 second-feet in mid-September. Parts of the Abejas channel were seen to be quite incompetent to carry any such discharge, and the additional menace of the rapidly rising detrital fan over a portion of what had recently been Volcano Lake was causing much uneasiness to those who were responsible for safeguarding the canal system of the rapidly growing Imperial Valley communities.

It was this, and associated hazards brought about by the fact that the river was unable to develop and maintain a stabilized channel through this region of indefinite drainage, which was in the meantime receiving heavy annual increments of detrital matter, that made the following years a period of unceasing vigilance on the part of the irrigation and conservation engineers and converted the investigation of the physiographic developments in the delta during the next decade largely into a study and appraisal of major engineering operations.

CHAPTER V

THE TREND SOUTHWESTWARD TO A BLIND OUTLET
(1910-1920)

The physiographic developments which took place in the several divisions of the delta region during the decade 1910-1920 may be briefly and broadly summarized as follows.

The river continued to occupy the Abejas basin and gradually filled and obliterated Volcano Lake, finding and occupying various minor and intricately connected channels as a means of outlet to the Hardy. Areas invaded in maintaining this generally southwesterly course were successively covered, and their surface relief was much changed, by the deposition of detrital matter. The entire period in this district may, in fact, be characterized as one of aggradation. No new permanent channels were developed.

In the Imperial Valley-Salton Basin area the dominant circumstance of physiographic importance was the continued diminution in volume of the water which occupied the deepest portion of the valley under the generally accepted name of " Salton Sea." This loss was almost wholly due to evaporation, being modified to some extent by rainfall and drainage and by overflow water from irrigated areas in the valley. The salinity of the water increased steadily in the diminishing lake, and some slight topographical changes took place through the extension by lateral cutting and erosion of the great channels which had been excavated through the southeastern part of the valley in 1906 by the inflowing water from the Colorado.

The Macuata Basin received flood waters in some considerable quantity several times during the 1910-1920 period, but information concerning the times and extent of these partial floodings is meager and somewhat conflicting. There is no record of a complete filling, and no extensive or important physiographic changes are believed to have taken place there within the period.

In the estuary region and the areas subject to tidal influence the pre-existing balance between tidal scour and deposition of detrital material from the river water was upset by the retention, by the vegetal screens which were impeding the free passage of water and silt in the district between Volcano Lake and the Hardy, of the greater portion of what would normally have reached the estuary. The proximate effect of this disturbance of long-established conditions was a deepening and simplification of the tidal channels in the estuary; the ultimate effect has been a general depletion of the material which had been deposited about the mouth of the river in the form of great tidal flats and of shoals and transitory islands in the tideway.

ESTABLISHMENT OF ABEJAS RIVER-VOLCANO LAKE OUTLET AND RESULTING PROTECTIVE MEASURES

Having selected the Abejas channel as an outlet towards the west in the summer of 1909, the river proceeded to enlarge the connection between its former alignment and its new course, with the result that, after two years of moderate flood conditions—1910 and 1911—this section had assumed the appearance and had attained the competence of an established channel. The bed of the Abejas itself was also cleared and slightly lowered, and fears began to be entertained that recessive cutting might take place which would extend upstream into the old channel of the Colorado and endanger the water supply for the Imperial Canal, or perhaps even the Laguna weir, which had been completed across the river some miles above Yuma in January, 1909.

With this hypothetical danger on the one hand and the more proximate peril of a direct and potentially devastating inbreak from the Volcano Lake region on the other, the dwellers in the Imperial Valley were placed in double jeopardy.

Protective measures were therefore taken upon both fronts. The Volcano Lake Levee (Fig. 28, Pl. I) had been built in the spring of 1908, when the river water was reaching this region through the Paredones and its associated sloughs (see p. 58). This protective line was strengthened, raised at low points, and vigilantly patrolled through the high-water period of 1910. Although the discharge at the peak of the summer flood barely reached 70,000 second-feet, the heavy deposition which had taken place during the two previous years raised the flood level against the levee to a dangerous height, and a break was averted only by bringing every resource to bear in the protective work.

Although the danger of recessive cutting taking place in the bed of the river was not so imminent, it was nevertheless considered at this time to constitute a real peril to the interests of the communities in the Imperial Valley and elsewhere along the Colorado River, and representations were made to President Taft for Federal aid in carrying out a scheme for preventive measures.

Although the work was to be carried out in foreign territory, an understanding had already been reached with the Mexican authorities for meeting the emergency, and the sum of $1,000,000 was set aside by a joint resolution of both branches of Congress, " to be expended by the President for the purpose of protecting the lands and property in the Imperial Valley and elsewhere along the Colorado River." Colonel J. A. Ockerson was appointed to carry out whatever works he might deem necessary in order to insure present relief for, and future protection to, the several irrigation enterprises.

A preliminary survey showed that the most pressing matter was a shortage of water in the Imperial Valley, brought about either by a lowering of the bed of the Colorado in the vicinity of the intake to the Imperial Canal, or a silting up of the head of the canal itself. As no dredger was immediately available for removing the obstruction in the canal, a submerged weir was placed across the Colorado channel immediately below the intake for the purpose of raising the water level to the required height to insure a free flow through the canal.

This operation was regarded merely as an emergency measure, and available resources were concentrated upon the work considered necessary farther down the river.

The plans, as formulated, called for a closure of the break into the Abejas and the construction of a line of protective levees at an average distance of 3,000 feet from the westerly bends of the river. The work was to be extended for about 25 miles, or at least as far as necessary to insure protection. Troubles, administrative and political, delayed operations, and it was not until the middle of May, 1911, and in the face of a fast rising river, that the rock dam closing the opening into the Abejas was considered to be complete and reasonably secure. Almost before this part of the work was accomplished, however, the entire scheme was seen to have failed. The dam was flanked by side cutting at both ends, and the 25 miles of levee which had also been built for the declared purpose of confining the Colorado to its former meander zone had been attacked and had failed at many places.

The summer flood of 1911 was not an especially high one, as the peak discharge barely reached 68,000 second-feet, but it remained above the 50,000 stage for a period of nearly two months, and above 40,000 for nearly three. Levee building, or even repairing, under such conditions of softened ground and general inaccessibility was practically impossible, and the whole scheme was allowed to lapse and the Colorado scored another victory.

Renewed attention was in the meantime devoted to the line of levees in the Volcano Lake area, and in 1912 extensive repairs and a general raising of the crest by $3\frac{1}{2}$ feet were undertaken as further protective measures.

The flood of 1912 reached a peak discharge of approximately 145,000 second-feet and tested all the protective works along the lower river very severely. The situation in the Abejas-Volcano Lake region was materially relieved by the tendency of the river to cut a rather definite relief channel for itself directly through the bed of the old lake, towards a junction with the upper Hardy. This channel maintained its identity until 1918 and represents the most extreme westerly swing of the river during the period of the investigation.

Developments in the Yuma Valley

Although some earlier irrigation upon a comparatively small scale, by means of a pumping plant raising water directly from the river into the distribution canal, had already been undertaken in the vicinity of Yuma, the real development of the portion of the delta area situated on the eastern side of the Colorado and between the mouth of the Gila and the international boundary line began with the completion of the Laguna weir in 1909.

This region had been subject to overflow at stages of the river exceeding a gauge height of 25 feet at the Yuma station and had been partially protected from inundation by local systems of light levees.

The Laguna weir was the first major project undertaken by the U. S. Reclamation Service and was in several respects of pioneer design and construction. It is situated at the extreme eastern confines of the delta, approximately 10 miles northeast of Yuma, upon the first site above the Colorado-Gila junction at which solid foundation material could be found upon both banks of the river. This was considered to be essential, although mid-river soundings disclosed no bed rock at any reasonable depth.

The dam is of the diversion type and is a low broad structure, with a length of approximately 4,500 feet between abutments. It is rock-filled and paved, has a heavy concrete crest, and three concrete core walls are embodied in the superstructure and carried well down into the river bed upon pile foundations. It raises the river level about 10 feet above its former low water level at this point and has proved to be a well-built and permanent diversion structure.

Although entirely successful in this sense, it failed to fulfil the expectations of its designers as furnishing an ample settling basin for the removal of silt from the river water before allowing it to enter the canal. The basin was filled with sediment practically to the lip of the dam within a few weeks after its completion, leaving available for water settlement and periodical sluicing only a small channel section above the sluicing gates which were provided at the western end of the dam. The process is effective in removing a certain proportion of the coarser and heavier detrital matter which is so objectionable to the irrigation engineer, but the limited space for stilling and settlement which it has been possible to maintain with the low head available for sluicing has resulted in practice in making the removal of such material only partial.

The effect of the dam upon the various phases of deposition in the delta may be considered as negligible.

The areas subject to gravity irrigation under the project lie partly on the western side of the river above and opposite the mouth of the Gila but principally on the eastern, or Arizona, side, in what is generally known as the Yuma Valley, which extends from Yuma, at the Colorado-

Gila junction, to the international line. The main canal is carried down upon the Californian side of the river to a point opposite the town of Yuma, then under the river bed through an inverted syphon 14 feet in diameter to the Arizona side, where it continues as a feeder to the general distribution system over the valley lands. The syphon was completed, and the Yuma Valley first reached by gravity flow, at the end of June, 1912.

The levee system for the protection of the project comprises lines of earth levees on the western side of the river from the dam to Yuma, along the southern bank of the Gila, and down the eastern side of the Colorado from Yuma to the international boundary. Construction of these protective works was carried on simultaneously with that of the dam, the sluicing and diversion works, and the syphon, and although some little trouble was experienced, especially along the Arizona bank of the Colorado, for a few years after they were first put into operation, a system of pole and brush abatis protection was worked out which proved to be very satisfactory.

Much of the Arizona area had been subject to inundation at times of high river, and in certain sections the ground-water level was very close to the surface. It was discovered after the levees had been finished that the water table was closely responsive to changes of level in the river, even in some localities two or three miles from the channels. The effect was that as the ground water approached the surface with the rise in the water table in the lower areas, the alkaline matter which it contained in solution was brought within the range of capillary attraction and surface evaporation, giving rise to a concentration of alkalies in the soil in quantities sufficient to make it unsuitable to support most forms of plant life. Soil leaching and drainage and the removal of the waste water from the irrigation system had to be planned upon a rather extensive scale, and this problem has continued to be one of the major ones in the district.

The matter of the permeability of the underlying strata, implied by the ready response of the ground water to hydrostatic pressure at some distance, was studied by the writer in some detail in 1912 and 1913 as a phase of the general investigation of delta phenomena, and the conclusion was reached that the super-sensitiveness was due principally to the presence of material derived in large part from the adjacent sands and gravels of the Sonoran Mesa, so called, which extends northwards as a topographical feature to the Gila valley. The presence of such material in the underlying measures might be accounted for either as a result of former eolian influence or of direct attacks by the river during some of its earlier alignments upon exposed salients of the escarpment, such as had occurred many miles to the south in 1904 and 1905.

After the completion of the Yuma project and the abandonment of any further attempt to revert the Colorado to its former alignment, no new engineering works of any magnitude or great importance were undertaken in any portion of the delta during the remainder of the decade under consideration.

The Yuma drainage system was further developed, the dangerous Volcano Lake sector of the western diversion was closely watched, the levee there was repaired and reinforced wherever necessary, and some spurs and connecting links were added to protective lines at other points. It was found necessary to add a revetment of heavy rock to several miles of the levee which protected the main canal from Laguna Dam to Yuma. Below Yuma and on the Arizona side of the river the question was largely one of the "shifting," or side-cutting, of the river and consequential attacks upon the levee line.

Political troubles in Mexico during the earlier years of this period interfered with development south of the international boundary, and the outbreak of the World War tended to discourage the launching of new enterprises in the delta region, as elsewhere.

INVESTIGATIONS IN THE IMPERIAL VALLEY

In the Imperial Valley the distribution system was extended and made more efficient as the growing needs of the Valley communities required. It was to this region that attention was chiefly directed for the next few years, as the river, following its recently developed alignment, maintained a fairly stable channel from its original diversion point to the foot slopes of the Cocopa Mountains and merely forecast further inevitable changes through the steady accumulation of detrital matter in the Volcano Lake region.

Studies undertaken by the writer and associates in the Imperial Valley region from 1915 to 1920 related chiefly to the dispersion and deposition of detrital matter entering the Salton Sea, allied problems in sedimentation, and periodical inspection of the areas uncovered by the receding water for the purpose of gathering data concerning wave action upon soft muddy foreshores and the resultant rearrangement of the material subjected to its influence. The work was done in connection with the general investigation of the botanical problems incidental to the filling and recession of the Salton Sea conducted by the Desert Laboratory of the Carnegie Institution of Washington under the direction of Dr. Mac Dougal.

DETRITAL DEPOSITIONS IN SALTON SEA

During the summer of 1906, when the whole volume of the Colorado was passing through the channel of the Alamo River, it overtopped the banks of the surcharged waterway for a distance of some miles, breaking away towards the south and southwest and flooding the country for many miles before finding a further outlet for the water through the New River drainage system and so into the Salton Sink. The partially impounded water lost much of its suspended load while its velocity was checked, and, upon entering the steeper grades which existed as the sink was approached, its competence for ablation was correspondingly increased. This fact, together with the friable and almost soluble nature of the material over which the inflow was taking place, caused some spectacular recessive cutting. The peak discharge entering the fast-growing " Sea " by way of New River was about 70,000 second-feet, and a much smaller, although considerable, quantity entered by way of the lower Alamo and its associated drainage system. The total yardage removed and transported by the two streams within a period of a few weeks was roughly computed at from 400,000,000 to 450,000,000 cubic yards.

The whole body of this detrital matter was quickly redeposited in and under the rapidly increasing waters of the lake, in the form of the foreset beds of a true delta. Little or no subaerial deposition took place at that time, as the rising water engulfed the material in transit almost as quickly as it reached the shore.

With the closure of the breach in the bank of the Colorado in February, 1907, direct flow from the river to the Salton basin ceased. It was found necessary, however, to maintain almost the maximum flow through the irrigation system in the valley, in order to check the deposition of silt in the canals, and this water continued to pass into the lake. By 1915 the lake level had fallen about 30 feet, and the shore line had receded more than 6 miles at the southeastern end, where the inflow had taken place at the highwater stage. The material brought in by the two streams united to form one general deposit while the lake level was rising, but by 1915 the medial lines of their deltas were over six miles apart.

An examination of the region made during the spring of 1915 showed that the delta-forming process was still in active operation about the mouths of both the New River and the Alamo, the New River delta being the larger and apparently increasing the more rapidly (Fig. 62).

It was realized that here in miniature, or at least upon a much reduced scale, the same processes were producing substantially the same effects as in the more general case of the entire delta. The same water, the same detrital material, the same climatic conditions, and practically the same types of vegetation were involved, and a further study of the region seemed to give promise of useful results and was at once undertaken.

RECEDING STRAND BELTS

The level of the lake water had fallen quite steadily at a rate of slightly more than 4 feet a year, and the areas which had been uncovered at

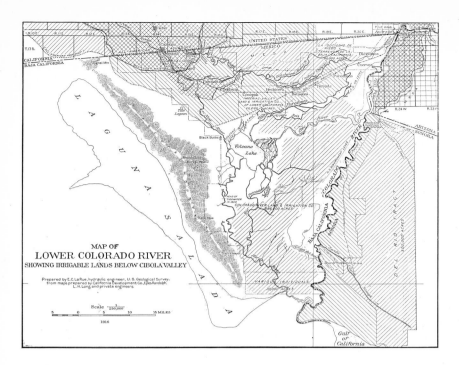

FIG. 28—Map showing the status of the drainage pattern in the Mexican portion of the Colorado Delta about in 1911, after the Colorado had been diverted into the Abejas (Bee) River, which emptied into Volcano Lake. The outline of Laguna Salada (or Macuata) represents approximately the contour of 12 feet above sea level. Cross ruling represents irrigated, single ruling irrigable land. (Much reduced, to 1 : 1,150,000, from map in E. C. La Rue's report, *U. S. Geol. Survey Water-Supply Paper 395, 1916*, based in this part on Bonillas and Urbina's map cited in note on Pl. I).

FIG. 29—'Mud volcanoes' on the western side of Volcano Lake in 1905. Cerro Prieto in left background. These volcanic mud cones and associated hot springs appear to lie on a line of structural weakness which represents a southeastern continuation of the San Jacinto fault of southern California and follows the western side of the Santa Rosa Mountains, crosses the boundary at Calexico, skirts Cerro Prieto, and passes into the Gulf along the northwest-southeast trending segment of the Sonoran Mesa escarpment.

Fig. 30—" Travertine Point," the end of a spur from the Santa Rosa Mountains projecting into Salton Sink at the northwestern shore of Salton Sea (near Fish Springs on map, Pl. I). The dark base of the hill, with the horizontal upper edge, is a coating of travertine which indicates the level of former protracted fillings of the basin.

Fig. 31—Partially submerged crescentic dunes on the southwestern shore of Salton Sea near mouth of Carrizo Creek in February, 1907 (highest level of the lake).

Fig. 32—A crescentic dune in the same vicinity in March, 1915. With the recession of the lake, many of the dunes became active again and resumed their advance toward the northeast.

FIG. 33—General near view of the travertine-covered rocks. The photograph was taken from a point some 25 feet below the present mean sea level as measured at the head of the Gulf of California and 50 feet below the surface level of the body of water which formerly filled the basin in which the travertine was deposited.

FIG. 34—Pattern incised in the surface of the travertine which has subsequently been partially obliterated by further deposition, indicating human occupation of the region antedating the later filling of the basin.

each annual growing season were quite clearly discernible by the gradu-
ated growth of vegetation which occupied them. Over the prevailing
steep gradient of 5 feet to the mile left at the time of subaqueous
deposition and rising lake level, there was not any great lateral dispersion of the more recently deposited foreset and topset beds, but channel
diversions and extensions, the upbuilding and overtopping of banks, and
the formation of obstructive dams and barriers through the agency of
profuse and rapidly growing vegetation could all be readily traced.

Although somewhat interfered with by war service, periodical examinations of this region were continued for a number of years in
connection with other observational work carried on in the basin, until the
increasing salinity of the water in the lake so changed the character and
quantity of the vegetation involved as clearly to make further study
in the immediate vicinity one of specialized local conditions rather than
of the more general factors governing the development of the larger
areas under investigation.

An examination of the strands uncovered annually at various selected
points around the diminishing lake (Fig. 62) was an important feature
of the work undertaken in the basin by the Desert Laboratory. Concerned more particularly with the botanical and ecological problems
involved in these seasonal and annual emergencies, the study also embraced the formation of beach lines and abrupt changes of level at the
shore line, caused, as it was surmised, either by wave action or pauses
or temporary reversals in the process of recession. Such lines, usually
made more prominent by the varying character and quantity of the
belts of vegetation which occupy them, may be counted by the score
at certain sections of the periphery of the sink, and are taken as evidence
of former fillings, or partial fillings, of the basin.

WAVE AND WIND ACTION ON BASIN SOILS

The detailed study of the beach lines was gradually further extended
to cover the broader questions of wave and eolian action as affecting,
or having affected, the general surface features of the basin areas.

The shore line of the lake, during the period under discussion, was
well above the comparatively flat floor of the sink, and material was then
being subjected to wave action which would fall within the categories of
" Imperial sandy loam " or " Imperial gravelly loam " as classified by
Holmes in a soil survey of the basin which was made in 1903.[1] The
two are defined as consisting of mixtures of sand or gravel with the
" Imperial loam " alluvium which formed the dry floor of the sink at
the time the survey was made. When subjected to wave action these

---

[1] J. G. Holmes: Soil Survey of the Imperial Valley, California, *Field Operations of the
Bureau of Soils, 1903*, Washington, 1904, pp. 1219-1248, with soil map and alkali map, 1: 126,
720.

CHEMICAL ANALYSES OF THE WATER OF SALTON SEA, 1907 TO 1916

(in parts per 100,000)

	1907 June 3	1908 May 25	1909 June 8	1910 May 22	1911 June 3	1912 June 10	1913 June 18	1914 June 12	1915 June 8	1916 June 10
Total solids (dried at 110° C.), plus water of occlusion and hydration	364.8	437.20	519.40	603.80	718.00	846.55	1002.56	1179.6	1377.4	1647.2
Water of occlusion and hydration	.....	.....	17.50	22.56	20.84	23.9	32.6	36.2	42.2	47.5
Sodium, Na	111.05	134.26	160.33	189.28	227.81	270.71	323.08	381.47	441.6	528.9
Potassium, K	2.30	2.78	3.24	3.53	3.81	3.81	3.45	4.01	5.2	5.71
Lithium, Li	trace	0.013	0.017	0.021	0.025	.....	.....	.....	.....	.....
Calcium, Ca	9.95	11.87	12.70	13.67	15.62	17.28	19.75	22.22	25.27	29.85
Magnesium, Mg	6.43	7.63	8.96	9.84	11.68	13.62	16.22	19.03	22.63	27.17
Aluminium, Al	0.030	0.035	0.062	0.040	0.089	0.100	0.125	0.140	0.032	0.034
Iron, Fe	0.005	0.006	0.010	0.008	0.036	0.042	0.038	0.012	0.020	0.060
Silicate radicle, SiO_4	1.41	1.43	1.59	1.55	1.83	1.79	2.18	2.42	1.55	1.21
Manganese, Mn	.....	.....	.....	.....	.....	.....	.....	.....	.....	.....
Lead, Pb	.....	.....	.....	.....	.....	.....	.....	.....	.....	.....
Copper, Cu	.....	.....	trace	trace	trace	.....	.....	trace	.....	.....
Chlorine, Cl	169.75	204.05	240.90	280.93	339.42	395.44	473.89	559.66	650.95	787.64
Bromine, Br	.....	.....	.....	.....	.....	.....	.....	.....	.....	.....
Iodine, I	.....	.....	.....	.....	.....	.....	.....	.....	.....	.....
Sulphate radicle, SO_4	47.60	56.74	65.87	76.36	91.67	106.83	124.65	148.10	174.47	207.89
Carbonate radicle, CO_3	6.58	7.66	7.34	6.38	5.78	12.09	11.28	10.96	11.92	11.40
Arsenate radicle, AsO_4	.....	.....	.....	.....	.....	.....	.....	.....	.....	.....
Phosphate radicle, PO_4	0.009	0.011	0.01	0.013	trace	trace	trace	.....	.....	doubtful
Nitrate radicle, NO_3	0.18	0.20	.....	.....	.....	trace	.....	.....	.....	.....
Nitrite radicle, NO_2	.....	.....	0.0006	.....	.....	.....	.....	.....	.....	trace
Oxygen consumed	0.093	0.059	0.068	0.045	0.063	0.072	0.110	0.110	0.208	0.170
Borate radicle, BO_2	.....	trace	trace	trace	trace	.....	trace	trace	trace	trace

compound soils were found to be undergoing a process of segregation, resulting generally in the shoreward movement of the larger and heavier particles and the contrary movement of the finer. Such selective tendencies, repeated over the basin surface at successive recessions of former ephemeral lakes which had occupied it, would result in the eventual movement toward and concentration in the bottom of the sink of the fine material carried in suspension in the river water and distributed with some uniformity throughout the basin area at times of inflow and filling. The information gained upon these points was deemed to be of importance as affecting plant distribution and soil texture.

The air circulation over the Salton area is fairly well defined, the prevailing westerly winds entering the region through the San Gorgonio Pass and sweeping down the valley of the Whitewater. The diurnal land and sea breeze movements about the head of the Gulf also affect the circulation to some extent. In passing over the sandy and gravelly areas which characterize the Whitewater the wind raises and carries forward a burden of sand and dust towards the basin. The movement is doubtless assisted and extended by the upward component introduced into the general circulation by convection currents rising from the heated surface of the desert. The result of this steady movement is the deposition of much arenaceous material upon the finer alluvial surfaces derived from the river.

As has been pointed out by Free,[2] the soil-forming actions of the wind fall under two headings, soil removal and soil mixing. Of the two actions, he claims for the mixing process by far the greater importance as a factor in the preparation of the surface layers of soil for supporting plant life. In the Salton region the mixture was found to be very complete. The resultant sandy loams of the Holmes classification are in every way, except for the high alkali content of the basic alluvium, suitable for development and cultivation, and the percentage of deleterious saline matter is correspondingly decreased by the admixture of clean wind-borne sand from the basin of a mountain streamway.

The examination, as conducted during the years in which this region was subjected to special scrutiny, was a mechanical rather than a chemical one, the soil texture being deemed to be of even more importance to the types of vegetation under investigation than the actual saline content.

CHEMICAL ANALYSES OF SALTON SEA WATER

Periodical analyses of the water remaining in the Salton Sea were nevertheless arranged for by the Desert Laboratory, beginning at the stage of maximum height and area in 1907 and continuing without intermission by means of samples taken in each summer season during the next ten years (see the accompanying table).

[2] E. E. Free: The Movement of Soil Material by the Wind, *Bureau of Soils Bull. No. 68*, Washington, 1911.

The results of these analyses, in regard to their bearing upon plant life in the emersed zones representing the annual recession of the water, were summarized by MacDougal in 1917 in a general review of the conditions and developments observed in the Salton area during the preceding decade.[3] The summary may be profitably quoted (pp. 467 and 469):

During the first year of the recession of the lake the chief mineral constituents increased so that the amount present was about 19 to nearly 21 per cent greater in 1908 than in 1907. This increase was shared by the calcium. In the following year, while the sodium increased 19.4 per cent and the potassium 16.5 per cent, calcium increased but 7 per cent and in the following year but slightly more. Coincidently the missing calcium was found as a lime deposit on the branches of submerged shrubs, stones, and other objects. The amount of calcium in solution had by no means reached the saturation point, and other causes must be brought into account for the deposition. The above applies also to some extent to the course of concentration of the magnesium. The only available inference is that the lime and magnesia were brought down by the action of a plexus of algæ and bacteria. The inferred presence of these organisms would carry with it the implication that the formation of the lake would be followed by their multiplication and development, which was such that the maximum formation of tufa or lime deposit was greatest in 1909 and 1910, during which period the amount thrown down was sufficient to account for about half of the expected increase in concentration of lime. In succeeding years this action was not so marked.

TRAVERTINE DEPOSITS

The question of the calcium content of the water, and the method of its separation therefrom and subsequent deposition upon available surfaces, had a direct bearing upon the investigation of some accumulations of travertine which was being carried on during 1915 to 1916.

These are to be found upon the vertical or undercut surfaces of a small rocky ridge (Fig. 30) which at its highest rises slightly above the highest and best marked "beach line" surrounding the basin and is situated at the northeastern extremity of a low spur of the Santa Rosa Mountains. It was to this ridge and spur that the preliminary expedition to the basin participated in by the Desert Laboratory and Dr. W. P. Blake had been directed, and the existence of the travertine was pointed out by Dr. Blake, who had originally noticed it in 1853, upon the occasion of his first visit to the region. It was not until 1915, however, that any opportunity under suitable light conditions had arisen for making a close examination of the deposit. It was then found that it had attained a maximum thickness of about 30 inches in a horizontal zone some 12 to 15 feet below its upper limit. This limit coincides with the conspicuous beach crest or shore line which surrounds the basin and doubtless represents the maximum level of filling within recent geological time.

[3] D. T. MacDougal: A Decade of the Salton Sea, *Geogr. Rev.*, Vol. 3, 1917, pp. 457-473.

In addition to data concerning thickness, development upon different exposures, and structural peculiarities, the examination revealed the presence of many incised patterns, apparently in conventional designs upon the surface of the travertine (Fig. 34). Although some were fairly conspicuous and would attract attention from some little distance, many could only be recognized upon the rough surface under optimum conditions of illumination. Sections were made, and it at once became obvious that the original lines had in many instances been traced some distance below the existing surface and covered by subsequent growth of the fibrous material. As the patterns were plainly artifacts, the question of their antiquity became interesting. Steps were taken to secure specimens of the travertine sufficiently large to show portions of several lines, and of sufficient depth to go beneath the original incised surface, in an effort to ascertain how many subsequent depositions had taken place in particular instances. The examination was not entirely successful, as the fibrous nature of the material was found to make identification of successive layers extremely difficult. The conclusion was, however, ultimately reached that a reasonable hypothesis would be that in some cases three or more layers with distinctive divisions between them had been superimposed upon the original incised surface.

The implication from these detailed examinations, incomplete and, in a sense, inconclusive though they might be, was that the basin had been filled to a level coincidental with the conspicuous beach line upon more than one occasion, for periods of sufficient length to allow for measurable travertine deposition, and that human occupancy of the region had antedated some of the later fillings.

CRESCENTIC DUNES

The recession of the lake from 1907 to 1917 had left the group of *barkhan* dunes, which had been partially submerged at the time of its greatest expansion (Fig. 31), many miles back from the 1917 shore line, and the development of a passable road along the southwestern side of the lake at about the 1907 water level had made them readily accessible from the land side in 1915. They were re-examined during 1916, and it was then found that many dunes which were recognized as having been partially submerged and reduced to mere mounds of sand in 1907 and 1908, had again assumed the typical crescentic form and become active. In some few instances they had been captured by vegetation and anchored, but the orientation of the reconstructed members of the group again corresponded with that of those at a higher level which had escaped submersion, and the general movement was, as before, towards the east.

This group is one of the few within the delta areas which appears to maintain a definite trend in direction of advance. This marked tendency is probably caused by a local peculiarity in air currents, due perhaps to the configuration of the mountain masses to the westward. In most of the dune areas and sand fields in and about the delta, as for instance in the great sand expanse which occupies the western part of the Macuata Basin, or the equally extensive Algodones Sand Hills which margin the northeastern side of Imperial Valley, any such united trend appears to be lacking.

Rate of Recession of Salton Sea, 1916-1920

The rate of recession of the Salton Sea slowed down appreciably during the period intervening between 1916 and 1920. The loss in volume became more irregular, and there were even actual reversals of the process at times, when gain instead of loss occurred. The new lowering of the water level between June 30, 1916, and November 30, 1920, was 11.5 feet, an average annual decrease of a little more than 2.5 feet. This was taken to indicate that the condition of equilibrium between inflow from the canal systems and rainfall, on the one hand, and evaporation from the water surface, on the other, was being approached. As the annual amount of evaporation from an open water surface in the basin may be reasonably estimated at about 8 feet under average meteorological conditions and as the area of the lake at that time was approximately 250 square miles, or 160,000 acres, a volume of inflowing water equivalent to 1,280,000 acre-feet was required in order to reduce the net loss to the amount indicated by the gauge figures.

CHAPTER VI

ARTIFICIAL DEFLECTION TO THE SOUTH-SOUTHWEST
(1920-1930)

At the opening of the decade 1920-1930 the Colorado River still continued to occupy the general alignment of the former Abejas channel into which it had broken twelve years previously.

Failing in the development of an unobstructed outlet towards tidewater by this route, it had ponded and deposited its load of suspended and transported detrital matter over extensive areas with heavy vegetal covering in the region of the former Volcano Lake, thus adding progressively to its difficulty in finding free egress. The further effect of the obstruction and ponding had been a general raising of the bed and banks along the Abejas section and a dangerous and increasing tendency of flood waters to escape from the channel on both sides. The condition of a surcharged and inadequate channel following the crest of a ridge, such as had existed along the abandoned navigable channel of former years, was again being approached.

The situation in the Volcano Lake area of deposition was causing much uneasiness to the staff of the Imperial Irrigation District in 1921. This body had acquired the management of and assumed the responsibility for water supply and conservation in Imperial Valley. By necessary agreements with the holding companies in Mexican territory, through whose lands the water for Imperial Valley use had to pass in order to reach the distributing system, it was also brought into a position of responsibility for averting or controlling flood damage in this critical district.

It was found that for corresponding discharge stages in the river, as indicated by the measurements obtained at the Yuma gauging station, the flood waters were rising higher each succeeding year against the Volcano Lake protective levee. The levee itself had been raised and strengthened from time to time in the effort to keep the protection in advance of the growing menace. The crest was $10\frac{1}{2}$ feet higher in 1920 than it had been in 1908, when the levee was built; the exposed face of the entire structure across the old lake area had also been revetted with rock as a protection against wave action at times of high water.

Two courses appeared to be open for safeguarding the Imperial Valley interests: either the levee line might be still further reinforced and raised, in the hope that the river might carve an adequate outlet for flood waters through the obstructive barriers, or relief might be sought through excavating an artificial channel towards the south, and away from the menaced sector.

Artificial Diversion of the Abejas Outlet Toward the Pescadero

This latter was the plan which received final consideration, as being the more likely to bring about the desired result. The basin of the Pescadero, which had heretofore existed as a drainage system for the central region between the Hardy and the old navigable channel of the Colorado during the after periods of high water, lay conveniently to the south of the Abejas sector of the river and was selected as the region towards which diversion should take place. The scheme involved, firstly, the excavation of a diversion channel from the Abejas bank to a point in the Pescadero basin to which an adequate fall might be obtained and, secondly, the construction of a dam across the Abejas in order to divert that river into and through the new cutting. It was fully realized, from earlier experiences in diverting and controlling the heavily laden Colorado water, that the success or failure of the plan would depend primarily upon the character of the excavated channel—whether it would tend to develop into a degrading or into an aggrading form through the factors of fall, cross section, and ability to pass an adequate flow to insure scour.

As the plan, as carried out, proved to be successful in relieving the pressure in the Volcano Lake region and maintaining a diversion in a general southerly direction for several years thereafter, it will be well to follow in some detail the engineering operations undertaken in excavating the cut and damming the river.

The point selected for diversion was approximately $7\frac{1}{2}$ miles west and 1 mile south of Monument 205 on the international boundary, which marks the termination of the Arizona-Sonora line. The river here passed between high and comparatively solid banks which would serve as favorable abutments for the diversion dam, and an even surface, falling about 4 feet to the mile for the first 4 miles and averaging about $2\frac{3}{4}$ feet for the first 15 miles, would carry the water into the Pescadero basin with a minimum of excavation. The hydraulic problem was to provide for sufficient initial flow through the excavated channel to insure rapid erosion of the bed and an increase in depth at its upper end. Owing to the limitation of equipment and also in order to insure such a flow, the new outlet was made in the first place in the form of three parallel cuttings with two spoil banks between them. The expectation was that these banks would be removed by scour as the flow increased and the three cuts be united into a single efficient channel. This expectation was very quickly fulfilled.

Fig. 35—Air view looking south across lower end of Pescadero Levee, built in 1922 and extended southwestward in 1923 and 1926 to prevent the escape of the river waters through the Pescadero Diversion Cut toward the Salton Sink. The waters are shown (July, 1926) as menacing and crossing the levee in that direction (northwest).

Fig. 36—General air view over part of the Colorado Delta proper, looking east-northeast from above the lower end of the dispersal channels on the inner side of Rodriguez Levee. The main features named on the photograph may be located by referring to the map, Plate I. Conditions shown are as in July, 1929. (Figs. 35-36 from air photographs by H. A. Erickson.)

FIGS. 37 and 38—Two views down the drying bed of the Pescadero Diversion Cut at periods of low river in 1925 (Fig. 37) and 1926. At both these times this immediate vicinity marked the termination of the Colorado, no water then reaching the estuary.

Fig. 39—Pescadero Diversion Cut, looking upstream from lower end while it was carrying the main discharge of the Colorado.

Fig. 40—Bank of the diversion cut at time of falling river.

Figs. 41 and 42—Suction inlets of syphon batteries abandoned by the river in 1929: left, at Pescadero Dam for delivery into the Delta irrigation canal system utilizing the remnant of the Bee River; to right, over the San Luis Levee (Baja California Canal Co. Levee) for delivery into the Vacanora Canal. (See map, Pl. I, and Fig. 48.)

Fig. 43—Dumping heavy revetment rock at a threatened point on the Pescadero Levee in 1926.

Fig. 44—Pescadero Levee extension breached and destroyed in 1926. The levee, with the track along its crest, extended into and through the timber in the background before the crevasse opened.

The cut was definitely directed toward a certain bend in the Pescadero arroyo approximately 4 miles from the Abejas bank. The difference in surface level at the two points was about 16 feet, the elevation above assumed mean sea level at the head of the Gulf being 76 feet at the river bank and 60 at the Pescadero. It was originally planned to tap the river channel by a cut 8 feet below bank level, but the depth was increased to 11 feet before the excavation was finished in order to insure a free passage for the water at lower stages of the river. The grade finally selected for the bed of the new channel was 2 feet to the mile. This gave an opening into the arroyo channel 5 feet below its average bank level. Its total depth at the selected point of entrance was about 12 feet, and it was at that time a well-cleared and scoured waterway leading towards, and serving as a high-water confluent to, the main channel of the Pescadero.

Following upon the gathering of the necessary data and the carrying out of the preliminary surveys and level traverses work was actively begun upon the project at the end of 1921. It was planned to have, before the end of January, 1922, the new channel opened to the river and the diversion dam carried near enough toward completion to insure the diversion of a sufficient quantity of water to keep it open.

Although the work had been well planned and was carried forward with great efficiency along the contemplated lines, it was somewhat interfered with by flash floods in the river. The preliminary structure for the diversion dam was carried away during one freshet and again seriously damaged during another. Advantage was taken of the high water, however, to cut the barrier at the head of the nearly completed new channel early in January and so begin the process of scour and erosion by which it was hoped to further develop it.

Success seemed to be assured from the initial opening. Following the first diversion of about 6,000 second-feet, the channel proved to be able to maintain itself under varying discharges of from 2,000 to 30,000 second-feet before the end of April and the beginning of the true spring rise in the river.

The dam across the river channel continued to be a source of anxiety all through the spring. It was flanked by a sudden rise in the river towards the end of March, and repairs were not completed until the middle of April, and it was again seriously menaced in June.

New Outlet Blocked by Developing Detrital Fan

Although the actual diversion of the river into the excavated channel continued to be successful, it was shortly discovered that the expected clearing of an outlet to tidewater from the lower end of the completed work was not taking place. The Pescadero arroyo proved to be quite incompetent to carry, or to develop into a channel capable of carrying, more than a limited quantity of water. It had formerly existed as a part of the general Pescadero drainage system, and its function had been to collect its share of the partially clarified water which remained upon the surface of the delta after each general flood and to pass it on towards the main Pescadero channel and tidewater. When it was filled to overflowing by the heavily laden water from the new cutting, silting and the building of obstructive bars and masses of drift began to diminish its cross-sectional area very rapidly. An inspection of the vicinity made during May, with a discharge of about 55,000 second-feet passing through the cut, showed no signs whatever of a definite channel but disclosed only a general inundation with a slow motion towards the south and every evidence of the rapid deposition of detrital matter amongst the dense vegetation which covered so much of the region.

The summer flood of 1922 reached a peak discharge of 115,000 second-feet at Yuma, and the total discharge for June was nearly 6,000,000 acre-feet. Adopting the formula used by the U. S. Reclamation Service at Yuma for estimating the suspended silt content of the Colorado water in terms of acre-feet and assuming a silt percentage for June of 0.66, as established by the mean for that month over a period of ten years, the total volume of detrital matter delivered into the region within the time would be somewhat in excess of 27,500 acre-feet, or approximately 45,000,000 cubic yards.

Opening the new cut had made an extensive area accessible to the heavily laden water coming directly from the river channel, which for some years previously had only been reached by the partially clarified water of the general overflow, and deposition was found to be correspondingly heavy. The blanket of deposited material began as a narrow belt almost at the head of the cut and gradually extended fanwise towards the southeast, south, and southwest. The area affected was perhaps 300 square miles, and the deposit from this flood alone was found to be 6 and 8 feet in thickness at certain points.

By the summer of 1923 the Pescadero arroyo had disappeared. It had been filled, covered, and obliterated by the fan of detrital matter which the floods of the two previous summers had spread about the lower end of the cut. As the 1923 flood receded it was found that the main outflow of the water was now towards the southwest, through a newly developed channel which split up into minor distributaries leading in the same general direction after a course of a few miles.

Extension of Levee System to Prevent Westward Migration of Pescadero Outlet

In order to guard against any general tendency of the newly diverted river to work back towards the Abejas channel and its former course towards the Volcano Lake area, the dam structure below the diversion point was extended during 1923, for 5 miles down the western bank of the diversion channel, in the form of a well-constructed and largely rock-revetted levee. Track was laid along the crest of the embankment, and gauging stations were established at several points on the bank of the channel.

A danger point existed in a deep bend in the Abejas (Fig. 35) 1½ miles to the westward of the diversion channel. The elevation above datum in the bed of this abandoned loop of the 1909-1921 river was only 48 feet, whereas, with a discharge of 90,000 second-feet passing through the diversion channel, a water-surface elevation of 69.95 was recorded on June 25, 1923.

The years 1924 and 1925 were years of comparatively moderate summer floods, and, although the fan of detrital matter below the end of the diversion cut continued to rise and spread, no decisive break towards the west took place. Rather indefinite paludal areas began to develop upon and about the new surface, and at this period the supply of silt in any form, derived from the river, was entirely cut off from tide-water.

In 1926 conditions changed again. The protective levee along the western bank of the diversion cut was extended for a distance of 2½ miles early in spring by the Imperial Irrigation District, and a further extension of 2 miles was to be added by Mexican interests whose lands would have been menaced by a break towards the west in that section. During the summer flood of the same year most of this additional length of 2 miles was practically destroyed before it was entirely completed (Fig. 44), and the main levee was also breached. The peak discharge at Yuma slightly exceeded 73,000 second-feet, with a run-off during the month of 3,560,000 acre-feet. Assuming as before a silt percentage for June of 0.66, deposition in the paludal areas in which the flood water was practically desilted at that time would be approximately 17,000 acre-feet for the month.

The main outflow channel issuing from the lower end of the diversion cut was now showing an increasing tendency to break away over the right flank of the fan or cone which it had been instrumental in depositing. The break through the levee extension, although largely a matter of side-cutting, was an indication of increasing pressure in that direction, and it was realized that, in order to safeguard the developments which were taking place in the western part of the delta, a more efficient and extensive barrier would have to be constructed.

The plan took shape early in 1927 in the building of an additional levee, based upon the bank levee along the diversion cut but striking off in a generally southwesterly direction between the Abejas channel and the area of active dispersal of the river water. In locating this new barrier the high-water mark of the previous summer's flood was generally followed, and sloughs and abandoned channels were avoided as much as possible. The work was pushed as an emergency measure, and the Mexican Government assumed a substantial portion of the cost. No rock revetting was used, as rock was not readily available, but pole and brush groins were built wherever it was necessary to protect the embankment against side-cutting. The total length of the work, as constructed, was about 15 miles.

Check measurements were recorded by engineers of the Mexican irrigation companies, and repeated during the two following years, of the flood level against the face of the levee, for integration with the discharge measurements of the river obtained at the Yuma gauging station, an interval of one day and a deduction of the amount passed into the Imperial intake being allowed for in making the computation as to the actual amount of water facing the embankment for corresponding stages of river flow. The curves plotted from these data showed graphically the amount of deposition which was taking place at that time along the levee, and were of great use in indicating where and to what extent betterments to the protective works were necessary.

The name of Rodriguez Levee was given to the new work, which continued, although at the cost of constant vigilance, to protect the lands to the northwestward of it and to prevent any incursion of water to the Abejas channel.

The great blanket of detrital material, the deposition of which had begun with the opening of the Abejas diversion cut in 1922, was thickening and extending rapidly during 1928 and 1929, and it was found to be necessary in each of these years to add to the height of the levee at certain critical points at which flood pressure was developing. For identical river discharge measurements of 20,000 second-feet, for instance, successive gauge readings, taken at a point on the face of the new levee about 5½ miles west of the original termination of the Abejas diversion cutting, showed water-surface elevations of 48.1, 50.7, and 53.1 feet respectively in May, 1927, May, 1928, and March, 1929, these heights in each case being above the assumed sea-level datum in use by the development companies operating in Mexican territory.

Construction of Vacanora Canal for Irrigation

Two further developments were taking place in the lower delta at this time. One was the grading and track laying of the Mexicali and Gulf Railroad, which had been promoted for the purpose of furnishing a seaport outlet in Mexican waters for the growing trade from the upper delta lands, and the other was the development by irrigation of a large body of land situated in the mesopotamian region between the old navigable channel alignment of the Colorado and the course as temporarily established by the Abejas diversion undertaking.

In furtherance of the irrigation scheme a levee was constructed paralleling the southern bank of the Abejas, beginning at the point of the

1909 diversion of the Colorado into it and continuing to, and terminating at, the eastern bank of the diversion channel of 1922. In the rear
of the levee, about one mile east of the diversion dam across the old
Abejas channel, was placed the head of a new main-line canal, which
was built for a distance of about 18 miles in a general south-southwest
direction and was intended to supply water to large areas situated between
it and the old navigable channel of the Colorado. The new channel was
excavated in the early part of 1929 and was called, and has since been
identified by the name, Vacanora.

A battery of syphons was installed over the crest of the river levee
for the purpose of supplying the new system with water. A larger
battery of seven units was also placed across the Abejas diversion dam
in 1928 in connection with a project for utilizing the old Abejas channel as a feeder for the Delta Canal, in the western part of the region
which was being developed behind the Rodriguez Levee.

The ultimate effect of the two projects would have been the diversion
into canal headings of practically the whole low-water flow of the river
without the necessity of constructing and maintaining costly diversion
works. The river itself would have formed a forebay for the two canal
systems, and the Abejas diversion cutting, a spillway. It was in contemplation at the same time to close this partially by means of a low
embankment or submerged diversion weir in order to maintain against
the suction side of the syphons the necessary head for effective working.

The summer flood in 1928 reached a peak of nearly 100,000 second-
feet in June, following upon a normal rise during May. The total discharge for the two months was somewhat in excess of 7,000,000 acre-
feet, but it fell off very rapidly during July, and, although the river
rose again and discharged rather heavily during October and November,
it remained at comparatively low stages during the 1928-1929 winter
season. Practically all the flood water had passed through the Abejas
diversion cutting and dispersed to the eastward of the Rodriguez Levee.
The effect was, as noted above, a progressive raising of the surface of
the ground over a large area and consequent higher levels of flood-water
surfaces for corresponding river discharges.

Appropriation of Vacanora Canal by the Colorado as Main Outlet

Changes were taking place also along the main river channel above
the point of diversion into the Abejas diversion cutting. They were
of the usual type incidental to a surcharged channel with bends of short
radius. Alignment was changing through the development of cut-offs
or the deepening of bends. A swing of the river towards the right, at
the point at which the Vacanora syphons had been installed, had the
effect of isolating them entirely from any practicable inflow (Fig. 42)
and so rendering the whole development project temporarily useless.

In an effort to maintain the water supply through the canal, a cutting
was made into it from the new alignment of the river in what was really
a backward direction. It was considered that this would safeguard the
canal works from destructive inflow.

The spring rise of the river in 1929 began in March with a peak discharge of 30,000 second-feet and a total discharge during the month
of 750,000 acre-feet. The rise was steady until the peak of the summer
flood in June, when a discharge of 89,000 second-feet was reached. July,
August, September, and October were all months of high discharge, the
aggregate for the eight months, March to October inclusive, being in
the neighborhood of 17,000,000 acre-feet. The effects of this long-
continued season of high river and heavy discharge were, firstly, a great
extension of the areas of silt deposition and, secondly, an increased
tendency of the river to carve new outlets for its water through the
softened ground. During the early autumn it began to enlarge the opening which had been cut into the Vacanora Canal, and by the beginning
of November the entire volume of the river was passing through the
new channel and entering the canal excavation.

Although this had been excavated as a main-line canal, it quickly
proved itself to be incompetent to carry the full volume of the river, and
side-cutting and breaching of the banks took place so rapidly, even with
the decreasing discharge, that its further usefulness as an irrigation
canal was practically destroyed and it became merely a part of the
Colorado River.

Another outbreak had occurred through the south bank of the main
channel of the Abejas during the summer, resulting in the temporary
wrecking of a portion of the levee constructed by the Baja California
Development Company at a point about one mile east of their syphons,
but, although the breach made in the levee was fully half a mile in width
and an immense volume of water entered the opening, no decisive
channel-cutting took place, the current velocity being checked in all
directions by the heavy growth of vegetation.

The new diversion of the river into the Vacanora Canal completely
altered its course from the diversion point to tidewater, an air line
distance of approximately 35 miles, and was, in fact, the most complete
abandonment of previous hydrological conditions that had occurred in
the delta since it had broken into and occupied the Abejas channel and
basin twenty years previously. By adopting the new course it entirely
ignored the Pescadero basin, through which it had for some time seemed
inevitable that an outlet towards the Hardy would be developed. Overflow pressure was now definitely towards the old navigable channel
meander zone, in the vicinity of Colonia Lerdo, with general high-water
flooding taking place towards the south and southeast rather than to
the southwest.

During the four winter months following upon October, 1929, the river discharge remained very low, and the whole volume of water that passed the Imperial intake turned into the Vacanora channel. The Abejas diversion cutting, which had formed the main river channel for seven years previously, was now entirely dry and both groups of syphons remained isolated.

The new section of the river was observed to be passing through the usual phases incidental to decreasing discharge and normal silt content of the water. Deposition was taking place upon bars and shoals in the channel and along the convex shores of bends, and there was a noticeable tendency towards the development of irregularities in alignment through bank-cutting and caving.

LESS DEPOSITION IN THE ESTUARY

Extensive and progressive changes were observed to be taking place in the estuary and upon the tidal flats surrounding the mouth of the river as the 1920-1930 period closed. Following upon the diversion of the river into the Abejas cutting in 1922, the water had encountered, and been compelled to spread over, a region densely covered with vegetation, with prevailing low gradients. Its velocity being checked by this vegetal screen, deposition of the matter held in suspension was correspondingly great, and the effluent from the paludal regions which shortly developed in the areas of interception and dispersal had lost the characteristic appearance of Colorado water and become partially or wholly clarified.

The process being continued, the delicate balance previously existing in the estuary between tidal sweep and scour on the one hand, and deposition of fresh detrital matter from the river, on the other, was upset. The visible consequences, as observed during the examination of the estuary made by the writer from the Sonoran shore in November and December, 1929, were a simplification and clearing of the tidal channels and a very marked decrease in the quantity of river drift upon the flood plains about the river entrance.

Estuarial channels were less obstructed by bars and shoals and appeared to be more efficient drainage outlets than when observed and navigated in previous years. No boat was available at the time the examination was made, but, as conducted from shore during several days and at all stages of the tide, the impression received of radical changes having occurred since former studies of the region had been made was very distinct. Extracts from notes made at the time will convey the impression:

" There is little doubt that practically the entire estuary now occupies a different position from that so carefully established and plainly mapped by Lieutenant Ives and his associates in 1857-1858 or even from the amended position and configuration shown by Commander Dewey in 1873-1875. Millions of cubic yards of friable material have repeatedly changed position along both shores of the estuary since the last detailed study was made from this shore twenty-five years ago. The shore lines themselves have advanced or receded, islands and shoals have been formed or have disappeared, and the drainage sloughs cutting back into the surrounding tidal flats have either been deepened and extended or shoaled and obliterated in accordance with the changing conditions. At the present time all change appears to be in one direction, namely toward depletion—the result undoubtedly of continual tidal inroads upon the accumulated detrital material consequent upon a different balance between tide and river."

The loss, through decay, storm, or general shore erosion, or other causes, of nearly all the leading or range marks and beacons which had been erected upon the shores of the estuary during the era of navigation, was found to add materially to the difficulty of precise identification of positions. Many had still been in existence during the earlier years of the investigation and had been made use of in estimating and plotting courses and distances when leaving or entering the river.

A visit made some months previously to the site of the old shipyard on " Shipyard Slough " had shown how completely traces of former occupancy and activity disappear when subjected to the high temperatures, alternating states of high and low humidity, and tidal activity of the river-mouth region. The slough was then found to have dwindled so in size as to be useless for navigation by anything larger than small skiffs, and but few traces were left of the shipyard itself.

DECREASE OF SIZE OF BORES

A further and associated hydrographical change observed in the estuary upon both of these visits was in the size and violence of the winter bores. These were witnessed upon several occasions and under varying circumstances of tide and wind; and the impression was received and recorded that, under similar conditions of these two contributory factors to their development, they were distinctly smaller and less violent in their advance than when observed and closely studied twenty-five years previously. The change in appearance and size was considered to be due principally to the fact that the incoming tide was meeting with little opposition from the river. This happened to be at extremely low stages on the occasions of both visits, and the periods of the ebb tides were noticeably shortened at certain definite points at which observations had been made during former studies of the phenomenon. The changed configuration and generally less obstructed character of the tidal channels were probably also contributory causes to the rapidity with which the impounded water of the last flood tide passed out of the estuary, and so were effective in reducing the head and back pressure against the succeeding incoming tide.

Tidal bores of great violence had been recorded as passing up the channels at times since the earlier observations had been made, notably an exceptionally heavy one in September, 1921, in which a small steamer was capsized and lost, with a loss of about 130 lives.

OTHER CHANGES IN ESTUARY

The observations made upon and from the Sonoran shore in 1929 were continued for a period of about ten days, covering two periods of spring tides, and the intervening neap tides. The general character of the changes in the tidal channels, as contrasted with the conditions twenty-five years previously, appeared to be towards the development of a main arterial outlet extending from the Colorado-Hardy junction to the vicinity of Montague Island. It was noticeably direct in alignment, fairly uniform in width, and apparently so in depth at extreme low water periods. The former tendency to cross the estuary from shore to shore seemed to be lacking. The western entrance to the river, between Montague Island and the Californian shore, although not very plainly discernible from observation points on the Sonoran side of the estuary, appeared to be passing most of the outflowing tide and to contain a continuous channel even at periods of extreme low water.

On the Sonoran flood-plain area, which could be examined in detail, radical changes were found to have taken place in the quantity and character of the driftwood and other river-derived matter with which the surface had formerly been so thickly covered. No recently deposited material was found except occasional loose masses of salt-grass, tule roots, and other transitory debris. Willow, cottonwood, poplar, and other light woods, which had formerly formed the bulk of the widely dispersed drift material, had disappeared entirely. Massive logs, timber-piling and railroad cross-ties of cedar, pitch pine, redwood, or oak, all of which are resistant to decay, alone remained of the larger and heavier matter.

Increased surface salinity was also very noticeable, and there was no appearance of recently deposited detrital matter along the beds or margins of drainage sloughs or channels.

The lower course of the Santa Clara Slough was also examined and was found to have lost its former appearance of a fresh-water stream-way and to have become a salt-water tidal channel. The entrance had shoaled somewhat, and the great expanse of tidal flats which lie across the narrow shore-channel opposite the entrance had increased in height and become better defined and existed as an island at nearly all periods of the tide.

7

The general appearance in this vicinity was that of stability or accretion, rather than of the depletion which was so noticeable in the upper reaches of the estuary.

Conditions in the Macuata Basin, 1920-1930

No marked changes or developments took place in the Macuata Basin during the 1920-1930 decade. The summer flood of 1923, reaching a maximum discharge of approximately 100,000 second-feet as measured at Yuma in June, caused an inundation over practically the entire alluvial area in the early autumn, with the development of some broad, shallow channels from the Hardy towards the head of the *barrancas*. These were observed at the end of 1924 as being still open and little obstructed by vegetation.

Some attempts were being made at about the same time by Mexican interests to open some of the region for development by means of artificial channels from the Hardy.

The varying phases of the distribution of the river water brought about by the diversion from the established channel in 1922 caused it to spread out over a wide frontal zone as it approached the Hardy, although the weight of the outflowing pressure was generally directed towards a point, or points, below the Macuata outflow.

A limited quantity of water reached the *barrancas* in 1927, and a somewhat greater quantity in 1928, but it was not until the great and sustained flood season of 1929 that the 1923 level was again approached.

During all this period the silt content of the invading water was low as the result of the straining and clarifying process that it had undergone through the penetration of dense thickets of vegetation, through the stilling and consequent settling in paludal areas, and by final escape towards the Hardy through further vegetal screens.

As the river entered and enlarged the newly excavated Vacanora Canal in the autumn of 1929, the flood pressure towards the Macuata Basin was definitely relieved, and it has since been negligible.

CHAPTER VII

PROSPECTS OF STABILITY AND A TIDEWATER OUTLET
(1930-1935)

No radical changes in channel development have taken place in the delta since 1930, activity having been confined to a restricted zone of which the eastern limit has been the approximate alignment of the old navigable channel of the Colorado River and the western limit has been the present course of the river through the Vacanora cutting. Such changes as have taken place have been practically confined to the development of minor distributaries in this mesopotamian region, with some slight adjustments in the series of bends through which the river enters the Vacanora channel and some recessive cutting and " fingering out " in the confluent system which finally delivers the residue of the water into tidewater in the Hardy.

The dominant morphographical feature of the period has been the upbuilding and lateral extension of the great deltaic fan which began to obstruct the lower end of the Vacanora cut soon after the water was admitted to it in 1929.

Ponding began to take place above this barrier, leading to the development of swamp and indeterminate drainage upon either flank but especially upon the eastern one. With the river discharge standing at 5,000 second-feet or less, practically all water reaching tidewater has since found an outlet in this direction, trespassing in part upon the abandoned meander zone of the old navigable channel and then following an almost due southerly course to tidewater. In seasons of flood the water spreads over and to both sides of the barrier, extending as far towards the west as the channel of the Pescadero but being still confined to the eastward by the slightly rising ground which defines the former alignments of the river down this side of the delta.

MODERATE FLOOD OF EARLY SUMMER, 1930

The period under consideration began, in 1930, with a summer flood of very moderate dimensions, the maximum discharge at Yuma during June only reaching 53,000 second-feet, the mean for the month 45,000 second-feet, and the total discharge 2,810,000 acre-feet.

Such subnormal conditions during the season when vegetational growth is at its height were favorable for the dispersal and deposition of the detrital burden of the water to the full extent of the limited overflow, although not for the development of new and more efficient drainage channels and distributaries. As the river discharge dropped rapidly during July and the lately inundated areas again became accessible for examination, it was found that deposition had noticeably increased over the surface and along the margins of the new fan and that the impounding of the river water and further development of the paludal areas was also very marked.

Although the flood had been moderate and of short duration, the comparative scantiness of the vegetal covering throughout the region subject to the annual inundation and the cumulative effect of the previous seasons of limited water supply had allowed water to find its way into the Pescadero in considerable volume for a period of two or more weeks, carrying a bank-to-bank flow into the Hardy through its deeply cut channel. This water reached the head of the Pescadero through the 1923 cutting from the Abejas channel and across the intervening expanses of partially dried swamp land, but flood pressure was already being definitely transferred from west to east, and the Pescadero and Rodriguez Levees no longer had to withstand direct attack except at periods of extremely high water.

Finding and Identification of the Hull of Ives's "Explorer"

As the region between the Vacanora channel and the meander zone of the old navigable channel of the Colorado was at this time becoming the more important, in view of possible developments, attention was concentrated in that direction, and it was subjected to periodical examination. In connection with this work an interesting bit of river history was revealed. During the winter of 1929-1930 a surveying party had found and reported their discovery of the partially buried hull of what had apparently been an iron shallow-draft steamer (Fig. 10). It was found at a considerable distance from any active river channel and had obviously been in the same position for many years. A further investigation was undertaken during July, the hull was visited and its position established approximately as latitude 32° 20' N. and longitude 114° 56' W. The interior had been cleared of sand and other deposits, and enough excavating had been done on the outside to show its construction and condition clearly. The dimensions were recognized as agreeing closely with those of the *Explorer* with which Lieutenant Ives made his exploratory voyage up the Colorado in 1858, but, other than this, there seemed at first little by which it could be identified. A closer examination showed, however, that the hull had been constructed in eight sections, as Ives had described the *Explorer,* and that these had been rather roughly, and perhaps hurriedly, assembled, suggesting such field conditions as are mentioned in his report.

A search for further clues and corroborative detail was still more successful and led to the identification of the hull as that of the *Explorer* beyond any reasonable doubt.

Serious misgivings had been entertained by Ives and his companions concerning the seaworthiness of the little steamer as she was being assembled at the mouth of the river, and the measures taken to remedy the trouble have been described above in Chapter I. It will be recalled that, in order to prevent risk of foundering, iron patches had been riveted over the lower ends of the too deeply cut slots in her transom through which passed the connecting rods that actuated her stern wheel. An examination of the fragments of the transom still remaining attached to the rest of the rediscovered hull showed the slots with rough patches still covering their lower ends (Fig. 11), precisely as described. Another structural defect, it will be remembered, was remedied by Ives by bolting two massive timbers longitudinally beneath her bottom, in the position of bilge keels to stiffen her hull. Although all traces of timber had disappeared at the time the examination of the remains was made, long loose bolts were found extending through her bilges, which had clearly supported some such strengthening structure. Her identity was, therefore, considered as having been fully established, and her present position became a matter of interest. She remains, as she was discovered, in an open flat, surrounded by dense thickets of brush and trees of mature growth, with no evidence in the immediate vicinity of any recent channel or lagoon.

Records were searched for further details concerning her history in an effort to discover how, or within what period, a section of active channel through which she might have reached her present situation had been transformed into an open glade with a level surface. The remains of a portion of the Ockerson Levee (see pp. 65-66), which had been hurriedly constructed in 1910-1911 at an average distance of about 3,000 feet west of the channel, were found near at hand, but apart from this there is no evidence of the proximity of the former river. According to Ives, the *Explorer* only remained in the possession of the Government for a period of about six months, and was in active service less than ninety days. She was then sold, at Yuma, to a local company. This completes her history, as given in his report.

Further investigation of contemporary newspapers disclosed the additional information that she was subsequently employed in carrying wood and other rough local freight in the vicinity of Yuma. She ultimately got out of control, probably during flood conditions, when coming out of the mouth of the Gila, was secured and made fast to the bank somewhere near Pilot Knob, but again broke away and drifted down into Mexican territory and was lost sight of. No details are available as to when or how her boiler or engines were salvaged, and unfortunately no direct information is available as to the date of her disappearance. Other ascertained facts, however, make it probable that it was not later than 1865.

The Ives map shows the main channel of the river more than a mile west of the position in which the hull was found, and the latest alignment of the navigable channel before the water abandoned it in 1909 was well to the eastward of it, so that, although it lies at some distance from any present or recent course of the river, it is well within the meander zone which has been occupied by recorded channel changes since the time of the Ives survey.

Short Flood of August, 1930

Following the very moderate flood of the early summer in 1930 another rapid rise took place early in August, the water coming principally from the Little Colorado and San Juan Rivers and being heavily burdened with the red silt which is characteristic of the basins of these two streams. This distinctive material was easily recognizable after the subsidence of the inundation, of which it clearly marked the limits. Each flood occurring at this time was observed to extend a little farther towards the east and towards the former river alignment for corresponding volume of discharge, indicating that the shallow trough between the Vacanora channel and the alignment of the old navigable channel was gradually filling up as each successive intervening zone had done with the eastward shifts of the river from the Paredones to the Vacanora. At this time the flood water from the west almost reached the hull of the *Explorer*.

The Vacanora channel had been excavated in the early part of 1929, with an average gradient of about $2\frac{1}{3}$ feet to the mile, or a total of approximately 40 feet to the point at which the barrier fan began to form. In comparison with the fall of about one foot to the mile in the original Abejas channel it afforded a more favorable outlet for the river water than either the Abejas or the later Pescadero cutting had done, and it was anticipated that it would speedily develop into a true degrading and scouring channel, perhaps into a direct cut into tidewater. In spite of the favorable gradient, however, lateral " whipping," with the development of abrupt crossings and short radius bends, began to take place almost as soon as the full weight of the river current entered it. This tendency was very plainly shown in an air photograph taken above the channel in July, 1931 (Fig. 50).

The August flood was of short duration, but was sufficient to refill the distributary channels and the associated paludal areas and to allow a moderate quantity of the settled and clarified water to reach the Hardy. The volume of this paludal effluent steadily decreased as winter approached.

Low Discharge of River in Early 1931 Increases Effect of Evaporation

The river remained at a very low stage until the last week in February, 1931, and the entire flow passing Yuma was diverted for several weeks into the Imperial Canal intake, the river bed below that point being entirely dry.

The February freshet was a local one, the water coming principally from the Gila, in sufficient volume to raise the discharge to about 17,000 second-feet, although very briefly, but not enough to do more in the distributary area than again to fill the swamps and replenish the dwindling stream into tidewater.

The prevailing and continuing low stage of the river during the early months of 1931 had the effect of adding marginally to the barriers of vegetation along the channels and around the lagoons, although without the development of any new relief channels. The net result, therefore, was a steady accumulation of impeded and trapped detrital matter in the region and an increasing difficulty for the water in finding an exit.

With the prevailing high temperatures and low humidity in the Colorado delta evaporation takes a heavy toll of water so widely distributed in shallow channels and lagoons. Percolation through the porous soil is also rapid, so that a flow of as much as 1,000 second-feet may disappear within the course of a few miles, under such conditions as existed about the lower end of the Vacanora channel during the dry spring months of 1931. Instances were observed and reported, in carrying out the field studies, where the steadily diminishing flow through an open channel appeared to end abruptly and absolutely against small masses of drift or other impediments, so that it was possible to step ashore literally from the end of a still-moving stream and find dry ground in all other directions.

The spring flood, which arrived towards the end of April, was again a very moderate one, only very briefly reaching a maximum discharge of 30,000 second-feet at Yuma and thereafter subsiding rapidly.

Absence of Summer Flood in 1931 and Its Effect on Plant and Animal Life

During August and September the river dropped far below any previously recorded stages for any season of the year. Minimum readings of less than 250 second-feet were obtained upon several occasions at the Yuma gauging station, while the maximum daily discharge barely reached 1,000 second-feet for some weeks. The entire residual flow passing Yuma was necessarily diverted into the Imperial Canal as soon as it fell below the normal daily requirements of the communities in the Imperial Valley, and, as the supply further diminished, a hastily drawn up international agreement was entered into by water-users upon both sides of the boundary for the rigid rationing of water. A brief flash flood, accompanied by heavy local rains, gave some temporary relief in August to domestic users and irrigation interests, but had little or no visible effect in changing conditions in the lower delta, and it was not until October that water in any quantity was again passing Yuma and flowing towards the Gulf.

This prolonged, and perhaps unprecedented, water shortage was observed to have reacted very severely upon plant life in those portions of the delta in which the only source of soil moisture is the periodical overflow from the river. Large tracts of country, untouched by inundation for two successive seasons, were bare and dry. Wild rice (*Uniola palmeri*), quelite (*Amaranthus palmeri*), wild flax (*Sesbania macrocarpa*), and other hygrophilous forms of plant life which normally cover such great areas had either failed to germinate or failed to mature, and the general aspect of the regions normally reached by flood waters, but which had, at that time, failed to receive more than the scantiest supply during the preceding two years, was one of arid desolation.

Extensive beds of tules (*Typha latifolia*) had died off or been burned and had failed to spring up again from the scorched roots. Cottonwoods and other trees dependent upon a readily accessible water supply and not sufficiently deeply rooted to withstand a prolonged dry period, had perished by the thousand, adding to the general forlorn appearance of the timbered sections. Even the belts of seedling willows which ordinarily cover the upper ends of bars and shoals, and line the banks and swales as the river falls after the spring floods, were noticeably scanty and stunted in growth. These quick-growing thickets are the most effective agency for checking bank erosion and the development of overflow channels when sudden freshets occur, by slackening the velocity of the rising water and allowing it to spread harmlessly amongst their roots and stems until the competence of the channel to accommodate the added volume has been increased by bottom scour.

Although vegetation had suffered so severely from the prolonged water shortage, some of the faunal readjustments were even more striking. The various varieties of river fish, which under previous conditions of ample space for development, plentiful food supply, and general optimum environment, had existed in almost incredible quantities in the river channels, had practically disappeared from the entire region between the intake of the Imperial Canal and tidewater. The river had been dry so frequently during 1930 and 1931 and so many changes had taken place in the distributing systems during the preceding years, with temporary development and subsequent desiccation of widely separated shallow lagoons and backwaters, that conditions had doubtless become intolerable for their continued existence, although occasional freshets had temporarily filled the channels.

Fig. 45—View across Laguna Macuata in the Macuata Basin. Lake level at intermediate stage (February, 1907). Steep wall of Sierra de Juárez in background. (See also *Carnegie Instn. Publ. 99*, Pl. 43.)

Fig. 46—Looking southward down the length of the Macuata Basin from the Mexicali-Ensenada road (at Paso Superior on map, Pl. I). The view extends from the slope of the Sierra de los Cocopas and the old alluvial fan at its foot across the vegetation-dotted piedmont alluvium and the smooth Colorado River alluvium to the Laguna Macuata in the distance. (Photograph by W. W. Weir.)

Fig. 47—The northern part of the rugged Sierra de Juárez seen across the northern end of the Macuata Basin. (Photograph by S. W. Cosby.)

FIG. 48—Air view southwards over the system of artificial channels cut through in the decade 1920-1930 to prevent the waters of the Colorado from flowing through the Rio Abejas artery toward the irrigated lands of the Imperial Valley. At the time of the photograph, July, 1929, the Vacanora Canal had only just been finished and the bulk of the discharge flowed (from left to right) down the Pescadero Diversion Cut. For later developments, see Figures 50 and 51. (Figs. 48-55 from air photographs by H. A. Erickson.)

FIG. 49—General air view southwards over the old meander zone of the Colorado (abandoned by the river after 1909) from a point slightly north of the intersection of the Mexicali-Gulf Railroad with the 115th meridian (see Pl. I). July, 1930.

Sierra   de   Juarez

Sierra del Mayor

de Pintas

Sierra de los Cocopas

Vacanora Canal

Pescadero Diversion Cut

Pescadero Levee

Rio Abejas channel now cut off

Pescadero Dam now cut off

Bee R. Levee

San Luis Levee

Rio Abejas

Fig. 50—The same locality as in Figure 48 looking southwest and showing conditions in July, 1931. Most of the water has abandoned the Pescadero Diversion Cut and is now going down the Vacanora Canal. The actual stream thread can be seen as a darker band " whipping " from one side to the other. (N. B. San Luis Levee on Figs. 48 and 50 is the Baja California Canal Co. Levee of Pl. I.)

Fig. 51—Further development of the invasion of the Vacanora Canal by the river discharge: view taken in August, 1933.

extension of cut

Pescadero

Vacanora Canal

Pescadero Diversion Cut

FIG. 52—General air view, taken in 1927, southwest across the meanders of the lower Río Hardy to the southern entrance to the Macuata Basin through which at times of high water the overflow finds its way northwestward (right) into the Laguna Macuata (Laguna Salada). The overflow channel probably lay farther to the right—nearer the southern end of the Sierra del Mayor—than indicated on the photograph.

FIG. 53—Looking southwest down the main channel by which the Vacanora drainage (see Figs. 69 and 74) discharges into the Río Hardy, seen in the background (the meander that carries the name is the same as the one marked by an arrow in Fig. 52). Identical points on Figures 53 and 55 are lettered A, B, C, D. July, 1931.

FIG. 54—General view in June, 1932, south-southeast down the meandering lower Río Hardy. In the right foreground a contact of the river with the Sierra del Mayor at El Mayor (Pl. I), shown in a ground view in Figure 57. Beyond, on the right margin, spurs of the range with intervening alluvial fans. Between the last spur and the range in the extreme background (Sierra de las Pintas) lies the southern entrance to the Macuata Basin. The junction of the main Vacanora discharge with the Hardy, shown on Figures 52 and 53, may be seen 2 inches from the left margin and about $\frac{3}{4}$ of an inch from the top of the photograph.

FIG. 55—Looking south down a secondary discharge channel which empties into the main Vacanora outlet at A (see also Fig. 53). August, 1933.

Fig. 56—Looking eastward across the mud flats of Ometepes Bay on the west shore of the head of the Gulf of California. The divergent reports as to the present existence of the bay may be due to the amphibious nature of the area as a result of the high tide range in the estuary (about 25 feet in this locality). (Photograph by Forrest Shreve.)

Fig. 57—Pumping station and landing at El Mayor on the Rio Hardy, where the river comes in contact with the Sierra del Mayor. This locality, seen from the air, is shown on Figure 54, right foreground. El Mayor is at the head of tidewater on the Hardy.

Fig. 58—Heavy growth of arrow-weed (*Pluchea sericea*), as met with in the areas that have been subjected to inundation.

In the brackish waters of the Hardy and the upper portion of the estuary, the gray mullet, carp, and a few other varieties adapted to, or tolerant of, such environment were at times observed to be quite plentiful, although even there the lack of the due proportion of fresh water and the loss of much of the former food supply from the river must have operated adversely both as to their numbers and distribution. With the increased salinity of the estuarial water, salt-water fish were observed in considerable numbers both there and as far up the Hardy as the limit of free tidal movement.

Although the rise in the river in October, 1931, was sufficient to relieve the situation of the acute water shortage which had existed with only brief intervals of amelioration throughout the year, it, too, proved to be of merely moderate duration, and it was followed by another period of extremely low river which lasted until the beginning of 1932.

Condition of Vacanora Fan During 1931

Very little physiographic change, other than progressive desiccation, had taken place in the subaërial portion of the delta during 1931. The fan of detrital material which blocked, although it did not yet entirely prevent, the direct passage of water from the Vacanora channel into the Hardy had nevertheless grown both in area and thickness with each pulsation in river volume during the year (Fig. 69).

A single small streamway, diverging slightly to the eastward of the original alignment of the Vacanora cutting, still crossed the recently deposited surface as late as the end of July, carrying water under the railroad grade and passing down the frontal slope a mile or more to the south. Most of the other distributaries left the central channel about where the " ponding " first became perceptible and avoided the growing central obstruction by making wider detours, principally to the eastward. Their continuity was in most cases lost as a zone of indefinite drainage—in reality a portion of the widely spread meander belt of the old navigable channel—was encountered. Swampy areas began to develop while water was still passing through the minor channels, but, as the winter season approached, the flow from the upper Colorado basins again dwindled and the whole distributary region became practically dry.

Heavy Flood of February, 1932, Characterized by Consecutive Instead of Cumulative Peaks

A series of heavy winter storms accompanied by rapidly rising temperatures occurred in southern and central Arizona early in February, 1932, causing a large volume of water to reach the delta within a few days and definitely terminating the long period of water shortage. The storm period lasted for about ten days and extended with modified intensity into both Utah and Nevada. Flood waters from the Little Colorado, the Virgin, Bill Williams Fork, and the Gila entered the river in quick succession and by their relative volume and sequence, and the character of the detrital material which was in each instance transported down stream, produced some remarkable results in the dispersal area.

The discharge from the Little Colorado reached a maximum of about 35,000 second-feet, the crest of the flood entering the Colorado on February 8-9. Bill Williams Fork contributed two peak discharges, each of about 50,000 second-feet, also on the 8th-9th, and the Gila flood, which was longer sustained, reached its maximum stage of 45,000 second-feet at its junction with the main stream on February 11. The flow from the Virgin was also heavy, but its identity amongst the other freshets was lost in passing down the river, before the delta was reached.

The discharge from the upper Colorado remained at about the ordinary winter minimum stage throughout the month, and the combined inflow from any one of the tributaries with the main stream hardly aggregated more than 55,000 second-feet at the Colorado-Gila junction at any time during the period of the flood, but it was sustained quite steadily at about that figure.

The manner in which the freshets reached the delta furnished an excellent example of one type of winter flood, in which the several increments to the total volume are so timed as to pass down the lower river separately, and therefore comparatively harmlessly, in contrast with the more common form, in which the maximum intensity is experienced with the passage of one well-defined crest. A consideration of the circumstances under which this February flood occurred will make the matter plain.

The focal point of the storm to which the flood was due was roughly in central and eastern Arizona, where the watersheds of the several tributaries through which the water reached the main stream approach each other very closely, forming a common plexus of drainage systems. Having entered one or the other of these, however, the storm water must travel by greatly varying distances in order to reach the common meeting point for all at the Colorado-Gila junction. A natural lag of from five to ten days, dependent upon the stage of the Colorado, will occur between the time at which storm water leaving this central region by way of the Hassayampa, Agua Fria or Verde, and the Gila, reaches the junction point and that which must find its way through some of the northward-flowing streams tributary to the Little Colorado. The Bill Williams quota would fall in somewhere between the other two, the actual amount again somewhat depending on the stage and rapidity of current in the Colorado.

The effects of a given volume of storm water, delivered either in the form of a single-crested, or of a multi-crested flood, may obviously vary very greatly. Floods of the first type practically destroyed Yuma in 1891 and have caused great local damage at other times. A flood of the multi-crested type may, on the other hand, be instrumental in moving a far larger yardage of detrital matter or of distributing it in an entirely different manner.

The Detrital Discharge of Bill Williams Fork in This Flood and Its Deposition on the Vacanora Fan

The most important feature of this severe winter storm, in its relationship to physiographic developments in the delta, was the great and rapid discharge from the Bill Williams Fork. This tributary of the Colorado, the only one entering it between its exit from the canyon section and the mouth of the Gila, is a typical desert waterway. It has a catchment area of approximately 5,500 square miles, drains nearly the whole of west-central Arizona, which is largely a sand and sandstone region, and contributes, during seasons of flood, a great quantity of coarse, heavy, detrital material to the rolling, saltatory, or bottom load in the river, as distinguished from the purely suspended matter which gives the Colorado its color and its name.

The junction with the Colorado is such that this load is projected into it almost at right angles, and at times of extreme flood conditions it has a tendency to accumulate as a great obstructive bar or shoal in the main channel. The " Bill Williams bar," following floods from the Fork, was well known to the steamboat men and was recognized as one of the possible hindrances to navigation.

The character of the material is such that, lacking coherence, it is readily swept away as a saltatory or rolling increment to the burden already being transported by the water. Under certain conditions of river-flow the movement seems to take place very rapidly, producing a loose shifting bottom, with rapid changes in water depth, as the mass advances.

In this case, sustained by the flood waters from the Little Colorado and the Virgin, the river remained in spate for a sufficient length of time to clear the channel and to carry the detrital load emerging from Bill Williams Fork down to the Gila junction, where a further reinforcement of the current and a fresh impetus to the moving load would take place. The steep gradient and direct course of the Vacanora channel assisted the further free movement of the load until the current virtually ceased at the breaking up of the main stream, and the water began to spread through the small branching channels and over the surface of the fan.

Deposition at and beyond this point began to take place very rapidly, the material, as was disclosed by an examination made later, being distinctive and differing in appearance and texture from that previously deposited over the same area.

The embankment of the Mexicali and Gulf Railroad, raised a few feet above the general ground surface, was quickly reached, invaded, and submerged by the advancing layer to a depth averaging two or more feet along a frontage of $1\frac{1}{2}$ to 2 miles.

As the river fell, it was found that the submersion of the previous ground surface had extended, as a gradually thinning tongue, for fully two miles beyond the line of the railroad grade and that the amount of new material brought in during the brief period of the flood was much greater than in any instance previously indicated and that fully 10,000,000 cubic yards of comparatively coarse and readily distinguishable material had been distributed.

Many of the smaller channels which had been developed upon and about the surface of the areas of deposition before these had been amalgamated and overlaid by the great February invasion had been filled, diverted, or wholly obliterated, and, as the vegetal covering had everywhere been sparse and stunted as a result of the prolonged period of inadequate water supply, the new material emerged as a great expanse of bare sand, with a surface mostly in low relief, but crossed here and there by deeper and better defined channels. This condition and appearance lasted until, with the approach of spring, the usual thick growth of annuals again took place.

FLOOD OF SPRING AND AUTUMN, 1932

The February flood was followed by a gradually falling river until the earlier part of May, when the discharge at Yuma had dropped to about 27,000 second-feet. The spring rise then began to appear from the upper basins, in which the snowfall during the 1931-1932 winter period had been extremely heavy, and rising temperatures unseasonably early.

The crest of the flood passed through the Grand Canyon in the middle of May, the discharge having doubled from 45,000 to 90,000 second-feet within a week and rapidly peaking up to over 100,000 second-feet. The passage of the flood through the lower valleys was nevertheless unusually slow, and it was not until early in June that it reached the delta. The resulting inundation there was very widespread, water finding its way into dry lagoons and other depressions in the region to the eastward of the Vacanora channel which had not received flood waters for a period of twenty years. To the westward it extended to the Rodriguez Levee, while to the southwestward it filled the lower Pescadero basin, flooded the Hardy channel and associated sloughs about the base of the Sierra Mayor, and escaped in considerable volume into the Macuata Basin, filling the Laguna Salada to a length of 8 or 9 miles.

As the water receded it was found that deposition had again been heavy over the surface of the Vacanora fan in the vicinity of the Mexicali and Gulf Railroad but that no important channel changes had taken place in the distributory system.

Another flash flood appeared in September, the result of heavy autumnal precipitation in the San Juan and other up-river basins. The peak discharge was about 50,000 second-feet as it emerged from the canyon section, but it flattened down to very moderate dimensions before reaching the dispersal area and produced little effect other than refilling a few more of the minor channels.

The winter of 1932-1933 passed with the river again at a low stage and no great change or surface deposition took place in the region in which the activity has been greatest during the three preceding years.

Contrasted Types of Deposition

Recent examinations of the surface layers of the newly deposited measures in the vicinity of the Mexicali-Gulf railroad grade, and a comparison between the material laid down from the summer flood of 1932 and that brought in during the February series of freshets, have again demonstrated the different character of the two. The more recent is the typical material which forms most of the fans, overlays, and riparian ridges throughout the delta, excessively fine, in fact almost impalpable in texture when dry and easily moved by the wind before it is secured by vegetation. The February accession, which at the point examined forms the bulk of the deposit, is coarser in grain, lacking in coherence when moistened, and, as viewed under low power with the microscope, is principally composed of minute angular or roughly spherical fragments of silica, which pack readily and are generally immobile in moderate air currents. Such material corresponds closely with that postulated by Gilbert [1] as being susceptible to transportation either by rolling or saltation, at current velocities equivalent to those in the lower Colorado. This is more fully discussed later (pp. 134-135).

The Hardy and Its Associated Drainage Systems

It is highly probable that when the Colorado diverged to the westward in 1909 and found an outlet to tidewater by way of the Hardy, it was again covering ground, and possibly occupying vestigial portions of channels, over or through which its waters had passed during earlier swings to this margin of the delta.

The material composing the surface layers, exposed in the banks of deeply cut channels in the region bordering the *bajadas* of the

---

[1] G. K. Gilbert: The Transportation of Debris by Running Water, *U. S. Geol. Survey Prof. Paper No. 86,* Washington, 1914, p. 11.

Cocopa Mountains and extending eastwardly towards the head of the estuary, differs materially from that present in the corresponding layers on the Sonoran side or in most other parts of the delta, in that it contains a much greater admixture of argillaceous matter, doubtless derived from the granites of the Cocopas and from the muds, marls, and beds of scoriae of the Cerro Prieto and its associated volcanic extrusions and overlays. In consequence of the presence of this tenacious component of the soil, bank-erosion and changes in channel alignment take place much more slowly than elsewhere, and the Hardy is enabled to maintain its general course and function as a well-defined drainage system irrespective of changes in the river.

The Colorado has doubtless found an outlet to the estuary and the sea in this direction more than once within comparatively recent times, and was probably doing so, at least for much of its water, when brought under the observation of Father Consag, Hardy, and the Patties. The common usage of the Hardy channel has now lasted continuously since 1909, the Colorado water entering it at different points, as detailed above. Since the diversion through the Vacanora channel in 1929, with the upbuilding of the great fan and the further detouring of the water around this growing obstruction, debouchment has taken place some 7 or 8 miles to the northwest of the point at which the junction existed in 1890. This corresponds to a channel distance of about 20 miles through the present convolutions of the Hardy channel, and for so far, at least, the Hardy is still the Colorado.

When the river broke away from the Abejas channel in 1929 and entered the Vacanora cutting, with its steep and favorable gradients and general direction somewhat to the west of south, there seemed to be a strong probability that a direct opening into tidewater at or about this old junction point would be developed within a flood season or two. The extremely low water stages of the river during 1930 and 1931, followed by the rapid upbuilding of the barrier fan around the foot of the open channel in the early spring of 1932, removed the immediate prospect of this and caused the water, as described above, to seek circuitous routes through a network of minor channels and partially swamped areas, in order to avoid the growing obstruction. This condition of indefinable drainage still exists, although the actual delivery of the residue of the river water into tidewater now takes place through one or the other of two roughly parallel drainage systems which have been developed across the zone of tule swamps and alkaline or semi-tidal flats which lie between the advancing " toe " of the barrier and the Hardy.

REVIVAL OF BOAT SLOUGH

A portion of Boat Slough, which formerly connected the Colorado channel with the Hardy, and which was first examined and roughly mapped in 1894 (Fig. 18), has been captured by the more direct and better defined of these two systems and has now become an active channel and the principal outlet to tidewater for the Colorado.

Prior to the abandonment of the old navigable channel of the river in 1909, Boat Slough averaged some 50 feet in width and had at least 5 feet of water in most places. The current was sluggish and set normally towards the west, although, as the whole channel came slightly within tidal influence, this was sometimes locally reversed at the periods of the spring tides. When the slough was first examined it was entered from the Colorado end through a thick growth of willows and cotton-woods, the belt of timber being about half a mile in width. The country then became open and savana-like in character and appeared for the most part to have been free from recent overflow. Tule swamps were afterwards encountered, and these became more frequent as the Hardy was approached. The total length of the main waterway was estimated at about 18 miles, the first 10 miles after leaving the Colorado channel having a general direction about 10° north of west (N 80° W) and the remaining 8 a course of about 10° west of south (S 10° W) to the Hardy. There were numerous connecting channels amongst the tules which materially increased the total length of the system and added to its complexity. These were only superficially examined, and none of them was explored. Although there was little current in the main channel there appeared to be a tendency, observable in some of the subsidiary channels, for a movement of water towards the south and down the general slope of the delta. This was taken to indicate that additional openings into tidewater might exist in that direction. The Colorado was in a condition of flood at the time of the initial journey through the channel, but no actual streams were observed bringing water from the north.

After the abandonment of the old navigable channel in 1909 the eastern end of this cross channel appears to have silted up or to have been filled, or at least lost its continuity, through local deposition. The southern arm, extending from the central bend in the system southwards into the Hardy, has probably always remained open and has carried a certain amount of flood water into tidewater. It was apparently functioning in this manner in 1931, when it was provisionally identified, in some air views taken above the region, as a part of Boat Slough. The identification was afterwards confirmed by an examination of former field notes covering the region. Other air views, taken in 1927, although not accessible until four years later, also showed it in practically the same condition at that time. It was then in communication with, and draining, the great paludal areas which had developed about the lower end of the Pescadero diversion.

When the supply of water from this course was cut off in 1930, by the full diversion of the river into the Vacanora channel, it appears to have gradually collected most of the drainage from both sides of the growing obstructive fan and to have retained its status as the most important tributary of the Hardy east of the Pescadero.

Had the river succeeded in reopening direct communication with the sea in 1930 by the way of the Vacanora channel, as appeared at that time quite possible, this remnant of Boat Slough would undoubtedly have developed into the connecting link with tidewater. With the further diversion of the water towards the east, however, an additional, although more indefinite, relief system has developed, which has since become capable of carrying a substantial proportion of the Colorado water to the sea. This, too, has probably developed in great part through pre-existing sloughs and vestigial remains of former channels. It is at the present time extremely tortuous and complicated and is interrupted in several places by tule swamps and thickets. It passes for some distance over ground which was occupied by the old main river channel at the time of the Ives survey but works off again into the tule beds towards a direct junction with the Hardy, ignoring the region of the old semi-tidal reaches of the river between the Colonia Lerdo mesa and the head of the estuary.

Both of these routes between the Vacanora swamp area and tidewater have been undergoing active, although intermittent, development since 1930, and heavy scour has been taking place in the beds of both, with the formation of temporary rapids and slight falls as the gradient of the *thalweg* has justified itself in the more or less friable material through which they are excavating their channels.

The presence of the great expanses of matted tule growth which cover most of the region is the principal cause of the intricacy of channel development. This surface covering is so dense and so resistant to removal by running water that channel enlargement and extension generally takes place by a process of undercutting and " fingering out " rather than by direct erosion and progression up the line of surface drainage.

ELEVATIONS IN THE LOWER DELTA IN THE LIGHT OF THE ACCEPTED FIGURE FOR SEA LEVEL

The comparatively steep fall, as evidenced by the rapid bed-cutting, of these active and still developing stream-ways has brought into prominence the question of elevations and relative levels in this part of the delta.

The general surface level of the region in which the Vacanora canal extension and the Mexicali and Gulf Railroad grade intersected in 1930 was at that time about 35 feet above reputed " sea level," based upon the datum in general use in the Imperial Valley and commonly accepted for practical purposes by all the irrigation organizations operating in the delta. It was originally derived from the accepted mean low water datum of the Pacific Coast and differs by something over 6 feet from an alternative basic level, presumably derived from the same source, recognized by the engineering staff of the Mexicali and Gulf Railroad.

The two systems came into conflict at the point at which the Rodriguez Levee crossed the railroad grade. The datum accepted by the irrigation companies has been adhered to in making the following brief analysis of the final adjustments which may be necessary in closing to sea level at the head of the Gulf.

Assuming the 35-foot surface level as correct in 1930, the surface level upon the crest, or apex, of the invading cone of detrital material rose sharply during the spring and summer of 1932, to approximately 44 feet, and was at the same time extended in a southerly direction without appreciable fall fully two miles beyond the Vacanora-railroad intersection. The distance from this intersection to the junction of the Hardy and the Boat Slough outlet is approximately 14 miles, and the difference in elevations, as they existed prior to the additional deposition, about 27 feet, or slightly less than 2 feet to the mile. The distance of the front edge of the comparatively level upper surface of the new deposition from the Hardy-Boat Slough junction is not more than 12 miles, and the difference in elevation between the two points fully 35 feet, or approximately 3 feet to the mile. This is a steeper grade than that under which the friable materials that form the upper layers of the delta formation will usually stand up when subjected to the action of running water. Recessive cutting and scouring-out of the beds of channels passing down this comparatively steep slope may therefore be anticipated.

Although these levels and gradients may be considered as being fairly well established with reference to the datum commonly used in the delta, their relationship to actual mean sea level at the head of the Gulf, and hence to the basic drainage level, is much more obscure.

" Sea level " at the mouth of the Colorado River is a very indefinite term, as its relationship to mean sea level upon the outer Pacific coast has not yet been established and can only be surmised until certain possible modifying factors have been satisfactorily determined and allowed for. In order of importance these are : (1) the elements of the semi-diurnal tidal waves as they approach the head of the Gulf of California, and as they are influenced by the depth and configuration of the Gulf itself ; (2) the actual, and still imperfectly established, tidal range ; and (3), perhaps equally as important as either of the others, the relationship between the enormous amount of evaporation which takes place from the surface of the Gulf water under the prevailing atmospheric conditions and the countervailing but varying inflow from the Colorado— almost the sole source of replenishment in a climate in which the annual precipitation is only 2 or 3 inches.

8

" Mean low water " may therefore, when accurately determined at the head of the Gulf, quite conceivably show a discrepancy from the established level of the outer coast, which has been provisionally projected into the delta, a discrepancy measurable not only in inches but possibly in feet. Such an error, great or small, will be concentrated into the narrowing zone between the established relative levels along the Mexicali and Gulf Railroad grade and the actual effective drainage level at the river mouth.

The fall of 40 to 45 feet which exists between the surface of the new deposition and low water in the Hardy is very unevenly distributed in the beds of the channels of the two drainage systems in their present stage of development. Both are undergoing an active process of degradation, but most of the erosion is taking place in certain sections in which the bed material is easily removable or in which local obstructions have previously arrested it. In the larger and more fully developed channel, mentioned above as connecting with the old Boat Slough outlet to the Hardy, a series of rapids, several miles in total length, occurs where the channel descends the frontal slope of the new deposition, while in the other channel a series still exists at the lower end which is periodically drowned by the tide. The beds of both channels have been examined in the vicinity of the railroad grade, and both were found to be exhibiting unmistakable signs of rapid erosion, having well-scoured surfaces of compacted material over which the current was flowing at comparatively uniform depth.

DEVELOPMENT OF A DEFINITE TIDAL CHANNEL OUTLET AT THE MOUTH OF THE HARDY

Depletion of previously laid-down deposits in the estuary and on the adjacent surfaces of the great tidal flats and flood plains was especially noticeable during the low-water period of 1930-1931, and, although greater quantities of water, containing appreciable amounts of suspended matter, reached tidewater in 1932, the general process of channel scour through the tidal zone was continued or at least merely locally and temporarily arrested.

A well-defined and unobstructed low-water tidal channel has been gradually developed the whole length of the estuary and now extends for at least twenty miles above the point at which the Colorado-Hardy junction took place at the time of the Ives survey. It is perhaps worthy of note that Hardy himself found and noted similar conditions when he designated as the Colorado the channel up which he worked with the *Bruja*. Being effectively scoured out, clear of drift and other obstructions, and direct in alignment, it operates as a very efficient drainage system, even at periods of extreme low tide and, if it has not already reached it, it is probably approaching very closely to the basic drainage level corresponding to actual low water at the head of the Gulf.

Above the outlet of the Pescadero, the Hardy shoals very rapidly and becomes a mere tidal backwater. No water now enters it directly except in seasons of very high river or while the paludal areas above are being drained. During the flood-season of 1932, when the river discharge reached a peak at Yuma of about 90,000 second-feet, much flood water crossed the channel and found its way into the Macuata Basin, filling the Laguna Salada to a higher level than it had reached since 1926. The movement of water in any considerable volume towards the west side of the Cocopa Mountains is nearly always due to the simultaneous presence, in the region from which overflow takes place, of river flood water in unusual volume and exceptional tidal pressure. The flood tide obstructs and reverses, in less or greater degree, the downward flow of the river water towards the sea, surcharging the channel by the development of a tidal wave with an upstream movement, which attains its culmination in the advancing zone in which the two forces neutralize each other. The presence or passage of such waves augment or sustain the overbank flow into and through the *barrancas,* and, as previously pointed out, their recurrence may have been instrumental in the excavation of these deeply cut channels. It should be remembered that under the conditions of great tidal impulses and excessively low gradients which obtain in and about the mouth of the Colorado, the momentum of the moving mass of water becomes relatively important, as compared with mere changes of static pressure, in controlling the topography of the region subject to tidal influence.

A further effect of the gradually increasing volume of tidal movement in the Hardy channel, due to continued depletion and scour, has been the correspondingly greater distance upstream at which the tidal influence has become perceptible. This tendency will doubtless reverse if and when increasing quantities of suspended and propelled detrital matter again reach the region through the re-opening of direct communication with the river above.

DEPLETION OF DEPOSITS AND DECREASE OF DRIFTWOOD ON ESTUARY FLOOD PLAIN

Depletion of previously laid-down deposits in the estuary has extended to the flood-plains upon either side. Upon the Sonoran side, especially, the effect has become very noticeable. The accumulations of driftwood and other river debris which were so widespread and conspicuous 30 or 40 years ago but which had already noticeably decreased when a previous examination of this side of the estuary was made in 1929, have since dwindled still more. The marvellous amount of this drift material when the river was carrying its several burdens freely into tidewater was one of the most striking features of the lower delta (Fig. 20) and was good evidence of the vigor with which deposition was proceeding at that time.

The drift which reached the northeastern shore of the estuary was chiefly deposited along a belt or zone some two miles or more back from the shore, which appeared to represent the " reach " of the average high tide. Here it accumulated in great fields and windrows which collectively formed a sort of low ridge or crest, roughly parallel to the shore, and barred further movement of the flood tide inland except at periods of exceptionally high spring tides.

The slope beyond drained inland towards Santa Clara Slough, and the seaward side drained back towards the estuary through occasional shallow depressions which here and there united to form deeper channels cutting through the shore line.

At the present time the fields of driftwood have almost disappeared, the slight ridge which they helped to form is barely discernible, the seaward slope has become steeper and is almost entirely free from debris, and the drainage channels have in general become deeper and less choked by deposits of soft mud.

Upon the opposite shore of the estuary depletion has taken place upon the same general lines, although much more water has sought an outlet towards the sea in this direction than upon the Sonoran side and has left more drift and other debris as evidence. Surplus flood-water entering and crossing the Hardy below the series of depressions leading into the Macuata Basin has always spread in the form of a sheet flood towards the southeast, much of it reaching the sea in a rather indefinite manner below Sargent's Point. Definite back-drainage has never, or at least not recently, existed upon this margin of the delta. Dunes and expanses of wind-blown sand, into which the alluvium merges almost imperceptibly in many places, have probably interfered with its development. While general surface denudation does not appear to have been so great upon this as upon the Sonoran side of the estuary, erosion and recession of the shore line below Sargent's Point has undoubtedly been extensive.

PRESENT STATUS OF OMETEPES BAY

In connection with the general changes which have undoubtedly taken place in the southwesterly prolongation of the areas containing alluvial deposits in recent years, Kniffen has reported [2] some interesting facts concerning the present status of the almost legendary Ometepes Bay, the entrance to which was featured in charts originating with the *Narragansett* expedition as existing in latitude 31° 29' N. upon the Californian shore. Kniffen states, upon the authority of a local fisherman, that three channels now connect it with the sea and that it again exists as a definite body of land-locked water.

[2] F. B. Kniffen: The Natural Landscape of the Colorado Delta, *Univ. of California Publs. in Geogr.*, 1932, p. 178.

Search was repeatedly and systematically made during the period of maximum deposition in the lower delta (1891 to 1904) for any sign of an opening in the shoreline in or about this latitude corresponding to the position and description given in the charts and "Gulf Pilot" current at that time, although entirely without success. Apparently, neither the entrance nor the bay itself was actually seen by members of the *Narragansett* party, but they were reported upon as having been discovered by the crew of a vessel named the *Ometepes* at some earlier, although unspecified time.

As searches ashore also failed to disclose anything more than a *salada* and extensive mud flats (Fig. 56) in the region supposed to be occupied by the bay, the evidence was considered to be conclusive that it had ceased to exist. This opinion was confirmed by a rather brief and not altogether satisfactory reconnaissance made from the landward side in 1925.

Kniffen's informant states that communication with the bay now exists through a long coastwise lagoon leading up from the south. This local feature has also been examined at times, although no inland opening from the northern end was ever observed. It extends from about latitude 31° 15′ to 31° 26′ N., following along the landward side of a barrier beach, capped here and there by dune sand. The floor of the depression, as exposed at low tide, has been observed to be principally composed of sedimentary matter, whether derived from the tidal water, which along this shore carries much river sediment in suspension, or from shore wash, is not clear.

This feature of the shoreline—a barrier beach capped with dune sand, with a lagoonlike depression paralleling it along the landward side—is characteristic of much of the coast below San Felipe Point and is doubtless due to some interaction of the excessive tidal range and currents and local conditions of wind circulation.

Taking into consideration the low and indefinite character of the shore for several miles south of Sargent's Point and the opportunity for flood water originating along the southern bank of the Hardy to escape in that direction, it is exceedingly improbable that either alluvium or drift are directly deposited by river water at the present time as far to the southward as the Ometepes area or the shorewise lagoon, even at seasons of high river. The tide is practically omnipotent below the Boat Slough channel.

Driftwood, plainly of Colorado River origin, has been observed as far to the southward as the San Luis Islands, along the Lower Californian shore (latitude 30° N.), and in this case the transporting agency was probably tidal current rather than wind.

CHAPTER VIII

THE IMPERIAL VALLEY

The pioneer emigrants, traveling to Southern California in 1850-1851, found two great natural obstacles opposing their progress westward as they were nearing the end of their journey. The first was the zone of desert, gradually increasing in aridity from the neighborhood of the last small settlements in New Mexico or Sonora and culminating in the belt of trackless sands and dusty loams to be traversed beyond the Colorado River; and the second, and perhaps most serious for worn-out stock and weary wayfarers, was the great escarpment which must be surmounted before the final journey down the short valleys and across the coastal plains was undertaken.

San Diego was the most important and by far the best of the Californian ports south of San Francisco and attracted much of the early travel directly toward it in spite of the formidable character of this mountain wall, which extended in an apparently unbroken line southward from the two great peaks of San Gorgonio and San Jacinto, the summits of which could be seen in clear weather from the Colorado crossing at the mouth of the Gila. Ascents of the escarpment were generally made from Vallecitos, San Felipe, or Carrizo Creek, at which places it was possible to obtain water at the foot of the grade.

It was not until a party under the leadership of Lieutenant R. S. Williamson, detailed to search for a practicable route across the Californian " backbone " for a transcontinental railroad, discovered in 1853 that a comparatively low and extremely easy pass existed between these two lofty peaks, that a really feasible southern route to the Pacific coast was found.[1]

DISCOVERY OF SALTON SINK AS DEPRESSION BELOW SEA LEVEL, 1853

It was owing to the scientific observational work of this expedition, and especially to the careful barometric readings of William P. Blake, the young geologist attached to it, that the true significance and possibilities of the great depression which extended eastward from the foot of the pass first became apparent.

Professor Blake's account of the discovery of the pass from the west and descent into the valley was written shortly before his death in 1910 and may be in part quoted [2] here:

Imagine, then, the enthusiasm with which the unknown great break in the mountain range between San Bernardino and San Jacinto was approached by the mem-

---

[1] See pp. 36-37 of Williamson report listed in the bibliography under " History of Exploration."
[2] D. T. MacDougal and collaborators: The Salton Sea, *Carnegie Instn. Publ. No. 193*, Washington, 1914, pp. 1-2.

bers of the party as we made our way eastward from the region, then practically unoccupied but now including the towns of Colton and Redlands, and found an easy grade and open country for our train of wagons to the summit, only 2,580 feet above the sea. Here, at last, was discovered the greatest break through the western Cordillera, leading from the slopes of Los Angeles and the Pacific into the interior wilderness. It had no place upon the maps and had not been traversed by surveying parties or wagons. From the summit we could look eastward and southward into a deep and apparently interminable valley stretching off in the direction of the Gulf of California. This pass was evidently the true gateway from the interior to the Pacific Ocean . . . .

We descended with eagerness into this great unknown valley, carefully reading the barometer at regular distances to ascertain the grade. Proceeding without obstacles, but with no trace of a road, and following the dry bed of a stream now known as the Whitewater, we reached the bed of a former lake and found it to be below the level of the sea.

Although the investigation by the Williamson expedition furnished the first actual proof that the lower portion of this great desert basin was below sea level, the fact had already been recognized that there was something abnormal about the overflow drainage west of the Colorado River. For instance, in August, 1851, a fairly correct description of New River, as it was already named, was sent in to San Diego and published in the *San Diego Herald*. Particulars were also given about " the overflow into the desert " which had failed to appear that year, although a flow towards the west and north had been noticed in the two preceding high-water seasons.

Public land surveys were made of a number of townships adjacent to the Mexican border between 1854 and 1856, although without any very precise establishment of a base line or adequate ties to established positions. Elevations were obtained approximately by barometric readings and so noted occasionally in the field notes, but no check levels were run through Mexican territory along the drainage channels and watercourses, to connect the data thus obtained with the actual surface level in the Colorado. Enough was learned, however, to confirm Blake's original discovery and place it upon official record.

PROJECTS FOR THE ECONOMIC DEVELOPMENT OF THE BASIN, 1859-1900

Projects for the future development of the region were already in the air. Dr. O. M. Wozencraft of San Francisco had become interested in its possibilities in the earlier years of the decade, presumably upon the basis of information obtained from members of the Williamson party, and began to formulate definite schemes for its reclamation on an ambitious scale. The plans were not finally perfected until 1859 and were never brought to the stage of actual accomplishment, as the necessary authorization was never obtained from Congress for acquiring title to the 3,000,000 acres of desert land which the promoters of the scheme desired. In its main features, however, the Wozencraft plan was based upon the already obvious course of utilizing the chain of natural connecting overflow channels existing between the river and the southeastern margin of the basin, for the purpose of introducing the water.

This original proposal was followed by several other abortive schemes for carrying out, by different methods and to different degrees, the same attractive-looking proposition. One such was outlined by Lieutenant Bergland in 1875-1876,[3] in which the Alamo channel, which by that time had become recognized as the principal waterway skirting the extensive sand areas which intervene between the river and the basin, was to be used as the main diversion canal.

The salt deposits in the deepest part of the depression were worked for a few years during the 1880-1890 decade, but the enterprise thereafter languished, and it terminated with the filling of the Salton Sink in 1905-1906.

Charles R. Rockwood reconnoitered the district in the winter of 1892-1893, and as a result of his preliminary examination he was instrumental in changing the name and objective of the Arizona and Sonora Land and Irrigation Company, with which he was then connected and which had been organized to explore and improve lands upon the east side of the Colorado, to that of the Colorado River Irrigation Company, with the declared purpose of developing the lands in the Colorado Desert.

Surveys were begun at once, starting from a proposed diversion point some 12 miles above Yuma, carrying the main canal down the western bank of the river as far as the Pilot Knob salient, and thence around the base of the sandy mesas into the basin. A complete distribution system was also worked out, designed to cover the entire basin and also most of the delta lands in Lower California which could be profitably reached with the water.

As the blockading sand hills and mesas which it was necessary to skirt extend for some distance into Lower California, a working agreement had to be reached with the Mexican owners of the lands through which the canal was obliged to pass. Unfortunately for the speedy fulfilment of the plans, these Mexican interests were antagonized by tactless approaches and refused for a while to grant the easements.

Before this difficulty could be satisfactorily settled, the financial upheaval of 1893 made the raising of the necessary capital for an ambitious scheme of this description, with so many unknown factors and possible contingencies, quite impossible. Although the author and promoter of the project, C. R. Rockwood, never lost faith in it or abandoned it, he was obliged for a while merely to mark time.

[3] Pp. 290-297 and 337-338 of his report cited in the bibliography under "History of Exploration."

Much financial juggling took place during the succeeding two years, with ramifications in Providence, R. I., Glasgow (Scotland), Denver, Los Angeles, and elsewhere, and when the air cleared again a modified plan appeared, changing the diversion point from 12 miles above to 8 miles below Yuma, thus eliminating some 20 miles of main canal. The headgates were to be located upon the American side of the boundary, although as close to the Mexican border as possible. An option upon a site for these works was secured after some lengthy negotiations, at a rather inflated price, and the company was reorganized in 1896 under the name of the California Development Company. An affiliated company, the Sociedad de Riego y Terrenos de la Baja California (generally known as the Mexican company) was also incorporated in the City of Mexico in 1898. This was done for the purpose of facilitating construction work and operation in Mexican territory.

Establishment of Irrigation System and Beginning of Settlement, 1901-1903

Early in 1900, the "Colorado Desert" of the earlier promotion prospectuses was officially changed to the "Imperial Valley" upon the suggestion of George Chaffey, the man to whom, above all others, credit is due for turning dreams into realities and actually bringing the Colorado water into the basin.

The situation, when, in April, 1900, he signed the contract and assumed the task of development, was far from encouraging. Options had expired, contracts had been broken, and agreements had lapsed by reason of the desperate financial straits to which the promoting company had been reduced. Little was left except Rockwood's original conception and surveys. Building upon this insecure foundation, however, Chaffey stretched his credit to the utmost, regained control of the essential keys to the situation, attacked the actual construction of the canals and control works with unbounded energy, and succeeded in turning the water into the headgates on May 14, 1901.

A separate company, the Imperial Land Company, had been organized in March, 1900, to handle the business of attracting and locating settlers and business enterprises into the valley. The operations of this subsidiary company were so successful that by February, 1902, when the Chaffey contract terminated, over 2,000 prospective settlers were ready to receive the water on their selected lands, more than 400 miles of canals and laterals had been built, and fully 100,000 acres of ground prepared for cultivation.

The following three years were strenuous ones for the settlers in the valley, and perhaps even more so for the promoters of the development. Funds were again at an exceedingly low ebb after the withdrawal of and settlement with the Chaffey interests, and other troubles ensued which seemed at the time to spell disaster and the speedy collapse of the entire enterprise.

In 1901 a necessarily hurried and incomplete soil examination was made in the valley by the U. S. Bureau of Soils. The report strongly discouraged any general attempt to cultivate the valley lands, as the alkali content of the soil was held to be prohibitive to the continued growth of crops. Information which was published in advance [4] as to the general tenor of the report had an effect upon the badly strained credit of the promoters, and upon the publicity campaign of the wing of the organization which attracted and located settlers, that was little short of disastrous.

In spite, however, of these adverse influences, the settlement of the valley went rapidly forward. Over 600 miles of distributing canals and " laterals " were brought into operation during 1903, and by 1904 fully 150,000 acres had been brought under active cultivation.

Cutting of Additional Openings from the River to the Irrigation Canal, 1903-1904

Even more serious trouble was yet in store. The enterprise was in a fair way to be swamped by prosperity. Settlers had arrived in such unexpected numbers, in spite of adverse reports, and were breaking ground so rapidly that an acute water shortage had been experienced during the 1903-1904 winter season, and numerous damage suits were filed against the development company for non-fulfilment of water contracts. The shortage was known to be largely due to the fact that the sill of the diversion gate was too high and that heavy silting had partially blocked the upper three or four miles of the canal. Ten thousand settlers were already in the valley, clamoring for water, their whole existence being dependent upon the supply from the Colorado.

Under these circumstances it was realized by the directorate that some steps must be taken to avoid more serious trouble during the forthcoming low-water season. The first expedient adopted was cutting a short bypass round the obstructing gate, but, although this was cut several feet below grade, it quickly silted up. An agreement was then sought with the Mexican Government whereby the river bank might be cut in Mexican territory. An opening was made shortly afterwards immediately below the international boundary under an informal and temporary arrangement. It, too, was quickly found to be inadequate for its designed purpose, as further heavy deposition took place in the first few miles of the intake canal. Both of these temporary openings were unprotected by head-gates.

The summer flood of 1904 was only a moderate one, although rather long-sustained, reaching peak discharges of 45,000, 50,000, and 38,000 second-feet in May, June, and July respectively, but thereafter falling

[4] *Bureau of Soils Circular No. 9,* Washington, Jan. 1902.

off rapidly. As the autumn approached and the river fell, it became evident that still more radical measures must be adopted in order to avoid more acute water shortages in the valley during the expected lower stages of the river.

In order to safeguard against this contingency a larger and more favorably situated opening was made between the river and the canal about

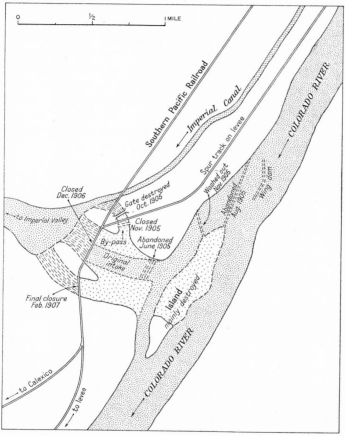

FIG. 59—Sketch map showing the engineering operations undertaken to close the openings in the western bank of the Colorado River, June, 1905, to February, 1907. Scale 1: 42,240. (Based on map by C. E. Tait, *60th Congr., 1st Sess., Senate Doc. No. 246*, Washington, 1908.)

4 miles below the border (Fig. 59). This opening, too, was left unprotected by a head-gate, pending the receipt of formal permission and approved working-drawings for the proposed structure from the Mexican Government. The new cutting was 3,300 feet in length, 50 feet in width, and from 5 to 6 feet in depth when first excavated, with a bottom gradient of approximately $2\frac{1}{2}$ feet to the mile.

Water was admitted through all three openings during the autumn months, temporary wing dams being placed in the river in order to deflect the current towards the intakes. The steamer *Cochan* was also chartered to tow a heavy drag along the canal bottom in the effort to loosen up the silt deposit and start it downstream. This expedient was not found to be very successful and was abandoned after a trial of a few weeks. The river fell to about 19.3 feet at the Yuma gauge early in October, and at that stage about 1,500 second-feet were found to be entering the canal, divided into approximately equal portions among the three headings. This was considered at the time to insure sufficient water to warrant extending the acreage to be brought under cultivation during the forthcoming winter to the desired extent to fulfill the needs of all newly arriving settlers.

The river rose sharply to about 23 feet at the middle of October, but it proved to be a short flashy flood, and did little more than scour out the new channel and confirm the assurance of plenty of water during the planting season.

Plans and estimates for the inlet gates for the new opening were completed early in November and forwarded to the City of Mexico for official approval. Until their return nothing could be done towards protecting this admittedly dangerous cutting.

The minimum height during the winter was approximately 19 feet, about the same as in the previous low-water season, but the new channel proved to be adequate to maintain the supply for the valley.

COMPLETE BREAK-THROUGH OF THE RIVER AND DIVERSION TO SALTON SINK, 1905

The first flood in 1905 came in the middle of January. It was brief and only reached to about 23.8 gauge height. It was followed, however, in February, by the first of a series of three violent flash floods, which occurred at intervals of two to three weeks and collectively rendered the outflow towards the west beyond the control of the development company with the resources and equipment then at its disposal. This was, indeed, the critical stage and turning point in the great westerly diversion of the Colorado which made physiographic and engineering history in the region for the succeeding five years and which has profoundly influenced the morphography of the delta until the present time. It has therefore been considered profitable to follow the incidents and developments preliminary to the loss of control in detail and to record the determining stages of the river in gauge heights rather than in discharge measurements.

Although the river was clearly out of control during the early spring months, the true danger of a total diversion into the Salton Basin and Imperial Valley was not yet fully realized by the engineers in charge of the situation. It was thought that it would be possible, as heretofore, to stop the crevasse, which had already reached such alarming proportions, during the expected period of low river before the usual spring rise. The possibility receded as the spring advanced, for the Yuma gauge height never fell below 23 feet for more than a few hours and remained above 25 feet most of the time.

A method which had previously been successfully used for closing openings of this description was again brought into use. By this plan the breach was contracted to a certain size by the construction of wing-dams from either bank, and a previously prepared plug of timber, brush, and sand-sacks, temporarily supported upon these structures, was then dropped into the central opening by the use of explosives. The method might have proved successful in this instance also, but the work was carried away, before the final closure could be attempted, by another sudden and great rise in the river. No reliable up-river reports were available at that time to engineers working in the delta, and they were generally forced to rely upon intuition, or upon the examination of past records, in anticipating future stages of the river. Following the failure of this attempt to close the fast widening opening, a proposal was made to the engineers in charge at the breach, by Captain Mellen of the steamer *Cochan,* to tow a large earth-loaded barge down from Yuma and scuttle it in the narrowest part of the cutting. This was towards the end of April, when the river had dropped temporarily to below 24 feet. Soundings and measurements were made at the selected point, and there is little doubt that this plan would have succeeded had it been adopted and that the whole course of river and valley history for several years thereafter would thereby have been changed. The river rose rapidly again in May and remained at flood stage until July. During this period one further attempt was made, in face of the rising water, to effect a closure by means of a piling and brush barrier.

Settlers in the valley were now thoroughly alarmed by the inflowing water, augmented by several serious breaches that had occurred in the headings and main canals. The development company was, however, in severe financial difficulties, with credit badly impaired in part by the filing of suits for heavy damages against it by the New Liverpool Salt Company and others. Under these circumstances the directors realized that they were entirely unable to cope with the situation without assistance. All further serious attempts to control the runaway river were therefore abandoned until the autumn, negotiations being entered into in the meantime with the Southern Pacific Company for the purpose of obtaining financial backing and the loan or use of men and equipment for carrying on the control work during the forthcoming winter.

The river rose during the summer (1905) flood to a sustained height of about 29 feet, corresponding to a discharge measurement of about 90,000 second-feet, of which at least 14,000 second-feet were flowing into the valley and basin. As the river fell again during the autumn, practically the entire flow was following the new course, so that by October 5,200 second-feet were entering the breach, and a mere trickle was passing down the former course towards the Gulf. Mr. Harriman and his associates of the Southern Pacific Company expressed willingness to come to the assistance of the development company upon certain terms, and an agreement was reached soon afterwards. Thereafter the railroad engineers were in charge of and directed the work of controlling the river. Its control was ultimately accomplished successfully in February, 1907.

Both technical and popular versions of this great engineering epic have been frequently published, and it is not considered to be necessary to enter more fully into the subject here than to trace briefly the several attempts at closure, in order to maintain the continuity of the account of the general development of the Imperial and Coachella Valleys.

Attempts to Close the Breach, with Final Success in 1907

Following the unsuccessful attempt, described above, in the spring of 1905 to close the breach in the river bank and the failure to come to terms with Captain Mellen to plug the opening with a loaded and scuttled barge, an effort was made, while negotiations with the Southern Pacific management were in progress, to deflect the weight of the river current away from the Mexican bank by means of a wing-dam, based upon a mid-stream island which had been a prominent feature in this long straight reach of the river for many years. This partial diversion was also unsuccessful in the face of the long-continued and unusually high river, and the last traces of it were carried away during August (1905), the upper end of the island also beginning to disintegrate at the same time.

In October a second and more extensively planned attempt was made, this time under railroad supervision and with the use of Southern Pacific equipment, to control, by means of a piling and brush-filled diversion dam, the heavy current between the island and the Mexican side. This barrier was built some distance down stream from the earlier attempt, as the island had, in the meantime, shortened considerably. The work failed and was totally destroyed by an extremely violent flash flood which reached the delta in November.

With the failure of this diversion attempt attention was concentrated upon engineering plans and structures of a more permanent and substantial character for finally controlling the inrush and at the same time keeping the growing communities in the valley supplied with water.

During the early months of 1906, and in accordance with these plans, work was begun upon two control gates, one, a permanent structure, being placed in the upper end of the original canal, north of the inter-

FIG. 60—Rockwood Gate, at the intake of the Imperial Canal. Looking downstream: Colorado River at left, canal at right, corner of Pilot Knob in extreme right. The United States-Mexico boundary is about 6,500 feet distant, beyond the tower on the right bank of the river. (See Fig. 61.)

FIG. 61—Temporary brush diversion dam (in this case only partially effective) as thrown across the Colorado River just below the intake of the Imperial Canal under annual permission from the United States War Department in order to retain sufficient of the residual flow of the river to fulfill the requirements of the Imperial Valley. The cableway towers, of which the left-hand one is here visible, are also to be seen in Figure 60.

national boundary. This was intended for use when the closure was effected and the main canal could again be brought into operation, and it is serving its purpose exceedingly well in a greatly enlarged form at the present time (Fig. 60). The other gate was to be a temporary one. It was built in an excavation near the north side of the breach, some distance back from the river bank, and was afterwards connected with the channel, both above and below, by a bypass. It was carried away in October, 1906, but the bypass was again successfully closed a week or two later by a supplementary structure.

The earthquake and great fire in April, 1906, which devastated San Francisco, sapped the energy of the construction and emergency departments of the Southern Pacific Company, but in spite of the preoccupation of the railroad executives over this great disaster they sanctioned the construction of a branch track to the scene of the proposed operations during the forthcoming winter and made other preparations for efficient working. The branch track proved to be invaluable in the later activities.

Serious work on the main closure was begun on October 1, and the water was shut off and turned down the old river channel on November 4. The victory was not a lasting one, however, for another violent flood arrived, flanked the south end of the newly completed closure dam on December 10, and again poured, in full volume, into the Alamo channel. The equipment was still on the ground, and a skeleton organization remained to patrol and repair levees, and the work was quickly resumed. A start was made upon actual dam building on December 20, and carried on with renewed energy. This attempt proved to be fully successful, and the breach was finally closed on February 11, 1907. Some levee construction remained to be done, and this was carried on with a reduced force during the spring.

Erosion of Gorges of New and Alamo Rivers During the Diversion

Conditions in the valley had been far from satisfactory during the protracted fight with the river. Recessive cutting up the two main drainage lines through which the water had found its way across the basin floor to the Salton Sink had resulted in the excavation of the great chasms that have since trisected the otherwise uniform surface of the expanse of irrigable land and added to the complexities of irrigation and water distribution. It was hardly realized at the time, in the face of disaster and imminent danger elsewhere and the loss of thousands of acres of valuable irrigable land, that they would afterwards form important parts of the completed irrigation system, in providing natural drainage channels for waterlogged land and conduits for the disposal of surplus water from the canal systems. They also served to localize the damage resulting from the overflow, as they were cut upstream towards the southern rim of the basin. Unfortunately, the recently established community of Calexico, on the border, and the sister town of Mexicali, on the Mexican side, were almost in the line of probable destruction, as both were situated on the eastern bank of New River,

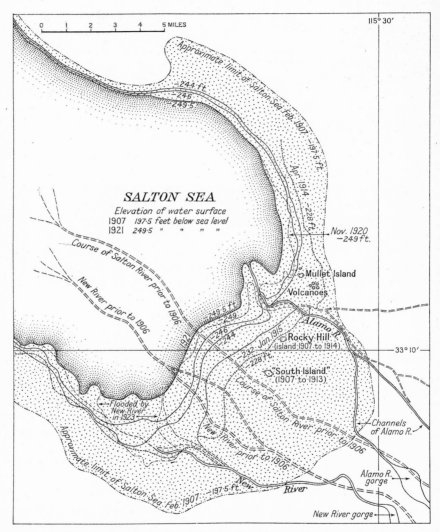

FIG. 62—Map showing the recession of the shoreline at the southeastern end of Salton Sea, 1907-1923. Scale 1: 253,440.

up which the most rapid and spectacular cutting was taking place. By strenuous and concerted work the inhabitants of Calexico succeeded, by liberal use of dynamite, in turning the course of the caving and recessive cutting away from their menaced western flank. Mexicali did not fare

Figs. 63 and 64—The two main channels through which the water of the Colorado River poured into Salton Sea after the break-through of 1905: the New River (Fig. 63) traversing its delta about one-fourth of a mile from the shore of Salton Sea, May, 1916, and the channel of the Alamo River (Fig. 64), upstream from the 1915 lake shoreline (see Fig. 62), carrying an average flow of water in May, 1916. (Photographs from D. T. MacDougal.)

so well. The head of the chasm approached the little group of buildings, lateral cutting began, and nearly all were undermined and engulfed within a few hours.

A similar gorge was developed up the course of the Alamo, beginning almost at the shore line of the fast-filling lake in the Salton Sink and ending several miles to the southward of the little settlement of Holtville.

The canal systems also suffered severely. The region to the west of New River was cut off from all water supply, and checks, headings, gates, and other works had been damaged or destroyed throughout the valley either by inundation or overfilling.

History of the Development Companies Since the Diversion

Serious as the physical damage to the young enterprise had been, the strain upon the financial standing and credit of the development company was even more a matter for concern. The Southern Pacific Company, nevertheless, continued to assume responsibility for safeguarding the valley against further danger from the river and used its resources and equipment liberally in reconstruction and protection work. It endeavored in the meanwhile, through its legal department, to secure itself against further commitments and entanglements in the maze of damage suits, Mexican claims and agreements, and other financial chaos in which the project had become involved. Various out-of-court agreements, restitution payments, and auditing of claims and accounts cleared up the situation somewhat and furnished a *modus operandi* which was reassuring to the settlers. Control by the Southern Pacific lasted until 1909, and the mere fact that it was able, as proved by its effective closure of the great breach, to avert further trouble, restored general confidence and promoted rapid and healthy growth throughout the valley.

The railroad executives, however, were more than willing to lay down the burden of an enterprise which was only remotely allied to the transportation business, and they plainly expressed their purpose to do so. The development company was still unable to stand alone, and the only solution of the situation appeared to be to allow it to pass into the hands of a receiver. This move was effected at the end of 1909.

The receivership was maintained until the spring of 1916, when control was assumed by the Imperial Irrigation District, organized under California state law in 1911 for the ultimate purpose of acquiring the water-distribution system. In 1922 this body was enabled to absorb the mutual water companies which had previously been responsible for distributing the water to the farmers, and it has since continued in full control of the business of irrigation throughout the valley. It also owns and manages the affairs of the subsidiary Mexican company and is responsible for the diversion of the water from the river and the maintenance of the protective levees in Mexican territory that are

9

most essential for the protection of the valley. Under its effective
control the project has developed into one of the major irrigation
enterprises in the world under a single management, and the cost of
water to the consumers has been kept down to a figure which compares
very favorably with that of most others.

TOPOGRAPHY OF IMPERIAL VALLEY AND RELATED AREAS

The area of the valley floor which is now under the direct control
of the Imperial Irrigation District for water service is approximately
600,000 acres. This consists almost entirely of deltaic alluvium, and it
slopes from sea level at the international border to about 250 feet below in
the deepest part of the great depression that is dry land, the rest being
covered by the water of the Salton Sea. Beyond this point the valley
floor rises again, although the alluvium still continues and extends for
some 20 miles more in a northwesterly direction, until it meets, and is
merged into, the sands and gravels of the Whitewater. This was the
gateway through which the Williamson expedition entered the valley
in 1853.

From the Salton Sea onwards to the northwest this portion of the
basin is known as the Coachella Valley, and its water supply at present
is obtained exclusively from artesian wells. Some 8,000 acres are now
under cultivation by this means. The water is undoubtedly derived
from the Whitewater drainage and the adjacent mountain slopes and is
entirely distinct from that found under the valley floor farther down.

The total area of the Coachella Valley is approximately 290 square
miles. Fully one-half is available for cultivation without any prohibitive
outlay for clearing and leveling, although, under any plan of distribution
now in contemplation, pumping will be necessary in order to bring the
water to some of the piedmont ground. The central portion of the purely
alluvial area is strongly impregnated with alkali, and an effective system
of leaching and drainage will be required before it can be utilized for
crop raising. Much of the alluvium around the margin of the valley
floor is obviously of local origin, having been derived from mountain
streams and washes draining towards the Salton Sink. With the exception of the drainage from Carrizo Creek, which has been mentioned in
another section (see p. 108), this is the only lateral drainage entering
the basin which has produced any marked effect upon the composition
of the surface and sub-surface soils.

At the extreme northwesterly end of the Coachella Basin eolian
influences have also been active, bringing in great quantities of wind-
blown sand, which is distributed in the form of sand fields, ridges, and
barkhan dunes. This accumulation has taken place at about sea level.

The regions which are now generally identified as the East Mesa,
the West Mesa, and the Dos Palmas district, although contained within

the physical limits of the basin, are not truly deltaic, but piedmont in character, and they do not, therefore, fall within the scope of this inquiry. Their surface soils are wind-blown sands, sandy loams, piedmont gravels, and compacted clays. The "old beach line," which delimits the deltaic portion of the basin upon its eastern and northeastern sides, forms the low escarpment of the East Mesa but becomes somewhat more indefinite and interrupted by low hills and mountain spurs where it separates the Dos Palmas mesa from the Coachella Valley. Although part of the West Mesa lies within the old beach, its gravels and clays are clearly derived from the mountain slopes surrounding the San Felipe Creek embayment and from Superstition Mountain, which separates most of the area from the valley.

THE ALL-AMERICAN CANAL

Although these three supplementary units do not come within the limits of the Imperial and Coachella Valleys, as at present constituted, they will be embraced within the areas to be irrigated under the All American Canal project, now in its preliminary stages of development, and will doubtless be identified collectively as Imperial Valley.

As early as 1912, certain movements were set on foot in the Imperial Valley looking towards the construction of a main line canal from the Colorado River which would lie wholly within the United States. Political reasons, and a desire to maintain complete control over the inflowing water from the river to the basin without the necessity for reciprocal agreements with a company organized under Mexican law and operating in Mexican territory, were the chief incentives for the agitation. The Imperial Irrigation District became officially interested and involved and passed certain resolutions and took steps towards making preliminary reconnaissances of the stretch of desert through which such a canal must pass.

A further and still more important idea began to supplement the original conception as it was realized that much additional acreage might be brought under the proposed canal system and the assessed cost per acre materially reduced, by holding the main channel to the highest practicable level from the diversion point on the river to the main distribution point in the valley. It was planned thus to cover the East Mesa, the Coachella Valley, and a substantial portion of the Dos Palmas district by gravity flow. The canal heading, according to this amended plan, was to be at the Laguna Dam, the point selected by Rockwood in his original scheme.

The scheme remained under consideration until 1918 without any definite progress being made, when, in response to requests from the Imperial Irrigation District board, the then Secretary of State of the United States outlined a proposal for a joint survey of the route with a view

to determining its practicability. The survey was made and the route
declared to be a feasible one,[5] but it was realized, as the scheme received
more study, that in order to be economically sound it must be linked with
a general plan for water-storage, and therefore for flood-control, upon
the Colorado River.

Such a scheme had of course received some general consideration
previously, but it was the All-American Canal plan, together with
insistent demands from the City of Los Angeles for water and power
from the Colorado, which at last crystallized into the Boulder Canyon
Project Act, which was signed by President Coolidge on December
21, 1928.

This greatest of Southwestern development projects, recently completed, may be confidently expected to bring about profound changes
both in the lower river and the delta, and is in itself a magnificent
conception. In view of the fact that the flood menace will, although not
entirely, practically cease to exist with the completion of the great dam,
it is unfortunate, from the strictly engineering and economic points of
view, that political and strategical considerations have made it desirable to
carry on the All-American Canal undertaking.

The opposition that the scheme had aroused, especially in the Coachella
Valley, is an indication that the question of cost and of the added burden
to the land is now receiving serious consideration. There is no doubt
whatever that the canal can be excavated along the selected alignment [6]
with modern equipment and the financial resources which will be available under the contemplated bonding plan, although the yardage will
be excessive for the first few miles after turning the Pilot Knob salient.
Maintenance through the difficult sand-hill region which bars the way
to the valley is likely to prove to be the most serious obstacle to successful
and continuous operation and will probably involve the oil-spraying of
berms and slopes, in order to arrest drifting sand, and possibly the
covering of certain critical sections of the canal.

The daily needs of the valley communities for their essential water
supply are so insistent and storage facilities are so limited that the total
cutting off of the canal flow, even for short periods, would be little
short of disastrous. It is conceivable that such interruptions may take
place either from drifting sand or from landslides and bank-caving in
some of the deep cuttings which the route necessitates.

Considered strictly as an engineering proposition, the Alamo route,
in use at the present time, is the logical one to serve as a conduit to the
Imperial Valley and the whole western slope of the delta. The channel
has already been cleared and straightened and could readily be dredged

---

[5] Report of the All-American Canal Board, July 22, 1919, by Elwood Mead, W. W. Schlecht,
and C. E. Grunsky. 98 pp. [Bureau of Reclamation], Washington, 1920.

[6] The latest report of the Bureau of Reclamation states that by June 30, 1936, 45.5 miles
of canal had been excavated (*Annual Rept. of the Secr. of the Interior for Fiscal Year 1935-1936*,
Washington, 1936, p. 62).—EDIT. NOTE.

to larger dimensions to meet increasing needs for water. Such lateral drainage as enters it during the infrequent storm periods experienced in the district does so through natural drainage channels and with minimum disturbance to banks or river bed. The route itself follows the natural drainage line to the rim of the valley basin, as was shown at the time of the flood of 1891. It will benefit equally with any other when the Boulder Dam reservoir produces the anticipated desilting of the Colorado water, and will be affected even more favorably than an excavated canal along a new alignment by the removal of the flood menace and regulation of river flow. Its continued use would, however, involve pumping in order to reach and irrigate the areas which it is contemplated to reclaim upon the East Mesa, the Dos Palmas mesa, and the sections of the West Mesa which lie behind the Superstition Mountain massif.

PART III
STREAM DYNAMICS

CHAPTER IX

THE DETRITAL LOAD OF THE COLORADO RIVER WATER

The definition of " silt " as given by Twenhofel,[1] somewhat freely interpreted, is an aggregation of matter of terrigenous origin in which the range of dimensions of the component particles is from 1/16 to 1/256 of a millimeter (0.06-0.004 mm). Although a rigid adherence to such specified dimensions may be somewhat arbitrary, it at least indicates the general conception of the term as applying to sedimentary matter, or matter in transit in running water, of a certain approximately uniform degree of fineness.

If restricted in this sense, a more comprehensive term would be preferable to describe the heterogeneous load carried by the Colorado. Although somewhat cumbersome, " detrital matter " is in many respects more suitable and has been made use of in the following discussions as the occasion has seemed to require.

Derivation and Composition of the Detrital Matter

The Colorado is a great river, and, in common with other large rivers in the temperate zones which flow in a meridional course, it passes through a great climatic range between source and mouth. Such conditions imply much diversity in the composition of the detrital material which enters and is transported through the system and involve seasonal variation in the times of its inflow.

Much of the freshly loosened lithoidal material starts upon its long journey towards the sea in the form of comparatively large and angular fragments, which in the swiftly running waters of the upper tributaries are subjected to a process of mutual friction and impact and to attrition against banks and stream bed which reduce the more friable almost to the condition of rock-flour before entering the long mixing-channel of the canyon section. Other and more resistant fragments survive as particles of measurable size until the delta is reached.

Another class of detrital material which bulks largely in the load carried by the lower river is that derived proximately from the arid surfaces of the lower basins, much of which is already in an extremely finely divided condition through being subjected to repeated wind action,

---

[1] W. H. Twenhofel and collaborators: Treatise on Sedimentation, National Research Council, Washington, 1926, p. 186.

exposure to varying degrees of temperature and humidity, and intermittent transit in desert streamways.

Fragments of organic matter, collected from the same sources as the
eroded material or having their origin in the riverside vegetation, are
likewise largely reduced to micronic dimensions while in transit and
form an appreciable fraction of the aggregate ultimately deposited in
the delta.

THE THREE CLASSES OF DETRITAL MATTER

The total load transported through the channel of the lower river
may be classified under three general groupings: (1) it is either so
excessively finely divided as to approach to or even exist in true colloidal
dimensions, capable of long-continued suspension in the transporting
water even when motion has ceased; or (2) the transported particles
may lie within the limits of size and weight which the current, moving
at its average velocity, is able to sustain and carry forward practically
in suspension but which fall rapidly with the cessation of motion; or
(3) the fragments, while too large and massive to be actually retained
in suspension, are nevertheless freely moved by the dynamic force of
the descending water, either by rolling or sliding along the river bed or,
being momentarily separated from it by momentum or inequalities in the
current, by advancing in a series of leaps or bounces in a method of
progression to which the term saltation has been applied. An additional
form of forward movement of the more massive material is found
to take place under certain conditions in a surcharged channel. A
rhythmic movement of the current is developed intermittently, and
masses of the river bed change position very rapidly in the resultant
turmoil. It is a phenomenon associated with a rapidly rising or flowing
river, and the method of progression is commonly designated as " sand
waves." All movement of the larger and heavier particles grouped
together under this classification also ceases as the transporting water
comes to rest.

COLLECTION, TRANSPORTATION, AND DEPOSITION OF QUASI-COLLOIDAL MATTER

The actual magnitudes and other physical properties of the finer
particles carried in suspension in the water of the Colorado River are
largely matters of conjecture. A certain portion of them undoubtedly
exists in true colloidal form and would therefore appear to be beyond
the scope of the ordinary methods of mechanical analysis and to be
recognizable only by chemical means.

The collection, transportation, and deposition of these minute bodies
through a river system in which the catchment areas vary as widely,
both physiographically and climatically, as do those composing the

drainage basin of the Colorado is obviously a process of much complexity. Soil conditions and features of run-off in the elevated mountain valleys in the north differ radically from those existing in the semi-arid areas in the south, and the chemical actions involved, as waters from such diverse sources pour into the water of the main stream, decrease or increase its capacity for free movement by modifying its colloidal phase.

Such contingencies and other questions involved in colloidal structure, together with inquiries into the physical properties of the deposited silts of the lower Colorado, have formed the subject of investigations by J. F. Breazeale and others at the Agricultural Experiment Station of the University of Arizona.[2] The laboratory studies were extended to cover observed and hypothetical conditions of high and low water, with progressive concentrations of sodium, calcium, and other salts, and they add materially to the available information concerning the transportation of this excessively comminuted material.

A distinction was drawn by the investigators between the regions in which sodium concentrations were likely to predominate and those in which calcium exists in excess. Fine sediments derived from the ordinary alumino-silicates of the soils of the upper valleys of the river system, and maintained in suspension in the swiftly flowing water, may previously have come in contact with soluble sodium salts and remain indefinitely in the disperse phase which such contact implies. If, on the other hand, they encounter water in which the calcium salts largely predominate, the colloidal phase changes and flocculation takes place. The process may conceivably be arrested or even reversed as storm waters of varying character from dissimilar catchment basins influence the general body of the stream. Conditions of high temperature, alternate desiccation and surface flooding, rapid evaporation from the surface of the soil, and other causes bring about excessive surface concentrations of soluble sodium, magnesium, or calcium salts in many of the areas from which such flood-waters are derived and thus influence the run-off and intensify the subsequent reactions. Flocculation implies deposition, or at least lessened capacity to remain in suspension in water moving at the average stream velocity, and so changes the manner in which material of this character is ultimately separated from the transporting medium. The primary magnitudes of particles which are acted upon in this manner may be almost molecular and are therefore far below the scale of the silt definition of Twenhofel. Colloidal entities in disperse phase constitute in the aggregate, nevertheless, one of the most important components of the delta structure.

A striking illustration of rapid and symmetrical deposition of the suspended load in the river water, by a process in which some colloidal

---

[2] J. F. Breazeale: A Study of the Colorado Silt, *Univ. of Arizona Techn. Bull. No. 8*, Tucson, 1926.

readjustment appeared to be involved, has been observed on several occasions in the zone of intermingling of the river and sea water in the lower estuary and in the Montague Island channels while open communication was still maintained with salt water. Contributing favorable conditions have been the ebb tide, a strong river current and heavy discharge, and almost perfect calm. Under such circumstances—the observations being carried on from a small boat dropping down in midchannel on the tide—the muddy river water has been seen at first beneath a thin film or shallow layer of clear salt water, and later, as the Gulf was approached, below a progressively deeper stratum, until the arm might be thrust down for a distance of 12 or 16 inches before the fingertips encountered the solid-looking surface of the silt-laden water. The phenomenon has appeared to extend over the entire width of the outflowing stream. The appearance of regularity and solidity of the subsiding or metamorphosed stratum has been very marked.

SUSPENDED SILT AND ITS TWO DOMINANT GROUPINGS ACCORDING TO SIZE OF PARTICLES

In approaching a consideration of the transported particles of the next scale of magnitudes, those which are sustained in suspension merely while the transporting water is in motion and which fulfill the specifications of " silt " in the Twenhofel definition, a useful tabulation of a mechanical analysis of samples of water taken from the river at the head of the delta may be profitably introduced. The analyses were made by Edward V. Winterer, by the Odén method of continuous sedimentation, at the University of California, and the results as published elsewhere [3] in tabular form are given in Table I. The samples analyzed were practically surface ones, taken at the same point, the intake of the Imperial Canal, 8 miles below Yuma, on February 28 and June 8, 1925, and may therefore be considered to be indicative of the suspended load in the current at representative periods of low and high water.

The columns have been separated for convenience of interpretation into three divisions which indicate approximately the proportions of matter falling above, into, or below the range of magnitudes specified above (p. 128) under (2) for classification by the manner of transportation. It will be noted that the upper, or " sand," group constitutes about 7.23 per cent of the whole, the middle, or " silt," group 87.75 per cent, and the lower, or " clay," grouping slightly over 5 per cent. Percentages are taken as the mean of the two columns giving the proportion by weight.

Samples obtained at this point may reasonably be expected to show slight discrepancies if taken at different periods, owing to the periodical flushing out of the settling basin at the Laguna Dam, some 23 river miles

[3] Samuel Fortier and H. F. Blaney: Silt in the Colorado River and Its Relation to Irrigation, *U. S. Dept. of Agric. Technical Bull. No. 67*, Washington, 1928, p. 75.

above. This process has at times a very marked effect upon the quantity
and character of the detrital matter entering the Imperial headgates or
passing onwards towards the dispersal areas in the delta.

Notwithstanding this and other possible causes of dissimilarity in
samples obtained at an interval of three months, the two series are strik-
ingly concordant in their main features and illustrate well the remarkable
uniformity of the suspended load in the water of the lower river.

A very significant point is the grouping, by percentages of the aggregate loading, of particles of certain dimensions into strongly marked
nodes. Approximately half of the matter in suspension which falls

TABLE I—MECHANICAL ANALYSIS OF SUSPENDED SILT IN THE COLORADO RIVER AT
INTAKE OF IMPERIAL CANAL, 1925

(by Edward V. Winterer)

	PROPORTION OF SILT BY WEIGHT	
DIAMETER OF PARTICLES	Feb. 28, 1925 (Low water)	June 8, 1925 (High water)
2.000-1.000 mm	1.34%	0.22%
1.000-0.500	0.89	0.32
0.500-0.250	1.94	0.39
0.250-0.100	3.73	5.64
0.100-0.050 mm	48.00%	56.90%
0.050-0.040	1.41	0.00
0.040-0.030	3.20	0.00
0.030-0.020	2.07	7.28
0.020-0.010	6.14	13.75
0.010-0.005	22.42	7.91
0.005-0.004	3.52	2.91
0.004-0.003 mm	2.21%	2.06%
0.003-0.000	3.15	2.60

within the " silt " classification consists of bodies 0.100-0.050 mm in
diameter, which may conveniently be designated as " very fine sand."
Another grouping occurs at about one-tenth of the diametrical magnitude
of the material fulfilling this description (0.020-0.010 and 0.010-0.005
mm) and practically at the lower dimensional limits of " silt." As the
double grouping appears so unmistakably in both series of analyses, with
only a slight shifting of actual magnitudes, it may reasonably be considered as a feature inherent in the suspended load in the water of the lower
Colorado and not merely as a fortuitous arrangement in a single sample.

A tentative hypothesis is advanced in explanation: The broad distinction between the two groupings is conceived to be primarily between
" sand " and " clay." The sand particles present, derived from original
rock surfaces by clastration, ablation, river or wind corrasion, or by

wind transportation from eolian deposits already existing in desert areas, and grouped together as of 0.100 to 0.050 mm in diameter, represent the residual fraction of detrital material of this description which the slackened current of the lower river is competent to maintain in suspension, the more massive and larger fragments being propelled down stream intermittently as a saltatory or bed load and not appearing prominently in a mechanical analysis of the suspended load alone. Owing to the increased viscosity of the heavily laden water of the stream and the cushioning effect and added inertia which this implies, but little further reduction in size of the particles once in suspension is likely to take place as a result of attrition or impact. With a slackening current they will merely subside, to be picked up and carried forward in suspension as the velocity again increases.

The excessively finely divided debris or rock dust produced by the abrasion, percussion, and mutual impact of the larger particles constituting the bed-load probably falls at once within the range of magnitudes subject to colloidal reactions, through the resultant increase in surface-volume ratio, and appears amongst the measured magnitudes only in combination with various zeolites, as argillaceous bodies of certain rather rigidly established dimensions, such as constitute the second group under consideration, namely those with diametric magnitudes ranging from 0.020 to 0.005 mm. The slight shifting of the center of gravity of this group discernible in the two analyses may be due to chemical causes or to some slight irregularity in the determination of percentages of weight.

Components of Suspended Silt

Numerous samples of detrital matter, obtained from the river water at various points in the delta, have been subjected to microscopical examination for the purpose of obtaining a general idea of the physical characteristics of the suspended load. The work has usually been done under field conditions and with moderate powers of magnification and has been extended from time to time to include samples from typical bodies of deposited material. The most striking fact revealed has been the remarkable uniformity of samples secured from widely separated sources and under greatly differing conditions. This uniformity was found to be so complete that it was not considered necessary to continue the work under laboratory standards of accuracy for the purpose of establishing minor distinctions in composition between individual samples.

The following digest of a number of examinations, made under the conditions outlined above, will present a reasonably accurate description of the more prominent components of the suspended load in the water as it flows on to the delta and a rough computation, based upon the mean of the series of observations, of the percentages of each (Table II).

TRANSPORTATION OF THE COARSER MATERIAL

Fragments which enter the current from various sources in sizes too large for transportation in suspension at the limited velocities imposed by the low gradients which exist between the foot of the canyon section and the Gulf fall into the third, and final, classification of detrital matter moved by the river, that which the descending water is competent to move forward, although not to return in suspension. Collectively, such material is frequently described as "bed silt" or sometimes as the "tractional load." The latter term is perhaps the more correctly descriptive, as it may be understood to embrace not only such particles

TABLE II—PHYSICAL CHARACTERISTICS AND PROPORTION OF COMPONENTS OF SUSPENDED DETRITAL LOAD IN LOWER COLORADO RIVER

COMPONENT, AS IDENTIFIED	APPEARANCE, AVERAGE MAGNITUDE, AND OTHER CHARACTERISTICS	PERCENTAGE OF TOTAL
Quartz, feldspar, chert(?), and other translucent grains, with a small admixture of garnet, hornblende, obsidian, and other dark-colored fragments	Rounded and abraded, average diameter about 0.010 mm	45
Calcite and other calcareous material	Approximately the same dimensions but of more diverse shapes	10
Scales and laminae of mica..........	Easily recognized by shape, sizes irregular	5
Hematite, limonite, etc..............	"Black sand"............	1
Argillaceous matter................	Partly as "nodules" but mainly as very fine particles	30
Organic and unclassified matter, with possible fragments of lignite	Shapes and sizes irregular...	9

as remain practically in contact with the stream bed and move forward by rolling or sliding along the semi-plastic surface but also those bodies of intermediate size and weight which the current can only retain in suspension intermittently.

Many points relative to the movement of this heavier material under the diverse conditions existing in actual rivers are still very obscure. The rate at which it travels, its volume ratio to that of the suspended load, and the mechanism of the mass movements which occur at times, are largely matters of surmise rather than precise knowledge.

COLOR OF THE DETRITAL MATTER

The distinctive color of the Colorado water is imparted to it almost entirely by the fine argillaceous component in the suspended load. In normal stages of the river it is a reddish brown, which becomes either more vividly red or tones down through the various shades of brown to a dark neutral-tinted gray as storm waters enter the system from certain tributaries. Thus, the inflow from the Little Colorado is a brighter and more vivid red, while that from certain confluents of the San Juan and Gila is almost black. Ferric oxides, carbon in various form and associations—much of it of proximate organic derivation—and, to a lesser extent, manganese are the principal sources of color.

Following deposition and dehydration upon the surface of the delta or elsewhere upon the flood-plains of the river valley, the distinctive color of the suspended load is generally lost and the dried sediments become a light yellowish brown. An exception to this occurs in situations in which the water has had an opportunity to deposit the finer particles of the suspended load quietly, through evaporation or the gradual draining away of lagoons or backwaters after the heavier and coarser material has settled out. The dried mud is in such cases a dark chocolate brown, which contracts, as further desiccation takes place, into polygonal horny-surfaced flakes, with deep intervening cracks or fissures. The dark color remains and extends through the mass. The lighter surface colors of areas where deposition has taken place from still moving water, or of those where re-arrangement of the material has taken place through wind action, is probably due to the removal of much of the finer material by the air currents, the decomposition of organic matter, and to true sun bleaching and weathering.

In the regions about the estuary the characteristic colors developed in the deposited muds range from dark chocolate browns to bluish grays. The color metamorphosis is probably due to differences in the processes of decomposition of the organic matter under the anaerobic conditions existing in the more compact tidal-deposited beds and to the conversion of the tincturing ferric oxides into sulphides.

The Mechanics of Silt Transportation According to Gilbert

Much experimental work covering the various phases of the transportation of debris by running water under controlled laboratory conditions was carried out by and under the supervision of the late G. K. Gilbert, at Berkeley, California, the results and conclusions being set forth in a publication of the U. S. Geological Survey.[4] While these studies are exhaustive and complete in establishing, by mathematical analysis and close observation, a sound basis for further investigation of the intricate questions involved in stream transportation, their chief value lies, perhaps, in the light they throw upon the innumerable and complex factors involved in the application of principles established

[4] G. K. Gilbert: The Transportation of Debris by Running Water, *U. S. Geol. Survey Prof. Paper No. 86*, Washington, 1914.

under laboratory restrictions, with a limited number of variants, to the constantly changing and interrelated conditions of discharge, alignment, cross-sectional channel area, and velocity incidental to a great river system.

The following extracts show in brief axiomatic form the conclusions reached by the monograph, which are pertinent to and corroborated by the present study: "The finer debris transported by a stream is borne in suspension. The coarser is swept along the channel bed. The suspended load is readily sampled and estimated, and much is known as to its quantity. The bed load is inaccessible and we are without definite information as to its amount" (p. 10). "Some particles of the bed load slide; many roll; the multitude make short skips or leaps, the process being called saltation. Saltation grades into suspension. When particles of many sizes are moved together the larger ones are rolled" (p. 11). "When the conditions are such that the bed load is small, the bed is molded into hills, called dunes, which travel down stream. Their mode of advance is like that of eolian dunes, the current eroding their upstream faces and depositing the eroded material on the downstream faces. With any progressive change of conditions tending to increase the load, the dunes eventually disappear and the debris surface becomes smooth. The smooth phase is in turn succeeded by a second rhythmic phase, in which a system of hills travel upstream. These are called anti-dunes, and their movement is accomplished by erosion on the downstream face and deposition on the upstream face. Both rhythms of debris movement are initiated by rhythms of water movement" (p. 11).

THE "SAND-WAVE" PHENOMENON OF STREAM-BED MATERIAL MOVEMENT

Although the above brief but comprehensive summary of the invaluable experimental and analytical work done at Berkeley appears to cover the process of silt transportation in full detail, the field work in the shifting channels of the lower Colorado soon made it evident that the "dune" theory of traction, as outlined, was still inadequate to explain many of the observed phases of rapid movement of detrital material which were encountered there. Concurrent studies by the writer in the bed of the Santa Cruz River near Tucson, Arizona, had revealed extensive and deep-seated movements in the stream bed as a result of a single violent storm and flood, and the observations were continued from time to time in the beds of other intermittent streams and desert washes as opportunity occurred and were generally confirmatory of the conclusions reached in connection with the Santa Cruz work.

Specifically, the observed facts in the Santa Cruz River had been as follows: Following upon a period of nearly a year of absolute dryness of the river bed, other than as moistened by occasional light rainfall, a

single violent storm had transformed the dry streamway into a raging
torrent for a few hours, with the development of typical " sand waves "
at intervals. The river in the vicinity of the observations has a fall of
approximately 5 feet to the mile, and prior to the flood had a bank-to-
bank width of about 150 feet and an excavated depth, below the flood-
plain level, of 8 to 10 feet. The necessity for digging in the again dry
bed arose shortly after the storm, and still-green willow leaves, twigs,
and other vegetable debris were encountered 6 to 8 feet below the
surface, which was again approximately at the same level as it had been
before the flood. In order to insure against an interpretation being based
upon a purely local condition, the stream bed was explored by excavating
at intervals for some distance both up and down stream, and fresh debris
was discovered several feet below the surface in most cases. The implication to be drawn from this manifold evidence is that the whole body of
the river bed had been practically in motion during its brief submergence
under the torrential flood.

Transferring the ideas gained at this time to the investigation of
apparently similar current conditions in the Colorado, although without
any possibility of a direct examination of the uncovered river bed, the
rather crude method was adopted upon numerous occasions of diving or
swimming in the turmoil of " sand waves " and " boils " in efforts to
reach the bottom and investigate conditions beneath the surface. The
efforts were not always or, indeed, predominantly successful, owing
to the extreme turbulence of the water at the times at which the information was most desired; but the fact was well established that during
certain phases of the rhythmic cycles of movement and wave development which accompany the sand-wave phenomenon, a deep-reaching
disturbance of the bed material takes place, followed by the rapid movement of much of the loosened matter down stream.

The method of investigation was persevered in and was supplemented
by other expedients for direct examination of representative portions
of the river under flood conditions, until the following general conclusions
were reached:

(1) That the fundamental condition causing the sand-wave development in stream flow is the overburdening of the water with detrital
material.

(2) That the observed rhythmic character of the phenomenon is due
to transitory changes in the fluidity or viscosity of the stream-water,
through temporary overburdening, and that this condition affects its
velocity and, therefore, its power of retaining matter in suspension.

(3) That an important contributing factor to the full development
of the rhythmic manifestation is the presence of an abundant supply of
detrital matter of approximately uniform size.

The phenomenon of " sand waves," as observed in the San Juan
River, the upper left tributary of the Colorado, is thus described by

Pierce:[5] " The usual length of the sand waves, crest to crest, on the deeper sections of the river, is 15 to 20 feet, and the height, trough to crest, is about 3 feet. However, waves of a height of at least 6 feet were observed. The sand waves are not continuous, but follow a rhythmic movement. . . . . At one moment the stream is running smoothly for a distance of perhaps several hundred yards. Then suddenly a number of waves, usually from six to ten, appear. They reach their full size in a few seconds, flow for perhaps two or three minutes, then suddenly disappear."

Waves of comparable size have been observed at times of rapid rise at various points upon the lower river and have been studied carefully through the several phases of the recurrent cycles of development and decline through which they pass.

The matter has appeared to be of vital importance as a feature of deltaic development, inasmuch as the volume of detrital material in a form readily retained in the dispersal areas, which passes down stream at such times, is known to be very great and yet not easily measurable by any of the ordinary methods of silt-content analysis.

THE SUCCESSIVE PHASES OF THE SAND-WAVE CYCLE

The successive phases of a cycle occur in the following relationship to each other. Assuming that at the first moment of observation the current is flowing swiftly and the water showing a slightly undulating surface, it is at the same time expending a portion of its accumulated energy of descent, or momentum, in raising from its lower layers a burden of detrital matter which already exists there in the readily accessible form of a more slowly moving bottom load—the product of a previous phase. This bottom load has been ascertained, by contact with it and actual immersion in it during certain parts of the cycle, to form a semi-fluid substratum which may vary in depth from a few inches to two feet or more, according to the irregularities of the harder layers of the bottom and the depth of the water.

The critical point of overburdening and loss of energy is in most cases reached very suddenly, as observed by Pierce on the San Juan, additional energy being obviously absorbed, as the speed decreases, in the accelerated subsidence of the suspended and saltatory particles due to gravity. Uniformity of size of the units of loading would also appear to be a factor in increasing the rapidity of the transition into the next phase of the cycle.

Although the quickly succeeding manifestation of the characteristic transverse wave system is so conspicuous at the surface, the sequence has not been clearly traced past this point of phase transition by direct

[5] R. C. Pierce: The Measurement of Silt-Laden Streams, *U. S. Geol. Survey Water-Supply Paper No. 400-C*, Washington, 1916, p. 42.

examination of the bottom, and reliance has been placed upon Gilbert's interpretation of his laboratory experiments for an explanation of the development of the "dune" and "anti-dune" systems of bed configuration which mark the succeeding phases. His explanation follows: "A particular relation between depth and velocity corresponds to a sort of equilibrium between the factors of turbulence and restraint, in accordance with which the sinuosity of the lines of flow is reduced to a minimum and the water surface and channel bed are approximately plane. This gives the smooth phase of traction. When the depth is increased without increase of velocity, the restraint permits the development of internal diversity, and this carries with it diversity of the plastic bed, giving the dune phase of traction. When the velocity is increased without increase of depth, the restraint is overpowered, and a diversified but systematic arrangement of flow lines develops, which carries with it systematic diversity of both water surface and channel bed and gives the anti-dune phase" (*op. cit.,* p. 34).

The transitional period under consideration is that from the comparatively placid "dune" stage, which is identified by the slightly undulating surface, to the sudden development of the steep and turbulent wave system which indicates and accompanies the growth of the anti-dunes. The conditions which Gilbert postulates for bringing about this transition, overpowering the restraint to free internal movement in the water through an alteration in the relationship between channel depth and current velocity, are apparently met by the decrease in effective depth due to the rapid subsidence of matter which has been in suspension and in saltatory movement during the previous phase and by the concurrent resumption of velocity by the transporting medium as it is relieved of its burden and as, in effect, its viscosity decreases.

The next stage in the cycle, clearly recognized by exploration in the stream, has been the transitory condition which may best be described as the phase of excavation. This brief recurrent period of rotary movement of the water and subjacent plastic bed layers perhaps constitutes the most important element in the mechanism for the rapid transportation of heavy detrital material down stream in times of flood, but its relationship to the other phases of the cycle has not been very clearly ascertained. Cause and effect are not readily distinguishable in the turbulence of the current, but the rapid loosening and throwing upwards of material by rotary movements of the water has been well established upon many occasions, and there would appear to be some close relationship between this subaqueous bombardment and the steep up-stream faces of the "anti-dune" ridges, which are always close at hand.

The transition from the phase of excavation to the succeeding phase of smoothly flowing current also takes place with great rapidity, as experienced in the current. The "dune" tops are levelled off, the loose mass of material at the bottom begins to move forward as a uniform layer, and the stream to gain speed.

This condition completes the cycle to the point of the assumed initial examination and marks the first stage in the accumulation of another overload.

MOVEMENT OF THE RIVER-BED MATERIAL

As the crest of a flood passes, the sand-wave phenomenon generally ceases except under purely local conditions of augmented current, due to channel changes, and material which is too coarse and heavy to be carried in suspension or by saltation continues to move along the *thalweg* of the channel at such times and in such quantities as the normal stream-flow is competent to roll or slide.

The difficulties which Gilbert experienced in his laboratory experiments in obtaining definite data concerning what he termed " bottom flow " naturally become still more formidable when the examination is to be made through the wholly opaque waters of a large and turbulent stream. It was thought, nevertheless, that the general impressions gained through direct subaqueous exploration of the current would have value in connection with information gained in other ways concerning the movement and other characteristics of this important portion of the stream load. Opportunities have been taken from time to time for continuing such examinations under more normal conditions of the current than exist during the " sand-wave " manifestation, for the immediate purpose of gauging the erosion and redeposition of bed material in shifting bars and shoals. By the use of stakes, floats, and other devices, combined with direct examination of the under-water conditions, it has been possible to obtain actual quantitative information concerning such local channel adjustments that it would have been difficult to acquire in any other way.

The results of several such examinations have been embodied below in the tabular matter descriptive of the dimensions and other physical properties of the bed material (Tables III and IV).

Some remarkable movements of bed material at times of high river have been observed and recorded at the Yuma gauging station of the U. S. Geological Survey. Such an instance occurred on the occasion of the great flood which issued from the Gila on January 21-22, 1916, with a peak discharge of 220,000 second-feet. A " scour " which was estimated to be equivalent to at least 1,600 acre-feet per channel mile—corresponding to a lowering of the bed by nearly 25 feet across the entire flood width of the river at the gauging point—was noted. The excavation extended for many miles down stream below the point of direct observation and caused an appreciable deepening through the upper portion of the Río Abejas, which at that time formed a part of the main river system.

The gauge height registered was about 20 feet above mean low-water level as the crest of the flood passed, and the bed scour was fully 32 feet in the *thalweg,* increasing the depth of the water from a normal low of about 8 feet to 60 feet. The channel rapidly shoaled again after the passage of the flood, but the summer rise of the same year, which crested up to 70,000 second-feet, cut it out to a depth of 20 feet at the end of June. By December it was once more at its normal stage.

None of the usual methods for estimating the passage of silt appear to be applicable in either of these cases of bodily movement of the river bed, and it is improbable that any figures based upon them would be of value in computing the yardage involved.

Basing his opinion upon the information available to him, Fortier [6] considers that fully one-fifth of the detrital load of the river passing Yuma does so in the form of bed-silt. It appears probable, however, that if due consideration be given to the " short haul " and intrinsically coarser material which enters the main artery of the river between the foot of the canyons and Yuma—that which comes from the Bill Williams Fork and from the lower confluents of the Gila—this estimate should be materially raised. Much of this matter undoubtedly passes Yuma and enters the delta, under extreme flood conditions and in a manner outlined above, and is not identified by the methods of the ordinary stream and silt analysis.

The River-Bed Material Grouped According to Size of Particles

In order to obtain a general and reasonably accurate idea of the physical characteristics of the detrital material which forms the river bed at the approach to the delta, a series of thirty samples which had been taken at various times between the site of the Laguna Dam and the termination of the Arizona-Sonora boundary were combined for mechanical analysis into five groups. The grading for sizes of particles was made through standard mesh sieves of 60, 100, 120, 200, and 300 interstices to the inch in each group. The division was made for the combined purposes of reducing the bulk to be examined at once and of providing additional comparisons for reaching a general average.

As will be noted, the results were sufficiently in accord to demonstrate the representative character of the material. The groupings were made entirely without reference to the date or locality at which the individual samples were obtained, as the intention was to gain an insight into the average composition, apart from any seasonal or purely local influences. The striking uniformity, as revealed by the percentages of magnitudes in the five groups as selected, is also worthy of note.

The sampling was terminated at the Arizona-Sonora line because at this point the river makes its first contact with the coarse gravel escarpment of the Sonoran Mesa, and it was clearly recognized that these

---

[6] Work cited above in footnote 3.

gravels, which were extensively attacked and eroded by the river, influenced the character of the bed-material from there on practically to tidewater.

Notwithstanding the general uniformity of the thirty samples of bed material of which the mechanical analyses are given in Table III, seven

TABLE III—MECHANICAL ANALYSES OF THIRTY SAMPLES OF COLORADO
RIVER BED MATERIAL

(Taken at various times from surface of mid-channel bars and shoals between Laguna Dam site and termination of the Arizona-Sonora boundary, generally at low water, 1900 to 1933)

Percentage in Given Sizes

Group	Retained on 60 Mesh	Retained on 100 Mesh	Retained on 120 Mesh	Retained on 200 Mesh	Retained on 300 Mesh	Passing 300 Mesh
A	1.0	3.6	26.3	62.5	5.0	1.6
	8.0	31.1	16.6	15.2	11.1	18.0
	6.1	15.4	23.4	40.1	7.6	7.4
	5.5	5.5	68.2	17.4	1.4	2.0
	0.0	4.2	34.7	26.7	10.0	24.4
	3.4	17.1	60.4	12.1	4.1	2.9
Group percentages	4.00	12.81	38.26	29.00	6.53	9.38
B	6.1	17.2	31.9	20.0	4.2	0.6
	10.7	14.2	29.4	17.6	17.8	10.3
	8.6	8.6	33.3	34.5	6.4	8.6
	6.3	5.2	50.1	15.7	15.4	7.3
	7.9	20.2	37.4	28.0	2.2	4.3
	13.3	15.4	63.1	1.5	2.4	4.2
Group percentages	9.15	13.46	40.86	19.55	8.06	5.88
C	2.0	6.3	10.1	40.2	37.4	4.0
	4.1	16.2	14.6	19.4	23.0	22.7
	3.0	11.4	67.1	14.5	1.0	3.0
	4.2	23.6	41.2	16.0	8.2	6.8
	7.6	2.4	43.7	34.4	5.6	6.2
	11.3	10.6	63.1	10.3	2.6	2.1
Group percentages	5.36	11.75	39.96	22.46	12.96	7.46
D	2.6	46.7	37.2	7.0	3.3	3.2
	9.3	36.0	22.4	14.6	10.7	7.0
	1.6	0.9	70.2	24.0	2.0	1.3
	0.9	2.6	18.1	31.0	27.4	20.0
	18.3	20.2	56.2	4.2	1.0	0.00
	4.7	42.6	30.0	14.3	6.2	2.2
Group percentages	6.23	24.83	39.00	15.85	8.43	5.61
E	4.2	6.7	20.4	14.7	21.7	32.3
	7.3	30.6	31.4	4.6	14.1	12.0
	7.8	13.2	47.3	19.4	10.3	2.0
	0.0	2.6	64.1	5.2	18.6	9.5
	26.0	40.1	10.2	6.4	9.3	8.0
	1.0	26.7	20.5	47.0	4.1	0.7
Group percentages	7.75	19.98	32.31	16.21	13.0	10.75
Total percentages	6.49	16.56	38.07	20.61	9.79	7.81

will be seen to contain a markedly higher percentage of particles fine enough to pass through the insterstices of a 300-mesh sieve (approximately 0.045 mm), while five show an opposite tendency by carrying percentages in excess of 10 per cent which were unable to pass a 60-mesh screen (approximately 0.25 mm). Ignoring the significance of these two divergences for the moment, it will be noted that about 85 per cent of the material represented by these samples existed in sizes between the limits stated and that the maximum percentage appears to have been slightly above the 120 mesh or as having a probable average diametrical magnitude of about 0.30 mm. This agrees well with the dimensions of bed-material sampled at various points in the dispersal areas in the delta during the recent years of irregular flow and doubtless indicates with fair accuracy the average bed composition where deposition has taken place directly from the tractional load.

The Sorting and Rearrangement Process of Bed Material

It has been found, by extending the actual stream-bed examinations to situations in which such direct deposition has recently taken place, that the conditions indicated by the divergent samples in the series have probably been due largely to purely local current movements and subsequent rearrangement of bodies of material already laid down. The manner in which such sorting and rearrangement is brought about will be briefly discussed.

A river, such as the Colorado, which has developed a meandering channel over an alluvial bed, is incessantly modifying the profile and relief of the deposited material over which it flows, in response to transitory changes in current intensity and direction. The moving body of water may be best visualized as being composed of a series of sinuous and interlocking filaments which generate transient resistances and eddy movements along their surfaces of contact. Variations in discharge, friction, temporary loss of momentum through following a circuitous path around or over obstructions, and divergences of the current around bends of the river, all contribute to the maintenance of the internal sinuous movement.

Differential velocities brought about by the interplay of these minor currents enhance or detract from the capacity of portions of the general moving body of water for transporting the bed load and mobile layers of the actual bed material, and irregularities in bottom contours and profiles result, through local deposition or depletion. Certain selective processes also take place, whereby the more massive particles tend to accumulate in the hollows, while the smaller and lighter ones are carried forward.

Such sequences of cause and effect are found to be in most complete and unrestricted operation during periods of comparatively steady or decreasing discharge. With substantially increased discharge, which usually implies an increase also in both the suspended and tractional loading of the water, a modified bed contour quickly results through the tendency of the more rapid current to short-cut across obstructive shoals or bank salients and to develop new deeps and shoals in order to mold the channel bed to its requirements.

With a view to determining the degree to which the selective and grading process may take place between points in the stream bed which are only separated by short distances, samples were taken in pairs from selected locations in the dry bed of the main channel of the river during a period of total diversion into the Imperial Canal. The brush diversion dam was in operation at the time and the river flow had been cut off at about 2,500 second-feet.

TABLE IV—MECHANICAL ANALYSES OF COLORADO RIVER BED MATERIAL
(Taken from dry bed below temporary diversion weir at Imperial Canal inlet)

SAMPLE*	LOCATION (Distance below weir)	DATE	RETAINED ON 200-MESH SCREEN	PASSING 200-MESH SCREEN
'A' 1	200 yards	Jan. 12, 1930	84%	16%
'A' 2	200 yards	Jan. 12, 1930	37	63
'B' 1	250 yards	Jan. 12, 1930	95	5
'B' 2	250 yards	Jan. 12, 1930	50	50
'C' 1	350 yards	Jan. 12, 1930	76	24
'C' 2	350 yards	Jan. 12, 1930	40	60

*The samples were selected in pairs, at points where there was evidence of local rearrangement of the deposited detrital matter.

The components of each pair were taken from points not exceeding 20 feet apart, in order to insure the operation of the same selective process in each case.

The results of the examination of three representative pairs are given in Table IV.

The 200-mesh screen, with interstices of approximately 0.075 mm, was used in making this examination, as it represents, more nearly than any of the others forming the series with which the standardized mechanical analyses of the bed-silt material have been made, the critical point in particle dimension at which the mode of transportation changes most markedly from bed-traction and saltation to suspension.

The fluctuating and intermittent filaments of current which were believed to be in operation in close proximity to the bottom in situations and under conditions such as were to be found here, where a gradually diminishing discharge of known volume from day to day had occupied a broad shallow channel with a well-stabilized bed, were considered to be likely to produce the most marked effects in assorting and segregating material of this intermediate character.

The results of the analysis, as set forth in the table, appear fully to justify this assumption, as the percentages of the finer and coarser components in the paired samples appearing upon either side of the critical dimension are very significant.

The dry river bed from which the samples were secured was left with a surface in low relief, and a cursory examination for some little distance up and down stream appeared to indicate that pairs of samples exhibiting the same features of finer and coarser material, and of about the same range of particle size, might have been obtained in great numbers.

CHAPTER X

FLUCTUATION AND RHYTHM IN THE MOVEMENT OF DEBRIS

The burden of detrital material transported by the Colorado is subject to many controlling conditions which influence the rate at which it passes towards the delta, apart from the fundamental one of stream volume. The varying silt-producing capacity of the confluent streams of the system, the seasonal frequency or comparative infrequency of torrential storms in certain sections of the drainage basin, and climatic conditions generally over a region some 900 miles in length by 500 miles in breadth are amongst the determining factors which regulate and apportion the supply down the main artery of the river. A curve developed to exhibit the influence of these determinants in full detail would in many respects resemble a tidal prediction curve and be extremely complex, and it would probably be impossible to plot it with any approximation to accuracy even with our present knowledge of the hydrography of the region. It is possible, however, to note the sources from which and the conditions under which much of the material is derived and to follow in general outline the seasonal and climatic influences to which it is subjected during its passage through the river system. This has been undertaken in the following digest.

Derivation Conditions and Time of Transport of Detrital Load

Such of the detrital material as is derived directly from exposed rock surfaces in the catchment areas is made available for transportation in various ways. Disintegration of the mantle rock is brought about by chemical decomposition, in the forms of oxidation or carbonation, in association with hydration, or by the solvent or corrosive action of certain organic substances or organisms.

Mechanical disintegration may occur as a result of root action, freezing, or differential expansion and contraction due to excessive temperature changes, or, in situations in which there is direct contact with running water, by attrition, percussion, or friction against other matter already in transit.

The products of disintegration in the more remote areas may not, however, be directly available for transportation through the river system except at times of invasion of areas in which they have accumulated, by floods, storm waters, or the run-off from melting snow-banks or snow-fields, and may exist for long periods exposed to atmospheric or other influences before actually entering the streamway.

By far the greater portion of the sedimentary matter which is water-borne through the lower reaches of the river is derived from such secondary deposits, or from sand, gravel, or clay measures which floor so many of the basins of the tributary streams. Much is wind-assorted or pulverized and enters the transporting water within the colloidal scale of magnitudes.

Owing largely to the disturbing influence of wind action and to the intermittent character of stream flow over most of the basin area, the time consumed in the passage of the material from the point at which it first comes within the influence of gravitation within the limiting watershed to its place of rest at sea level must be extremely irregular. A month, a year, or a century may conceivably elapse between the initial loosening of a given fragment at some remote stream-head and its incorporation in the delta or delivery into the sea, although it remains throughout the period within the limits of the banks of the transporting waterways. A particle derived from one of the great arid areas common in the lower basins of the river system, and which is dependent for its downward progress upon such uncertain factors as wind, intermittent flow through desert washes, or periods of sheet-flooding due to excessive precipitation, may take less or infinitely more time before its redeposition in the delta.

The Constituent Drainage Basins of the Colorado System and Their Run-Off Régime

The drainage basin of the Colorado River system is shaped roughly like a trapezoid, with an extreme length of nearly 900 miles and an extreme width of more than 500 miles, and has an area of about 243,000 square miles. Its eastern and northeastern margins practically coincide with the crest of the main continental divide, its northern angle is situated amongst the mountain plexus in southwestern Wyoming, and its western and southern sides terminate rather indefinitely amongst the detached ranges and open desert spaces which lie between it and the great enclosed basins of Utah, Nevada, and California, and the heads of the south-flowing rivers of Sonora.

The system below the union of the Green and the Upper Colorado (formerly the Grand) is practically a unilateral one, as only two tributaries of any size, the Fremont and the Virgin, and a few small and unimportant streams under the northern rim of the Grand Canyon, the Paria, Bright Angel, and Kanab, enter the river from the western bank between that point and the Gulf.

The basins of the four larger tributary streams, including the Upper Colorado, all lie to the eastward of the main channel (considered as beginning at the head of the Green River). The aggregate area of the four (Upper Colorado, San Juan, Little Colorado, Gila) is approximately 135,000 square miles. Their individual areas and other characteristics more immediately pertinent to delta accretion, as well as those of other tributaries, are summarized below.[1]

GREEN RIVER BASIN (area, 44,400 square miles; altitude, 14,000 to 3,900 feet).

General Character. The Green River system comprises six major confluents and several smaller tributaries. The Yampa and the Duchesne are the most important. Including the Green River itself, most of the confluents head high in the mountains, are principally snow-fed, and are essentially mountain streams. Much of the lower course of the main stream is through canyons.

Run-off. The greater portion of the discharge is the result of melting snow upon the high mountain slopes. Irrigation requirements now take a heavy toll of the water of several of the confluents during the short growing season, but a secondary period of precipitation which occasionally occurs during the early autumn months is at times the cause of rapid erosion of the sedimentary floors of the valleys in the mid-basin region. This leads to a great temporary increase in the percentage of detrital matter carried through the main channel and delivered towards the lower river and delta.

UPPER COLORADO BASIN (area, 25,900 square miles; altitude, 14,000 to 3,900 feet).

General Character. Fully half of the basin area consists of high, rugged mountain slopes and spurs at elevations from 7,000 feet upwards, heavily timbered in many localities. The remaining half contains much broken tableland and foothill country which erodes readily. The Upper Colorado River (formerly the Grand River), with its tributaries, is distinctly a mountain system.

Run-off. Principally from melting snow from the western slopes of the continental divide in Colorado. Maximum volume in May and early June, according to the advance of the season. A secondary rise, due to summer rains, also frequently occurs. Discharge from this system is heavy, amounting to about 40 per cent of the total discharge through the lower Colorado.

SAN JUAN BASIN (area, 25,800 square miles; altitude, 14,000 to 3,400 feet, with most of the area at from 8,000 to 5,000 feet).

General Character. The north and northeastern portions of the basin consist generally of steep mountain sides and spurs, with the streams occupying deeply eroded canyons and valleys. The central portion contains much broken tableland, easily eroded and composed in great measure of talus material and sedimentary measures. The main stream leaves the basin through a deeply-cut canyon.

Run-off. Maximum in early spring owing to melting snows, with a well-marked summer run-off resultant from the seasonal rains which usually occur in the central districts. The silt content of the water from this tributary is nearly always high. The use of water for irrigation already materially curtails the normal flow from the system during the growing season.

LITTLE COLORADO BASIN (area, 25,900 square miles; altitude, 7,000 to 2,780 feet).

General Character. The main stream and most of the tributaries flow through broad shallow valleys with sedimentary floors. The basin contains extensive areas in which the surface concentration of alkaline matter is very pronounced, others in which wind-swept expanses of sand or sandy loam, with occasional *pedregales,* or desert pavements, exist. As a whole, the region is very sparsely covered by vegetation of any description, although heavy stands of yellow pine cover portions

---

[1] For isopleth maps of annual run-off, evaporation, and denudation in the Colorado drainage basin, with the relevant discussion, see Eberhard Reichel: Der Wasserhaushalt des Colorado-gebietes, *Geogr. Abhandl.,* Series 2, No. 4, Stuttgart, 1928.—EDIT. NOTE.

of the Mogollon and Datil Mountains, which form parts of the watershed between this basin and that of the Gila. The Little Colorado itself drops into a deep and narrow canyon for many miles before entering the main river.

Run-off. The run-off is entirely characteristic of the climatic conditions prevailing throughout most of Arizona and northern Sonora, having two well-marked peaks of discharge corresponding to the mid-winter and summer periods of maximum precipitation. The silt content is always very high.

VIRGIN RIVER BASIN (area, 11,000 square miles; altitude, 9,000 to 940 feet).

General Character. The basin occupied by the Virgin River and its chief confluent, the Muddy, is essentially a desert one. Precipitation is light, ranging from 20 inches annually in limited areas at the headwaters of the two streams, to less than 3 inches in the lower part of the basin. Most of the area is very sparsely occupied by vegetation, and erosion during the torrential rains which occasionally occur is in consequence very heavy.

Run-off. Very irregular. Most of the normal flow has been appropriated and is being used for irrigation during the growing season. Violent floods have occurred at different seasons of the year, which have carried great quantities of detrital matter into the Colorado.

BILL WILLIAMS BASIN (area, 5,400 square miles; altitude, 8,000 to 375 feet).

General Character. This is also principally a region of sparse vegetation. Some comparatively light wooded cover, mostly juniper and scrub oak, is reached at the higher elevations, but in general the basin may be classified as a typical semi-arid area. The hydrological system is composed chiefly of sandy-bedded channels passing through broad shallow valleys and only occupied intermittently by flowing streams. The surface soils are largely loose and sandy, eroding readily.

Run-off. The run-off is essentially that of a desert stream system of this Southwestern region. Winter rains and occasional snow usually produce a flow, at least in some of the confluents, during the early weeks of the year, and the other seasonal flow is in the late summer. Occasional heavy rains at irregular intervals also produce flash floods. Erosion is generally rapid, and the silt content of the run-off is high.

GILA BASIN (area, 56,000 square miles; altitude, 8,000 to 120 feet).

General Character. The Gila basin, which contains the two principal systems of the Gila River and the Salt River, together with a number of smaller secondary streamways, principally of the intermittent desert type, is by far the largest unit in the entire Colorado drainage area. The upper portion is mountainous, with elevated and dissected tablelands as a prominent feature about the heads of the two principal confluents and their feeders. The Roosevelt Dam and subsidiary dams and storage basins on Salt River and the San Carlos Dam on the Gila now practically control the entire flow from the upper parts of both. The uppermost tributary now delivering an unimpeded flow into the system is the San Pedro, which rises south of the Mexican border and flows north to a junction with the Gila near Winkelman, Arizona. The only other tributary of any size which enters the system from the south is the Santa Cruz, which rises on the eastern slopes of the Santa Rita Mountains in southern Arizona, loops down through Sonora, and comes to a rather indefinite ending in the Gila valley without maintaining a permanent channel into the main streamway. Other confluents, entering from the north, are the Hassayampa and the Agua Fria. Both rise in the mountainous district in central Arizona and are typical dry desert streamways during most of the year, but are subject to violent flash-floods in the rainy seasons. Other desert washes of minor importance enter on both sides below the mouth of the Hassayampa, but none carries a permanent stream.

Run-off. Although incomplete records appear to indicate that the Gila used to join the Colorado as a stream of some considerable volume during most of the year, the discharge has been very small for many years except at times of heavy storms somewhere within the basin. The best-marked period of flood condition is in mid-winter, even under the present curtailed area available for unrestricted run-off. Summer storms are common, however, and produce flash-floods of some violence. Both spring and autumn rains of "cloudburst" intensity have also occurred in sections of the lower basin, which have given a flash discharge of upwards of 50,000 second-feet at the junction. The silt content of the outflowing water is always high, especially under flood conditions, and has been known to amount to almost 10 per cent by volume of freshly precipitated solid matter.

The several comparatively small tributary creeks that enter the canyon section of the river between the San Juan and the Virgin, namely the Paria, the Bright Angel, and Kanab Creek from the north and Cataract Creek from the south, are all subject to similar seasonal variations in discharge: an early spring freshet, or series of freshets, due to winter storms and melting snow on the high plateaus, and occasional flash floods in the summer rain season. The perennial flow of those in the depths of the canyon is generally clear, but some lithoidal debris and a high proportion of organic matter is brought down at times of freshets.

THE CANYON AND DOWNSTREAM SECTIONS AS GRINDING AND STORAGE CHAMBERS RESPECTIVELY

The fundamental difference between the Colorado River and other heavy carriers of detrital matter is the long, steep canyon section which intervenes between the chief silt-producing tributaries and the areas of deposition. This constitutes, in effect, a great grinding, mixing, and forwarding chamber for matter already in transit, although, in the passage through it, practically nothing is added to the load. Owing to the physical features of the gorges there are few sites within them upon which sedimentary material can be even temporarily deposited. Little is retained, therefore, even during periods of diminishing flow.

The 250 miles of placid river of low gradient, largely bordered by extensive flood plains and in which the only tributary is the intermittent and relatively unimportant Bill Williams Fork, form, on the other hand, a sort of storage bin into which much of the suspended load and practically all the coarser saltatory or rolling load which has survived the grinding process in the canyons is temporarily deposited during low-water periods, to be picked up and moved forward intermittently in times of rising river and flood. These controlling factors must be given due weight in constructing a hypothetical annual flow-sheet of the delivery of the debris on to the delta.

ANNUAL RÉGIME OF COLORADO DISCHARGE: WINTER AND SPRING

At the commencement of the calendar year, the river may be assumed to be at its lowest stage, with its detrital burden also at a minimum.

Discharge from the higher mountain tributaries in the Green, Upper Colorado, and San Juan basins is also likely to be impeded by ice. Deposition upon the aggrading of the bed is usually taking place during mid-winter in the lower reaches of the river, owing to the diminution and lessening carrying capacity of the current and aside from any introduction of fresh detrital material into the main channel. The earliest increase in the detrital content of the water to appear in the year is usually the result of winter storms in the semi-arid lower basins. At times, and in certain sections, melting snow which has fallen earlier in the season is also involved in the run-off. Such storms have frequently given rise to sharp flashy floods at the Gila-Colorado junction, and, as they represent in most instances the scavenging of areas which have been dry for several months previously, in which the surface material has been disturbed and distributed by wind and is readily accessible to denudation and transportation, the detrital content of the flood waters from the streams affected is generally very high. Although floods of this description usually enter the main artery of the river system with some violence, their momentum is quickly absorbed by the partially dried river bed and the lower portions of the flood plain, and deposition, rather than channel scouring, takes place during the first few hours in the section immediately below the point of inflow.

While local deposition from the heavily charged advance waters of such brief winter floods frequently occurs and its removal down stream through the agency of the same storm period is not uncommon, the first three months of the year are usually marked by a continuation of the seasonal low-water period and general light deposition. Much of the heavier recently introduced matter undoubtedly remains practically unmoved during the usual lull of early spring, merely serving as a feeder to such slowly moving bottom load as the varying conditions of current may be competent to keep in motion. With the steadily increasing flow of the main river during the later spring months, the real movement of these local deposits begins, together with that of the fresh detrital matter brought from the upper basins as a consequence of the melting snows. The increase in discharge through the lower river continues usually with little interruption until the end of May, or early part of June, and it is during these weeks of steadily augmenting current that the delta receives its greatest annual loading of detrital matter. Although there does not appear to be any close relationship between the volume of discharge and the percentage of suspended material in transit in the current, the total quantity transported during the season of high water is very large. The general scouring of the channel to accommodate the increasing flow also sets in motion a great volume of bed material which has accumulated during the preceding months. Local deposits, left in the main channel by brief floods from the lower tributaries, are gathered up and swept forward as the surface gradient and velocity of the stream increase.

Sand waves and other evidences of disturbed bottom conditions become common, and bank erosion and the development of cut-offs add to the detrital burden.

THE MAY-JULY PEAK

No satisfactory method has yet been devised for directly estimating the tonnage, yardage, or acreage of this mass of bed material, although indirectly its passage down the channel is fully evident. The relationship between gauge heights and discharge, as measured at the Yuma station, almost immediately below the point of inflow of detrital matter from the Gila, has long been recognized as an indication of the rapid movement of bed material at that point at times of rapidly rising river. The discharge capacity below the 25-foot gauge height, which represents the critical level of overflow of the lower Yuma valley, has varied from 38,000 to over 105,000 second-feet within a twenty-year period, which implies heavy scour and movement. A specific instance showed a doubling of channel capacity below the critical figure, or from 41,000 to 82,000 second-feet, during the three-month period from April 20 to July 21, 1907, a heavy summer rise to a peak gauge height of 29 feet having intervened.

Although the occurrence of the summer rains is one of the most strongly marked climatic features of the arid southwestern region which embraces most of the Colorado Basin, the brief but frequently violent storms which characterize it are generally purely local disturbances. They occur almost daily, however, and similar heavy precipitation may take place in several areas simultaneously. Small tributaries with steep gradients will rise to flood stage within a few minutes, and the movement of detrital matter in the initial rush of the water is at times very remarkable. As the downpour is usually only a matter of minutes, the flood momentum is soon lost when flatter gradients are reached, unless reinforced by inflow from confluents, and deposition takes place as the transporting current decreases in velocity or is absorbed into the stream bed. Temporary local deposits are thus left here and there, partially obstructing streamways. These are gathered up, distributed, or overlaid by further accumulations of detrital matter, until the next general scavenging of that portion of the system takes place through more widely distributed precipitation.

THE AUTUMN FRESHETS AND THEIR HEAVY SILT LOAD

Autumnal floods, with an amplitude of discharge at Yuma of 50,000 second-feet or over, pass down the lower river at average intervals of about two years, and when they occur they usually carry a capacity burden of suspended matter and cause much movement of the bed mate-

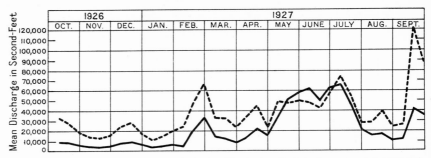

FIG. 65—Graph showing amount of dissolved solids (broken line) in the water of the Colorado River at Yuma, Ariz., and the discharge of the river at that point October 1, 1926, to

rial. A violent flood of this type, which reached a maximum of somewhat over 93,000 second-feet in September, 1909, was instrumental in completing the filling of the basin above the Laguna Dam with detrital material within six months after the completion of the dam itself.

A well-recognized characteristic of the early autumnal flow through the lower river and into the canal system of the Imperial Valley, whether the season is marked by excessive discharge conditions or not, is the prevailing high percentage of finely divided suspended matter carried by the water, together with much organic debris. This is clearly the result of the heavily charged run-off from the upper catchment areas of the system, received during these brief but violent summer rain storms and distributed through the main stream during the passage through the canyons (Figs. 66 and 67).

Remarkable instances of rapid changes in the character and quantity of the suspended solids carried during the season of minor autumnal freshets have been observed by and have given trouble to the engineers in charge of the water-purifying and softening plant serving Boulder City, which pipes its water from the Colorado above Boulder Dam. Preliminary studies of the water to be treated at this point had showed variation in the matter in suspension of from 350 to about 60,000 parts per million (p.p.m.), with an average content of 6,000 p.p.m. In order to handle the influent successfully, a large presedimentation basin is used, allowing for a detention period of two and a half hours at full capacity of the plant. This is found to be sufficient under ordinary circumstances to furnish comparatively clear water to be pumped up to the filtering and softening units.

During the last few days of August, 1932, and accompanying a sudden rise in the river from an unusually low seasonal discharge of about 6,000 second-feet, to nearly 50,000, the amount of suspended solids rose from 5,200 p.p.m. on the 26th, to 41,000 p.p.m. on the 27th, and 84,000 p.p.m. on September 1. The amount thereafter slowly decreased. The matter in suspension was found to be excessively finely divided, and only a very small proportion settled out in the presedimentation reservoir, even after

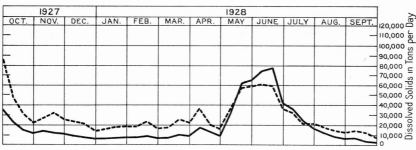

September 30, 1928. (Based on C. S. Howard, *U. S. Geol. Survey Water-Supply Paper 636,* Washington, 1930, pp. 10-11 and 13-14, Table 2, analyses Nos. 89-126 and 178-213.)

seven and a half hours' detention. The water in this case came principally from the San Juan and the lower portion of the Little Colorado basin. The crest of the rise passed Yuma and proceeded on to the delta on September 6, the discharge having been reduced to about 40,000 second-feet by evaporation and irrigation requirements in the lower valleys. The large amount of debris carried in suspension was still very noticeable. There was no evidence, however, of any unusual movement of bed material.

The conditions observed, both at Boulder City and Yuma, on this occasion were entirely typical of silt movement at this period of the year. Closely following, as it does, the general scavenging of the river bed [2] by the chief annual rise and before any great replenishing can take place through aggradation, the minor autumnal rise, if it occurs, is usually noticeable in the lower valleys and upon the delta for an increase in suspended matter alone, if the flood waters have originated above the canyons and the debris in transit has been subjected to the inevitable grinding process. The excessively finely divided condition observed at this time was doubtless due, in addition, to some local peculiarities in the area from which it has been derived.

San Pedro River the Only Unobstructed Purveyor of Silt to the Delta

The Virgin River, Bill Williams Fork, and certain confluents of the Gila, have at times discharged heavy loads of detrital material on to the delta as the result of summer storms of sufficient intensity and duration to carry the flood waters past the Colorado-Gila junction. All the coarser and heavier debris entering the upper part of the Gila system is,

[2] Dr. Leighly suggests that, in addition to the scavenging of stream beds, another process is involved, namely a "preparation" (in Walther Penck's terminology: Die morphologische Analyse, *Geogr. Abhandl.*, Series 2, No. 2, Stuttgart, 1924, Ch. 2) on the interstream areas. As noted by Hjulström (see bibliography at end of this volume) in the case of the Fyris, the early discharge carries more material, though the run-off be less than at the highest stage. He interprets the process as having its seat in the interstream areas, where in resting periods fine material is made accessible to the first run-off after a period of quiescence.—Edit. Note.

however, now retained behind the Roosevelt and San Carlos Dams, and
the San Pedro alone, of all the heavy silt carriers of the Gila basin, has
still free run-off to the lower river. This stream, which has a drainage
area, partly in Mexico, of about 3,450 square miles, has long been
notorious for the amount of fine silt and other debris which its flood
waters carry. Its valley has been settled and largely used for cattle
grazing for many years, and the natural covering of vegetation has
been irreparably damaged upon most of the steep lateral slopes, and
heavy erosion has followed. With the completion of Boulder Dam and
the construction of Parker Dam, the Los Angeles Aqueduct storage and
diversion dam below the mouth of Bill Williams Fork, the San Pedro will
remain as the sole source in the entire Colorado drainage system from
which the heavier detrital matter can reach the delta in any considerable
quantity.

OCTOBER-DECEMBER DECLINE, WITH OCCASIONAL FLOODS

A less strongly marked period of floods has occurred at irregular
intervals during the latter part of November or early December. Such
floods have at times continued in sufficient volume to cause further extensive scouring of the channel and the rapid removal down stream of
the accumulating masses of bed materials. Notable instances occurred
in 1905, when the great flood of November peaked up to 103,000
second-feet, and again in 1919, when a discharge of 82,000 second-
feet was reached. In both cases the rise was rapid, subsidence comparatively slow, and the amount of bed material moved very remarkable.

In general, however, the annual movement of the heavier debris has
practically ceased by the end of September, and the gradually falling
river is flowing over a slowing aggrading bed. Normally this condition
continues until the recognized storm period during January and February
initiates the movement from the lower basin areas for the ensuing year.

RATES OF PROGRESSION OF THE DIFFERENT TYPES OF DETRITAL LOAD

Emphasis should be placed upon the differences in the rate of progression through the system of the suspended, the saltatory, and the
true bed loads. That in free suspension may travel practically at the
average rate of the current, which even through the lower valleys
may be taken at from $2\frac{1}{2}$ to 3 miles per hour. The saltatory load may
be assumed to attain under favorable conditions about half the current
speed, while the forward motion of the still heavier and more immobile
bed material may be more readily measured in feet per minute than
in miles per hour, except during such occasional flood conditions as
were outlined in the preceding chapter, when practically the entire bed of
the stream is in motion.

FIGS. 66 and 67—Two views showing water heavily charged with silt derived from summer rain storms flowing over the Grand Falls on the Little Colorado River where this intermittent stream drops into its first canyon section preparatory to entering the Grand Canyon about 65 miles farther down. This supply of detrital matter has been cut off from the delta since the completion of Boulder Dam.

CHAPTER XI

DEPOSITION OF THE DETRITAL MATERIAL

PHYSICAL FEATURES OF THE HEAD OF THE GULF OF CALIFORNIA

Certain regional features and conditions existing about the head of the Gulf of California have determined the size and character of the Colorado delta. The comparatively narrow space available for sub-aerial deposition, the form of the pre-existing marine basin toward and into which the river flow was directed, and, perhaps most important of all, the great tidal impulses which the outflowing water with its detrital load is now compelled to meet head-on as the transporting power of the river ceases—all have contributed to the upbuilding and shaping of the delta.

The Gulf of California itself is a typical funnel sea, of the littoral-abyssal type, 600 miles in length at the existing coastal level and of unknown original depth, but at least of the order of magnitude of 1,500 fathoms (9,000 feet), about its entrance.

Into this submarine trough, near its upper extremity, almost in an axial direction, and for a period extending back into probably Tertiary time, the Colorado has carried its vast volume of detrital material. The result of this long-continued process has been the deposition of a prism of sedimentary matter practically covering the Gulf floor and having a present average gradient on its upper surface of some 15 feet to the mile from the river mouth to the vicinity of Cape San Lucas at the southern end of the peninsula of Lower California.

The deposited mass has a reasonably even slope for the first 200 miles, dropping from low tidal level at the river bar to approximately 1,250 feet in latitude 29° N. Soundings over this area have disclosed at most stations the characteristic soft mud indicative of fluviatile deposition. Just south of the 29th parallel the Gulf is much constricted by islands—San Lorenzo, San Esteban, and Tiburón—with passages not exceeding 10 miles in width between them, all unfavorably known by mariners for their strong tidal currents. The bottom in this vicinity is extremely irregular, the deepest water being found in the Salsipuedes Channel, between San Lorenzo and the Lower California shore. From the vicinity of this archipelago down to latitude 27° 40', a distance of approximately 100 miles along the axis of the Gulf, the floor drops rapidly, at about 48 feet to the mile, to 6,000 feet. A stretch of 100 miles of comparatively level bottom follows, and then comes another steep incline for 40 miles, with a terminal depth of somewhat over 9,000 feet at the Gulf entrance. Muddy bottom is found in nearly all the deeper soundings down the *thalweg* of the Gulf floor, and soundings in the still deeper water to the southwest and west of Cape San Lucas (10,000 to 11,000 feet) have also revealed mud of the same general character and almost certainly of continental and fluviatile origin.

The upper basin of the Gulf, from the plexus of islands to the mouth of the Colorado, has an area of approximately 20,000 square miles at present coastal levels and is probably underlaid almost entirely by the foreset and bottomset beds of the delta. In their developed form these beds are the proximate cause of the progressive shoaling of the water as the head of the Gulf is approached, and this, in turn, is the condition which augments tidal intensity at the river mouth.

In its passage between the islands a spring tide has a range of some $10\frac{1}{2}$ feet, about double that of an equivalent tide at Cape San Lucas. At the river mouth the range has increased to over 30 feet, and the tidal currents have grown correspondingly in violence. The time consumed by the tidal crest in traversing the upper basin—a distance of about 200 miles—is approximately two hours and forty minutes. In the presence of such violent tidal movement as these figures indicate it appears probable that the ascertained gradient of the floor of the basin represents about the limit of stability or angle of repose of the deposited material, and that a surplus, when such exists or temporarily accumulates, will be carried by further tidal movement through the inter-island passages and into the deeper portions of the Gulf.

Decrease of Estuarial Deposits Due to Cessation of Sea Outlets of the Colorado

Under the usual conditions of delta upbuilding, in which one or more channels cross the delta in free communication with the sea or other receiving body of water, such of the heavier detrital material as is not previously disposed of by bed aggradation or lateral dispersion is carried directly forward to the sub-aqueous foreset and bottomset beds for final deposition. When, on the other hand, free communication between the river and the sea ceases or is interrupted, all such material is retained within the sub-aerial portion of the delta.

During the past thirty years practically no detrital matter of the heavier, coarser, bed-silt type, such as is incapable of being maintained in suspension more than momentarily by the current, has entered the Gulf from the river.

As previously described, deposition has taken place successively in the Salton basin (1905-1907), the Volcano Lake district (1909-1923), the Pescadero basin (1923-1929), and since 1929 in the region about the lower end of the Vacanora cutting. In the short interregnum between the reversion of the river to its previously occupied channel and its diversion into the Río Abejas (1907-1909), the escape of any considerable portion of the tractional load to tidewater was prevented by the choked and shoaled condition of the river-bed through the lower delta.

As tidal action in the Gulf has remained unimpaired during this period of curtailment of the supply of river-borne detrital matter at its head, depletion of accumulated estuarial deposits has taken place as a natural result. The existence of this abstractive activity has been fully confirmed by observation, as described elsewhere. Depletion will undoubtedly continue when the full effect of the Boulder Dam and the other control structures now in contemplation is felt upon the lower reaches, until a new balance is struck between river and tide.

DEVELOPMENT OF VACANORA CHANNEL DELTA AS SHOWN ON AIR PHOTOGRAPHS

The process of dispersal and deposition of the heavier detrital matter about the lower end of the Vacanora channel during the 1929-1933 period can be more readily illustrated and explained with the aid of a series of three aerial photographs of the region, taken by Major Erickson in July, 1931, March, 1932, and August, 1933 (Figs. 69, 70, 74) than by a detailed description based solely upon ground observations. Substantially the same field is shown in each picture, although the direction and angle at which the exposure was made has varied.

Beginning with the first in the series, taken on July 28, 1931, two years after the channel was excavated and deposition in the area began, the following points may be noted. Dispersal, as indicated by the light-colored areas, had up to that time been very moderate, concentrating about the end of the original excavated cutting, which had terminated at the unfinished railroad grade which may be seen crossing the lower portion of the picture in a slightly diagonal direction. The original alignment of the cutting may be seen as a slightly lighter band on the photograph extending as far as the railroad grade, although it was impossible to distinguish it upon the ground at the time the picture was made.

A small amount of water, distinguishable as a slightly darker sinuous line, still followed the crest of the deposit along the channel alignment, for about half the distance to the railroad grade, and was then diverted down the left flank. It may then be seen crossing the grade, following the crest of an extension of the newly deposited mass, and at length reaching the lower margin of the photograph.

The channel which carried this small stream was discontinuous, being interrupted by swampy areas after passing down the flank of the main deposit, but it formed a part of the most direct link between the Colorado River and the Gulf at the time. The larger distributary branches, leaving the main channel in the middle distance, were all lost in the swampy region which was developing above the railroad grade. Evidence of the

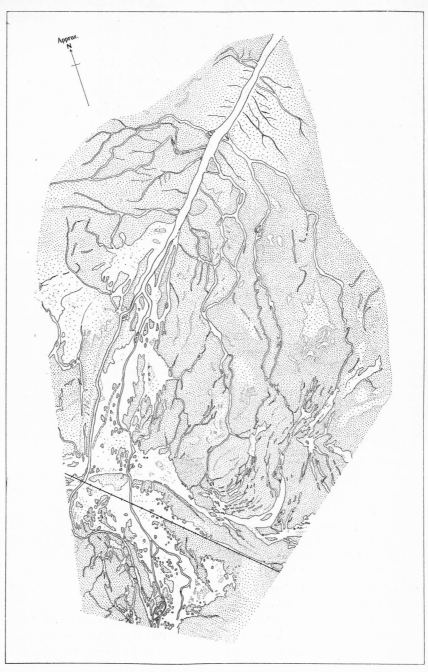

FIG. 68—Map of secondary delta fan at lower end of Vacanora channel, July, 1931, plotted from the oblique air photograph on the opposite page (Fig. 69). Scale, 1:57,000. Stippling indicates approximately the distribution and density of the vegetation. White areas are largely sand, gravel, and silt of the distributary channels. (Drawn at the American Geographical Society by means of a single-eyepiece plotter by O. M. Miller and C. B. Hitchcock.)

FIG. 69—Air view of the secondary deltaic fan built up since 1929 at the lower end of the Vacanora Canal. Looking north-northeast from behind the Mexicali-Gulf Railroad embankment, July 28, 1931. Cf. the map, Figure 68, and the discussion in the text, pp. 157 and 159. For the broader relationships of the features shown in the background, see also Figure 36. The three mountain masses on the left horizon are, from left to right, Chocolate Mts., Cargo Muchacho Mts., Pilot Knob.

FIG. 70—The same fan slightly closer by, photographed on March 18, 1932, showing the increased deposit of detrital material, due to the February flood of that year. For discussion, see text, p. 159. (Figs. 69 and 70 from air photographs by H. A. Erickson.)

FIGS. 71 and 72—Various aspects of vegetation in the delta: (upper) in the old channel of the Colorado, abandoned since 1909 (photograph taken in 1925); (lower) on the new delta, showing secondary growth extending among the upper portions of trees of an earlier growth, the original surface of the ground being some 10 feet below the present level. Vegetation has played an important role in the formation of the Colorado Delta, through the fixation of detrital material.

Fig. 73—Bank of a distributary channel in the delta showing newly deposited mud on the foreshore and stands of willow seedlings on the edges of the bank. This photograph is typical of a falling river following upon a moderate rise.

Fig. 74—The deltaic cone at the lower end of the Vacanora Canal seen from the opposite direction to that of Figures 69 and 70. Air view taken on August 25, 1933, showing the recapture by vegetation of the areas of detrital invasion of a year and a half previously. See text, pp. 159 and 160. (From air photograph by H. A. Erickson.)

indefinite drainage thereabouts may be seen in the frequently retrograde direction in which they terminate amongst the dense vegetation.

The process of the overwhelming of the vegetal covering of the region by the detrital invasion is clearly shown at many points, where small stands or even isolated bushes still exist within the frontal margins of the advancing waves of the debris.

Turning to the second photograph of the series (Fig. 70), taken from almost the same view-point little less than eight months later (March 18, 1932), the remarkable effects of a single additional invasion at once become apparent. This was the February flood of the same year, which carried down the mass of sedimentary matter ejected from Bill Williams Fork and which has already been fully described (p. 97).

The discharge of the river at the time the picture was taken was about 15,000 second-feet, and the surface of much of the newly deposited material was still moist. The extension of the invaded area is very obvious from the aerial view, but the most remarkable fact brought out by examination on the ground after the inundation had drained away and disappeared was the thickening of the mass along the crest of the main cone and of the principal lines and areas of deposition. This may be seen at the extreme left-hand margin of the picture, where a light-colored area covers the railroad grade. The surface was dry at that point, the unfinished track was buried to a depth of nearly 3 feet, and the underpass which had been constructed across original drainage lines with 16 to 18 feet headroom was wholly obliterated.

Although the discharge of the river had nearly reached 50,000 second-feet during this winter flood and although the flood itself was a comparatively brief one, the volume of detrital matter carried on to this dispersal area was very striking. Vegetation was generally overwhelmed, and the invasion took the form of a sheet flooding over the whole surface of the cone, rather than the more common building up in detail along dispersal channels. This is made very manifest in this view from above.

The third picture in the series (Fig. 74), taken on August 25, 1933, and showing practically the same foreground and mid-distance field as the previous pair, although in a contrary direction, was made at a time of slightly lower river and during the height of the summer season of vegetational growth.

The discharge at Yuma on the previous day had been 13,400 second-feet and was slowly decreasing. Diversion into the Imperial Canal, between the gauging point and the section of channel shown in the picture, together with seepage, evaporation, and other wastage, would in all probability account for 3,000 or 4,000 second-feet, leaving a net flow, at the time and point shown in the foreground, of from 9,000 to 10,000 second-feet. The crest of the summer flood, reaching a maximum discharge of nearly 70,000 second-feet, had passed Yuma a month earlier, and during the intervening weeks the river had been steadily falling.

In striking contrast to the view taken seventeen months earlier, a dense stand of vegetation once more covers the greater part of the areas devastated and submerged by the detrital invasion of February, 1932, entirely altering the aspect of the region of dispersal. It will be realized at once what an all-important part a vegetal covering of such density and vigor plays in controlling the distribution of detrital material, and therefore in the development of the delta. Actual deposition of the tractional loading of the current would be practically confined, under the conditions illustrated in this view, to the distributaries and the innumerable small outlets which fringe the banks of the partially ponded main channel.

Delta Upbuilding by Distributary Channels

The process of delta upbuilding by means of the development and multiplication of distributary channels upon the sub-aerial surface is well understood and need be only briefly referred to.

A channel which is temporarily surcharged through overwhelming flood conditions, or by reason of a checking of free discharge by obstructions, soon develops a transriparian flow at such points as afford opportunities for relief at the then existing levels. As the outflow takes place, organic and other light debris is carried bankwards and lodges against vegetation or other impeding surfaces until a more or less impervious barrier is formed, cresting the bank and virtually adding to its height. As the surcharged condition passes and the transporting power of the current decreases, deposition takes place upon the stream bed. The process may be repeated during and following upon succeeding highwater periods until the entire channel is materially higher than the surrounding region. When this stage is reached a breach in the bank may permit the development of an outflowing current of sufficient velocity to move bed material and open for itself a definite divergent channel. Further subdividings take place in like manner, and the complexity of the distributory system increases until the intervening spaces between and surrounding the channels are filled and a general rise in level has taken place.

As a measure of such accretive activity within the immediate area, and during the period embraced by the three air views under discussion, it may be reasonably assumed that a deposition of fully 12 feet has taken place along most of the larger channels and the general elevation has increased at least 8 feet over an area of 40 or 50 square miles.

Wherever a light area appears in any one of the photographs, whether it is in the form of the broad expanses in the vicinity of the railroad grade or the delicate pencilings of the minor distributaries fringing the main channel, it signifies the deposition of heavy material of the type which has been retained above tidewater during the western excursion of the river. Such material forms the bulk of the Vacanora deposit or semi-cone and has been a most important factor in the rapid accumulation of the deposits about the lower ends of the Río Abejas and the Pescadero diversion cutting.

RETENTION OF THE SUSPENDED LOAD IN AREAS OF INDEFINITE DRAINAGE

The distribution of the suspended load by the river water—such of it as has been retained within the field of the pictures—is not so obvious. At times of flood much of this finer material passes directly out to sea or at least is arrested and precipitated in the estuary by contact with the saline constituents of the sea water. During periods of moderate and minimum discharge, and while the delta remains in its present condition of arrested development, practically all this is held, either in paludal areas, zones of vegetation, or in ephemeral lagoons or other surface irregularities. Retention of this portion of the river's burden within the sub-aerial regions of the delta is due to prolonged cessation of motion of the transporting water or to its diminution or disappearance through seepage, evaporation, or transpiration from the leaf surfaces of growing plants.

The dense thicket of arrow weed (*Pluchea sericea*), poplar seedlings (*Populus macdougalii*), carrizo (*Calamagrostis gigantea*), or of one or more of the several species of willow common in this part of the delta form effective sieves for retaining much of the material of intermediate, or saltatory, size that is carried into them by the overflowing waters in times of floods. Still finer particles are deposited as the effective hydrostatic head, and hence the velocity, of the outflowing water decreases with the continuing friction. Thus arises the commonly observed condition of progressive fineness of the surface material with increase of distance from the banks of built-up main channels or distributaries.

Areas of enclosed, restricted, or indeterminate drainage, such as commonly develop during the formation of secondary deltaic fans, tend to become paludal in character, either ephemerally or perennially so, as the inflow of water is intermittent or constant. Several such areas of both types exist within the field of the photographs but are indistinguishable amongst the covering and surrounding vegetation when one is on the ground.

Two well-defined distributaries which leave the main channel through its left bank at about the upper limit of the ponded section and which are plainly discernible in the views of 1931 and 1932 have carried fairly constant streams into the region of indefinite drainage shown in the right-hand portion of both pictures. A great volume of detrital matter, largely of the coarser and heavier type in making the initial fill over the more depressed portions of the invaded ground but afterwards of progressively finer texture as the gradient decreased, has been carried into and deposited within this section ever since these distributaries developed.

Overflow in this direction is, however, apparently failing somewhat at the present time (1934), as there is an increasing tendency for a direct flow to establish itself along the crest of the recently deposited semicone and to develop direct communication with the Hardy through the two new channels which have been described elsewhere, both of which may be plainly seen crossing the upper portion of the 1933 view in roughly parallel courses towards tidewater.

DIFFERENTIATION BETWEEN TRACTIONAL AND SUSPENDED LOAD ON BASIS OF SILT INVESTIGATIONS

Silt investigations of the Colorado water in the canal systems of the Imperial Valley have demonstrated [1] that detrital material capable of passing through the interstices of a 200-mesh sieve (approximately 0.076 mm on a side) is carried forwards without notable deposition at current speeds of 40 feet per minute, or less than half a mile per hour. Laboratory experiments with still finer material, such as passes freely through a 300-mesh sieve (which is the finest sieve in practical use) and of which the component particles are less than 0.053 mm in diameter, have shown that it will remain in suspension almost indefinitely at much lower rates of motion, such as that induced by a slight breeze blowing over an open expanse of shallow water. The 200-mesh sieve has been commonly accepted as a somewhat arbitrary division between the tractional and suspended loads, and the studies in the Imperial Valley canals appear to indicate that such a division is substantially correct, it having been found, for instance, that with proper flashboard manipulation at the canal heading fully 90 per cent of the matter in suspension which enters the canal is below this size.

The application of these facts to the deposition of detrital matter in the delta is that a broad distinction exists in the manner of distribution between that which is of tractional or bed-silt size and that which may be classified as suspended. Accepting the arbitrary 200-mesh division as correct, particles which would be retained thereon may be considered as restricted in distribution to channels and other areas reached by *running* water moving with some velocity, while below that critical size they will be freely distributed by water which merely *flows* in the manner of a general inundation or sheet flood.

WASTAGE OF FLOOD WATERS IN PALUDAL AREAS THROUGH SEEPAGE, EVAPORATION, AND ABSORPTION BY VEGETATION

Swamp conditions in enclosed areas are generally maintained by the inflow of slowly moving water, and in a region of prevailing low surface relief and gentle gradients such as are found in this portion of the delta,

---

[1] Samuel Fortier and H. F. Blaney: Silt in the Colorado River and Its Relation to Irrigation, *Dept. of Agric. Technical Bull. No. 67,* Washington, 1928, pp. 46-49.

the periodical inundations—except along lines of natural drainage—are usually featured by a gradual rise, maintenance for some time at or near the crest level, and slow subsidence. Water which ultimately reaches tidewater by slow passage across flooded areas carries a certain amount of the finer portion of its burden to the sea, although much is deposited during the transit; but such as fails to escape must deposit all.

Three main causes are recognized for the disappearance of flood waters in paludal areas similar to those under discussion. Gradual seepage into the underlying strata is perhaps the most important. It should be remembered, however, that percolation through deposited bodies of the excessively fine material, of which the residual deposition from the Colorado water is composed, is exceedingly slow. Wastage through evaporation from open water surfaces and from the surrounding zones of moist soil is doubtless more rapid, in view of the prevailing high temperatures and low humidity at the time of year at which the swamps are most extensive.

The studies of Bigelow [2] in the Salton Sink in 1907-1908 indicated that fully half an inch per diem might be evaporated from open water surfaces in this region under optimum conditions of temperature and air movement. A daily loss of half an inch over a water surface of one square mile is equivalent to a constant inflow of approximately 16 second-feet, and this may be accepted as a reasonable amount of wastage due to this cause under summer conditions in the lower delta region, for each square mile of impounded water. The solid matter in suspension in this quantity of water is probably about 20,000 cubic feet, as computed upon the basis of dried silt, so that this volume is available for deposition through the process of evaporation alone, each twenty-four hours, beneath each square mile of water surface from which evaporation is taking place freely. The resultant deposited layer is something less than 1/100 of an inch in thickness, or 5 inches in the course of the year, should the wastage from this cause proceed uninterruptedly.

The third cause of wastage is one to which comparatively little attention appears to have been paid until recently, in connection with problems such as those we have presented with regard to the Colorado delta: this is the absorbtion of water by massed vegetation in paludal areas and its ultimate loss through transpiration from leaf surfaces. Recent researches in the *sudd* regions of the upper Nile have focussed the attention of the investigators of the Physical Department of the Egyptian Ministry of Public Works [3] upon this process as being probably the chief cause of the remarkable loss of water from the associated series of waterways which unite to form the White Nile, while they are passing through

[2] F. H. Bigelow: Studies on the Rate of Evaporation at Reno, Nevada, and in the Salton Sink, *Natl. Geogr. Mag.*, Vol. 19, 1908, pp. 20-28.

[3] H. E. Hurst: The Sudd Region of the Nile, *Journ. Royal Soc. of Arts*, Vol. 81, 1933, pp. 721-734; reference on p. 731.

this zone of profuse vegetation. Although no very definite figures or analyses of the actual causes of this loss are at present available, it appears that between latitudes 5° and 10° N. the Nile system loses as much water through swamp wastage as it gains from its tributary streams—the round figures being approximately 27,000,000,000 cubic meters per annum—and that this loss is largely due to passage through plant tissue.

Studies carried out by, or on behalf of the California Division of Water Resources,[4] have indicated a direct water loss of as much as 4½ inches per week as due to transpiration alone in paludal areas in south-central California. The conditions of humidity and temperature and also the character of the vegetation are in this instance very similar to those found in the delta.

In the aggregate, and with the closest possible estimate of the paludal areas appurtenant to the Vacanora channel, it seems necessary to account for a continual surface loss of from 4 to 5 inches a day. This figure is based upon actual estimates of the inflow towards, and the effluence from, the region on several occasions and under circumstances which would imply a more or less constant area of wastage; and it may be accepted as reasonably accurate. The equivalent total deposition of suspended matter per week (the week being taken as a convenient unit of time) is approximately half an inch, as computed for these enclosed drainage areas into which everything is carried but nothing leaves except water vapor and such water as penetrates the underlying stratum of deposited mud and the waterlogged subsoil.

Ponded sections of channels in which through flow has ceased are of course subject to the same wastage from seepage and evaporation as equivalent bodies of water in strictly paludal areas. Transpiration, however, will, except in cases of extremely narrow channels, seldom be operative to the same extent, even if riparian seepage and the passage of moisture by capillary action to adjacent root-masses and zones of vegetation be taken into account. As the through current ceases, further movement of the tractional load will also cease and deposited matter thereafter will consist wholly of such as is retained readily in suspension at extremely low rates of water movement.

COMPLEXITY OF DELTA FORMATION PROCESS

The upbuilding of the delta body by the dispersal and deposition of the detrital material furnished by the river is thus found to be a matter of much complexity, even when activity is restricted, as it is at the present time, to a limited area. Through the practical severance of direct communication between the river and the sea, the usual process of the free passage of coarse and heavy bed material into tidewater has latterly

[4] " Rainfall Penetration and Consumptive Use of Water," *California Div. of Water Resources Bull. No. 33.*

been wholly arrested, and its total deposition has perforce taken place within the zone in which the transporting water still retained sufficient velocity to move it. It has thus appeared, after the subsidence of successive floods, either as extensive new topset beds upon the surface of previous deposits or as innumerable invading tongues amidst the dense vegetation which so quickly covers surface scars in this region.

Deposition of the finer, and suspended, matter has also been affected by the recent developments. Extensive areas of indefinite drainage, which have in some instances received steadily inflowing streams, have retained their entire residual loads.

While these conditions appear to be the proximate and dominant ones in determining distribution in the Vacanora dispersal area, there are innumerable interacting influences, operative throughout the Colorado drainage basin, which collectively regulate the quantity, character, and periods of minimum or maximum movement of detrital matter towards the delta.

CONCLUSION

CHAPTER XII

RETROSPECT AND OUTLOOK

Although our earliest historical information concerning the region about the mouth of the Colorado River dates back nearly four hundred years, it remained almost a *terra incognita* for fully two centuries thereafter. The fragmentary records left by the infrequent Spanish explorers during that time merely afford us fleeting glimpses of an unattractive land, traversed by a great river which was difficult of access, surrounded by inhospitable deserts of unknown extent, and guarded from a sea approach by great and violent tides.

EVIDENCES OF SHIFTING OF COLORADO RIVER CHANNEL SINCE EARLY EXPLORATION

While much general information concerning the river was secured during the succeeding hundred years, the region between the Colorado-Gila junction and the sea still remained practically unknown. Certain deductions can be made, however, from the meager accounts left by explorers during the first two centuries and from the hardly more precise information that has come to us from travelers who entered or crossed the delta during the following century, which make it reasonably certain that the portion of the river contained therein was then—as it has proved to be since being subjected to closer scrutiny—an erratic stream, discharging into tidewater through different channels and doubtless in response to the same influences that now govern its movements. Evidences of periods of diversion of the main stream to the western side of the delta appear to be discernible in the accounts of Consag, Pattie, and Hardy, while those of Alarcón, Díaz, and Kino all indicate that they found it following the eastern margin.

During the sixth decade of the last century the lower river came under direct and continuous observation and was mapped twice, first by Derby, as the result of a joint reconnaissance by Major Heintzelman and himself in 1851, and again by Lieutenant Ives in 1858. During the intervening years commercial navigation had been developed between the head of the Gulf and Fort Yuma, and this activity continued until the mid-seventies, when the completion of the Southern Pacific Railroad from the Pacific coast to the bank of the Colorado caused its abandonment.

Derby and Heintzelman had found that the main channel, which they reported upon as being capable of navigation by light-draft vessels, was apparently well established down the eastern margin of the delta. It maintained approximately the same alignment within the limits of a meander zone some two or three miles in width for more than fifty years thereafter.

Navigation was begun upon a very moderate scale and reached the climax of its development about at the outbreak of the Civil War. At that time a regular service of some considerable magnitude was maintained, with scheduled sea connections, between San Francisco and other coast ports on the one hand and Fort Yuma on the other. Freight on the river was handled both as deck-loads on the steamers and in towed barges. A shipyard, capable of undertaking repairs to hulls and machinery, was maintained by the Colorado Steam Navigation Company near the mouth of the river, and this enterprise, although in Mexican territory, was allowed to operate without any interference by the Mexican authorities.

With the cessation of the river service this yard was dismantled and abandoned, and the delta south of the international boundary almost at once reverted to the condition of an untraveled wilderness. The river, although continuing in the same general alignment, was undoubtedly steadily raising both its bed and banks during the fifteen years following upon the withdrawal of the river men and their vessels. It had plainly reached a condition of instability in 1890, when the first examination of the channel between Yuma and the Gulf was made in connection with the investigation detailed in the foregoing pages. The entire river system was still at that time practically unaffected by human enterprise, so that conditions as observed in the delta region were those of purely natural development.

The Great Westward Diversion and Attempts to Check It

In the winter of 1890-1891, and consequent upon a heavy flood from the Gila, the river broke bounds towards the west, at the head of the delta, the flood waters reaching the Salton depression and forming a temporary lake several square miles in extent. The breach in the bank healed itself during the year, but it was the forerunner of many others during the following years, at various points along the western bank at which some temporary weakness existed.

In 1901 a canal was opened into the Salton depression—shortly afterwards to be known as the Imperial Valley. The intake proved to be unsuccessful and quickly silted up. A second and third were excavated in 1902 and 1904, respectively, but still failed to admit sufficient water to fulfill the needs of the many settlers who were already flocking into the valley. A fourth and more direct opening was therefore cut into the head of the Alamo in the autumn of 1904. With the rise of the river in the spring of 1905, the opening began to enlarge, and by the middle of August the entire river was flowing through the opening and into the Salton Sink.

Repeated efforts were made during the following year and a half to close the opening, control the inflow to the valley, and return the river to its former course. The efforts at closure were crowned with success in February, 1907, and the abandoned channel was again occupied. The reversion was not permanently successful, however, and the river persisted in escaping towards the west, first through the Paredones and afterwards through the parallel channel of the Abejas. Both these diversions carried the water towards the Hardy. The decisive abandonment of the former navigable channel took place in 1909, and since that time it has never been re-occupied by a running stream at any point between the termination of the Arizona-Sonora international boundary and tidewater and has, in fact, almost disappeared.

BUILDING OF SECONDARY DELTA FAN AT ENDS OF SUCCESSIVE DIVERSION CHANNELS

The newly selected course of the river extended for fully 45 miles in a southwesterly direction, approximately 65° to the right of its previous alignment, and ended somewhat indefinitely in the region which had formerly been occupied by an ephemeral sheet of water known as Volcano Lake. Heavy deposition began almost at once, covering the lake area and rapidly obliterating all former drainage channels in the surrounding districts. No through and definite channel communication ever developed with the lower Hardy and tidewater during the thirteen years of river discharge in this direction, dispersion of water and debris taking place over a more extended frontage as the deposit grew amidst the scattering vegetation with which the region was normally covered.

The proximity of dangerous downward slopes towards the Imperial Valley was the cause of increasing concern to the engineers of the Imperial Irrigation District, and an effort at control was determined upon. A cutting was excavated in 1921, beginning at a point in the south bank of the Abejas channel some 10 miles west of the termination of the Arizona-Sonora boundary and extending southwards into the drainage basin of the Río Pescadero, a confluent of the Hardy. The river was dammed and diverted into this cutting early in 1922, but, notwithstanding favorable downward slopes and the proximity of the Pescadero, widespread deposition once more took place along both banks and around and beyond the termination of the new channel, without the development of any definite connection with tidewater.

In the summer of 1929 a further major diversion of the river took place. It broke into, and at once occupied, a newly excavated (Vacanora) canal, some 17 miles in length, which headed a mile or two to the eastward of the previous cutting and extended towards the south-southwest in a direction roughly parallel to the old navigation channel. It has since continued to maintain the same approximate alignment through a single definite channel for a distance of about 14 miles below the diversion point but has again been prevented from establishing free communication with the sea by the growth of a great barrier fan of detritus, around and across which the ponded water is forced to find an exit by means of numerous minor distributaries. In the zone between the dispersion area and the Hardy many of these small channels unite to form two arterial waterways which carry the greater portion of the flow of the river into tidewater. A certain quantity of flood water is also diverted round the western side of the detrital deposits and finds its way into the Hardy through the Pescadero—the rejected route towards which the previous diversion of the river was directed.

The building up of this latest barrier has presented some features not previously observed in the study of the development of the delta. The rapidity of the accumulation of the central mass was very remarkable. It clearly resulted from two definite and readily identified sources of detrital matter. The first was the result of the heavy scour of the Vacanora channel itself, incidental to the passage of a flood of some 90,000 second-feet through a recently excavated and unconsolidated channel in the summer of 1929. The second, two and a half years later, was the great and suddenly projected volume of detrital material which could be traced, with almost absolute certainty, to an outrush of heavily laden flood water which issued from Bill Williams Fork in the early part of February, 1932. By the beginning of 1934 the total volume of detrital material of the heavy, or " bed-silt," type which had been spread over this great semi-cone, almost wholly submerging the heavy stand of vegetation which has previously occupied the site, was estimated as being substantially in excess of 100,000,000 cubic yards.

Only moderate and gently rising floods had occurred during the summer of 1930, and 1931 was remarkable as passing without any summer rise whatever, so that little was added to the deposit in the interval between the primary scouring of the Vacanora channel and the rapid accumulation of fresh material which was so noticeable immediately after the sudden outrush from Bill Williams Fork.

Much of the surface of the area of recent deposition was left bare and uneven as a result of the passage of the second flood, but during the ensuing growing season the natural covering of luxuriant vegetation, which is normal to this part of the delta, again sprang up, impeding or blocking the free flow of flood water and being instrumental in causing the formation of local swamps and various complexities of surface drainage.

Later and detailed examinations of the region showed that a further great increase in the volume and a real extent of the deposited mass took place as the result of the long-sustained flood conditions during the late summer of 1932, the material added being also mainly of the " bed-silt " type. The extension in lateral dimensions was almost entirely in a general up-stream direction—to the north, northwest, and northeast. This was doubtless due to the fact that the nucleus of the deposited body has formed an effective barrier against which all additional material of the heavier and less mobile types must necessarily come to rest.

The area of the deposit at the end of 1932 was estimated as being substantially in excess of 60 square miles.

As is usual during the formation of one of these great secondary fans or semi-cones of detrital matter, minor distributary channels to a total length of at least some hundreds of miles were formed, developed, overgrown, abandoned, and obliterated, as successive floods fought for mastery with the impeding vegetation upon the uneven and shifting surface.

PROSPECT OF A THROUGH OUTLET TO THE SEA

There are indications at the present time (August, 1935) that a definite waterway is at last developing across the crest of the barrier and opening a connection down its forward slope with one of the two main gathering channels which empty into the Hardy. Active recessive cutting and degradation is taking place in both of these in the manner which has been long foreseen, in consideration of the difference between the ponded level of the lower Vacanora channel and mean low water level in the Hardy. Through the united activity of these two processes it appears probable that communication between the river and tidewater by means of a continuous channel may shortly be reestablished.

For the past twenty-five years practically all detrital material too massive to be maintained in suspension in the sluggish currents of the lower river has been retained upon the sub-aerial portion of the delta, the greater part having been deposited upon and incorporated with the three accumulations which have successively barred the way to the Gulf.

The opening of a channel of sufficient capacity and fall to establish itself as the main outlet for the river system will again allow such matter to pass freely into the estuary and sphere of tidal action and terminate the present conditions of barrier building and general channel instability.

EFFECT OF COMPLETION OF BOULDER DAM

In consequence of the recent completion of Boulder Dam and the further construction of an impounding and diversion dam (Parker Dam) across the river below the mouth of Bill Williams Fork for the Los Angeles Aqueduct, thus practically ending the movement of fresh detrital matter of the coarser type down the main stream, it is improbable that the development of another localized deposit at all comparable in size and importance with the one which has recently accumulated about the lower end of the Vacanora channel will ever again take place within the delta area.

Flood hazard along the lower Colorado, except for flash freshets originating in the still uncontrolled confluents of the Gila, will be practically eliminated by the vast storage capacity behind the Boulder Dam, and the controlled stream will undergo further settlement and additional clarification 155 miles farther down behind Parker Dam. This dam has an impounding capacity, according to the present tentative plans, of approximately 717,000 acre-feet and an effective height, at full storage level, of about 70 feet above the present stream bed.

Only 150 miles of channel remain between this barrage and the present Laguna Dam, and 15 miles more from that point to the Colorado-Gila junction and head of the delta. A certain amount of adjustment from existing gradients in this section will undoubtedly take place to meet the requirements of the clarified and controlled stream, and a considerable volume of bed material is likely to be moved forwards while the adjustment is taking place, but for all practical purposes the closure of the construction by-passes at the Boulder Dam, on February 1, 1935, has spelled the end of the growth of the delta body as a major phenomenon.

Minor developments resulting from the new order of hydrological conditions along the lower course of the river have, however, already made their appearance. The great beds of temporary deposited detritus which form the channel bed between the dam and the dispersal areas are now being subjected to processes of erosion, assorting, and redistribution which is resulting in the release of a body of extremely mobile detritus which clogs irrigating canals and minor distributory channels into which it gains entrance. The investigation of these conditions by means of a series of mechanical analyses of the affected material has constituted the basis of the continued study of the region by the writer during 1934 and 1935. The work has again been done under the aegis of the Carnegie Institution.

SOME OTHER PROSPECTS

In conclusion, brief speculation may be indulged in as to the future development of the region in other ways.

International agreements between the United States Government and the Republic of Mexico regarding the division of the residual discharge of the river are still incomplete, but it appears improbable that any great surplus of the impounded and stored water will be available for the extension of the cultivated areas south of the international boundary if existing and recognized water rights upon the American side are fully exercised.

De-silted flood water from the Colorado and such flash floods as may issue from the lower Gila from time to time will in all probability pass through a channel in which aggradation will have ceased and in which degradation may have become active and capacity for the passage of all ordinary flood ample.

The present process of depletion by tidal action will continue in the estuary, and the stoppage of further supplies of detrital material from the river may be instrumental in modifying the sub-aqueous contours at the head of the Gulf.

Curtailment of the surface water supply and its restriction to the cultivated areas and a narrow channel zone will eventually result in the reversion to the condition of the surrounding deserts of much of the region which is at present occupied by luxuriant vegetation.

BIBLIOGRAPHY *

History of Exploration

(ALARCÓN) Relatione della navigatione & scoperta che fece il Capitano Fernando Alarcone per ordine dello Illustrissimo Signor Don Antonio de Mendozza Vice Re della nuoua Spagna, data in Colima, porto della nuoua Spagna. In Ramusio's " Navigationi et Viaggi ", first edition of Vol. 3, Venice, 1556, leaves 363-370. [From copy in library of American Geographical Society, New York.]

(ALARCÓN) The relation of the navigation and discovery which Captaine Fernando Alarchon made by order of the right honourable Lord Don Antonio de Mendoça Vizeroy of New Spaine, dated in Colima, an haven of New Spaine. Reprinted from Hakluyt's " Principal Navigations " in *Hakluyt Soc. Publs.*, Extra Series, Vol. 9, Glasgow, 1904, pp. 279-318. [Translation of the account in Ramusio.]

BANCROFT, H. H. History of the Pacific States of North America, Vol. 10: North Mexican States, Vol. 1 (1531-1800). San Francisco, 1883. [Among others, Chapters 4, 10, 11, and 16 deal with exploration referred to in the present work.]

BERGLAND, ERIC. Preliminary report upon the operations of Party No. 3, California Section, season of 1875-76, with a view to determine the feasibility of diverting the Colorado River for purposes of irrigation. *Annual Rept. Geogr. Surveys West of the 100th Meridian, for 1876*, 1876, Appendix B (pp. 109-125); also in *Annual Rept. Chief of Engineers for 1876*, Part 3, pp. 329-345; both with general map in 1: 1,013,760 and map of the 'depressed area in the Colorado Desert', same scale.

BROWNE, J. ROSS. A sketch of the settlement and exploration of Lower California. 200 pp. San Francisco, 1869. [Bound with the same author's " Resources of the Pacific Slope ", same place and date. Pages 5-77 contain a historical summary of Lower California, 1532-1867, by Alexander S. Taylor.]

(CONSAG) Account of the voyage of father Fernando Consag, missionary of California, performed for surveying the eastern coast of California to its extremity, the river Colorado, by order of father Christoval de Escobar and Llamas, provincial of New Spain, in the year 1746. In " A Natural and Civil History of California . . . translated from the original Spanish of Miguel Venegas . . ." (2 vols., London, 1759), Vol. 2, Appendix 3 on pp. 308-353, without map. [English translation of the Spanish original published in Madrid, 1757, listed immediately below. It is this translation apparently, that without citation of source, is reproduced, with slight verbal changes and errors, in Monsignor Krmpotic's book, passages from which are quoted above on pp. 11-13. This more authentic source was not available while Chapter 1 of the present work was being written.—EDIT. NOTE.]

(CONSAG) Derrotero del viage, que en descubrimiento de la Costa Oriental de Californias, hasta el Rio Colorado, en donde se acaba su Estrecho, hizo el Padre Fernando Consag, de la Compañia de Jesus, Missionero de Californias, por orden del Padre Christoval de Escobar y Llamas, Provincial de Nueva-España, de la Compañia de Jesus. Año de 1746. In " Noticia de la California y su conquista temporal y espiritual hasta el tiempo presente, sacada de la historia manuscrita formada en Mexico año de 1739 por el Padre Miguel Venegas . . ." (3 vols., Madrid, 1757), Vol. 3, Appendix 3 on pp. 140-194, with map of upper half of the Gulf of California on a scale of about 1: 2,300,000.

(CONSAG) Krmpotic, M. D. Life and works of the Reverend Ferdinand Konsćak, S. J., 1703-1759, an early missionary in California. 167 pp., Boston, 1923. [See comment to entry above under Consag, English translation of Venegas, London, 1759.]

COOKE, [P. ST.] GEORGE. A winter's work of a captain of dragoons. *Magazine of Amer. Hist.*, Dec. 1887. [See below under Emory.]

DERBY, G. H. Report of the expedition of the United States transport " Invincible " . . . to the Gulf of California and River Colorado . . . , 1850 and 1851. *32nd Congr., 1st Sess., Senate Exec. Doc. No. 81.* 28 pp., with map in 1: 253,440. 1852.

(DÍAZ, MELCHIOR) [Account of his expedition by land around the head of the Gulf of California in 1540.] In chapters 10 and 17 of the First Part of: Relacion de la Jornada de Cibola conpuesta por Pedro de Castañeda de Naçera donde se trata de todos aquellos poblados y ritos y costumbres, la qual fue el Año de 1540. Spanish text, with English translation by G. P. Winship, *14th Annual Rept. Bur. of Ethnol. 1892-93*, 1896, Part I, pp. 414-469 and 470-546 (relevant chapters on pp. 425-428 and 438-439 and pp. 484-487 and 501-502 respectively); and in: Relacion del suceso de la jornada que Francisco Vazquez [de Coronado] hizo en el descubrimiento de Cibola, English translation in *ibid.*, pp. 572-579. [The Spanish text of Castañeda is printed from the manuscript in the New York Public Library, which is a copy that was made at Seville in 1596. A French translation, not as close as Winship's English translation, was made from the same copy,

---

* Expanded, annotated, and classified by the American Geographical Society from the author's list.—EDIT. NOTE.

then in Paris, and published by Ternaux-Compans in his " Voyages, relations, et mémoires originaux pour servir à l'histoire de la découverte de l'Amérique " (20 vols., Paris 1837-1841), Vol. 9, 1838, pp. vii-xvi and 1-246. Winship's translation is also printed in his " The Journey of Coronado " (in Trail Makers Series), New York, 1904, and in " Spanish Explorers in the Southern United States, 1528-1573 ", edited by F. W. Hodge and T. H. Lewis, New York, 1907.]

EMORY, W. H. Notes of a military reconnaissance from Fort Leavenworth, in Missouri, to San Diego, California, . . . made in 1846-7 with the advanced guard of the " Army of the West ". *30th Congr., 1st Sess., Senate Exec. Doc. No. 7* (or *House Exec. Doc. No. 41*). 614 pp. 1848. [On this military expedition during the Mexican War the Salton Basin was crossed on Nov. 24-28, 1846. This part of the journey is described in Lieut. Emory's report, pp. 97-103, in Lieut. P. St. G. Cooke's report, pp. 538-539, and in the journal of Capt. A. R. Johnston, pp. 608-611, and shown on the main map on the scale of 1 : 1,500,000 accompanying Emory's report.]

FERGUSON, D. Report on the country, its resources, and the route between Tucson and Lobos Bay. Actually in *37th Congr., 3rd Sess., Serial 1150,* although should read *38th Congr., Spec. Sess., Senate Misc. Doc. No. 1.* 22 pp., with 2 maps of Lobos Bay (on the Gulf of California in Sonora). Washington, 1863.

HARDY, R. W. H. Travels in the interior of Mexico in 1825, 1826, 1827, & 1828. London, 1829. [Chapters 13 and 14 and part of 15, pp. 312-384, deal with the stay in the Colorado estuary.]

HEINTZELMAN, S. P. (Letter concerning his running survey of the Colorado River in 1851 for about 80 miles below Yuma). *San Francisco Daily Herald,* Oct. 22, 1851. [For text, see above, pp. 18-19.]

IVES, J. C. Report upon the Colorado River of the West, explored in 1857 and 1858. *36th Congr., 1st Sess.,* [*House*] *Exec. Doc. No. 90.* Five parts separately paginated and appendices (total 368 pp.), with a topographical map of the area tributary to the Colorado River, 1 : 380,160 in lower course, 1 : 760,320 in middle course. 1861. [The estuary and Colorado Delta up to Yuma are discussed in Part 1 (general report), pp. 19-44, and Part 2 (hydrography), pp. 7-10.]

KINO, EUSEBIO FRANCISCO. Celestial favors . . . experienced in the new conquests and new conversions of the new kingdom of New Navarra of this unknown North America, and the land-passage to California in 35 degrees of latitude, with the new cosmographic map of these new and extensive lands which hitherto have been unknown . . . English translation in H. E. Bolton's " Kino's Historical Memoir of Primería Alta ", 2 vols., Cleveland, 1919. [Father Kino's two journeys of 1701 and 1702 in the Colorado Delta are described in Book III, Chapters 4-6 (Bolton, Vol. 1, pp. 312-322) and Book IV, Chapters 4-5 (*ibid.,* pp. 340-346). Of Kino's " new cosmographic map ", which showed the region about the upper part of the Gulf of California, a manuscript version was in 1900 in the Archivo General de Indias in Seville (Estante 67, Cajon 3, Legajo 29). It was first published in 1705 in *Mémoires pour l'Histoire des Sciences et des Beaux-Arts,* Trévoux, May, 1705, p. 764, and in " Lettres édifiantes et curieuses écrites des missions étrangères par quelques missionaires de la Compagnie de Jésus ", Vol. 5, Paris, 1705. Both the manuscript version and the published Trévoux version are reproduced in Bolton, Vol. 1, p. 331 and frontispiece, respectively.]

KINO, EUSEBIO FRANCISCO. Favores celestiales . . . experimentados en las nuevas conquistas y nuevas conversiones del nuevo reino de la Nueva Navarra desta America Septentrional yncognita y passo por tierra a la California en 35 grados de altura, con su nuevo mapa cosmografico de estas nuevas y dilitadas tierras que hasta aora havian sido yncognitas . . . (finished in 1710). Spanish text in *Publicaciones del Archivo General de la Nación,* Vol. 8, Secretaría de Gobernación, Mexico City, 1913-1922. [See comment under Kino, Bolton translation.]

(PATTIE) The personal narrative of James O. Pattie of Kentucky . . . , edited by Timothy Flint, Cincinnati, 1831. Reprinted and edited with notes by R. G. Thwaites in series " Early Western Travels, 1748-1846 ", Vol. 18, Cleveland, 1905. [The journeyings in the Colorado Delta region are described on pp. 133-165 of the 1831 edition and pp. 181-220 of the Thwaites reprint.]

POOLE, C. H. Report upon the route from San Diego to Fort Yuma via San Diego River, Warner's Pass, and San Felipe Cañon. *Pacific Railroad Survey Reports,* Vol. 5, Appendix B (Appendices, pp. 15-28). 1857.

(ULLOA) A relation of the discovery, which . . . the Fleete of the right noble Fernando Cortez . . . made, . . . of which Fleete was Captaine the right worshipfull knight Francis de Ulloa . . . Taken out of the third volume of the voyages gathered by M. John Baptista Ramusio. Reprinted from Hakluyt's " Principal Navigations " in *Hakluyt Soc. Publs.,* Extra Series, Vol. 9, Glasgow, 1904, pp. 206-278; passage dealing with head of the Gulf of California on pp. 214-215. [Translation of Preciado's account in Ramusio; see next item.]

(ULLOA) Relatione dello scoprimento che . . . va à far l'armata dell' illustrissimo Fernando Cortese, . . . della quale armata fu Capitano il molto magnifico Caualliero Francesco di Ulloa . . . In Ramusio's " Navigationi et Viaggi ", first edition of Vol. 3, Venice, 1556, leaves 339-354. [Account of Ulloa's voyage by Francisco Preciado, a participant. From copy in library of American Geographical Society, New York.]

ULLOA, FRANCISCO DE. Record and narrative of the voyage and discovery which, in the name of Our Lord, was made after this, your lordship's fleet, had left the Puerto de Acapulco, July 8, 1539, as far as this, Isla de Cedros, where I now am, April 5, 1540. In:

(1) "California Voyages, 1539-1541: Translation of Original Documents", edited by Henry R. Wagner, San Francisco, 1925 (also as *Quart. California Hist. Soc.,* Vol. 3, No. 4, Dec. 1924), pp. 14-60; and (2) "Spanish Voyages to the Northwest Coast of America in the Sixteenth Century" by Henry R. Wagner (*California Hist. Soc. Spec. Publ. No. 4*), San Francisco, 1929, pp. 16-46. [Translation, by Irene A. Wright, of a document of 35 small folio leaves written on both sides that "a few years" prior to 1924 was in the Archivo General de Indias in Seville, under the designation Legajo 1-1-1/20, No. 5, Ramo 11. It is a legally attested copy made in Mexico City, May 29, 1540, of Ulloa's original report. This is the first published version of that report. Prior to its publication in 1924 the primary source was Francisco Preciado's account as published in Ramusio, 1556 (see that entry).]

WILLIAMSON, R. S. Report of explorations in California for railroad routes to connect with the routes near the 35th and 32nd parallels of north latitude. *Pacific Railroad Survey Reports,* Vol. 5, Part 1. 43 pp. 1857. [Region between San Gorgonio Pass and Yuma discussed on pp. 36-40. The general map, illustrating this report, on the scale of 1:600,000, is in Vol. 11, published in 1861. For geological report see below first W. P. Blake entry under Geology.]

GEOGRAPHY

ARROWSMITH, AARON. A new map of Mexico and adjacent provinces compiled from original documents. Various editions and dates. London, 1800 to 1830, e. g. 1810 and 1816.

BARROWS, D. P. The Colorado Desert. *Natl. Geogr. Mag.,* Vol. 11, 1900, pp. 337-351.

BONILLAS, Y. S., and F. URBINA. Informe acerca de los recursos naturales de la parte norte de la Baja California, especialmente del Delta del Río Colorado. *Parergones del Inst. Geol. de México,* Vol. 4, 1912-1913, pp. 161-235, with two maps in 1:500,000 and 1:250,000.

BONNER, JOHN. The new desert lake. *Cosmopolitan Magazine,* Vol. 11, 1891, pp. 674-681.

BROWN, J. S. Routes to desert watering places in the Salton Sea region, California. *U. S. Geol. Survey Water-Supply Paper 490-A.* 86 pp. 1920. With shaded relief map of the Salton Sea region, 1:250,000, in 2 sheets.

BROWN, J. S. The Salton Sea region, California: A geographic, geologic, and hydrologic reconnaissance, with a guide to desert watering places. *U. S. Geol. Survey Water-Supply Paper 497.* 292 pp. 1923. With shaded relief map of the Salton Sea region, 1:250,000, in 2 sheets (same as the map accompanying *Water-Supply Paper 490-A*). [The standard work on the region and the most comprehensive discussion by the U. S. Geological Survey. Bibliography, pp. 125-128.]

BRYAN, KIRK. Routes to desert watering places in the Papago country, Arizona. *U. S. Geol. Survey Water-Supply Paper 490-D.* 117 pp. 1922. With shaded relief map of the Papago country, 1:250,000, in 3 sheets. [Barely touches upon the region under consideration in the present work.]

BRYAN, KIRK. The Papago country, Arizona: A geographic, geologic, and hydrologic reconnaissance, with a guide to desert watering places. *U. S. Geol. Survey Water-Supply Paper 499.* 436 pp. 1925. With shaded relief map of the Papago country, 1:250,000, in 3 sheets (same as the map in *Water-Supply Paper 490-D*). [Comprehensive discussion of the geography and physiography of the region, the westernmost tip of which falls within the area under consideration in the present work.]

BYERS, C. A. The possibilities of Salton Sea. *Popular Sci. Monthly,* Vol. 70, 1907, pp. 5-18.

CECIL-STEPHENS, B. A. The Colorado Desert and its recent flooding. *Bull. Amer. Geogr. Soc.,* Vol. 23, 1891, pp. 367-376, with note by J. W. Powell, pp. 376-377, reprinted from *New York Times.*

[Chart of] Mouth of the Colorado River surveyed by the officers of the U. S. S. Narragansett, Comdr. Geo. Dewey comdg., March, 1875. 1:58,000. U. S. Hydrographic Office Chart No. 800, edition of July, 1877.

[Chart of] The coasts of Lower California and of the Gulf of California from a survey by Commander Geo. Dewey, U. S. N., and officers of the U. S. S. Narragansett in 1873-74 (1873-75), Sheet I. 1:625,000. U. S. Hydrographic Office Chart No. 619, edition of Oct., 1874 (respectively Sept., 1877).

CORY, H. T. The Imperial Valley and Salton Sink. xiii and 452 pp. San Francisco, 1915. [Consists mainly of reprints and abstracts of published papers by various authors as follows: pp. 1-35, Sketch of the Region at the Head of the Gulf of California: A Review and History, by W. P. Blake (original and complete version of *Carnegie Instn. Publ. No. 193,* pp. 1-12); pp. 37-51, abstracts by H. T. Cory of papers in *Carnegie Instn. Publ. No. 193;* pp. 53-61, The Colorado River Watershed, by H. T. Cory; pp. 1204-1571 (sic), reprint of Irrigation and River Control in the Colorado River Delta, by H. T. Cory, *Trans. Amer. Soc. Civil Engineers,* Vol. 76, 1914, pp. 1204-1571 (discussion pp. 1454-1571); pp. 1573-1581 (sic), Developments, September, 1913, to July, 1915, by W. T. Cory.]

COSBY, S. W. Notes on a map of the Laguna Salada basin, Baja California, Mexico. *Geogr. Rev.,* Vol. 19, 1929, pp. 613-620, with map in 1:500,000.

COSBY, S. W., and L. G. COAR. Soils and crops of the Imperial Valley. See under Soils.

DARTON, N. H. Guidebook of the Western United States, Part F: The Southern Pacific lines, New Orleans to Los Angeles. *U. S. Geol. Survey Bull. 845.* 300 pp. 1933. [The territory along the railroads between Yuma and San Gorgonio Pass and between Yuma and San Diego is described on pp. 239-264 and 287-292 respectively and reproduced on Sheets 26 and 27 of the accompanying topographic-geologic strip map in 1:500,000.]

DAVIS, A. P. The new inland sea. *Natl. Geogr. Mag.,* Vol. 18, 1907, pp. 37-49, with photograph, 1:1,500,000, on p. 36 of relief model by Reclamation Service of U. S. Geol. Survey.

DEWEY, GEORGE. Remarks on the coasts of Lower California and Mexico. *U. S. Hydrogr. Office [Publ.] No. 56.* 60 pp. 1874. [Deals with the surveys of the U. S. S. *Narragansett.*]

DOWD, M. J. Map of the Imperial Irrigation District, California. 1:60,000. Imperial, Calif., 1925. [Blue-line print.]

FAVELA, J. L. Plano de la región del delta del Río Colorado y de los terrenos irrigables con aguas derivadas del mismo río en el Dto. Norte, B. Caf., y Dto. de Altar, Son. 1: 200,000. Agencia General de la Secretaría de Agricultura y Fomento, Zaragoza, B. C. [1929]. [Blue-line print.]

FOX, C. K. The Colorado Delta: A discussion of the Spanish explorations, the Colorado River silt load and its seismic effect on the Southwest. 75 pp. mimeographed. Los Angeles, 1936.

FREE, E. E. The topographic features of the desert basins of the United States with reference to the possible occurrence of potash. *Bull. U. S. Dept. of Agr. 54.* 65 pp., with map of the desert basins of the western United States, 1: 2,500,000. 1914. [The Salton Basin is discussed on pp. 45-48.]

GORDON, J. H. Problems of the lower Colorado River. *Monthly Weather Rev.,* Vol. 52, 1924, pp. 95-98.

GORDON, J. H. The Colorado River situation. *Monthly Weather Rev.,* Vol. 56, 1928, pp. 211-215.

GORDON, J. H. Tidal bore at mouth of Colorado River, December 8 to 10, 1923. *Monthly Weather Rev.,* Vol. 52, 1924, pp. 98-99.

IMRAY, JAMES, and son. North Pacific Pilot; various charts and sailing directions. London, 1850 to 1870.

KNIFFEN, F. B. The natural landscape of the Colorado Delta (Lower California Studies, IV). *Univ. of California Publs. in Geogr.,* Vol. 5, 1932, pp. 149-244, with geomorphologic map in 1: 600,000.

KNIFFEN, F. B. The primitive cultural landscape of the Colorado Delta (Lower California Studies, III). *Univ. of California Publs. in Geogr.,* Vol. 5, pp. 43-66. 1931.

LARUE, E. C. Map of lower Colorado River showing irrigable lands below Cibola Valley. 1: 250,000. Pl. 12 of author's work in *U. S. Geol. Survey Water-Supply Paper 395.* 1916. [Reproduced, greatly reduced, in Fig. 28 of the present work.]

MACDOUGAL, D. T. A cycle of the Salton Sea. In "Festschrift Carl Schröter" (*Veröffentl. des Geobotan. Inst. in Zürich,* No. 3, 1925), pp. 354-363.

MACDOUGAL, D. T. A decade of the Salton Sea. *Geogr. Rev.,* Vol. 3, 1917, pp. 457-473.

MACDOUGAL, D. T. Botanical exploration in Arizona, Sonora, California, and Baja California. *Journ. New York Botan. Garden,* Vol. 6, 1905, pp. 91-102.

MACDOUGAL, D. T. Botanical exploration in the Southwest. *Journ. New York Botan. Garden,* Vol. 5, 1904, pp. 89-98. [Boat trip from Yuma to San Felipe Bay.]

MACDOUGAL, D. T. Botanical features of North American deserts. *Carnegie Instn. Publ. No. 99.* 111 pp., with map, 1: 900,000, by Godfrey Sykes. Washington, 1908. [Pages 33-44 deal with the Colorado Delta and region.]

MACDOUGAL, D. T. Delta and desert vegetation. *Botanical Gazette,* Vol. 38, 1904, pp. 44-63.

MACDOUGAL, D. T. More changes in the Colorado River. *Natl. Geogr. Mag.,* Vol. 19, 1908, pp. 52-54.

MACDOUGAL, D. T. Movements of vegetation due to submersion and desiccation of land areas in Salton Sink. In *idem, Carnegie Instn. Publ. No. 193,* pp. 115-172. 1914.

MACDOUGAL, D. T. The delta of the Rio Colorado. *Bull. Amer. Geogr. Soc.,* Vol. 38, 1906, pp. 1-16, with map, 1: 650,000, by Godfrey Sykes.

MACDOUGAL, D. T. The desert basins of the Colorado Delta. *Bull. Amer. Geogr. Soc.,* Vol. 39, 1907, pp. 705-729, with map, 1: 1,500,000, by Godfrey Sykes.

MACDOUGAL, D. T. The Salton Sea. *Amer. Journ. of Sci.,* 4th Ser., Vol. 39, 1915, pp. 231-250.

MACDOUGAL, D. T., and collaborators. The Salton Sea: A study of the geography, the geology, the floristics, and the ecology of a desert basin. *Carnegie Instn. Publ. 193.* 182 pp. Washington, 1914. [Deals with Salton Sink as a whole. Includes, among others, sections by W. P. Blake (geology), Godfrey Sykes (geography), E. E. Free (soils), W. K. Rose (chemical composition of Salton Sea water), S. B. Parish (plant ecology), and D. T. MacDougal (movements of vegetation).]

[Map of] Lower Colorado River, Imperial Valley, and Boulder Canyon Reservoir. [1: 575,000]. Bureau of Reclamation Map No. 23530. 1929. [Extends from Boulder Canyon and Coachella Valley to mouth of Colorado River. 50-foot contours in delta and Salton Sink. Also edition No. 23530-A with marginal statements in red explaining various features of map.]

[Map showing] All America Canals System, Boulder Canyon Project. 1: 316,880. Bureau of Reclamation Map No. 25190-A. 1935.

MCGLASHAN, H. D., and H. J. DEAN. Water resources of California, Part III: Stream measurements in the Great Basin and Pacific Coast basins. *U. S. Geol. Survey Water-Supply Paper 300.* 1913. [Pages 29-33, 405-417, and 423-479 deal with watercourses of the Salton Sink and the basin of the lower Colorado River below Yuma.]

MEARNS, E. A. Mammals of the Mexican boundary of the United States: A descriptive catalogue . . . with a general summary of the natural history . . . *U. S. Natl. Museum Bull. 56.* 1907. [Dr. Mearns served as medical officer, 1892-94, of the International Boundary Commission, United States and Mexico. His report contains sections on the general character of the region explored (pp. 23-32) and life areas of the Mexican boundary region (pp. 70-74). Passages in these deal with the Colorado Delta region; also other passages in the reports, viz. p. 20 (collecting trip from Yuma along the Colorado to the mouth of the Hardy in March, 1894) and pp. 125-131.]

MENDENHALL, W. C. Ground waters of the Indio region, California, with a sketch of the Colorado Desert. *U. S. Geol. Survey Water-Supply Paper 225,* with map of the Salton Sink in 1: 500,000. 1909.

MENDENHALL, W. C. Some desert watering places in southeastern California and southwestern Nevada. *U. S. Geol. Survey Water-Supply Paper 224.* 1909. [Contains a detailed description of springs which gives local topographical details. The springs in the Salton Basin are described on pp. 77, 79-80, and 82-87.]

MENDENHALL, W. C. The Colorado Desert. *Natl. Geogr. Mag.,* Vol. 20, 1909, pp. 681-701.

Mexico and Central America Pilot. U. S. Hydrographic Office. 2nd edition, 1893; 6th edition, 1920; 7th edition, 1928.

MITCHELL, EDMUND. The Salton Sea. *North Amer. Rev.,* Aug. 1906, pp. 224-236.

MURPHY, R. C. Natural history observations from the Mexican portion of the Colorado Desert, with a note on the Lower California pronghorn and a list of birds. *Abstract of Proc. Linnaean Soc. of New York,* No. 29, 1916-17, pp. 43-101.

MURPHY, R. C. The desert life group and an account of the Museum expedition into Lower California. *Brooklyn Museum Quart.,* Vol. 5 (i. e. 4), 1917, pp. 179-210.

NELSON, E. W. A land of drought and desert: Lower California. *Natl. Geogr. Mag.,* Vol. 22, 1911, pp. 443-474.

NELSON, E. W. Lower California and its natural resources. *Memoirs Natl. Acad. Sci.,* Vol. 16, No. 1. 194 pp., with bibliography, pp. 147-171, and map in 1: 2,000,000. Washington, 1921.

NELSON, HELGE. Coloradofloden: Kanjonernas flod och dess framtida utnyttjande. *Svensk Geogr. Arsbok* (Lund), 1927, pp. 179-207 (also *Meddel. fran Lunds Universitets Geogr. Instn.,* Series C, No. 28).

NEWELL, F. H. The Salton Sea. *Annual Rept. Smithsonian Instn. for 1907,* pp. 331-345. 1908.

ORCUTT, C. R. A visit to Lake Maquata. *West American Scientist,* Vol. 7, 1891, pp. 158-164.

ORCUTT, C. R. The Colorado Desert. *10th Rept. (for 1890) of the California State Mining Bur.,* pp. 899-919.

PARISH, S. B. Plant ecology and floristics of Salton Sink (in D. T. MacDougal, *Carnegie Instn. Publ. No. 193,* 1914, pp. 85-114).

POWELL, J. W. Of the physical features of the valley of the Colorado. Part 2 (pp. 149-214) of his "Exploration of the Colorado River of the West and Its Tributaries . . . ," Smithsonian Instn., Washington, 1875.

POWELL, J. W. The new lake in the desert. *Scribner's Mag.,* Vol. 10, 1891, pp. 463-468.

PRESTON, E. B. Salton Lake. *11th Rept. (for 1890-92) of the California State Mining Bur.,* pp. 387-393. [Describes the nature of Salton Basin and its connection with Colorado River.]

REICHEL, EBERHARD. Der Wasserhaushalt des Coloradogebietes im südwestlichen Nordamerika. Mit einem Anhang: Untersuchungen über die Denudation dieses Gebietes, von Sr. M.-Mercedes Leiter. *Geogr. Abhandlungen,* 2nd Ser., No. 4. Stuttgart, 1928.

Report of the Boundary Commission upon the survey and re-making of the boundary between the United States and Mexico west of the Rio Grande, 1891 to 1896. Part I: Report of the International Commission, pp. 1-56. Part II: Report of the United States Section, pp. 1-240. Washington, 1898. Accompanied separately by an album of 258 views of monuments and characteristic scenes along the boundary and a folio atlas containing 2 index maps in 1: 600,000, 19 sheets of the boundary in 1: 60,000, and 5 sheets of profiles in 1: 60,000 horizontal and 1: 6000 vertical. Editions in Spanish have also been published of text, album, and atlas. [Sheets 2-6 of the 1: 60,000 series relate to the area of the map accompanying the present work. Sheet 5 shows, superposed, the boundary segment of the Colorado River as surveyed by the U. S. party in March, 1893, and by the Mexican party in March, 1894.]

RIQUELME INDA, JULIO. El territorio norte de la Baja California y sus principales problemas. In: "Primer Centenario de la Sociedad Mexicana de Geografía y Estadística, 1833-1933," Vol. 1, pp. 187-207. Mexico, 1933.

ROSS, C. P. Routes to desert watering places in the lower Gila region, Arizona. *U. S. Geol. Survey Water-Supply Paper 490-C.* 1922. With shaded relief map of the lower Gila region, 1: 250,000, in 3 sheets. [Barely touches upon the region under consideration in the present work.]

ROSS, C. P. The lower Gila region, Arizona: A geographic, geologic, and hydrologic reconnaissance, with a guide to desert watering places. *U. S. Geol. Survey Water-Supply Paper 498.* 1923. With shaded relief map of the lower Gila region, 1: 250,000, in 2 sheets (same as map in *Water-Supply Paper 490-C*). [Only the southwesternmost tip of the area here discussed falls under the region under consideration in the present work.]

ROUSE, H. M. Map of developed area of lands of the Colorado River Land Co., S. A., and of adjacent lands. [1: 75,000.] Mexicali, Sept. 1929, partially revised April and Nov., 1931. [Blue-line print.]

SYKES, GODFREY. Geographical features of the Cahuilla Basin (in D. T. MacDougal, *Carnegie Instn. Publ. No. 193,* 1914, pp. 13-20). [Also as abridged reprint in H. T. Cory's "The Imperial Valley and the Salton Sink," 1915, pp. 43-51.]

SYKES, GODFREY. The delta and estuary of the Colorado River. *Geogr. Rev.,* Vol. 16, 1926, pp. 232-255, with map in 1: 600,000.

SYKES, GODFREY. The reclamation of a desert. *Geogr. Journ.,* Vol. 46, 1915, pp. 447-457.

TUTTLE, E. D. The River Colorado. *Arizona Hist. Rev.,* July 1928.

VELASCO, ADOLFO. El Valle Imperial. *Magazine de Geografía Nacional,* Vol. 1, No. 4, Oct., 1925, pp. 31-52. Mexico.

WEBSTER, E. B. Report on the northern district of Lower California. 359 pp., with folder of blueprint maps. San Diego, 1913. [Compilation based on various sources that are not cited, including Bonillas and Urbina (see above).]

POPULAR TRAVEL AND DESCRIPTION

DELLENBAUGH, F. S. The romance of the Colorado River. New York, 1902.
FREEMAN, L. R. The Colorado River, yesterday, today, and tomorrow. New York, 1923.
HORNADAY, W. T. Camp fires on desert and lava. New York, 1908.
JAMES, G. W. Wonders of the Colorado Desert. Boston, 1906.
KENNAN, GEORGE. The Salton Sea. New York, 1917.
KOLB, E. L. Through the Grand Canyon from Wyoming to Mexico. New York, 1914.
LUMHOLTZ, CARL. New trails in Mexico. New York, 1912.

NEWSPAPER FILES

San Diego Herald. May 29, 1851, to April 7, 1860.
San Diego Union. October 31, 1868, to the present.
San Francisco Herald. Portions of 1851 and 1852.
Yuma Sun.

GEOLOGY
(see also under Geography)

ANTISELL, THOMAS. Geological report (Part 2 of "Report of Explorations for Railroad
    Routes . . . near the 32d Parallel . . ."). *Pacific Railroad Survey Reports*, Vol. 7, Part 2.
    33rd Congr., 2nd Sess., Senate Doc. 78. 1857. [Chapter 18, pp. 119-129, entitled " Geology
    of the District from San Diego to Yuma ", deals with the region here under consideration.]
BLAKE, W. P. Geological report [Williamson's reconnaissance in California]. *Pacific Railroad
    Survey Reports*, Vol. 5, Part 2. 370 pp. 1857. [Chapter 17, pp. 228-252, devoted to the
    Colorado Desert, with geological map of Colorado Desert, 1 : 1,650,000, facing p. 228.]
BLAKE, W. P. Preliminary geological report [Williamson's reconnaissance in California]. *Pacific
    Railroad Survey Reports*, octavo edition. *33rd Congr., 1st Sess., House Exec. Doc. 129.*
    80 pp. 1855.
BLAKE, W. P. Report of a geological reconnaissance in California. New York, 1858. [A
    separate edition of the report in *Pacific Railroad Survey Reports*, Vol. 5, Part 2.]
BLAKE, W. P. Sketch of the region at the head of the Gulf of California (in H. T. Cory's
    " The Imperial Valley and the Salton Sink ", San Francisco, 1915, pp. 1-35).
BLAKE, W. P. The Cahuilla Basin and Desert of the Colorado (in D. T. MacDougal, *Carnegie
    Instn. Publ. No. 193*, 1914, pp. 1-12).
BROWN, J. S. Fault features of Salton Basin, California, *Journ. of Geol.*, Vol. 30, 1922, pp.
    217-226, with geological map in 1 : 887,040.
BUWALDA, J. P., and W. L. STANTON. Geological events in the history of the Indio Hills and
    the Salton Basin, southern California. *Science*, New Series, Vol. 71, 1930, pp. 104-106.
EMMONS, S. F., and G. P. MERRILL. Geological sketch of Lower California. *Bull. Geol. Soc. of
    Amer.*, Vol. 5, 1894, pp. 489-514.
FAIRBANKS, H. W. Geology of San Diego County, also of portions of Orange and San Ber-
    nardino Counties. *11th Rept. (for 1890-92) of the California State Mining Bureau*, pp. 76-120.
    Sacramento, 1893.
LE CONTE, J. L. Account of some volcanic springs in the Desert of the Colorado in southern
    California. *Amer. Journ. Sci.*, 2nd Ser., Vol. 19, May, 1855, pp. 1-6.
LINDGREN, W. S. (a) Notes on the geology of Baja California, Mexico; (b) Petrographical notes
    from Baja California, Mexico; (c) Notes on the geology and petrography of Baja California,
    Mexico. *Proc. California Acad. of Sci.*, 2nd Ser.: (a) Vol. 1, 1888-89, pp. 173-196, with
    map of northernmost Lower California, 1 : 633,600, and geological profile, 1 : 316,800, from
    Ensenada to the Colorado River; (b) Vol. 2, 1889, pp. 1-17; (c) Vol. 3, 1890-92, pp. 25-33.
MENDENHALL, W. C. Notes on the geology of Carrizo Mountain and vicinity, San Diego County,
    Cal. *Journ. of Geol.*, Vol. 18, 1910, pp. 336-355, with contour sketch map, 1 : 700,000, of
    area southwest of Salton Sea to Mexican boundary.
MERRILL, F. J. H. [Geology and mineral resources of] The counties of San Diego [and]
    Imperial. *14th Rept. (for 1896) of the California State Mining Bur.*, pp. 635-743.
MILLER, W. J. Geomorphology of the southern Peninsular Range of California. *Bull. Geol.
    Soc. of Amer.*, Vol. 46, 1935, pp. 1535-1561, with topographic and fault map, 1 : 316,800.
NEWBERRY, J. S. Geological report. Part 3 of J. C. Ives's " Report upon the Colorado River of
    the West ", *36th Congr., 1st Sess., [House] Exec. Doc. No. 90.* 154 pp., with a geological
    map of the area tributary to the Colorado River, 1 : 380,160 in lower course, 1 : 760,320 in
    middle course. 1861. [Colorado Delta region is discussed on pp. 13-28, *passim*.]
VEATCH, J. A. Notes of a visit to the ' mud volcanoes ' in the Colorado Desert in the month
    of July, 1857. *Amer. Journ. Science*, 2nd Ser., Vol. 26, 1858, pp. 288-295. [From *Proc.
    California Acad. Nat. Sci.*, 1857, p. 104.]

SOILS

COSBY, S. W., and L. G. COAR. Soils and crops of the Imperial Valley. *Univ. of California
    Agric. Exp. Sta. Circular 334.* 108 pp. Berkeley, 1934.
FREE, E. E. Sketch of the geology and soils of the Cahuilla Basin (in D. T. MacDougal,
    Carnegie Instn. Publ. No. 193, 1914, pp. 21-33). [Soils discussed on pp. 29-33.]
HOLMES, J. G. [Soil survey of the Colorado Delta in Lower California]. Accompanied by blue-
    line map in 1 : 50,000. 1902. [Unpublished report on soils of Mexican portion of delta

prepared for Colorado River Land Co. The map shows the areas north, south, and east of the Paredones River. Above data from H. M. Rouse, Chief Engineer of C. R. L. Co., and Bonillas and Urbina, *Parergones Inst. Geol. México*, Vol. 4, 1912-1913, pp. 202 and 213.]

HOLMES, J. G. Soil survey of the Yuma area, Arizona. *Field Operations Bur. of Soils 1902*, pp. 777-791, with two maps in 1: 63,360. 1903.

HOLMES, J. G., and others. Soil survey of the Yuma area, Arizona-California. *Field Operations Bur. of Soils 1904*, pp. 1025-1047, with map in 1: 63,360. 1905.

HOLMES, J. G., and party. Soil survey of the Imperial area, California (extending the survey of 1901). *Field Operations Bur. of Soils 1903*, pp. 1219-1248, with two maps in 1: 126,720. 1904.

HOLMES, J. G., and party. Soil survey of the Indio area, California. *Field Operations Bur. of Soils 1903*, pp. 1249-1262, with two maps in 1: 63,360. 1904.

KOCHER, A. E., and others. Soil survey of the Brawley area, California. *Field Operations Bur. of Soils 1920*, pp. 641-716, with map in 1: 63,360. 1925.

KOCHER, A. E., and W. G. HARPER. Soil survey of the Coachella Valley area, California. *Advance Sheets, Field Operations Bur. of Soils 1923*, pp. 485-535, with map in 1: 63,360. 1927.

MEANS, T. H., and J. G. HOLMES. Soil survey around Imperial, California. *Bur. of Soils Circular No. 9*. 20 pp.; 2 maps. Jan. 10, 1902. [Preliminary advance edition of report listed next below.]

MEANS, T. H., and J. G. HOLMES. Soil survey around Imperial, California. *Field Operations Bur. of Soils 1901*, pp. 587-606, with soil map and alkali map, each in 1: 63,360. 1902.

SHAW, C. F. Classification of soils bordering the Imperial Valley. In " Problems of Imperial Valley and Vicinity ", *67th Congr., 2nd Sess., Senate Doc. No. 142*, 1922, pp. 93-95.

STRAHORN, A. T. Summary of soil survey of Imperial Valley. In " Problems of Imperial Valley and Vicinity ", *67th Congr., 2nd Sess., Senate Doc. No. 142*, 1922, pp. 95-98.

STRAHORN, A. T., and others. Soil survey of the El Centro area, California. *Field Operations Bur. of Soils 1918*, pp. 1633-1687, with map in 1: 63,360. 1924.

YOUNGS, F. O., W. G. HARPER, and JAMES THORP. Soil survey of the Yuma-Wellton area, Arizona-California. *Bur. of Chemistry and Soils Series 1929*, No. 20. 37 pp., map in 1: 62,500. [1933.]

ECONOMIC UTILIZATION
(including Engineering and Irrigation)

ADAMS, FRANK. Irrigation from Colorado River in Lower California. *71st Congr., 2nd Sess., House Doc. 359*, pp. 159-177, with map of lands irrigable and irrigated from Colorado River in Lower California, 1: 243,000. 1930.

ADAMS, FRANK. Progress report of special Colorado River investigations. *71st Congr., 2nd Sess., House Doc. 359*, pp. 94-158. 1930.

ADAMS, FRANK. Report of inspection trip over Colorado River levee systems below Yuma, Ariz., September 17, 18, and 19, 1929. *71st Congr., 2nd Sess., House Doc. 359*, pp. 178-191, with map of Colorado River levee systems below Yuma, Arizona, 1: 57,000, furnished by Colorado River Land Co., Oct., 1929. 1930.

ADAMS, FRANK, J. L. FAVELA, and ARMANDO SANTACRUZ, JR. Data on irrigated areas, stream flow, use of water, etc., in the United States and Mexico, Colorado River basin. *71st Congr., 2nd Sess., House Doc. 359*, pp. 85-93. 1930.

ALLISON, J. C. Control of the Colorado River as related to the protection of Imperial Valley. *Trans. Amer. Soc. Civil Engineers*, Vol. 81, 1917, pp. 297-340.

BROWN, R. M. Complications in the utilization of the Colorado River water. *Geogr. Rev.*, Vol. 22, 1932, pp. 315-317. [Note summarizing recent publications.]

BROWN, R. M. The utilization of the Colorado River. *Geogr. Rev.*, Vol. 17, 1927, pp. 453-466.

Bureau of Reclamation, Department of the Interior (prior to 1922, Reclamation Service), *Annual Reports*.

Colorado River and the Boulder Canyon project: Historical and physical facts in connection with the Colorado River and lower basin development. 400 pp. Sacramento, 1931.

Colorado River basin: Hearings before the Committee on Irrigation and Reclamation, United States Senate, 68th Congress, 2nd Session, on S. 727, a bill to provide for the protection and development of the lower Colorado River basin. In 2 parts. 1925.

Colorado River basin: Hearings before the Committee on Irrigation and Reclamation, House of Representatives, 69th Congress, 1st Session, on H. R. 6251 and H. R. 9826 by Mr. Swing, bills to provide for the protection and development of the lower Colorado River basin. In 2 parts. 1926.

Colorado River basin: Hearings pursuant to Senate Resolution 320, 68th Congress, 2nd Session, directing the Committee on Irrigation and Reclamation, United States Senate, . . . to make complete investigation with respect to proposed legislation relating to protection and development of Colorado River basin. In 6 parts, 931 pp., consecutive pagination. 1925-26.

Colorado River development: Colorado River investigations, water storage and power development, Grand Canyon to the Imperial Valley. *70th Congr., 2nd Sess., Senate Doc. No. 186*. 231 pp. 1929.

CORY, H. T. Irrigation and river control in the Colorado River delta. *Trans. Amer. Soc. Civil Engineers*, Vol. 76, 1913, pp. 1204-1453, with discussion pp. 1454-1571. [Also included in the author's volume " The Imperial Valley and Salton Sink ", listed under Geography, above.]

DYKSTRA, C. A., editor. Colorado River development and related problems. *Annals Amer. Acad. of Polit. and Soc. Sci.,* Vol. 148, Part II, 1930, pp. i-vi and 1-42.

GRUNSKY, C. E. Report on the utilization of the waters of the Colorado River for irrigation and its relation to the Imperial Valley, California. *65th Congr., 1st Sess., Senate Doc. No. 103.* 39 pp., with map in 1: 750,000. 1917.

GRUNSKY, C. E. The lower Colorado River and the Salton Basin. *Trans. Amer. Soc. Civil Engineers,* Vol. 59, 1907, pp. 1-51, with discussion pp. 52-62.

Irrigation map of the State of California. 1: 506,880. Revised and redrawn 1920 in cooperation with California State Department of Engineering, College of Agriculture, University of California, and California State Water Commission. Bur. of Public Roads, U. S. Dept. of Agric., 1922. [On the standard relief-shaded base map of the state are shown the irrigated areas and three kinds of non-irrigated agricultural lands, as well as irrigation and power canals.]

KELLY, WILLIAM. The Colorado River problem. *Proc. Amer. Soc. Civil Engineers,* Vol. 50, 1924, pp. 795-836, with discussion in Vol. 50, pp. 1436-1499, and Vol. 51, 1925, pp. 262-288.

KELLY, WILLIAM. The Colorado River problem. *Trans. Amer. Soc. Civil Engineers,* Vol. 88, 1925, pp. 306-437, with discussion.

LA RUE, E. C. Colorado River and its utilization. *U. S. Geol. Survey Water-Supply Paper 395.* 231 pp. 1916. [The basic report on the question.]

LA RUE, E. C. Water power and flood control of Colorado River. *U. S. Geol. Survey Water-Supply Paper 556.* 1925.

MARSHALL, W. L. Plan for protection of Imperial Valley. *64th Congr., 1st Sess., House Doc. 586.* 1916. [Describes levees and work done in Mexico to protect Imperial Valley from overflows of the Colorado.]

Problems of Imperial Valley and vicinity: Letter . . . transmitting . . . report by director of Reclamation Service on problems of Imperial Valley and vicinity with respect to irrigation from Colorado River together with proceedings of the conference on construction of Boulder Canyon Dam held at San Diego, Calif., 1922. *67th Congr., 2nd Sess., Senate Doc. 142.* 326 pp. 1922. [Pages 62-98, with map, deal with the Colorado Delta area.]

Protection and development of lower Colorado River basin: Hearings before the Committee on Irrigation of Arid Lands, 67th Congress, 2nd Session, on H. R. 11449. In 4 parts. 210 pp., consecutive pagination. 1922.

Protection and development of lower Colorado River basin: Hearings before the Committee on Irrigation and Reclamation, House of Representatives, 68th Congress, 1st Session, in connection with H. R. 2903 by Mr. Swing, a bill to provide for the protection and development of the lower Colorado River basin. In 8 parts. 1980 pp., consecutive pagination. 1924.

Protection and development of lower Colorado River basin: Hearings before the Committee on Irrigation and Reclamation, House of Representatives, 70th Congress, 1st Session, on H. R. 5773. In 4 parts. 1928.

Protection and development of lower Colorado River basin: Information presented to the Committee on Irrigation and Reclamation, House of Representatives, 68th Congress, 1st Session, in connection with H. R. 2903: Statements by citizens of Arizona relative to the Colorado River problem and opinions on the legal questions involved. Printed for the use of the Committee. 152 pp. 1924.

Report of the American Section of the International Water Commission, United States and Mexico. *71st Congr., 2nd Sess., House Doc. 359.* 492 pp., with maps. 1930. [Pages 12, 17-23, 85-283 deal with the Colorado River.]

Report based on reconnaissance investigation of Arizona land irrigable from the Colorado River. 72 pp. Arizona Engineering Commission, Phoenix, 1923.

ROADHOUSE, J. E. Irrigation conditions in the Imperial Valley of California. *Office of Exper. Stations Bull. No. 158.* Dept. of Agric., 1905.

ROTHERY, S. L. A river diversion of Colorado River in relation to Imperial Valley, California. *Proc. Amer. Soc. Civil Engineers,* Vol. 49, 1923, pp. 671-697, with discussion, pp. 1285-1291.

ROTHERY, S. L. A river diversion on the delta of the Colorado in relation to Imperial Valley, California. *Trans. Amer. Soc. Civil Engineers,* Vol. 86, 1923, pp. 1412-1447, with discussion. [On the Pescadero Diversion Cut.]

SMITH, G. E. P. A discussion of certain Colorado River problems. *Univ. of Arizona College of Agric. Bull. No. 100* (pp. 139-175). 1925.

SMITH, G. E. P. Harnessing of the Colorado River. *Pan-American Geologist,* Vol. 54, 1930, pp. 31-64.

TAIT, C. E. Investigation of wells in Imperial Valley. *California Dept. of Engin. Bull. 1.* Sacramento, 1915.

TAIT, C. E. Irrigation in Imperial Valley, California: Its problems and possibilities. *60th Congr., 1st Sess., Senate Doc. No. 246.* 56 pp. 1908.

TAIT, C. E. Irrigation resources of southern California. *California Conservation Comm. Rept. 1912,* pp. 241-327. [Portions of this paper summarize developments in the desert region.]

TAIT, C. E. Preliminary report on the conservation and control of flood waters in Coachella Valley, California. *California Dept. of Engin. 5th Bienn. Rept.,* Appendix D. Sacramento, 1917.

RELATED ENGINEERING STRUCTURES

All-American Canal in Imperial Valley, California: Hearings before House of Representatives Committee on Irrigation of Arid Lands, 66th Congress, 1st Session. 1919.

BACON, J. L. Some problems of the Boulder Canyon-Colorado River development. *Monthly Weather Rev.,* Vol. 59, 1931, pp. 295-297. [Deals in part with silt of Colorado River.]

BARBOUR, G. B. Boulder Dam and its geographical setting. *Geogr. Journ.*, Vol. 86, 1935, pp. 498-504.

BELLOLI, G. La diga di Boulder sul fiume Colorado. *Le Vie d'Italia*, Vol. 3, 1935, pp. 71-90. Milan.

Boulder Canyon reclamation project. *69th Congress, 1st Sess., Senate. Calendar No. 666, Report 654.* In 2 parts. [1927?]

Boulder Canyon reclamation project. *69th Congr., 2nd Sess., House of Repr. Report No. 1657.* 1927.

Colorado River and the Boulder Canyon project: Historical and physical facts in connection with the Colorado River and lower basin development. Colorado River Commission of State of California, Sacramento, 1931.

Colorado River aqueduct . . . : History, design, and construction of huge water supply project for southern California. *Civil Engineering*, Vol. 5, 1935, pp. 72-77.

FERTIG, J. H. Construction of All-American Canal. *Military Engineer*, Vol. 27, 1935, pp. 467-469.

FORESTER, D. M. Water softening plant for Boulder City. *Engineering News Record*, Sept. 7, 1933.

GAULT, H. J. The All-American Canal. *Military Engineer*, Vol. 25, 1933, pp. 379-382.

HINDS, JULIAN. The Colorado River aqueduct. *Military Engineer*, Vol. 24, 1932, pp. 115-119.

HOMAN, P. T. Economic aspects of the Boulder Dam project. *Quart. Journ. of Econ.*, Vol. 45, 1931, pp. 177-217.

[Map of] All-American Canal system. 1: 316,800. Bur. of Reclamation Map No. 25190-A. 1935. [Also on half the scale, 1: 633,600, as Map No. 25190.]

MEAD, ELWOOD. Hoover Dam: The Boulder Canyon project, a colossal enterprise. *Civil Engineering*, Vol. 1, 1930, pp. 3-8.

MEAD, ELWOOD, W. W. SCHLECHT, C. E. GRUNSKY. Report of the All-American Canal Board, July 22, 1919. 98 pp. 1920. [Pages 26-31 (The Flood Menace) contain review of river's shifts, p. 28 mainly; p. 30 discusses building of levees.]

NELSON, W. R. The Boulder Canyon project. *Smithsonian Instn. Annual Rept. for 1935*, pp. 429-452.

WEYMOUTH, F. E. Colorado River aqueduct. *Civil Engineering*, Vol. 1, 1931, pp. 371-376.

WYER, S. S. Study of Boulder Dam project, with special reference to flood control, irrigation, Los Angeles water supply, and electric power. Ohio Chamber of Commerce, Columbus, 1928.

YOUNG, W. R. Significance of Boulder Canyon project: Considerations leading to vast undertaking for regulation, water supply, and power. *Civil Engineering*, Vol. 5, 1935, pp. 279-283.

POLITICAL ASPECTS

Colorado River Compact. Letter from the chairman of the Colorado River Commission transmitting report of the proceedings of the Colorado River Commission and the compact or agreement entered into between the States of Arizona, California, Colorado, Nevada, New Mexico, Utah, and Wyoming respecting the apportionment of the waters of the Colorado River. *67th Congr., 4th Sess., House Doc. 605.* 12 pp. 1923.

FAVOUR, A. H. Arizona's rights in the Colorado River: Proposals of Arizona and the counter proposals of California submitted to the Tri-state Conference now in progress. Arizona Colorado River Commission, [Phoenix], 1929.

GRUNSKY, C. E. International and interstate aspects of the Colorado River Problem. *Science*, Vol. 56, 1922, pp. 521-527.

KEELER, K. F. Memorandum on treaty rights of the United States and Mexico in Colorado River. *71st Congr., 2nd Sess., House Doc. 359*, pp. 234-283. 1930.

KEELER, K. F. Memorandum on the Convention of November 12, 1884, and navigation of the Colorado River. *71st Congr., 2nd Sess., House Doc. 359*, pp. 192-233. 1930.

Official report of the proceedings of the Colorado River conference between delegates representing California, Nevada, and Arizona, at the state capital, Phoenix, Arizona, Monday, August 17th, 1925. 36 pp. Phoenix, [1925].

OLSON, R. L. The Colorado River Compact. Los Angeles, 1926. [Based on the author's doctoral dissertation at Harvard University.]

Report and supplemental report of Delph E. Carpenter, commissioner for Colorado, on the Colorado River Commission. 40 pp. [Denver, 1923.]

SMITH, G. E. P. The Colorado River and Arizona's interest in its development. *Univ. of Arizona College of Agriculture Agric. Exper. Sta. Bull. No. 95*=pp. 529-546. 1922.

STREAM DYNAMICS

BROWN, R. M. The movement of load in streams of variable flow. *Bull. Amer. Geogr. Soc.*, Vol. 39, 1907, pp. 147-158.

CHRISTIANSEN, J. E. Distribution of silt in open channels. *Trans. Amer. Geophys. Union*, 1935, pp. 478-485.

COOK, H. L. Outline of the energetics of stream-transportation of solids. *Trans. Amer. Geophys. Union*, 1935, pp. 456-463.

EAKIN, H. M. Diversity of current-direction and load-distribution on stream-bends. *Trans. Amer. Geophys. Union*, 1935, pp. 467-472.

GILBERT, G. K. The transportation of débris by running water. *U. S. Geol. Survey Prof. Paper 86.* 263 pp. 1914. [The standard treatise of its time.]

GROVER, N. C. United States Geological Survey records of suspended and dissolved matter in surface-waters. *Trans. Amer. Geophys. Union*, 1936, pp. 444-446.

HJULSTRÖM, FILIP. Das Transportvermögen der Flüsse und die Bestimmung des Erosionsbetrages. *Geografiske Annaler*, Vol. 14, 1932, pp. 244-258. Stockholm.

HJULSTRÖM, FILIP. Studies of the morphological activity of rivers as illustrated by the River Fyris. *Bull. Geol. Inst. of Univ. of Upsala*, Vol. 25, 1935, pp. 221-527 (bibliography, pp. 442-452; see below under " Bibliographies "), with map in 1: 333,333 and silt graphs.

KERNE, F. W., and WARREN EGBERT. Discussion of " The Removal of Bed-Load from Artificial Channels " and notes on the removal of suspended load, silt, and fine sand by spiral flow. *Trans. Amer. Geophys. Union*, 1934, pp. 606-611. [See under Parshall, below.]

LEIGHLY, JOHN. Turbulence and the transportation of rock débris by streams. *Geogr. Rev.*, Vol. 24, 1934, pp. 453-464; abstracted in *Trans. Amer. Geophys. Union*, 1934, pp. 453-454.

MUSGRAVE, G. W. Some relationships between slope-length, surface-runoff, and the silt-load of surface-runoff. *Trans. Amer. Geophys. Union*, 1935, pp. 472-478.

O'BRIEN, M. P. Notes on the transportation of silt by streams. *Trans. Amer. Geophys. Union*, 1936, pp. 431-436.

O'BRIEN, M. P., and B. D. RINDLAUB. The transportation of bed-load by streams. *Trans. Amer. Geophys. Union*, 1934, pp. 593-603.

PARSHALL, R. L. The removal of bed-load from artificial channels. *Trans. Amer. Geophys. Union*, 1934, pp. 603-606.

PIERCE, R. C. The measurement of silt-laden streams. *U. S. Geol. Survey Water-Supply Paper No. 400*, pp. 39-51. 1917.

SCHOKLITSCH, A. Geschiebebewegung in Flüssen und an Stauwerken. Vienna, 1926.

SHULITS, SAMUEL. Fluvial morphology in terms of slope, abrasion, and bed-load. *Trans. Amer. Geophys. Union*, 1936, pp. 440-444.

SHULITS, SAMUEL. The Schoklitsch bed-load formula. *Engineering*, June 21 and 28, 1935, pp. 644-646 and 687.

STERNBERG, H. Untersuchungen über das Längen- und Querprofil geschiebeführender Flüsse. *Zeitschr. für Bauwesen*, 1875.

STRAUB, L. G. Hydraulic and sedimentary characteristics of rivers. *Trans. Amer. Geophys. Union*, 1932, pp. 375-382.

STRAUB, L. G. Some observations of sorting of river-sediments. *Trans. Amer. Geophys. Union*, 1935, pp. 463-467.

STRAUB, L. G., chairman. Report of the Committee on Dynamics of Streams, 1933-34. *Trans. Amer. Geophys. Union*, 1934, pp. 320-321.

STRAUB, L. G., chairman. Report of the Committee on Dynamics of Streams, 1934-35. *Trans. Amer. Geophys. Union*, 1935, pp. 443-451 (bibliography, pp. 447-451; see below under " Bibliographies ").

STRAUB, L. G., chairman. Report of the Committee on Dynamics of Streams, 1935-36. *Trans. Amer. Geophys. Union*, 1936, p. 334.

WRIGHT, C. A. Experimental study of the scour of a sandy river-bed by clear and by muddy water. *Trans. Amer. Geophys. Union*, 1936, pp. 439-440.

SILT IN COLORADO RIVER

BREAZEALE, J. F. A study of the Colorado River silt. *Arizona Univ. Coll. of Agric. Techn. Bull. 8* (pp. 159-185). 1926.

COLLINGWOOD, C. B. Soil and waters. *Arizona Agric. Exper. Sta. Bull. 6*, pp. 4-8, 1892. [Determination of quantity of suspended matter carried by Colorado River at Yuma.]

COLLINS, W. D., and C. S. HOWARD. Quality of water of Colorado River in 1925-1926. *U. S. Geol. Survey Water-Supply Paper 596*, pp. 33-43. 1927.

FORBES, R. H. Irrigating sediments and their effects upon crops. *Univ. Arizona Agric. Exper. Sta. Bull. 53*. 1906.

FORBES, R. H. The lower courses of the Colorado River. *Univ. of Arizona Monthly*, Vol. 7, 1906 (Feb.).

FORBES, R. H. The river-irrigating waters of Arizona: Their character and effects. *Arizona Agric. Exper. Sta. Bull. 44* (pp. 143-214). 1902.

FORTIER, SAMUEL, and H. F. BLANEY. Silt in the Colorado River and its relation to irrigation. *U. S. Dept. of Agric. Techn. Bull. 67*. 94 pp., 1928.

GRUNSKY, C. E. Silt transportation by Sacramento and Colorado Rivers and by the Imperial Canal. *Proc. Amer. Soc. Civil Engineers*, Part I, August, 1929, pp. 1473-1502.

GRUNSKY, C. E. Silt transportation by Sacramento and Colorado Rivers and by the Imperial Canal. *Trans. Amer. Soc. Civil Engineers*, Vol. 94, 1930, pp. 1104-1115.

HOWARD, C. S. Quality of water of the Colorado River in 1926-1928. *U. S. Geol. Survey Water-Supply Paper 636*, pp. 1-14. 1930.

HOWARD, C. S. Suspended matter in the Colorado River in 1925-1928. *U. S. Geol. Survey Water-Supply Paper 636*, pp. 15-44. 1930.

HOWARD, C. S. Suspended matter in the Colorado River, 1925-1935. *Trans. Amer. Geophys. Union*, 1936, pp. 446-447.

[LAWSON, L. M.] Silt observations at Yuma gaging station. *Reclamation Record*, Vol. 8, 1917, pp. 240-241.

LAWSON, L. M. The Yuma project silt problem. *Reclamation Record*, Vol. 7, 1916, pp. 358-359.

LIPPINCOTT, J. B. Investigations in California [on suspended matter carried by the Colorado River at Yuma]. *U. S. Reclamation Service, 2nd Annual Rept.*, 1904, pp. 153-154.

ROTHERY, S. L. A problem of soil in transportation in the Colorado River. *Proc. Amer. Soc. Civil Engineers,* Vol. 60, No. 8, Part 2.

ROTHERY, S. L. A problem of soil in transportation in the Colorado River. *Trans. Amer. Soc. Civil Engineers,* Vol. 99, 1934, pp. 524-543, with discussion, pp. 544-575.

STABLER, HERMAN. Some stream waters of the western United States. *U. S. Geol. Survey Water-Supply Paper 274.* 1911. [Pages 25-28 contain results of investigation of Colorado River water at Yuma.]

GENERAL PHYSIOGRAPHIC PROCESSES

BRYAN, KIRK. Erosion and sedimentation in the Papago country, Arizona, with a sketch of the geology. *U. S. Geol. Survey Bull. 730-B.* 90 pp. 1922.

CORNISH, VAUGHAN. Waves of sand and snow. London, 1914.

CORNISH, VAUGHAN, and others. On the formation of sand dunes. *Geogr. Journ.,* Vol. 9, 1897, pp. 279-309.

DUTTON, C. E. Tertiary history of the Grand Cañon district. *U. S. Geol. Survey Monogr. 2.* With atlas of 23 sheets. 1882.

FREE, E. E. The movement of soil material by the wind. *Bur. of Soils Bull. No. 68.* 1911.

GILBERT, G. K. On the glacial epoch in Utah and Nevada. *Bull. Philos. Soc. of Washington,* (abstract of paper read on April 26, 1873), 1871-74, pp. 84-85.

GRABAU, A. W. Principles of stratigraphy. New York, 1924.

MC GEE, W J. Sheet flood erosion. *Bull. Geol. Soc. of America,* Vol. 8, 1897, pp. 87-112.

MC GEE, W J. The formation of arkose. *Science,* New Series, Vol. 4, 1896, pp. 962-963.

TWENHOFEL, W. H., and collaborators. Treatise on sedimentation. Prepared under the auspices of the Committee on Sedimentation, Division of Geology and Geography, National Research Council of the National Academy of Sciences. Baltimore, 1926.

EVAPORATION

BIGELOW, F. H. Studies on the phenomena of the evaporation of water over lakes and reservoirs, V, VI, VII. *Monthly Weather Rev.,* Vol. 38, 1910, pp. 307-316 and 1133-1135. [These sections deal with studies at Salton Sea.]

BIGELOW, F. H. Studies on the rate of evaporation at Reno, Nevada, and in the Salton Sink. *Natl. Geogr. Mag.,* Vol. 19, 1908, pp. 20-28.

ROHWEN, CARL. Evaporation from free water surfaces. *Dept. of Agric. Techn. Bull. No. 231.* 96 pp. 1931.

SHREVE, FORREST. Rainfall, runoff, and soil moisture under desert conditions. *Annals Assn. Amer. Geogrs.,* Vol. 24, 1934, pp. 131-156.

SHREVE, FORREST. The vegetation of a desert mountain range as conditioned by climatic factors. *Carnegie Instn. Publ. No. 217.* Washington, 1915.

STUDIES OF DELTAS

CREDNER, RUDOLF. Die Deltas, ihre Morphologie, geographische Verteilung, und Entstehungs-bedingungen: Eine Studie auf dem Gebiet der physischen Erdkunde. 74 pp., with world map in Mercator's projection, equat. scale 1 : 135,000,000, and detailed maps of typical deltas on various scales. *Ergänzungsheft No. 56 zu Petermanns Mitt.* Gotha, 1878.

JOHNSON, W. A. Sedimentation of the Fraser River delta. *Geol. Survey of Canada Memoir 125.* 46 pp., with map in 1 : 190,080. Ottawa, 1921. [The outstanding modern discussion of a North American delta.]

HUMPHREYS, A. A., and H. L. ABBOTT. Report upon the physics and hydraulics of the Mississippi River, upon the protection of the alluvial region against overflow, and upon the deepening of the mouths, based upon surveys and investigations . . . Submitted to the Bureau of Topographical Engineers, War Department, 1861. 456 and cxlvi pp. Philadelphia, 1861.

BIBLIOGRAPHIES

(California) Bibliography of southeastern California. In J. S. Brown: The Salton Sea Region, California (*U. S. Geol. Survey Water-Supply Paper 497*), pp. 125-128. 1923. [Classified and annotated.]

(Colorado River) Bibliography: Selected classified list of references and sources relating to utilization of lower Colorado River. In: Report of the American Section of the International Water Commission, United States and Mexico (*71st Congr., 2nd Session, House Doc. No. 359*), pp. 97-98.

(Colorado River) HELLMAN, F. S. List of references on the Colorado River and its tributaries. (Supplementing bibliography compiled in 1922 by Bertha L. Walsworth, Riverside Public Library, Riverside, California). 1926.

(Colorado River) WALSWORTH, BERTHA L. The Colorado River and its tributaries: A bibliography of books, magazine articles, and government documents in the Riverside Public Library. Riverside, Calif., 1922.

(Colorado River Basin) Bibliography of books and principal magazine articles relating to Colorado River Basin, arranged by subjects. In: Problems of Imperial Valley and Vicinity (*67th Congr., 2nd Session, Senate Doc. 142*), pp. 223-233. 1922. [Strong on articles in engineering journals and general magazines.]

(Colorado River Basin) List of references on geography, precipitation, evaporation, and hydrographic régime of Colorado River Basin. In Eberhard Reichel: Der Wasserhaushalt des Coloradogebietes (*Geogr. Abhandl.*, 2nd Series, No. 4, Stuttgart, 1928), pp. 69-74. [Alphabetical list of 182 items.]

(Colorado River Basin) List of references on the water resources of the Colorado River Basin. In E. C. La Rue: Colorado River and Its Utilization (*U. S. Geol. Survey Water-Supply Paper 395*), pp. 31-36. 1916.

(Lower California) Bibliography of Lower California. In E. W. Nelson: Lower California and its natural resources (*Memoirs Natl. Acad. Sci.*, Vol. 16, No. 1), pp. 147-171. 1921. [Excellent, full chronological list of references from 1686 to 1919, critically annotated. Of the scientific expeditions the published results of which form the bulk of the bibliography a chronological account is given on pp. 141-147.]

(Lower California) Lower California: A bibliographical list . . . 1913. Div. of Bibliography, Library of Congress. 13 typewritten leaves. On cover: Public Affairs Information Service.

(Stream Dynamics) Bibliography of stream dynamics. In Filip Hjulström: Studies of the morphological activity of rivers as illustrated by the River Fyris (*Bull. Geol. Inst. of Univ. of Upsala*, Vol. 25, 1935, pp. 221-527), pp. 442-452.

(Stream Dynamics) Bibliography of stream dynamics. In L. G. Straub: Report of the Committee on Dynamics of Streams, 1934-1935 (*Trans. Amer. Geophysical Union*, 1935, pp. 443-451), pp. 447-451. [List of 155 items substantiating the references in the body of the report in which the subject is discussed according to its various subdivisions.]

INDEX

Abejas, Rio, 52, 58, 62, 63, 139, 171; artificial diversion toward the Pescadero, 78; danger point in deep bend, 81
Abejas basin, 64
Abejas River-Volcano Lake outlet, protective measures and, 65
Acknowledgments, iv
Adams, Frank, iv
Agriculture, 37
Agua Fria, 148
Alamo River, 39, 40, 44, 51, 56, 57, 69, 170; channel, 122; channel after break of 1905 in Colorado River, 117, opp. 118 (Fig. 64)
Alarcón, Hernando, exploration, 8, 9
Algodones Sand Hills, 76
All-American Canal, 121; report of Board, 122
American Geographical Society, iv
Ancón, term, 7
Ancón de San Andrés y Mar Bermejo, 7, 8
Anian, Strait of, 10
Aridity, 94
Arizona, storms of February, 1932, 95
Arizona-Sonora boundary line, 43-44
Arrowsmith chart, 13
Arrowweed, 161; heavy growth, opp. 95 (Fig. 58)
Artificial channels. *See* Channels
Artificial deflection to the south-southwest (1920-1930), 77

Baja California Development Co., 84
Bajadas, 3
Barges, 28; list of those used in river trade, 33
Barrancas, 61, 62, 88, 105
Bell, W. A., 30
Benicia, 25
Bergland, Eric, 110
Bibliography, 177
Bigelow, F. H., 163
Bill Williams bar, 97
Bill Williams Basin, altitude, area, character, run-off, 148
Bill Williams Fork, 34, 96, 140, 149, 153, 154, 159, 172, 173; detrital discharge in February, 1932, 97
Biological investigation, 54, 56
Black Crook (barge), 28, 33
Blake, W. P., 59; discovery of Salton Sink, 108
Blaney, H. F., 130, 162
Blind outlet, 64
Boat journey on River in the 1890's, 40, opp. 40 (Fig. 16)
Boat on mud bank (ill.), opp. 40 (Fig. 17)
Boat Slough, 43, 44 (with map), 50, 103, 104, 107; revival, 100
Bolsón, 3
Bore, 30; decrease in size of bores, 86; formation, 49, opp. 54 (Fig. 19); *Retta* and (ill.), opp. 30 (Fig. 14)
Botanical expeditions, investigations of 1903-1904, 53; second expedition (1905), flood conditions, 54
Bottom flow, 139
Boulder City, 152, 153
Boulder Dam, iii, 34, 152, 154; effect of completion, 157, 173
Boulder Dam Project Act, 122
Boulder Dam reservoir, 123
Breazeale, J. F., 129

Bright Angel Creek, 146, 149
Bruja (sloop), 13, 14, 33, 104

Calexico, iv, 56, 62, 118
California, Gulf of, iii, 10; physical features of the head of, 155; tides, 2, 3, 7, 8, 13, 15, 20, 30, 156
California, Island of, 10
California Development Co., 111
California Division of Water Resources, 164
Camp Yuma, 24, 25, 26, 31
Canyons of the Colorado, 1; as grinding chambers, 149; water charged with silt, 152, opp. 154 (Figs. 66, 67)
Capacity (schooner), 25, 33
Carnegie Institution, iii, iv, 59, 69, 174
Carrizo, 48, 50, 161
Carrizo Creek, 120
Carrizo-San Felipe drainage basin, 60
Castillo, Domingo del, chart, 8, opp. 10 (Fig. 1)
Cecil-Stephens, B. A., 40
Cerro Prieto, 3, 9, 100
Chaffey, George, 111
Channel of the Colorado River, during early navigation period, 31; Ives (1858) and author's (1891) surveys compared (with map), 38; survey (1891), 37
Channels, air view over system cut in 1929-1930 to save the Imperial Valley, opp. 94 (Fig. 48); distributary channel of a falling river showing mud and willow on bank, opp. 158 (Fig. 73)
Civil War, 28
Clarence Island, 22
Coachella Valley, 3, 120, 121, 122
Cochan (steamer), 33, opp. 26 (Fig. 9), 114, 115; *Silas J. Lewis* and, opp. 30 (Fig. 12)
Cocopa Indians, 37, 43, 54, 55
Cocopa Mountains, 3, 16, 43, 51, 55, 56, 62, 100, 105
Cocopah (steamer), 27, 28, 33
Colonia Lerdo, 19, 37, 38, 44, 49, 53, 84; earthquake shocks, 52
Colorado Basin, storms, 151
Colorado City (Yuma), 27
Colorado Delta. *See* Delta
Colorado Desert, 110; change of name, 111
Colorado-Gila junction, 20, 67; military post, 24, 25
Colorado No. 1 (steamer), 26, 33
Colorado No. 2 (steamer), 27, 28, 33
Colorado River, annual régime of discharge: winter and spring, 149; autumn freshets and heavy silt load, 152; beginning of commercial navigation, 24; break-through into Salton Sink in 1905, 114; canyon and downstream sections as grinding and storage chambers, 149; canyons, 1; changes in 1893-1894, 42; channel, shifting of, 169; closing of breach in 1907, 116; color of water, 133; constituent drainage basins of the system and their run-off régime, 146; decade of the great diversion (1900-1910), 47; detrital load, 127; detrital material, amount, 4; discharges at *Yuma,* 39, 42; dispersal of detrital matter, 1; dissolved solids in, at Yuma, and discharge, 1926-1928 (graph), 152-153; lateral channels, 50; low discharge early in 1931 and evaporation, 93; lower

DATE DUE

APR 30 1989		APR 22 '89	RET
MAY 23 1989		APR 24 '89	RET

Demco, Inc. 38-293

The Price of Money, 1946 to 1969

THE PRICE
OF MONEY

1946 to 1969

An Analytical Study of United States and Foreign Interest Rates

by SIDNEY HOMER *and*
RICHARD I. JOHANNESEN

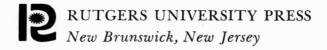 RUTGERS UNIVERSITY PRESS
New Brunswick, New Jersey

Preface

This book is a summation of the research work we have done over the years on bond prices, trends, relative values, yields, yield spreads, and yield curves, on behalf of the investment firm of Salomon Brothers & Hutzler. While we have published all of these data and much more in that firm's periodical reviews, this book for the first time sums it all up in the form of an analytical narrative account of the entire postwar bond market in the United States. A summary of simultaneous interest rates in several key foreign markets has been included in order to put United States interest rates into an international context.

We anticipate that next year another book will be published on another vital aspect of our bond market research, namely *Supply and Demand for Credit,* to be written by our associates, Dr. Henry Kaufman and Mr. James J. McKeon.

As we go to press, interest rates in the United States are still rising rapidly and, therefore, the story we tell of the greatest of all bear bond markets may be incomplete. However, rather than wait for a better market climate, we are publishing this analysis now because it is apt to be most useful in a period of high bond yields.

We should like to express our appreciation to the partners of Salomon Brothers & Hutzler for the enthusiastic support they have given to their Bond Market Research Department over the years in its experimental efforts to develop accurate analytical tools for measuring and studying the bond market. We are also most grateful to those many bond market participants and students who have actively employed our data in their own studies as a basis for investment decisions, and who have repeatedly encouraged us to continue and to expand these forms of market analysis. We should like to thank our publisher, Mr. William Sloane, of the Rutgers University Press for his early encouragement of this book; Dr. Sidney Klein for reading a preliminary version and offering useful suggestions; and Miss Therese Shay for typing and retyping this manuscript.

Finally, we should like to dedicate this book to that large group of institutional bond portfolio managers throughout this country who have loyally and persistently devoted their best efforts over these years of adverse markets to a task which is vital both to their institutions and to the economic health of our country.

Sidney Homer
Richard I. Johannesen

New York
June, 1969

Contents

Tables

Charts

The Price of Money, 1946 to 1969

Introduction

This book tells the story through early 1969 of the greatest bear bond market in the history of the United States and of concurrent bear bond markets in several, but not all, of the principal trading nations of the western world. During the past twenty-three years, prime American bond yields have risen from their all-time lows to levels close to the highest in this country's history. Simultaneously, prime bond yields in Great Britain have risen even more, to reach by far the highest levels in two hundred and fifty years. As this book goes to press, yields are still rising in both countries.

A blow-by-blow account of the sequence of dramatic episodes that go to make up the history of this or any other major bear market is bound to evoke a morbid fascination in some readers, is apt to repel others, but is sure to be instructive to all. These momentous events, with their long series of surprises and precedents, will profoundly influence the behavior of market participants for decades to come.

In all periods of sustained revolutionary change, our precise memory of events and their sequence is likely with time to become blurred and distorted. Few investors today have a clear picture of the prophetic sequence of events during the crisis of 1920–21, or during the stock market boom of 1927–29, or during the crash of 1929–32, or during the great depression. Error and confusion on the real facts of past crises is common and leads to false expectations of future events. Hence, it is hoped that this book will serve a useful purpose by describing these years of bear bond market in some detail and also by placing them in the context of simultaneous events in major foreign markets.

The Organization of This Book

Part I of this book reports in summary form the trends and levels of both short-term and long-term interest rates since 1945 in eight countries: the United States, the United Kingdom, Canada, France, Germany, the Netherlands, Belgium, and Switzerland. It includes comparisons of annual averages of each country's rates with American rates, and a brief discussion of the relationship in all eight countries of long-term rates to short-term rates.

Part II of this book reports in much greater detail on the market in the United States, and includes an analysis of the monthly record of rates since 1945 for all the leading types of short-term market securities and for all the leading types of high-grade long-term bonds. Cyclical bull and bear phases are measured, described, and compared with each other, and are analyzed against the background of economic and political events. The various departments of the market are compared; and the frequent distortions within the market whereby one class of securities became out of line with others and presented relatively attractive or unattractive values are analyzed. The effect of quality on yield is studied. A number of yield curves that depict the relationship of long yields to medium and short yields are charted and their significance is discussed. Finally, the implications of recent market events for the longer-range future are briefly explored.

From time to time in the chapters of this book, various background events, such as wars, or inflations, or cyclical business trends, are mentioned as possible causes of interest-rate trends; however, such attempted correlations are tentative. This book is not intended to be a theoretical discussion of the economic causes or consequences of interest-rate trends. It does not attempt to explore the various economic theories of the role of interest rates in a capitalist economy. Its primary purpose is to set down and analyze an empirical record of interest-rate levels, trends, and relationships during the twenty-three years since the end of World War II.

This book is so constructed that the chapters do not have to be read consecutively. Thus, Part II, "The United States" is largely independent of Part I, "International." Chapter IX, "Long-Term [United States] Bond Yields," is largely independent of all other chapters, and is the only chapter that correlates market trends in some detail with the political and economic environment.

The foreign yields used in Part I are all derived from publications of the Federal Reserve Board and of the International Monetary Fund. The United States yields are from a number of series compiled and published by the firm of Salomon Brothers & Hutzler. The Appendix contains the basic statistics on United States rates used in the charts and tables, and explains the nature of these series. The Appendix also reports yields to June 1969; while most of the tables and charts in the book are complete only to January of 1969. The text occasionally refers to data as late as June.

The Relationship of This Book to A History of Interest Rates

This book is not intended to be a supplement to Sidney Homer's *A History of Interest Rates* (Rutgers University Press, 1963), which covers a very long time span (forty centuries) and a wide geographic area (forty countries). Although it does bring up to 1969 a number of the interest-rate series in the older book, this book is much more limited in both time and space, but much more intensively analytical. It is essentially intended to be a working document, providing economists, bond-portfolio managers, and others with a history of recent trends in all principal departments of the American bond and money market, an analysis of the interrelationships among the different types of yields, and an account of the surrounding economic and political environment.

It would seem pertinent here to quote a few comments from *A History of Interest Rates*.

A history of interest rates should not fail to be dramatic. Most readers will be startled merely by the high level and low level of many ancient and modern interest rates. (Page 3)

Almost every generation is eventually shocked by the behavior of interest rates, because, in fact, market rates of interest in modern times have rarely been stable for long. Usually they are rising or falling to unexpected extremes. A student of the history of interest rates will not be surprised by volatility. His backward-looking knowledge will not tell him where interest rates will be in the future, but it will permit him to distinguish a truly unusual level of rates from a mere change. (Page 5)

The major political and economic events of two or three centuries may be observed in terms of their impact on various rates of interest. The result is a fever chart of the economic and political health of nations. Although the doctors do not always agree on how to read the chart, especially on how to define normal, the extremes stand out, the direction of change is plain, and political and economic calamities are often recognizable at sight. (Page 489)

Historical Perspective

At this point it should be useful to put the subject matter of this book into a broad historical perspective. Chart I * provides a rough sketch

* NOTE: This chart and all other yield charts in this book are plotted vertically in ratio scale. This has the advantage of equalizing yield fluctuations

of long-term prime bond yields in the United States from the days of Alexander Hamilton. Early data are not precise and not exactly comparable with modern data; nevertheless, the over-all picture seems valid.

The chart shows clearly a succession of protracted secular trends in long-term prime yields: five great bull markets, each succeeded by a great sustained bear market. The time spans and the scope of fluctuation of these secular bull or bear bond markets are highly varied, so that they do not lend themselves to any "great-cycle" theory. The use of annual averages, or estimates, in this chart emphasizes the long-term trends, but also tends to obscure some large inter-year fluctuations; therefore, cyclical trends tend to be minimized.

The chart suggests that from 1797 until 1946, in addition to a succession of great secular bull and bear markets, there was a broad suprasecular trend toward lower yields, in the sense that at each succeeding peak and trough the extreme yields were progressively lower. This could be attributed, in part, to the historic evolution of a new young frontier country into a dominant financial power. In some measure this highly irregular trend toward lower yields was world-wide for at least two centuries. However, the chart shows that in 1967 this trend line toward lower yields in the United States was broken when yields rose decisively above the extreme high yields of 1920, and came close to the high yields of the Civil War period. Indeed, the chart shows that the great secular bear bond market of 1946–69 was by far the largest in our financial history.

In the chart, all major wars stand out clearly. We see the War of 1812, the Civil War, World War I, the aftereffects of World War II and, no doubt, the sustained effect of the Cold War, Korea, Vietnam, and high defense expenditures.

Chart II pictures the yields of British Consols from 1752, when they were originally floated as 3's (they were exchanged for the present 2½'s in 1888), and of some earlier securities. Here again we see a succession of great secular bear and bull bond markets ending in the greatest of all bear bond markets, that of 1946–69. The timing of these British market trends after 1800 was roughly similar to that in the United States, except that the large Civil War rise in American yields did not occur in Great Britain. British yields were always below American yields until World War I. Thereafter they were usually close to or above American yields, and since World War II they have at times risen to levels far

---

in low yield areas with proportionate fluctuations in high yield areas. Thus, for example, a doubling of yield from, say, 1% to 2%, will occupy the same vertical space as a doubling from, say, 3% to 6%.

Chart I

YIELDS OF LONG-TERM HIGH GRADE AMERICAN BONDS

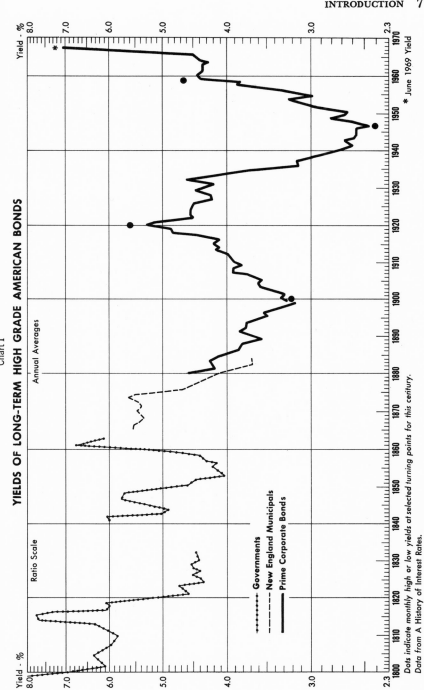

Annual Averages

Ratio Scale

Governments
New England Municipals
Prime Corporate Bonds

* June 1969 Yield

Dots indicate monthly high or low yields at selected turning points for this century.

Data from A History of Interest Rates.

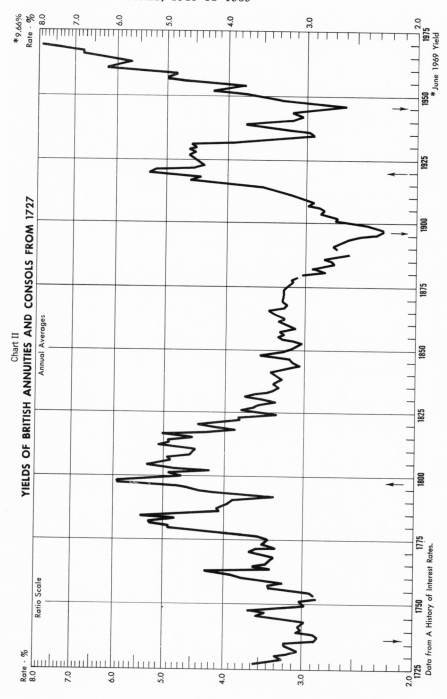

Chart II
YIELDS OF BRITISH ANNUITIES AND CONSOLS FROM 1727
Annual Averages

Ratio Scale

Data from A History of Interest Rates.

* June 1969 Yield

* 9.66%
Rate - %

above American yields. Nevertheless, the dates of highs and lows of the secular trends in this century were very similar.

In the British chart, major wars also stand out sharply. Every major war was accompanied or immediately followed by a bear bond market, and there are few or no major bear bond markets without a war. We see the bulge in yields at the time of the Seven Years' War and the American Revolution, and the much larger rise during the Napoleonic Wars. The succeeding one hundred years of peace were accompanied by almost steadily declining yields. We see the huge yield rise at the time of World War I, the decline during peace and depression and, finally, the record rise following World War II. In the case of World War II, the economic and financial controls in Britain, as in the United States, postponed the effects of the war on commodity prices and on bond yields until the postwar period. Also, no doubt, the adverse aftereffects of World War II on British bond prices were importantly supplemented by the Cold War, its occasional heatings, the breakup of the empire, and the constant threat of world-wide disorders.

Long-range charts of wholesale commodity prices in both America and Britain show patterns roughly similar to those of the bond-yield charts, with commodity prices usually rising when bond yields were rising, and falling or stable when bond yields were falling. It seems probable that the wars caused commodity prices to rise, and rising commodity prices caused bond yields to rise. We shall see in Part II that commodity-price trends in the United States from 1945 through 1968 seemed most of the time to be closely related to the trends of long-term interest rates.

Part I—International

Short-Term Interest Rates
in Eight Countries

Short-term market rates of interest in the eight leading financial markets of the western world have followed diverse trends since 1946. Chart III shows that only in the three English-speaking countries, the United States, the United Kingdom, and Canada, have short-term interest rates fluctuated in a similar pattern, rising most of the time, and all reaching their highs in 1968 and 1969. In contrast, French short rates reached their highs in 1958, the year de Gaulle ascended, and fluctuated in a moderate range until 1968. German short rates reached their highs as long ago as 1951, zigzagged thereafter much more persistently than the others, and in 1968 were near the bottom of their range. In Switzerland and Belgium short rates followed another distinct pattern, fluctuating at very low levels until 1959, and thereafter rising to peaks in 1966, which were not very high. The Netherlands pattern was unique, with very low and declining rates until 1955 and thereafter two sharp peaks, one in 1957 and the other in 1966.

Chart III is based on the annual averages of short-term rates of interest in each of these eight countries. It therefore misses inter-year highs and lows, but for the purposes of general perspective this technique seems appropriate. The data are derived from Table I. The series used are those published by the Federal Reserve and the International Monetary Fund.

The various rates pictured in Chart III are not perfectly comparable; that is to say, U.S. "3-month Treasury bills" are not exactly the same as French "day money" or German "call money." Actually very few, if any, short credit instruments are precisely duplicated in any two countries, and the institutional structures within which the rates fluctuate

Chart III
SHORT-TERM INTEREST RATES
(Annual Averages)

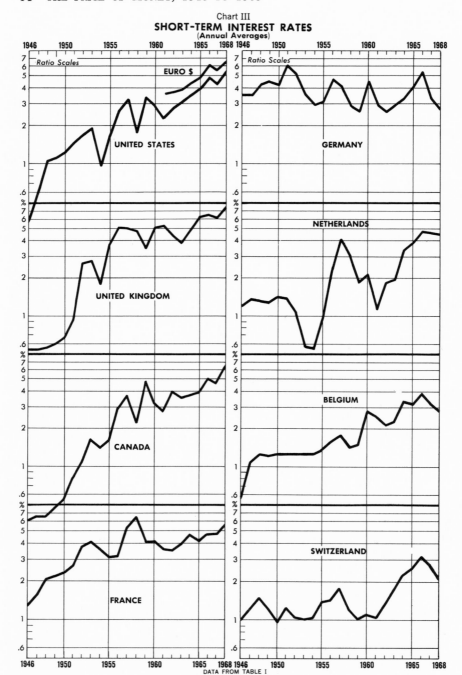

DATA FROM TABLE I

Table I

Short-Term Interest Rates
(Annual averages)

	U.S. 3-Month Bills	U.K. Open Mkt.	Canada Treas. Bills *	France Day Money	Germany Call Money †	Nethlds. 3-Month Bills	Belgium Call Money	Switzld. Call Money	Euro-$ 3 Month
1946	0.37	0.53	0.39	1.31	3.50	1.20	0.58	1.00	
1947	0.59	0.53	0.41	1.57	3.50	1.35	1.08	1.11	
1948	1.04	0.56	0.41	2.09	4.25	1.30	1.25	1.50	
1949	1.10	0.60	0.48	2.26	4.46	1.27	1.23	1.12	
1950	1.22	0.67	0.55	2.43	4.20	1.40	1.25	0.96	
1951	1.55	0.92	0.80	2.70	6.02	1.36	1.25	1.13	
1952	1.77	2.70	1.07	3.85	5.17	1.08	1.25	1.05	
1953	1.93	2.78	1.69	4.04	3.58	0.57	1.25	1.01	
1954	0.95	1.84	1.44	3.59	2.94	0.55	1.25	1.03	
1955	1.75	3.75	1.62	3.16	3.13	0.96	1.35	1.38	
1956	2.66	5.05	2.92	3.18	4.70	2.38	1.58	1.45	
1957	3.28	4.98	3.76	5.35	4.08	4.06	1.78	1.80	
1958	1.84	4.75	2.25	6.48	2.93	3.01	1.41	1.19	
1959	3.40	3.49	4.81	4.07	2.67	1.85	1.47	1.01	
1960	2.93	5.05	3.32	4.08	4.54	2.14	2.79	1.10	
1961	2.38	5.28	2.82	3.65	2.94	1.12	2.56	1.03	3.60
1962	2.78	4.41	4.00	3.61	2.66	1.84	2.13	1.33	3.73
1963	3.16	3.83	3.57	3.98	2.97	1.94	2.28	1.75	3.91
1964	3.54	4.81	3.74	4.70	3.29	3.37	3.34	2.35	4.35
1965	3.95	6.29	3.97	4.18	4.11	3.83	3.14	2.63	4.79
1966	4.85	6.42	5.00	4.78	5.41	4.74	3.89	3.18	6.17
1967	4.30	6.08	4.60	4.77	3.33	4.58	3.22	2.72	5.53
1968	5.33	7.48	6.35	5.56	2.75	4.41	2.81	2.08	6.47

* Includes all bills through 1954, 3-month bill thereafter.
† Official discount rate through 1949, call-money rate thereafter.
Source: *Federal Reserve Bulletin, International Financial Statistics* (IMF).

are always very different.   Therefore, we cannot conclude from these tables and charts, when short-term rates or even one specific short-term rate appears to be "higher in country A than in country B," that the comparison is between identical instruments in different countries. However, most of these series are internally uniform and self-consistent, so that each pattern over time is valid, and the patterns can be compared.   The rates quoted are all "unhedged" internal rates payable to nationals with no allowance for the cost of cover to foreigners or for taxation.   In most of these countries there are many other short-term market rates of interest, and these are usually at different levels from the series used here.   The series chosen by the Federal Reserve and the International Monetary Fund and reported here are considered standard.

Table II

Central Bank Discount Rates
(Annual averages)

	U.S.	U.K.	Can-ada	France	Ger-many	Nethlds.	Bel-gium	Switzld.
1946	1.00	0.53	1.50	1.63	3.50	2.50	2.25	1.50
1947	1.00	0.53	1.50	2.19	3.50	2.50	3.25	1.50
1948	1.35	0.56	1.50	2.98	4.25	2.50	3.50	1.50
1949	1.50	0.60	1.50	3.00	4.46	2.50	3.38	1.50
1950	1.60	0.67	1.62	2.54	4.33	2.62	3.50	1.50
1951	1.75	0.92	2.00	2.79	6.00	3.71	3.50	1.50
1952	1.75	2.70	2.00	4.00	5.25	3.33	3.13	1.50
1953	2.00	2.78	2.00	3.83	3.71	2.63	2.88	1.50
1954	1.58	1.84	2.00	3.25	3.21	2.50	2.75	1.50
1955	1.92	3.75	2.10	3.00	3.21	2.50	2.88	1.50
1956	2.79	5.05	3.12	3.00	4.83	3.12	3.25	1.50
1957	3.12	4.98	4.01	4.17	4.33	4.26	4.00	2.16
1958	2.12	4.75	2.50	4.88	3.21	3.83	4.00	2.50
1959	3.38	3.49	5.06	4.08	3.08	2.87	3.63	2.04
1960	3.50	5.05	3.57	3.90	4.83	3.50	4.50	2.00
1961	3.00	5.28	3.09	3.50	3.17	3.50	4.75	2.00
1962	3.00	4.41	4.89	3.50	3.00	3.88	3.88	2.00
1963	3.23	3.83	3.87	3.58	3.00	3.50	3.88	2.00
1964	3.54	4.81	4.02	4.00	3.00	4.21	4.50	2.21
1965	4.04	6.29	4.52	3.63	3.70	4.50	4.75	2.50
1966	4.50	6.42	5.17	3.50	4.67	4.83	5.00	3.00
1967	4.17	6.08	4.96	3.50	3.33	4.58	4.63	3.25
1968	5.15	7.42	6.75	4.42	3.00	4.50	3.79	3.00

Source: *Federal Reserve Bulletin, International Financial Statistics* (IMF). Authors' averaging.

Probably in most countries other short-term market rates fluctuate similarly to these, but usually are a bit higher by varying differentials.

Finally, Table II shows the central bank discount rates in each of these eight countries. These are also on an annual average basis.

The United States *

The history of United States bill rates depicted in Chart III can be divided into three parts: (1) From 1946 to 1953 there was a steady rise

* In Chapter VII of this book, short-term interest rates in the United States are charted and analyzed in detail with monthly data on many leading types of rates.

from the low controlled wartime level of ⅜% to 1.93%; the average every year was higher than the year before. (2) From 1953 to 1961 there was a series of sharp swings that achieved only a small net further gain, i.e., from 1.93% to 2.38%. (3) From 1961 to 1969 there was another, almost uninterrupted rise in the annual average of rates during six of seven years, which carried them up from 2.38% to 6.80%, a historically very high level not seen since 1920.

Politically minded analysts will note that the first period, 1946–53, was largely a period of Democratic administration, the latter part of which was dominated by the Korean War. The low-interest-rate-minded Democrats fought the rise in interest rates and gave ground stubbornly. Rates, nevertheless, rose steadily each year both before and after the "Accord" in February, 1951. Commodity prices rose substantially during this first period. It was during these inflationary years that the widespread fears of a traditional postwar depression gradually faded. They were years dominated by the Cold War and "the Bomb."

The second period, 1953 to 1961, was the period of the zigzags. These were the Eisenhower years. They were years of peace. Monetary and fiscal policy were both actively employed to cushion recessions and to restrain booms, and there was less effort to create sustained rapid growth. The wide interest-rate fluctuations were all cyclical, with the three dips (1954, 1958, 1960–61) all roughly coinciding with small inventory recessions and the three peaks (1953, 1957, 1959) all coinciding with booms, either capital-goods booms or inventory booms. Inflation was brought to a halt in 1958, not to resume until 1965, but rising unemployment, slow growth, and high interest rates created dissatisfaction with the monetary and fiscal techniques employed.

The third period, 1961–69, was Democratic and, like the earlier Democratic period, these years were marked by steadily escalating interest rates, in spite of an easy-money bias and in spite of a monetary policy that was usually very expansive. Thus, again, expansive monetary policy and a political bias for low interest rates actually coincided with steadily rising short-term interest rates. Though the verbal Cold War seemed to subside, Vietnam dominated the latter three years of this period. The rise in rates, however, began long before that war. With the war, inflation was renewed and grew severe. Excessive unemployment was eliminated. In spite of a usually expansive monetary policy, the credit markets suffered repeated severe dislocations and there were important liquidity problems. Furthermore, the international position of the dollar eroded. Nevertheless, these were years of exceptional growth.

It can be argued that the rise in American short-term interest rates until 1959 was merely a readjustment to normal levels following the abnormalities of the depression and of World War II. The highest short rate of the 1950's, a 3.40% annual average, was moderate compared with short rates in many foreign countries and with pre-depression American short rates.   On the other hand, the sustained rise since 1961 and especially that following 1965 was of extraordinary magnitude, reflecting severe underlying pressures of far greater significance than the incidence of the Vietnam War.   Although causative factors are not easy to isolate and many causes can be cited for this extraordinary period of rate escalation, such as the renewed inflation, the sustained business boom, and the war, no doubt the deterioration in our balance of payments was basic.

The United Kingdom

The pattern of United Kingdom short rates pictured in Chart III was very similar in shape, but not similar in level, to that of United States short rates, with a few small differences in the dates of turning points. In the first period, 1946–51, the Labor government of the United Kingdom clung to wartime nominal interest rates for several years longer than did the United States authorities, in spite of the 1949 devaluation. However, soon after the 1951 Tory victory, United Kingdom rates readjusted upward abruptly. From 1951 until 1963 United Kingdom rates zigzagged very much as they did in the United States, but in a wider range and rising much more rapidly on balance.   The dating of these United Kingdom peaks and troughs was similar to those in the United States, but not identical, and a lag of a year or so gradually developed behind U.S. turning points.   In England at this time a Tory government was attempting to maximize economic growth without destroying the pound, and it used contra-cyclical monetary policy vigorously.   The third period, that from 1963 to 1969, closely resembled that of the United States: under a new Labor government and a sustained sterling crisis, rates escalated almost continuously, although there was a small dip in the annual average in 1967.   In the United Kingdom, as in the United States, this third period was dominated by a deteriorating currency and a government which, up to each moment of crisis, gave top priority to growth and tolerated inflation.   Unlike the United States, the United Kingdom had no war on its hands, but nevertheless its interest-rate pattern in the 1960's was very much like that of the United States.

Canada

The pattern for Canadian short-term interest rates since 1946 was broadly similar to those of the United States and the United Kingdom: From 1946 to 1953 there was a steady rise from very low levels; from 1953 to 1961 there was a series of ascending zigzags; from 1961 to 1969 there was an almost continuous rise.   However, in Canada the 1954 cyclical rate decline was much less than in the United States and the United Kingdom, and the 1959 peak was much more pronounced than in the United States and coincided with a cyclical trough in the United Kingdom.

France

French short-term rates of interest also rose steadily from 1946 to 1953 and then declined but thereafter they followed a unique pattern by reaching their high in 1958.   The period 1946 to 1953, when they rose persistently and very sharply, was a period of repeated devaluations of the franc and of political turmoil.   In the 1953–56 period, when the Indo-China War ended, rates declined, but soon thereafter they shot up, reaching extreme highs in 1958.   It was during these years that the Common Market was created and the situation in Algeria deteriorated. In 1958, de Gaulle became Premier and then President, the franc was sharply devalued, and a program of political and economic stabilization was inaugurated.   Interest rates promptly came down almost as sharply as they had risen, and rate fluctuations were moderate until 1968.   From 1962 to 1967, rates tended to rise gently, and they soared in the 1968 crisis.

Germany

The German pattern of short-term interest rates from 1946 to 1969 was also very different from all others.   During the period of occupation, 1946 to 1949, interest rates, which were relatively high, rose moderately further.   After the formation of the West German Republic in 1949, rates soared to their highest levels on the chart.   In 1952–54, a period of recovery and growth, rates came down even more sharply, almost to their lows.   Thereafter from 1954 to 1968 there was a series of three large cyclical swings in a very wide but stable band.   Monetary policy, it seems, was used more vigorously than in other countries to offset cyclical swings and to promote growth without inflation.   German rates were the only rates that closed the period under review at close to their lows.

The Netherlands

Short-term market rates of interest in the Netherlands were the only ones in this group that declined in the period 1946 to 1953, in spite of a low starting level. This perhaps represented an attempt to return to the ancient tradition of low Dutch interest rates. After 1953, however, there were two sharp peaks. From 1955 to 1957 rates rose rapidly, together with rates in most other countries. From 1957 to 1961 they declined more sharply and over a longer period than in other countries, and in 1961 reached a level actually below that of 1946. From 1961 to 1966, rates moved up persistently and rapidly, even more than they did in the three English-speaking markets. Finally, in 1966–68 rates declined a little in a manner more typical of Common Market countries than of the English-speaking countries.

Belgium

The Belgian and Swiss patterns were similar to each other and in many respects different from the others. Very low Belgian rates, not far above the wartime rates, persisted until 1959. There were no pronounced cyclical swings in the 1940's or 1950's. Thus, the Belgian interest-rate pattern, which before the war often followed the French pattern, moved quite independently in the period under review. Finally, however, in 1960 Belgian rates rose, but not to very high levels. After receding in 1962, they rose again in a series of moderate cyclical swings and peaked at relatively low levels in 1966. Thereafter, unlike the rates in English-speaking countries but like most Common Market rates, they declined.

Switzerland

Swiss money market rates remained close to wartime low levels from 1946 to as late as 1963, with only two short periods of small rise. Thus, they remained low for several years longer even than did Belgian rates. After 1963 Swiss rates rose persistently until 1966 and then came down. Thus, they followed the Common Market pattern of peaking in 1966 and receding in 1967, but they never reached levels much above 3%.

Euro-Dollars

During the early 1960's a large market for short-term Euro-dollar loans developed. While these loans were most often of a very short maturity, they ranged out to a year or longer. For purposes of comparison, we have recorded on Table I and Chart III the rates on 3-month prime Euro-dollar deposits.

In 1961, when the series began, the Euro-dollar rates, at 3.60%, were well below the United Kingdom rates, about equal to the French rates, and well above United States rates and all other rates. Thereafter, until

1966 the Euro-dollar rates rose steadily and substantially in a pattern similar to those of the English-speaking markets. They declined briefly in 1967, and then soared again in 1968. This sharp rise in 1968 followed the British devaluation and the two-tier gold system. It was, no doubt, heavily influenced by the high American rates, demand by American banks, and restrictions on capital exports. Thus, over its entire short history the Euro-dollar rate has been rising in every year except one. In May of 1969, in an American liquidity crisis, it touched 13%, which was about twice the U.S. bill rate.

III

International Short-Term
Rate Comparisons

During the twenty-three years covered by this history, not only have short-term interest rates in most countries fluctuated dramatically, but fundamental changes have taken place in the comparative levels of rates among the eight countries discussed in Chapter II. In some cases, historically low-rate markets have achieved the highest rates, while some high-rate markets have developed relatively low rates. These changes of relative status may be summarized as follows:

In Order of Rate	1946	1967	1968
1st: Highest	Germany	United Kingdom	United Kingdom
2nd	France	France	Canada
3rd	Netherlands	Canada	France
4th	Switzerland	Netherlands	United States
5th	Belgium	United States	Netherlands
6th	United Kingdom	Germany	Belgium
7th	Canada	Belgium	Germany
8th: Lowest	United States	Switzerland	Switzerland

The most obvious change over these years is the shift of the three English-speaking markets (the United States, the United Kingdom, and Canada) from lowest short rates to medium or highest short rates. Conversely, Germany shifted from highest rates to second-lowest. Switzerland and Belgium moved from medium-rate positions to low or lowest.

Chart IV shows the relative rank of all eight rates annually since 1946 in terms of the short-term annual average yields from Table I. In the chart, each country is plotted solely in terms of rank: 1 = highest rate,

Chart IV

RELATIVE RANKINGS OF SHORT-TERM INTEREST RATES - Annual Averages
(No. 1 equals highest yield, No. 2 the next highest yield, etc.)

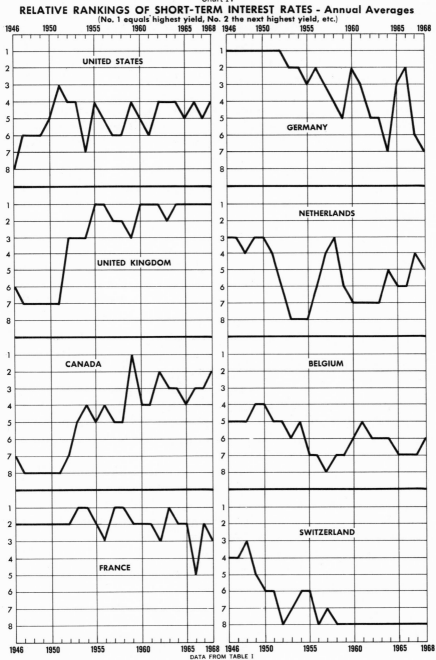

DATA FROM TABLE I

2 = second-highest rate, etc.   In Chapter II we noted that these eight rates are not strictly comparable with each other, so that from spot comparisons it is difficult to say arbitrarily that rate A is above or below rate B, especially if the difference is moderate.   However, most of these series are internally consistent and, therefore, comparisons of relative standing over time should yield valid generalities such as, "Rate A had risen more than rate B," etc.

Chart V attempts to measure the shifts in rate differentials more precisely by charting annual yield spreads in basis points between each foreign rate and the simultaneous United States rate, and then between the rate in the United States and a simultaneous average of these seven foreign rates.   Again, the differentials themselves, tabulated in Table III, have only rough absolute significance, but their shift over time should be meaningful.

United States

In 1946 the United States short-term rate was the lowest of these eight rates.   Between 1946 and 1951 the relative rank of the United States short rates, as indicated in Chart IV, moved up sharply.   Thereafter, until 1969 its rank fluctuated between medium and low, but it never again was lowest.

Chart V and Table III show that the United States rate started the period under review about 80 basis points below the average of the seven other rates.   This differential narrowed most of the time until 1953, but widened again in both 1954 and 1958; this seems to mean that our cyclical easy-money spells in the 1950's were not matched in the seven-market average.   Actually, in those years the timing of business cycles here and in Europe synchronized poorly.   In 1959, for the first time, United States rates rose far above the average of foreign rates; but the spread came down, and the short United States rate was close to average from 1960 until 1967.   In 1968, the United States rate rose far more than foreign rates and became substantially above average.   Thus, in the entire period from 1946 to 1968, the United States rate rose an aggregate of 168 basis points more than the seven-market average, that is to say, the United States rate rose 496 basis points from .37% to 5.33%, while the average was rising 328 basis points from 1.21% to 4.49%.

United Kingdom

Chart IV shows that from 1946 until 1952 the United Kingdom short market rate of interest was almost the lowest of these eight rates.   It

Chart V

SHORT-TERM INTEREST-RATE SPREADS
(Annual Averages in Basis Points)

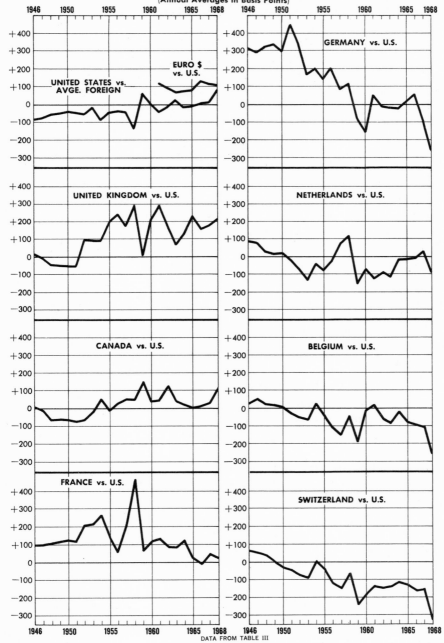

DATA FROM TABLE III

retained this rank before, during, and after the 1949 devaluation. Between 1951 and 1955, however, it rose from second-lowest rank to highest rank and it has remained the highest, or close to the highest, most of the time ever since. As long ago as 1955, the United Kingdom rate achieved its present top rank, but this fact did not serve to avoid a succession of monetary crises ending in devaluation.

Chart V, which measures the yield spread from the United States rate, follows a somewhat different pattern. The United Kingdom rate in 1951 and 1952 moved from 63 basis points below the United States rate to 93 basis points above the United States rate. This, however, was just the start of an era of wide positive spreads. By 1955 the United Kingdom rate was 200 basis points above the United States rate; the spread reached 291 basis points in 1958, came down almost to 0 in 1959, and reached 290 basis points again in 1961. During this erratic period of the 1950's both the United States and the United Kingdom rates were zigzagging upward; but the range of United Kingdom cyclical upswings was much larger than the range of United States cyclical upswings, and the cycles were badly out of phase. After 1961 the spread continued to swing widely, but it tended to decline. In other words, since 1961 the United States rate on balance has risen more than the United Kingdom rate. It was during this period that currency pressures spread to the United States.

Canada

The Canadian rate, like those in the United States and United Kingdom, started this period, as Chart IV shows, among the lowest of this group of rates and ended it among the highest. A large part of the change in rank occurred between 1951 and 1954, when the Canadian rate rose net and some others declined. Thereafter the Canadian rate for a while occupied a medium rank, but it became highest in 1959 and second highest in 1962 and 1968.

The spread of the Canadian rate from the U.S. rate, as pictured in Chart V, was more stable than any of the other spreads, ranging from −75 basis points in 1951 to +141 basis points in 1959, and usually holding in a + or −50 basis-point range. The Canadian rate was below the United States rate in the years 1947 to 1953. Thereafter it was usually above the United States rate. In 1959, 1962, and again in 1968 it moved sharply above the United States rate by over 100 basis points.

France

Chart IV shows that France began the period under review with a relatively very high short-interest rate, and that the French rate remained relatively high until 1966. Thereafter its rank came down to medium.

The yield spread of the French short rate from the United States short rate since 1946 covered a very wide range. It started at plus 100 basis points, and more than doubled by 1954, then declined sharply. However, in 1958, the year of de Gaulle, the spread rose to a remarkable plus 464 basis points—the highest spread of any of these countries during this period. In 1959, however, the spread fell equally abruptly, as the United States rate rose while the French rate declined from its crisis levels. After a few years of stability at a spread of around +100 basis points, the spread came down sharply again in the 1965–68 period. By 1966 the French rate was a trifle below the United States rate; by 1968, it was a little above the United States rate.

Germany

Chart IV shows that the German rate was the highest of all these rates until 1952 and then came down in rank almost steadily, reaching 5th rank in 1959. After a spurt in 1960 to the rank of second highest, it came down steadily again, until by 1964 it was the second-lowest. The German rate peaked again in 1966, reaching second-highest and then in 1968 it again became second-lowest. This rapid shifting in rank reflected the fact that German cyclical interest-rate swings ever since 1954 have been far larger than the cyclical interest-rate swings in most other countries. Unlike those of most other countries, the German cyclical interest-rate swings were in a band, the borders of which neither rose nor fell; this, no doubt, reflected successful economic stabilization, rapid growth, and a favorable balance of payments.

Chart V shows the extraordinary swing in the relationship of the German rate to the United States rate. From a peak of +447 basis points above the United States rate in 1951, the spread came down almost steadily, and by 1960 the German short rate was a remarkable 161 basis points below the United States rate. It rose briefly and was moderately above the United States rate in 1961, and again in 1966, and then came down by 1968 to a level of 258 basis points below the United States rate. Thus, over-all from 1951 to 1968 the German rate declined by 327 basis points from 6.02% to 2.75%, while simultaneously the United States rate rose by 378 basis points from 1.55% to 5.33%. The spread, therefore, changed by an aggregate of 705 basis points!

The Netherlands

The rank of the Dutch short-term interest rate, as pictured in Chart IV, was third-highest most of the time from 1946 through 1950, and thereafter dropped steadily, becoming the lowest by 1953. From 1955 to 1958, it gained in rank and then fell back, so that by 1960 it was almost the lowest. Since then, it has risen to medium rank.

Chart V shows that the Dutch short-term interest rate has swung around the United States rate ever since 1946. The spread moved from +83 basis points in 1946 to −136 basis points in 1953, to +117 basis points in 1958, and back to −155 basis points in 1959. Since 1959, it has usually been negative.

Belgium

The Belgian short-term interest rate, as illustrated by Chart IV, was never relatively very high over these years. It started in a medium rank, and lost rank almost steadily after 1950, becoming the lowest by 1957. Thereafter, until 1961, it returned to a medium position, but by 1968 it was the third-lowest.

Chart V shows that this Belgian rate was never much above the United States interest rate and was usually below it, often far below. From 1946 to 1953 the Belgian rate was stabilized at a low level while the United States rate was rising; however, the Belgian rate did not decline in 1954 as the United States rate did, and so the spread again became briefly positive. Thereafter, the Belgian rate rose slowly, but its spread below the United States rate tended to widen until 1960–61, when it was again briefly positive. From 1964 to 1968, however, the Belgian rate did not participate in the sharp upswing in the United States and a number of other countries; therefore, by 1968 the negative spread became very wide at −252 basis points.

Switzerland

The Swiss interest rate, like the Belgian interest rate, started this period in a medium rank. However, after 1948 it held to its low wartime levels, while most other rates were advancing and, therefore, it lost rank until it became the lowest of all eight rates in 1952. From 1953 to 1957, the Swiss rate rose moderately above a few other rates, but by 1958 it was again the lowest. From then through 1968, it was the lowest, because it was rising less than the other short rates.

Chart V shows that the Swiss short-term rate lagged behind the rise in the United States short-term rate most of the time since 1946. In the early years the shift in spread from positive to negative was steady year by year. From 1953 through 1961, however, the spread swung widely because the big cyclical swings in the United States rate were accompanied by comparative stability in Switzerland. Thereafter, rates rose very similarly in both countries, and the spread in favor of the United States rate was stable until 1968. From 1965 to 1968 the Swiss rate declined, while the United States rate soared so that the spread widened to −325 basis points.

Euro-Dollar

When our Euro-dollar series began in 1961, the Euro-dollar rate was below only two national rates. It soon became second to only one of these national rates, and held there. It was generally well below the United Kingdom rate, but above the United States and Canadian rates and, of course, in these recent years, very much above all other rates.

Chart V and Table III show that in 1961 the Euro-dollar rate was 122 basis points above the United States rate. In 1962 and 1963, the

Table III

Foreign Short-Term Interest Rates vs. U.S. Bill Rates
(Annual averages)
(Spread in basis points; rates from Table I)

	U.S. vs. Avg.	Euro-$ vs. U.S.	U.K. vs. U.S.	Canada vs. U.S.	France vs. U.S.	Germany vs. U.S.	Nethlds. vs. U.S.	Belgium vs. U.S.	Switzld. vs. U.S.
1946	−84	−	+16	+2	+94	+313	+83	+21	+63
1947	−77	−	−6	−17	+98	+291	+76	+49	+52
1948	−58	−	−48	−63	+105	+321	+26	+21	+46
1949	−52	−	−50	−62	+116	+336	+17	+13	+2
1950	−41	−	−55	−67	+121	+298	+18	+3	−26
1951	−47	−	−63	−75	+115	+447	−19	−30	−42
1952	−54	−	+93	−70	+208	+340	−69	−52	−72
1953	−20	−	+85	−24	+211	+165	−136	−68	−92
1954	−85	−	+89	+49	+264	+199	−40	+30	+8
1955	−44	−	+200	−13	+141	+138	−79	−40	−37
1956	−38	−	+239	+26	+52	+204	−28	−108	−121
1957	−41	−	+170	+48	+207	+80	+78	−150	−148
1958	−131	−	+291	+41	+464	+109	+117	−43	−65
1959	+62	−	+9	+141	+67	−73	−155	−193	−239
1960	+10	−	+212	+39	+115	−161	−79	−14	−183
1961	−38	+122	+290	+44	+127	+56	−126	+18	−135
1962	−10	+95	+163	+122	+83	−12	−94	−65	−145
1963	+25	+75	+67	+41	+82	−19	−122	−88	−141
1964	−11	+81	+127	+20	+116	−25	−17	−20	−119
1965	−7	+84	+234	+2	+23	+16	−12	−81	−132
1966	+8	+132	+157	+15	−7	+56	−11	−96	−167
1967	+11	+123	+178	+30	+47	−97	+28	−108	−158
1968	+84	+114	+215	+102	+23	−258	−92	−252	−325

United States rate rose more than the Euro-dollar rate, and the spread came down to +75 basis points and then recovered. In 1966, 1967, and 1968, when U.S. banks borrowed a large volume of Euro-dollars, the spread remained at about +125 basis points but at times exceeded 200 basis points. In May 1969 the spread rose at one time to over +600 basis points when the Euro-dollar rate rose to the unprecedented level of 13%.

Long-Term Interest Rates
in Eight Countries

The trends of long-term market rates of interest on prime bonds in these eight leading financial markets of the western world have shown more uniformity than the corresponding eight short-term rates discussed and compared in Chapters II and III. As illustrated in Chart VI and tabulated in Table IV, all but two of these bond yield series tended to rise most of the time in the period 1946 to 1969. The sizes of the fluctuations, however, and the timings were highly variable.

French long-bond yields, for example, peaked as long ago as 1951, and Belgian yields peaked in 1961. German and Dutch yields peaked in 1966, Swiss in 1967, and only the yields in the English-speaking markets, the United States, the United Kingdom, and Canada, peaked in 1968.

The size of most net long-term yield increases from 1946 to 1969 was distinctly less than the net increases of corresponding short-term rates over the same period, as we shall see in detail in Chapter VI. Cyclical swings against the uptrend were much less noticeable in long yields than in short rates. Therefore, long-term trends are much smoother and more quickly recognizable in the charts of long-term yields than in the charts of short rates.

The greater economic significance of long-term yields, in spite of their smaller range of fluctuations, is the result of two factors: (1) Short-term rates are largely controlled by official monetary policy, but long-term yields are usually created by the independent decisions of thousands of uncontrolled borrowers and lenders. Government, indeed, influences these decisions largely through its power over short rates, but its means of influencing long rates are imperfect and often prove unsuccessful. Only in wartime does government actually control long rates. (2) Long-

Table IV

Long-Term Interest Rates
(Annual averages)

	U.S.		U.K. Con-sols	Can-ada Long Govts.	France Rentes *	Ger-many Mtg. Bonds	Neth-lds.†	Bel-gium Long Govts.**	Switzld. Govts.
	Corp. Bonds	Long Govts.							
1946	2.45	2.19	2.60	2.61	3.17	—	2.99	4.17	3.10
1947	2.57	2.25	2.76	2.56	3.91	—	3.06	4.44	3.17
1948	2.82	2.44	3.21	2.93	4.62	5.39	3.09	4.75	3.42
1949	2.68	2.31	3.30	2.82	6.28	5.22	3.12	4.60	2.94
1950	2.62	2.32	3.55	2.78	6.52	5.78 ‡	3.28	4.42	2.67
1951	2.90	2.57	3.79	3.24	6.54	6.33 ‡	3.88	4.62	2.95
1952	3.03	2.68	4.23	3.59	5.60	5.28 ‡	3.95	4.51	2.84
1953	3.27	2.92	4.08	3.68	5.41	5.67 ‡	3.43	4.40	2.55
1954	2.97	2.54	3.76	3.14	5.38	—	3.31	4.27	2.62
1955	3.10	2.84	4.17	3.08	5.21	—	3.26	4.16	2.97
1956	3.35	3.08	4.74	3.61	5.28	6.23	3.84	4.21	3.11
1957	3.93	3.47	4.98	4.17	5.92	6.64	4.58	4.69	3.64
1958	3.81	3.43	4.98	4.26	5.68	6.28	4.32	4.57	3.19
1959	4.37	4.07	4.82	5.17	5.27	5.86	4.12	4.27	3.08
1960	4.39	4.01	5.40	5.26	5.15	6.50	4.20	4.30	3.09
1961	4.32	3.90	6.20	5.08	5.07	6.00	3.91	5.90	2.96
1962	4.32	3.95	6.03	5.09	5.03	6.03	4.21	5.24	3.12
1963	4.23	4.00	5.68	5.06	4.97	6.10	4.22	4.98	3.24
1964	4.36	4.15	6.02	5.19	5.08	6.20	4.92	5.58	3.97
1965	4.43	4.21	6.41	5.22	5.27	6.70	5.21	5.59	3.95
1966	5.13	4.66	6.80	5.74	5.40	7.60	6.24	5.80	4.16
1967	5.47	4.85	6.73	5.96	5.66	7.00	6.00	5.83	4.61
1968	6.06	5.26	7.46	6.81	5.85	6.80	6.21	5.55	4.37

* 3% Rentes through 1948, 5% Rentes thereafter.
† 2½'s Perpetuals through 1949, 3¼'s 98 thereafter.
‡ With tax privileges.
** New series in 1961.
Source: *United Nations Statistical Year Book, International Financial Statistics* (IMF).
U.S. corporate bonds based on "Durand Basic Yields." (See *A History of Interest Rates*.)

term credit contracts establish rates and, hence, affect both borrowers and lenders over a period of years, often several decades. In contrast, short-term credit contracts establish rates for only a period of months and, therefore, their effect on borrowers and lenders is apt to be transitory.

Thus, the charts on short-term rates in Chapter II gave us a history of eight monetary policies. In contrast, the charts on long-term yields give us a composite history of the effects of fundamental shifts in economic environment, in investor preferences and expectations, in supply

Chart VI
LONG-TERM INTEREST RATES
(Annual Averages)

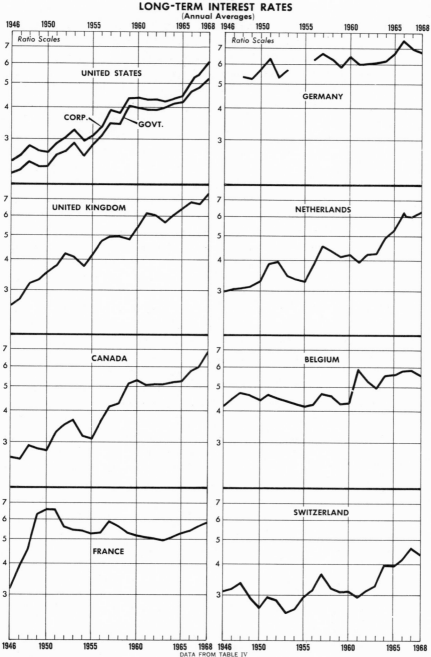

DATA FROM TABLE IV

and demand for credit, and also of the capital-market effects of monetary policy.

The fact that the broad direction of change for both long and short rates in most countries has usually, but not always, been the same over a period of years, is probably because both are influenced simultaneously by the same economic environment. Factors, such as inflation or excessive credit growth, which naturally favor rising long yields, have usually moved monetary authorities to attempt restraint and, hence, have also pushed up short rates. Sluggish economic activity, which favors declining credit demands and declining bond yields, has usually moved monetary authorities to reflate and thus to lower short rates. When, on rare occasions, monetary policy has run counter to natural interest-rate trends, it has not for long reversed the natural trends of long-term bond yields and indeed has only temporarily modified short-term rate trends. Most of the time monetary policy in most countries has "leaned against the wind." This means it has pushed short rates in the direction they would naturally go. Therefore, short rates usually fluctuate in the same direction as bond yields, only more so.

The structures of the long-term bond markets in these eight countries are even more different from each other than are the various short-term market structures. Thus, in the United Kingdom the market for long-term governments is a relatively massive affair, which dominates all other bond markets. In the United States, on the other hand, long governments are created very sparingly except in wartime, and they often have large scarcity premiums; therefore, in America prime long corporate bond yields are more representative than long government yields. However, American governments are charted in this chapter for purposes of comparison. For Germany, the series used in Table IV is for mortgage bonds, which usually yield a little more than governments; the German bond series was almost meaningless before 1956, because the capital markets were chaotic. The French bond yield series changed radically in 1949, and from time to time is distorted by conversions and other fiscal measures. The Belgian bond yield series was changed drastically in 1961. In spite of these imperfections, the charts, based on annual averages, seem to provide usable pictures of the broad trends of yields in all eight countries.

The United States *

The period under review again seems to divide into three parts: (1) From 1946 to 1953 there was an irregular rise from the immediate

---

* In Chapter IX of this book many types of long-term interest rates in the United States are charted and analyzed in detail from monthly data.

postwar yields, which were below the controlled yields of wartime. This rise in yields began five years before the "Accord" of 1951. In all, it carried long government bond yields up from an annual average of 2.19% to an annual average of 2.92%. (2) From 1953 until 1961, there was a series of cyclical swings with declines against the trend in 1954, 1958, and 1960. These cyclical declines, however, were much less vigorous than those for short rates (see Chart III). Therefore, the net rise in long government yields in this period, from 2.92% to 3.90%, amounted to 98 basis points, while simultaneously the net rise of short United States rates was only 45 basis points. (3) From 1961 to 1968 there was a sustained rise in long United States government yields, during which they advanced from 3.90% to 5.26%. However, as late as 1964–65 yields were not much above their cyclical peak in 1959, so that most of this large 136-basis-point rise occurred in 1966, 1967, and 1968. The rise in long yields in this period was far less than the 295-basis-point rise in short rates.

Here again, as in the case of short United States rates, we see yields rising persistently, regardless of the interest-rate preferences of the various administrations in power, and sometimes in defiance of the interest-rate policies they invoked. The first two steps of the rise in yields, that is, from 2.19% in 1946 to 2.92% in 1953 and to 3.90% in 1961, may be described as a return to normal peacetime rates from the artificially low wartime rates. It was the period from mid-1965 to 1969, when long governments rose to a monthly peak of over 6% and new prime long corporate bond yields rose even more spectacularly to 8% or so, that carried yields altogether out of their conventional range and back to levels not seen since the Civil War. On the other hand, short rates, although rising much more than long yields in the 1965–68 period, did not reach historically extraordinarily high levels. This is because in the 1920's and earlier, short rates often ranged far higher than long rates—by 100, 200, and more basis points—whereas since 1930 short rates have averaged below long rates.

The United Kingdom

Long-term government bond yields in the United Kingdom rose sharply during most of the period under review. They rose more than the long yields in any other of these eight countries, and they rose to well above the highest previous yields in the long history of their market, which dates back to 1752. Immediately after World War II, British government policy tried to restrain the rise in United Kingdom yields, but with no success. Then, in the 1950's, a policy was adopted of promoting high long yields through frequent fundings as a means to induce saving, fight inflation, and defend the pound. None of these policy objectives was achieved. In fact, the massive protracted bear bond market in the United Kingdom, during which capital values of prime long bonds declined, over 70%, went too far, and was self-defeating. In time, it discouraged saving through bond investment, and thus it diverted funds to equities or to other so-called inflation hedges, or discouraged savings. During these years, the price of Consol 2½'s declined from 99¾ to 25, while equities soared and savings were attracted by past performance rather than by income.

The pattern of the United Kingdom long yields also seemed to fall into three parts: (1) 1946 to 1952, when yields rose steadily from 2.60% to 4.23%; (2) 1952 to 1963, when the continued uptrend from 4.23% to 5.68% was interrupted by a series of cyclical dips (1954, 1959, 1963); and (3) 1963 to 1968, when yields rose sharply in every year but one, going from a 5.68% to a 7.46% annual average, and over 9% in May of 1969.

Canada

Canadian bond yields also rose very sharply during the period under review, as did those of the other two English-speaking countries. However, the pattern of the Canadian rise in yields was less smooth. Most of the increase took place in three big swings: 1950 to 1953, 1955 to 1960, and 1965 to 1968. There were important periods of stability or decline, such as 1946 to 1950, 1953 to 1955, and 1960 to 1965. The cyclical pattern of Canadian yields was similar to that in the United States, but by no means exactly parallel. No doubt the close financial, commercial, and cultural ties of Canada to both the United States and to the United Kingdom helped account for the basically similar patterns of yields in the period under review.

France

The pattern of French bond yields during the period 1946 to 1969 was very different from that in any other country. Although the early yields in the chart are probably distorted by fiscal gimmicks, French long-term bond yields seem to have reached their peak as long ago as 1951. We saw in Chapter II that French short rates peaked in 1958. After 1951, French bond yields have tended irregularly downward on balance, with a temporary rise in 1956–57 and a steady rise from 1963 to 1969. Since 1946, French bond yields have never been very low, and until 1961 they were relatively and absolutely very high. Until 1958 the government had great difficulty funding its debt because of the inflation and distrust, but thereafter economic stability led to stabilization in the bond market. The rise in French yields in the 1960's was less than the rise in most other countries. The French did not employ high bond yields, as the British and Germans did, as an anti-inflation weapon.

Germany

Long-term bond yields in Germany were very high throughout the period under review. In spite of very high yields immediately after the war and great progress from chaos and occupation to prosperous sovereignty, yields rose further as time passed. The net yield increase, however, from 1948 to 1969 was far less than in most countries. In the early years, there was no functioning capital market in Germany. Bonds were issued with very attractive tax advantages, no doubt because regular issues were unsalable. A really useful bond-yield series did not begin until 1956; had it been possible to extend it backward it might well have made a pattern more like the French with peak yields sometime in the period 1946–53.

We saw in Chapter II that during the period 1956 to 1968 short German rates swung widely in response to a vigorous contra-cyclical monetary policy, which succeeded in creating relative price stability and rapid growth. No such great cyclical swings were visible in the pattern of German bond yields. Yields were always very high, and market congestion led to a peak in 1966. Even when short rates came down sharply to around 3%, as in 1968, bond yields stayed close to their peaks.

Few German bond issues are long-term in the American sense of the word. They are usually at medium-term and this is often due to heavy sinking funds. Since in these recent years there was in Germany no balance of payments problem to require high yields, and since the government from time to time insulated its bond market from foreign investment, it seems probable that the very high German yields reflected in part the savings habits of the German people. Memories of two wars and two almost total inflations, and the fact of a divided country directly confronting the Communist world probably discourages the German flow of funds into really long-term bonds at reasonable rates. Exceptionally large capital requirements have also favored high rates.

The Netherlands

Long-term bond yields in the Netherlands followed a pattern during the period under review somewhat similar to the German pattern, but at lower levels. The over-all rise in yields was not as great as in the English-speaking markets nor was it as persistent. There were three peaks: 1951–52, 1957, and 1966–68. There were long periods of decline or stability in 1953–55 and 1957–63. Until 1961, Dutch yields had advanced only very moderately. However, after 1963 long Dutch yields advanced more sharply than any other long yields in these eight countries.

Belgium

In the late 1940's, long-term bond yields in Belgium were far higher than all other long yields except German. Instead of rising from low wartime levels, therefore, as most did, Belgian yields fluctuated in a narrow band until 1960. The series breaks in 1961, and the new series reveals much higher yields. A decline in the yields of the new series in 1961–63 was not matched elsewhere. Thereafter, a moderate rise in Belgian yields coincided with a rise in most other markets, but was much milder than in most. In general, Belgian yields have avoided extremes and have fluctuated much less than most other yields.

Switzerland

Long-term bond yields in Switzerland were relatively stable and never very high in the period under review. They declined from 1948 to 1953. They bulged to a modest peak in 1957, which also saw a peak in many other countries, including the United States and the United Kingdom. However, they came down in 1957–61, reaching a level slightly below that of 1946. This decline was concurrent with yield declines in most of the Common Market countries, but contrasted with sharp gains in yields in the English-speaking countries. From 1961 to 1967, Swiss yields rose steadily in keeping with trends in most of the other countries, but nevertheless they remained relatively low.

International Long-Term Yield Comparisons

During the stretch of years from 1946 to 1969, there were a few important changes in the relative levels of long-term bond yields among these eight markets, but they were not as many or as striking as the changes of rank among the eight short-term markets. In the long-term markets, countries tended to follow their yield traditions more than in the short-term markets.

The following summary shows that Germany remained a high-yield country throughout, in spite of a trend toward relatively very low short rates; and that the United States remained a low-yield country throughout, in spite of a trend toward medium short rates. The United Kingdom and Canada, however, both moved from relatively very low yields to relatively very high yields. On the other hand, Belgium, France, and Switzerland moved from high or medium bond yields to relatively low bond yields.

In Order of Rate		1946	1967	1968
1st:	Highest	Germany *	Germany	United Kingdom
2nd		Belgium	United Kingdom	Canada
3rd		France	Netherlands	Germany
4th		Switzerland	Canada	Netherlands
5th		Netherlands	Belgium	France
6th		Canada	France	Belgium
7th		United Kingdom	United States	United States
8th:	Lowest	United States	Switzerland	Switzerland

* Estimated.

Chart VII plots the history of the rank of each country's annual average of long bond yields just as Chart IV reported the history of the rank of each short yield.   Chart VIII and Table V show the yield spreads of each long-term yield above or below the simultaneous yields of U.S. government bonds, and the yield spread of U.S. government bonds below the average of the other seven yields.

United States

In spite of the fact that the U.S. short rate in this period of twenty-three years moved from the lowest to medium rank, Chart VII shows that the U.S. government long yields remained among the lowest of the eight countries.   This was in part because long U.S. government bonds have not been offered in large volume in the postwar period, partly because of the 4¼% rate ceiling and partly because of a policy of encouraging long-term private financing.   Though at times monetary policy has turned stringent and forced up short rates to relatively and absolutely high levels, debt-management policy has rarely acted vigorously to soak up investment funds by offering high-yielding long governments, and after 1965 it could not do so because of the rate ceiling.

It has been said that for the United States, prime corporate bond yields are more representative, because they have no rate ceiling and are offered on the market in volume almost continuously.   However, if we compare the yields of U.S. seasoned long-term corporate bonds in 1967 and 1968 with the government bond yields of the other seven countries, we shall see that the United States would still be fifth in rank, with only France, Belgium, and Switzerland lower.

Chart VIII and Table V show the spread between United States long government bond yields and the average of the long yields in the seven other countries.   It shows that the United States yields ranged from 58 basis points to 191 basis points below that average, and never approached it closely.   Furthermore, the spread was about the same in 1946 as it was in 1968.   The chart also shows the spread of prime U.S. seasoned corporate bond yields from the average of seven foreign government bond yields.   This spread was also always negative.   It followed a very similar course to the government spread until 1966, when it narrowed much more than the government spread and indeed almost vanished in 1968.

Between 1946 and 1951 the U.S. government spread rose from −91 to −191 in basis points (its maximum), when foreign yields, especially in France and the United Kingdom, rose much faster than U.S. yields. After the Accord of 1951, the spread narrowed as U.S. yields tended to rise faster than foreign yields.   The spread reached its minimum at

Chart VII
RELATIVE RANKINGS OF LONG-TERM INTEREST RATES - Annual Averages
(No. 1 equals highest yield, No. 2 the next highest yield, etc.)

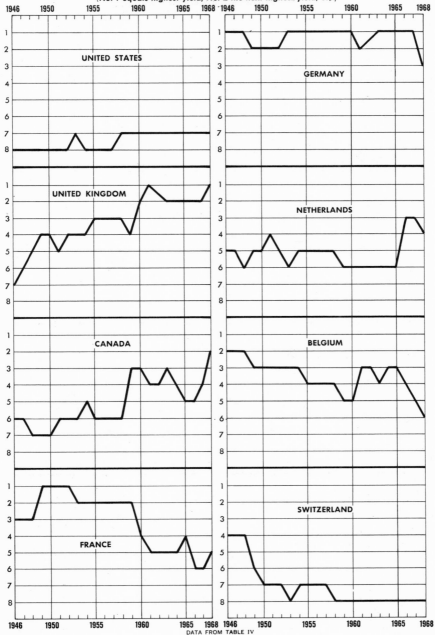

DATA FROM TABLE IV

Chart VIII
LONG-TERM INTEREST RATE SPREADS
(Annual Averages in Basis Points)

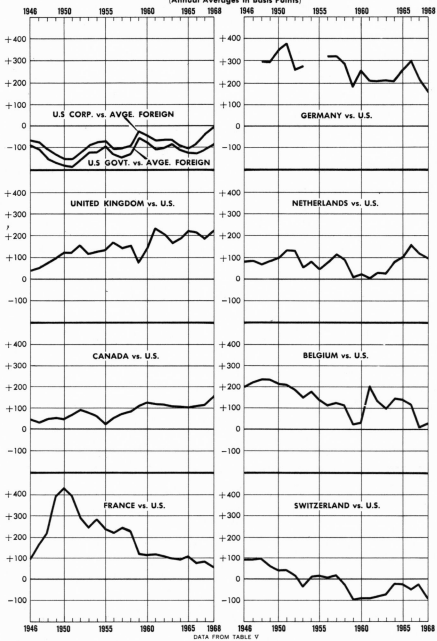

DATA FROM TABLE V

Table V

Foreign Long-Term Interest Rates vs. U.S. Governments
(Annual averages)
(Spread in basis points; rates from Table IV)

	U.S. Corp. vs. Avg. Foreign	U.S. Govt. vs. Avg. Foreign	U.K. vs. U.S.	Can- ada vs. U.S.	France vs. U.S.	Ger- many vs. U.S.	Nethlds. vs. U.S.	Bel- gium vs. U.S.	Switzld. vs. U.S.
1946	−65	−91	+41	+42	+98	−	+80	+198	+91
1947	−75	−107	+51	+31	+166	−	+81	+219	+92
1948	−110	−148	+77	+49	+218	+295	+65	+231	+98
1949	−136	−173	+99	+51	+397	+291	+81	+229	+63
1950	−154	−184	+123	+46	+420	+346	+96	+210	+35
1951	−158	−191	+122	+67	+397	+376	+131	+205	+38
1952	−125	−160	+155	+91	+292	+260	+127	+183	+16
1953	−90	−125	+116	+76	+249	+275	+51	+148	−37
1954	−78	−121	+122	+60	+284	−	+77	+173	+8
1955	−71	−97	+133	+24	+237	−	+42	+132	+13
1956	−108	−135	+166	+53	+220	+315	+76	+113	+3
1957	−101	−147	+151	+70	+245	+317	+111	+122	+17
1958	−94	−132	+155	+83	+225	+285	+89	+114	−24
1959	−28	−58	+75	+110	+120	+179	+5	+20	−99
1960	−45	−83	+139	+125	+114	+249	+19	+29	−92
1961	−70	−112	+230	+118	+117	+210	+1	+200	−94
1962	−64	−101	+208	+114	+108	+208	+26	+129	−83
1963	−66	−89	+168	+106	+97	+210	+22	+98	−76
1964	−92	−113	+187	+104	+93	+205	+77	+143	−18
1965	−106	−128	+220	+101	+106	+259	+100	+138	−26
1966	−83	−130	+214	+108	+74	+294	+158	+114	−50
1967	−40	−112	+188	+111	+81	+215	+115	+98	−24
1968	−9	−89	+220	+155	+59	+154	+95	+29	−89

−58 basis points in 1959, when United States yields reached a temporary peak, widened again to −130 basis points in 1965–66, and then declined to −89 basis points in 1968.

The swings in this spread over a twenty-three-year period when all yields were fluctuating dynamically were not large. The United States government yields have rarely strayed very far from a 100-basis-point spread below the foreign average.

United Kingdom

In the United Kingdom both long-term bond yields and short-term interest rates moved in the postwar period from almost the lowest to the highest, or almost the highest, among these eight countries. Chart

VII shows that the rise in rank for long yields began in the period 1946–49. From 1949 until 1959, United Kingdom long yields tended to remain at a medium rank, but from 1960 to 1968 they were either highest or second-highest.

Since United States yields throughout this twenty-three-year period rose less spectacularly, it followed that the spread of United Kingdom yields over United States yields, as pictured in Chart VIII, widened. The increase in the spread in favor of United Kingdom yields was, however, not a steady year-by-year trend. It almost all happened in two periods, i.e., 1946 to 1952, and 1959 to 1961. Since 1961, there has been no lasting change in the spread, which has zigzagged in a narrow band at a time when yields in both countries were tending upward by close to the same amounts.

Comparison of Chart VIII with Chart V shows that the spreads between the United States and the United Kingdom long-term markets after 1951 followed a pattern similar to the spreads between the two short-term markets, but the short-term spreads, like the short-term yields, swung over a much wider range. There has also been a trend since 1961 for the short-term spreads to narrow that is not discernible in the chart of the long-term spreads, since the latter have remained close to their peak.

Canada

Chart VII shows that the rank of Canadian long yields was relatively low in 1946–58, moved up sharply in 1959, and has been medium or close to the highest ever since. The rise in rank has been less than that of the United Kingdom, but is more impressive than that of any other country.

Compared with long United States yields, Canadian yields have always been higher, and the spread has tended to rise since 1955. It moved, in fact, from +24 basis points in 1955 to +155 basis points in 1968, as shown in Chart VIII. However, this spread of long yields has actually been stable for long periods of years and does not show the year-to-year shifts shown by the short-term rate spread pictured in Chart V. Every now and again Canadian short rates have been below United States short rates, but Canadian bond yields have never been below United States bond yields.

France

Chart VII suggests that long yields in France have lost rank since 1952 more persistently than those of any other country. French yields were highest in 1949–52 and almost the highest until 1960.   In that year, they came down to a medium rank, where they have remained ever since.

The yield spread of French long bond yields above those of the United States soared from 1946 to 1950, rising from +98 basis points to over +400 basis points.   This reflected a French inflationary crisis, when long yields in 1951 rose to their peak of 6.54%, while United States long yields were still around 2.50%.   Thus, French yields reached their peak long before yields peaked in any other country.   From 1951 right through to 1968, the spread in favor of French yields declined almost steadily until it became small.

Germany

Chart VII shows that German long-term yields have been the highest or near to the highest throughout these twenty-three years, while United States yields have remained close to the lowest.   Nevertheless, as Chart VIII shows, the yield spread in favor of German yields over United States yields has declined since 1957 from over 300 basis points to about 150 basis points.   (The German data before 1956 were not very meaningful.)   The spread in favor of German yields declined sharply in 1957–59, rose a bit in 1964–66, and declined sharply again in 1966–68.   German long yields, however, remained far above United States long yields throughout this period, whereas Chart V shows that German short yields have moved from over 400 basis points above United States short yields in 1951 to about 250 basis points below United States short yields in 1968, and have been below short-term United States yields most of the time since 1958.

The Netherlands

Long-term bond yields in the Netherlands were never among the lowest or among the highest during these twenty-three years.   Chart VII shows that from 1946 until 1966 they almost always ranked fifth- or sixth-highest among these eight yields.   After 1965, however, they rose in rank.

Chart VIII shows that these Netherlands yields have always been above these United States yields, the spread varying from nominal up to 158 basis points.   From 1957 until 1961, the spread tended to decline as United States yields rose faster than Netherlands yields.   From 1961 to 1966, the Netherlands yields rose faster than American yields, but thereafter American yields rose faster, and the spread came down to about its 1946 level.

Belgium

An abrupt break in the Belgian series in 1961 makes comparisons difficult. However, it is evident from Chart VII that the long-term Belgian yields were relatively very high at the beginning of this twenty-three-year period and tended to lose rank, ending the period not far from the lowest. Short-term Belgian rates similarly lost rank during this period. This means that short and long Belgian rates rose less than most other rates.

Chart VIII shows that long-term Belgian bond yields most of the time rose less than long-term United States bond yields. They were always above United States yields, but the spread came down from 231 basis points in 1948 to about 29 basis points in 1968.

Switzerland

The Swiss long-term bond yields were of about medium rank in 1946–48, and then came down abruptly, to become the lowest of all eight yields. This is about the same pattern of rank that Swiss short-term rates followed. Ever since 1958, the Swiss long-term yields were the lowest, and the United States long-term yields were second-lowest.

Chart VIII shows that Swiss long-bond yields started the period under review at 90 basis points or so above long United States yields. This spread came down sharply in 1953 to −37 basis points, when the Swiss yields fell briefly below United States yields and then rebounded. Again, in 1958, a negative spread appeared. It became as much as −99 basis points in 1959, and Swiss yields have remained below United States yields ever since.

A Comparison of Long-Term Rates with Short-Term Rates in Eight Countries

Complete yield curves, plotted from the yields of homogeneous securities with a wide variety of maturities, are not available for most of these eight countries. In this chapter, therefore, we analyze only the differentials between the two extremes of the curves, i.e., the long-term bond yields tabulated in Table IV, Chapter IV; and the short-term money-market rates tabulated in Table I, Chapter II. These long yields and their corresponding short rates are not always derived from completely comparable instruments, but since they are mostly government securities or prime money-market paper no important quality difference was likely to exist.

Table VI provides the long–short spreads based on the data in Tables I and IV. Chart IX pictures the history of these spreads since 1946. Again, since these are annual averages, the data fail to show large temporary deviations from the average.

There seems at present to be at least four theories that attempt to explain the relationship of long rates to short rates.*

(1) The classical "expectations theory" holds that a chain of expected future short-term rates, stretching years ahead, compared with present long-term rates, determines borrowers and lender preferences between short and long. Therefore, if it is thought (at the margin of the market) that future short rates will average below present long rates, investors will prefer longs, and borrowers will prefer shorts. However, if it is thought that future short rates will average above present long rates,

---

* See Chapter XI for a further analysis of the yield curve and for complete sets of United States curves.

Table VI

Long-Term vs. Short-Term Interest Rates
(Annual averages in basis points; rates from Tables I and IV)

	U.S.	U.K.	Can-ada	France	Ger-many	Nethlds.	Bel-gium	Switzld.
1946	+182	+207	+222	+186	–	+179	+359	+210
1947	+166	+223	+215	+234	–	+171	+336	+206
1948	+140	+265	+252	+253	+114	+179	+350	+192
1949	+121	+270	+234	+402	+76	+185	+337	+182
1950	+110	+288	+223	+409	+158	+188	+317	+171
1951	+102	+287	+244	+384	+31	+252	+337	+182
1952	+91	+153	+252	+175	+11	+287	+326	+179
1953	+99	+130	+199	+137	+209	+286	+315	+154
1954	+159	+192	+170	+179	–	+276	+302	+159
1955	+109	+42	+146	+205	–	+230	+281	+159
1956	+42	–31	+69	+210	+153	+146	+263	+166
1957	+19	0	+41	+57	+256	+52	+291	+184
1958	+159	+23	+201	–80	+335	+131	+316	+200
1959	+67	+133	+36	+120	+319	+227	+280	+207
1960	+108	+35	+194	+107	+196	+206	+151	+199
1961	+152	+92	+226	+142	+306	+279	+334	+193
1962	+117	+162	+109	+142	+437	+237	+311	+179
1963	+84	+185	+149	+99	+313	+228	+270	+149
1964	+61	+121	+145	+38	+291	+155	+224	+162
1965	+26	+12	+125	+109	+259	+138	+245	+132
1966	–19	+38	+74	+62	+219	+150	+191	+98
1967	+55	+65	+136	+89	+367	+142	+261	+189
1968	–6	–2	+46	+29	+405	+180	+274	+229

investors will prefer shorts, and borrowers will prefer longs. These preferences will create sharply positive yield curves if higher short rates are expected, and flat or negative yield curves if lower short rates are expected. In other words, the expectation of lower-than-present short rates will itself raise present short rates and lower present long rates as investors hasten to switch shorts into longs. The opposite will be true if higher short rates are expected: investors will hasten to switch longs into shorts. There are many modifications of this old theory, including one that combines it with a supposed permanent preference for shorts for purposes of liquidity. Because of this preference, long rates will tend to average well above the average of expected future short rates.

(2) A drastic modification of the old expectations theory holds that present maturity preferences and, therefore, the present yield curve, are

Chart IX
LONG-TERM VS. SHORT-TERM INTEREST RATES
(Annual Averages in Basis Points)

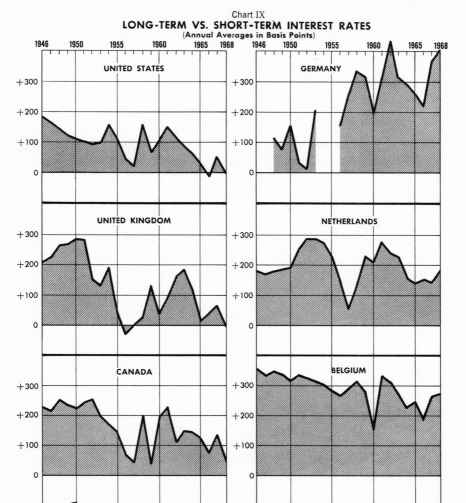

DATA FROM TABLE VI

created by expectations of medium-term future changes in long yields. If long yields are expected to rise, investors prefer shorts and have to be coaxed into longs by a large positive curve. If long yields are expected to decline, investors prefer longs and will not hold shorts except if they are coaxed by a large negative curve. This theory does not envision a precise conscious forecast of long yields, but assumes merely a general market consensus that present long yields are "unusually high," or "unusually low," or "about normal." Both of these expectations theories ignore the institutional structure, which forces many borrowers and many lenders to favor shorts or longs almost regardless of the shape of the curve.

(3) A third theory is based on a market structure that is heavily compartmentalized. It assumes, for exan.ple, that pension funds and life insurance companies will almost always buy longs, and that corporate treasurers with tax reserves will almost always buy shorts. It admits that there are some types of investors with a wide choice of maturity, but nevertheless it explains the curve largely by contrasting supply and demand factors in the different segments of the market. For example, if there is an unusually large volume of new short borrowing and not too much long borrowing, short rates will rise much more than long rates, and vice versa.

(4) A fourth theory goes even further than the third and looks upon short- and long-term bonds as fundamentally very different types of investment that are only accidentally linked by the artificial concept of the yield curve. It suggests that the chief reason short and long rates usually move in the same direction is that they are both independently influenced by the same economic environment. Short rates have much less inertia than long yields because their life is so brief. Therefore, short rates would naturally fluctuate in a wider range than long yields. Hence, in periods when both suffer protracted declines a positive curve is created, and in periods when both suffer protracted increases a negative curve is created.

It seems probable to us that the yield curves are created by the interaction of the several forces detailed above in theories 2, 3, and 4. The differentials in Chart IX for eight countries over a period of twenty-three years should help to illustrate the theoretical problem, but will not by themselves solve it.

Chart IX and Table VI show conclusively that positive curves (long yields above short yields) were almost but not quite universal throughout these twenty-three years and that the positive spreads were usually very large. This was a period when monetary policy was actively used by most countries as a stabilizer, and hence a period when the short end of the curve was determined by monetary policy. The long end of the curve, however, soon gained freedom from wartime pegs, and for most of these years was a good reflection of the free decisions of an army of investors and borrowers.

In the three English-speaking markets we see similar patterns of spreads. This pattern almost always produced wide positive spreads in periods of easy money, and smaller positive or negative spreads in periods of monetary stringency. This is the classical pattern. Very simply, if short and long rates almost always move in the same direction, and if short rates are almost always more volatile than long rates, then automatically the spread will move toward positive when rates decline and toward negative when rates rise. In these three countries, just this has happened most of the time—but not always. There have been important exceptions, when long and short rates moved in opposite directions (1939–46; 1967, 1968 in the United States), and occasions when long rates were as volatile or more volatile than short rates. A glance at the other markets in Chart IX will suggest that the exceptions were more frequent elsewhere. Indeed, it is hard to formulate any generalized theory that would fit all of these countries.

Thus in Germany, as long yields rose, short yields fell, and the higher the long yields the more the market seemed to "prefer" shorts. Again, in most of these European markets the curve ended the period under review just about as sharply positive as when it began in 1946, in spite of the enormous rise in rates. In Switzerland, there was very little variance in the long–short spread throughout. We must conclude that the familiar curve pattern of modest or negative spreads at high yields and big positive spreads at low yields was somehow a characteristic of the English-speaking markets, and not a universal phenomenon.

The United States

Chart IX shows that the yield-curve pattern during this period fell into the same three parts discussed in Chapters II and IV: (1) 1946–53, when all rates rose and the positive spread declined steadily; (2) 1953–61, when short rates swung vigorously and so did the long–short spread swing without a trend; (3) 1961–68, when short rates rose steadily and long rates rose less and belatedly, and the long–short spread declined persistently and finally became negative in 1966 (negative inter-year spreads also occurred in 1957, 1959, 1966, 1967, and 1968). The chart shows that actually the peak positive spreads that occurred in 1946, 1954, 1958, and 1961 were not very different and, therefore, the three dips that occurred in 1953, 1957, and 1959 could all be called cyclical developments. After 1961, a more lasting change in the spread occurred, as short rates rose more than long rates in every year but one.

United Kingdom

In the United Kingdom a similar decline in the long–short spread oc-curred, but with a very different time pattern. Indeed, the entire shift from large positive to small negative occurred in 1951–56, when the government was funding vigorously and attempting to exercise an anti-inflationary fiscal policy with the aid of extraordinarily high long yields. No great success was achieved, and thereafter short rates swung vigor-ously, while long rates continued to rise. A large positive spread was re-established by 1962–63. Thereafter, in the crisis years short rates rose sharply while long yields moved up much more gradually, so that the spread again became negative.

Canada

The history of the Canadian long–short spread was roughly similar to that of the United States spread, but with a few differences. The positive spread in Canada peaked in 1952, later than the peak in either the United States or the United Kingdom. It came down in 1952–57 very sharply, more like the United Kingdom pattern than the United States pattern. After 1957, it fluctuated very similarly to the United States spread, but the size of the swings were larger than in the United States, suggesting a more vigorous use of monetary policy. The decline in the spread from 1961 to 1968 was more irregular than in the United States, and did not become negative in terms of annual averages.

France

The long–short spread in France followed a unique pattern in these twenty-three years. This was largely because of the fact that French long-term rates reached their peak in 1951, when short-term rates re-mained very low; and French short-term rates reached their peak in 1958, when long rates declined. It is hard to read market expectations into either of these extreme curves. In the immediate postwar years there was in France, as in Germany, great difficulty in re-establishing any sort of a capital market in the face of a history of currency debase-ment and war. Indeed, in France the government employed bonds convertible into gold and into equities. Gradually, however, a market for straight debt was re-established and was greatly aided after 1958 by de Gaulle's stabilization of the economy.

The crisis of 1958, when de Gaulle assumed power, was characterized by an extraordinary rise in short rates as a result of a vigorous stabiliza-tion policy when the franc was devalued. Although long yields also rose during this crisis, they rose much less, and hence a negative spread was briefly created. Within a year, short rates declined and a positive spread was re-established, and has remained with only moderate variations ever since.

Germany

The long–short yield-spread chart for Germany probably should begin in 1956, because earlier data seem faulty. It is evident, however, that there was always a positive spread, and it was always very large and tended to rise irregularly from 1956 to its peak in 1962. German long rates were always among the highest; whereas, in contrast, German short rates swung in a wide band from relatively high to relatively low, but always far below long yields. As mentioned previously, two wars and two inflations have made it very difficult to sell really long-term bonds to the public, and German maturities were usually moderate and sinking funds large. Even so, heavy capital demands were difficult to finance, and long-term credit at times was in effect rationed. Again if this chart is to be interpreted in terms of expectations, then the higher the long yields have been in Germany, even up to 8%, the more the German public has expected still higher yields.

Netherlands

The Netherlands spread history also showed very little similarity to that of other countries. It was dominated by three very wide swings in short rates, while long rates rose more persistently. Peak positive spreads occurred around 1952 and 1961, but in 1957 there was a sharp decline in the spread; this was caused by a steep rise in short rates, which by 1961 was lost. Thereafter in the 1960's, the spread tended downward, because short rates were rising more than long. Except for 1957, the chart showed very little of the cyclical swings in the spread that dominated the English-speaking markets.

Belgium

The long–short spread in Belgium was on a high plateau throughout these twenty-three years. The plateau was interrupted only by two temporary dips, one in 1960 and one in 1966. The dip in 1960 was probably nothing but a statistical fluke based on a new higher-yielding series of long rates. The dip in 1966 was caused by a sharp rise in short-term rates not matched in the bond market. Thus, the Belgian spread, like Belgian rates, was relatively stable throughout and suggested nothing but differences in market structure or an effective opinion that long yields should usually be 250 basis points above short money-market rates of interest.

Switzerland

The Swiss spread was also very stable until 1961, but was much smaller than the Belgian spread. It dipped moderately from 1962 to 1966 and rose again, but in general showed less cyclicality than existed in the English-speaking markets. Swiss rates, both long and short, were relatively low throughout, but it is hard to discover until 1961 that changing rates had much effect on the spread, which was always fairly large. After 1961, when both long and short Swiss rates joined in the international trend upward, short rates moved up a bit more than long rates until 1966.

Part II — The United States

Short-Term Interest Rates

The short-term money market in the United States since World War II has been characterized by a rise in rates from extraordinarily low wartime levels to the highest levels since early in the 1920's. This prolonged rise from less than 1.00% to above 8.00%, constituted the longest period of rising rates in our economic history. The following table shows that the duration of this period of rising rates was almost double that of any other.

Periods of Rising Short-Term Interest Rates
(As measured by 4- to 6-month commercial paper rates)

| | Annual Average Yields | | Change in Basis Pts. | Duration in Years |
	Trough	Peak		
1831	6.12			
1836		18.00	+11.88	5
1843	4.41			
1848		15.10	+10.69	5
1858	4.81			
1873		10.27	+5.46	15
1895	2.83			
1907		6.66	+3.83	12
1916	3.84			
1920		7.50	+3.66	4
1941	0.54			
June 1969		8.00	+7.46	28

Data from the Federal Reserve and *A History of Interest Rates.*

The commercial-paper rate of 8.00%, reached in June 1969 was historically high, but nevertheless was below the monthly peak in 1920. In contrast, the peak long-term corporate bond yields reached in 1969, as illustrated by Chart I, were well above other peak yields back to 1815. The above table also suggests that in spite of recent very high short rates, something of a long-term secular downtrend in our short-term money-market rates has prevailed since the early nineteenth century. This is noticeable especially in the series of troughs.

Chart X,* "Short-Term Interest Rates—1945–1969," suggests that these postwar years can be usefully broken down into three distinctly different periods according to money-market behavior, as follows:

(1) *The period from 1945 to 1953* was characterized by steadily rising short-term interest rates. The nation first underwent demobilization and then the lifting of both price and interest-rate controls. It witnessed the deferred inflationary influences of World War II. Instead of the usual postwar depression, there was the Cold War and the nuclear arms race. Then came the stress, mobilization, and inflation of the Korean War. During this period, most money rates rose by more than 150 basis points to over 2.00%.

(2) *The period from 1953 to 1961* in contrast, was marked by a series of sharp interest-rate fluctuations superimposed on a slower trend toward higher rates. This was a period in which the Federal Reserve assumed a much more active role in offsetting three booms and three recessions. During this period the net rise in rates was at most 100 basis points, i.e., from 2% to 3%, but cyclical rate fluctuations were as great as 350 basis points.

(3) *In the period 1961 to 1969,* short-term interest rates rose almost as steadily as they had in the first period. At first it was a time of gradual, sustainable growth marked by an unusual degree of commodity-price stability. In spite of this stable economic environment, money rates rose steadily. Then in 1965 the burden of the boom and the Vietnam War led to overheating in the economy and renewed inflation. This caused a sharper rise in money rates to historically high levels. During this period of unprecedented uninterrupted prosperity, short-term rates rose from roughly the 3.00% level to the 6.00% level in 1968 and to more than 8.00% in 1969.

* NOTE: This chart and all other yield charts in this book are plotted vertically in ratio scale. This has the advantage of equalizing yield fluctuations in low yield areas with proportionate fluctuations in high yield areas. Thus, for example, a doubling of yield from, say, 1% to 2%, will occupy the same vertical space as a doubling from, say, 3% to 6%.

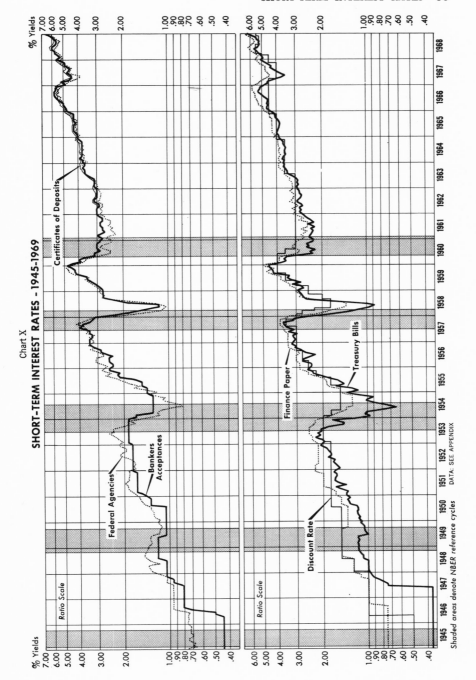

Chart X
SHORT-TERM INTEREST RATES – 1945-1969

Shaded areas denote NBER reference cycles   DATA: SEE APPENDIX

Chart XI

SHORT-TERM INTEREST RATES - 1945-1953

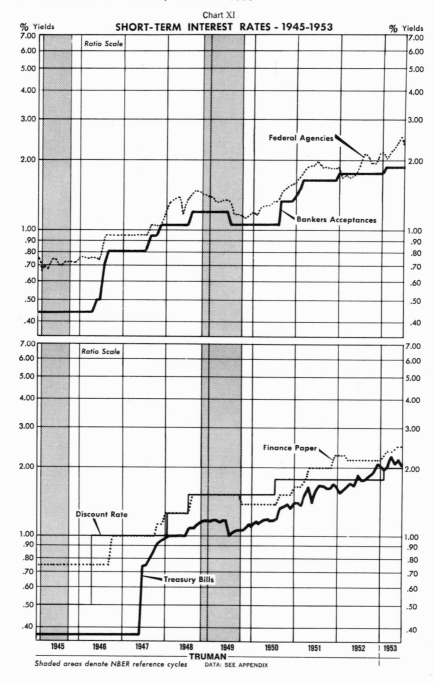

Federal Agencies

Bankers Acceptances

Ratio Scale

Finance Paper

Discount Rate

Treasury Bills

TRUMAN

Shaded areas denote NBER reference cycles   DATA: SEE APPENDIX

1945–53

Chart XI shows that in the year of demobilization immediately following the war, short-term money rates remained unchanged at nominal levels. In mid-1946, however, when price controls were lifted and commodity prices jumped upward, there was a sharp rise in bankers' acceptance rates from the wartime level of 0.44% to 0.81%; in finance-paper rates from 0.75% to 1.00%; and in federal agency rates from 0.75% to 0.95%. Treasury-bill rates did not participate in the increase, as the Federal Reserve continued to support this market at the pegged, 0.375%, level. Then in mid-1947 the Federal Reserve finally modified this support program, and Treasury bill rates rose to 0.75%. From that point until the beginning of the 1948–49 recession, most money rates rose by another 50 basis points.

A recession began in November, 1948, and continued until the following October, but short-term rates did not turn down until mid-1949. Rate declines even then were modest and brief, amounting to no more than 20 basis points and lasting no more than one year.

From late 1949 until the outbreak of the Korean War in June, 1950, Treasury-bill and agency rates rose gradually, while most other rates remained steady. The war, however, set off another sharp rise in all rates. They moved up again after March, 1951, when the Treasury and the Federal Reserve reached their "Accord," in which the Federal Reserve no longer pegged the long-term government market at 2.50%. Several rates rose further in 1952. In 1953 the economy boomed, and all rates rose again until the end of the Korean War at mid-year.

In 1953, in the early months of the Eisenhower administration, the Federal Reserve tightened money further. This resulted in what some economists considered the closest thing to a money-market crisis since 1933. Rates were by no means historically high, but the contrast of the new mildly restrictive monetary and fiscal policies with twenty years of easy money shocked market sentiment. At their peaks of 1953, three-month Treasury bills had risen 118 basis points from their 1949 recession lows, bankers' acceptances about 82 basis points, and finance paper 112 basis points.

A topping out of short-term rates in mid-1953 coincided with the end of the Korean War and the beginning of the 1953–54 recession. At their high rates of 1953, bills, agencies, and commercial paper all were about 180 basis points above their levels at the end of World War II, and acceptance rates were up 145 basis points. These were fourfold to sixfold rate increases.

Summary of Short-Term Rate Changes, 1945–53
(In basis points)

	Rates 1/45	1/45 to 1/47	1/47 to 1/48	1/48 to 6/49	6/49 to 8/50	8/50 to 2/52	2/52 to 6/53	Rates at 6/53 Peak	Net Change from 1/45 to 6/53
Treas. Bills 3 Mos.	0.37%	0	+60	+20	+1	+33	+67	2.18	+181
Bankers' Accept. 3 Mos.	0.44	+37	+25	+13	−13	+69	+13	1.88	+144
Agencies 3 Mos.	0.75	+20	+25	+12	−2	+38	+90	2.58	+183
Finan. Paper 3 Mos.	0.75	+25	+25	+25	−12	+87	+25	2.50	+175
Discount Rate	0.50	+50	0	+50	0	+25	+25	2.00	+150

1953–61

The decline in short-term rates during the recession of 1953–54, as shown in Chart XII, ranged from 63 basis points for bankers' acceptances to 178 basis points for agencies. Treasury bills lost 150 basis points whereas, in contrast, the Federal Reserve cut the discount rate twice, for a total of only 50 basis points. Short-term interest-rate levels dropped from 2–½% to ¾–1¼%. Just as the Federal Reserve's refusal to cut the discount rate in the 1948–49 recession helped then to minimize rate declines in short-term instruments, its more active easy-money policy in the 1953–54 recession undoubtedly contributed to the far greater declines in short-term rates.

The excess profits tax ran out at the end of 1953, and shortly thereafter stock prices began to rise. Short-term rates, however, continued to decline in early 1954, bottoming out about a month or so before the recession ended in August. At their low rates most instruments had given up over a half of their gross postwar rate advance. Agencies were only about 15 basis points above their wartime rate lows whereas, at the other extreme, bankers' acceptances were still about 80 basis points above their 1945–46 lows.

In the three-year business-recovery period that began in the summer of 1954, the advance in commodity prices was moderate. Short-term interest rates, however, rose sharply and by June, 1955, the rates on most short-term obligations were back at their previous highs of 1953. In fact, the major part of the cyclical rate rise took place in 1955.

Stock prices rose more in 1954 than they had in the previous ten years. Not even the raising of margin requirements from 50% to 70% in the first half of 1955 appreciably dampened speculation. In April of 1955, the Federal Reserve raised the discount rate from 1½% to 1¾% in what was the first of six quarter-point increases in a period of 16 months. From August, 1956, the discount rate remained at the 3% level for exactly one year, but in August, 1957, the Federal Reserve, feeling that the economy was still advancing too rapidly, acted dramatically by boosting the discount rate to 3½%. It soon became apparent, however, that the economy had already topped out, and by November the discount rate was back at 3% again.

By the end of the business recovery in July, 1957, most short-term interest rates were at about the 3½%–4% level, or about 100 to 200 basis points above their highs of 1953, and 210 to 260 basis points above their lows of 1954. For most short-term instruments the rise in rates during this recovery period was about twice the magnitude of the declines during the previous recession.

Chart XII

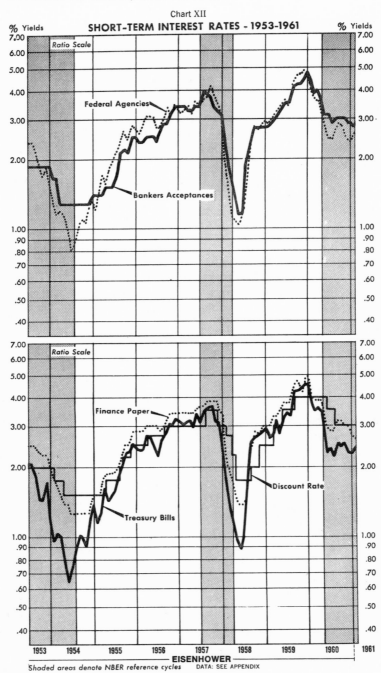

% Yields   **SHORT-TERM INTEREST RATES - 1953-1961**   % Yields

Federal Agencies

Bankers Acceptances

Ratio Scale

Finance Paper

Treasury Bills

Discount Rate

1953   1954   1955   1956   1957   1958   1959   1960   1961

EISENHOWER

Shaded areas denote NBER reference cycles   DATA: SEE APPENDIX

Summary of Short-Term Rate Changes, 1953 to 1961

	Rates 6/53	6/53 to Summer '54	Summer '54 to Fall '57	Fall '57 to 6/58	6/58 to 1/60	1/60 to 1/61	Rates 1/61 Trough	Net Change from 6/53
Treas. Bills 3 Mos.	2.18%	−154	+301	−276	+363	−224	2.28%	+10
Bankers' Accept. 3 Mos.	1.88	−63	+275	−287	+375	−213	2.75	+87
Agencies 3 Mos.	2.58	−178	+341	−318	+379	−247	2.35	−23
Finan. Paper 3 Mos.	2.50	−125	+263	−250	+362	−237	2.63	+13
Discount Rate	2.00	−50	+150	−125	+225	−100	3.00	+100

The 1957–58 recession adjustment was a sharp one. In less than a year from October, 1957, most short-term rates declined by almost as much as they had gained in the three previous years. Many rates dropped from about the 4% level to the 1% to 1½% level. Most short-term yields at their 1958 recession lows were only about 25 basis points above their 1954 lows. The Federal Reserve during this recession period cut the discount rate four times for a total of 175 basis points.

Following the successful Sputnik launching by the Russians in the fall of 1957, and a 20% lowering in the margin rate to 50% at the end of the year, stock prices once again rose sharply and steadily. The last cut in the discount rate in April, 1958, coincided with the end of the recession. In the subsequent short, sharp two-year business recovery, money rates climbed even more than they had during the previous three-year recovery. Rate levels rose from 1%–2% to as much as 5%, or about 1% above the previous highs of 1957.

The Federal Reserve moved to restraint more quickly and intensively in 1958–59 than in the previous recoveries. From September, 1958, to September, 1959, the discount rate was increased five times, for a total of 225 basis points. Perhaps because of this prompt, vigorous action, the topping-out of money rates in early 1960 did not occur after the business downturn had begun, but instead several months before it had begun.

The economic downturn that started in May, 1960, was the third recession period of the Eisenhower administration. Its severity, measured in terms of money-rate declines, was less than that of the 1957–58 recession. The sizes of the rate declines were again unusually uniform and brought prevailing rate levels down from 5% to 2½%–3%. The discount rate was cut only twice, for a total of 100 basis points. At their lows of January, 1961, all short-term rates except agencies' were higher than they were at their highs in 1953.

1961–69

Following the 1960–61 recession, the economy entered into the longest uninterrupted period of prosperity in our nation's history. Chart XIII shows that money rates started to rise promptly in mid-1961, were flat in 1962, rose sharply in 1963, flattened again in 1964, and rose sharply after the Vietnam War buildup in late 1965. Rates soared in 1966, continuing to rise even after the credit crunch in August, 1966, but turned down in late 1966 and declined significantly for six months. In late 1967 and 1968, they rose once again and reached very high levels at mid-year. Following the passage of the new surtax in 1968, money rates declined

Chart XIII

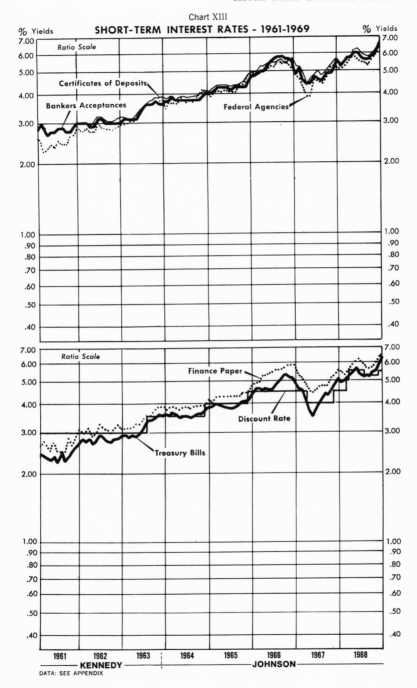

% Yields **SHORT-TERM INTEREST RATES - 1961-1969** % Yields

Ratio Scale

Certificates of Deposits

Bankers Acceptances

Federal Agencies

Ratio Scale

Finance Paper

Discount Rate

Treasury Bills

1961 1962 1963 1964 1965 1966 1967 1968

KENNEDY ─────────────── JOHNSON ───────────

DATA: SEE APPENDIX

briefly and moderately, and then rose sharply to new highs in early 1969. As we go to press in June, they are still rising.

In the period from early 1961 to the first half of 1965, the country benefited from steady economic growth and steady commodity prices. The table below shows that most short-term rates were in the 2¼%–¾% range as the 1961 recovery began. Two years later, by the spring of 1963, they had risen to the 2¾%–3¼% range, while the discount rate had remained steady at 3.00%.

During 1963 the economy began to anticipate the probable effects of the $11 billion tax cut. Short-term rates rose significantly from 3% to over 3½% until January, 1964, when the first stage of the tax reduction went into effect. During 1964, money rates fluctuated within a very narrow range. This was the first full year of the Johnson administration. Some small increases in rates occurred in late 1964 and early 1965, but the market then steadied until the start of the Vietnam buildup later in the year. In the period from the spring of 1963 to August, 1965, short-term rates rose by another 100 basis points on average, or about twice the magnitude of the advance from 1961 to 1963. The discount rate was raised twice during this period, for a total of 100 basis points, once in July, 1963, and again in November, 1964. It then stood at 4%. Balance-of-payments problems, no doubt, greatly influenced the Federal Reserve's decisions to raise the discount rate during this period.

In late 1965 the buildup in military expenditures for Vietnam put pressure on an already prospering economy, which could not be supported without imbalances. In the twelve months after mid-1965, industrial production advanced sharply. Government expenditures rose from $128 billion in 1965 to $151 billion in 1966. The demand for capital expanded rapidly, monetary policy became increasingly restrictive and, as a result, short-term money rates soared, rising above long-term bond yields. In August of 1966 short-term rates rose to above 5.50%. This was a very severe credit squeeze, and was dubbed the "crunch." The disrupting effects of the rechanneled money-flows during this period were everywhere in evidence. The phenomenon of "disintermediation" became widespread, that is, the process by which individual savings are redirected from institutional intermediaries to direct market investments at higher yields. The squeeze on savings institutions cut savings flows at these institutions to a mere trickle. In addition, a substantial increase in fixed-interest policy loans at life insurance companies forced these institutions to curtail new investments. As a result, the housing industry, unable to get sufficient funds from traditional sources, had to reduce its activities drastically. Commercial banks, effectively excluded from the CD market because of a rate ceiling of 5.50%, put added pressure on short-term rates by selling secondary reserves in order to satisfy a burgeoning loan demand and to pay off maturing CD's.

At their peaks in the fall of 1966, short-term rates at 5¼%–5¾% were 150 to 175 basis points higher than they had been a year earlier. The discount rate, however, was only increased 50 basis points in 1965 and not at all in 1966. Instead, the Federal Reserve chose to use a more qualitative approach. Among other things, it combined a campaign of urging banks to make only productive loans with a more discriminating policy at the discount window.

The breaking effects of the August, 1966 crunch on the economy began to be felt by late 1966. In early 1967, fears of a recession, along with a desire to strengthen the British pound and to revive the housing industry, paved the way for an easy monetary posture. Three other factors also operated in early 1967 to reduce money rates substantially. The first was a relative scarcity of Treasury bills and short-term governments because of refunding operations. The second was the increased short-term investment stemming from the repatriation of funds from abroad by United States corporations and banks. Finally, corporations seized upon the increased availability of funds to rebuild their liquidity, which had been so drastically reduced during the crunch. As a result, some of the proceeds from a record volume of new long-term corporate bond issues were invested in the short-term market as well as being used to repay bank loans and to finance growth.

In early 1967 short-term rates declined sharply until June, at which point most money rates were at their pre-Vietnam levels of 3½%–4½%. The Federal Reserve, however, refrained from lowering the discount rate until April, when it lowered the rate by 50 basis points to 4%. During this period of declining short-term rates in the first half of 1967, long-term bond yields were moving up to record levels.

In January of 1967, President Johnson expressed the urgent need for a surtax to help bring the federal budget into balance. The Federal Reserve, nevertheless, elected to keep monetary conditions easy. However, in spite of monetary ease, money rates in the last half of 1967 again rose sharply. At that time an international monetary crisis exerted a greater adverse influence on the short-term market than did domestic events. In November of 1967, following the devaluation of the pound and the raising of the British bank rate to a crisis level of 8%, the Federal Reserve increased the discount rate by ½%. The discount rate was twice again raised by ½% in early 1968, when bearish sentiment caused some short-term rates to climb to above 6%, a new postwar record. By the end of May, 1968, Treasury-bill rates had risen in a year's time by more than 220 basis points.

Summary of Short-Term Rate Changes, 1961–69
(In basis points)

	Rates Early 1961	Early '61 to 3/63	3/63 to 8/65	8/65 to Fall '66	Fall '66 to 6/67	6/67 to 6/68	6/68 to 10/68	10/68 to 1/69	Rates 1/1/69	Net Change from Early 1961	Net Change from 1945
Treas. Bills 3 Mos.	2.28%	+60	+92	+154	−187	+221	−52	+109	6.25%	+397	+588
Bankers' Accept. 3 Mos.	2.75	+38	+100	+175	−150	+162	−37	+87	6.50	+375	+606
Agencies 3 Mos.	2.35	+63	+109	+168	−187	+206	−53	+115	6.56	+421	+581
Fin. Paper 3 Mos.	2.63	+50	+112	+163	−150	+175	−50	+75	6.38	+375	+563
CD's 3 Mos.	–	–	+134	+157	−150	+185	−60	+105	6.65	+371*	
Discount Rate	3.00	–	+100	+50	−50	+150	−25	+25	5.50	+250	+500

* Early 1962.

Statements by key congressmen in late May, 1968, indicating that the surtax would be passed, caused short-term rates to turn down once again. The surtax was finally passed and put into effect in July. However, the continued strength in the economy in the last half of 1968 made it plain that the long-sought fiscal measure would not be sufficient to slow it down. As a result, the decline in short-term rates in mid-1968 was brief and was reversed in September, and by year-end they were at new highs. Finally, in December 1968, the Federal Reserve adopted a restrictive policy that promised to put great pressure on the banking system. By June of 1969 it seemed that another crunch had developed. Bill rates rose to 6.80%, most other market rates rose above 8%.* Federal funds traded at 10% and Euro-dollars at 13%. These were traditional crisis rates.

* For interest rates in early 1969, see Appendix.

VIII

Short-Term Yield Spreads

The interest-rate trends discussed in the previous chapter resulted in frequent changes in the yield relationships among these various short-term instruments. In this chapter, yield relationships will be described and measured in terms of yield differentials, called yield spreads, between the yield of each instrument and the simultaneous yield of United States Treasury bills of the same maturity. All of the data are for three months' maturity. Since the Treasury bill yields used throughout are on the bid side and all other yields are on the offer side, the spread of any instrument at any one point in time approximates the yield gain to a tax-free investor from switching out of Treasury bills into that instrument.*

Chart XIV summarizes the four most important spreads in terms of annual averages. It can be seen that bankers'-acceptance spreads fluctuated more than other spreads. Acceptance, and finance spreads were especially wide during recent recession periods, whereas agency spreads, on the other hand, tended to widen in periods of prosperity and, in fact, often acted in an opposite manner to the other spreads.

Charts XVI, XVII, XVIII, and XIX show these same spreads in terms of monthly averages. They show that the spreads in most periods fluctuated within fairly well defined ranges, regardless of the underlying yield

---

* Bills, acceptances and finance-paper yields are reported on a discount basis and are, therefore, not precisely comparable with agencies and CD's, which are on a bond yield basis. The difference for 3-months' maturity adds 2 basis points to 20 basis points to discount yields.

Chart XIV
SHORT-TERM SPREADS FROM BILLS
(Annual Averages)

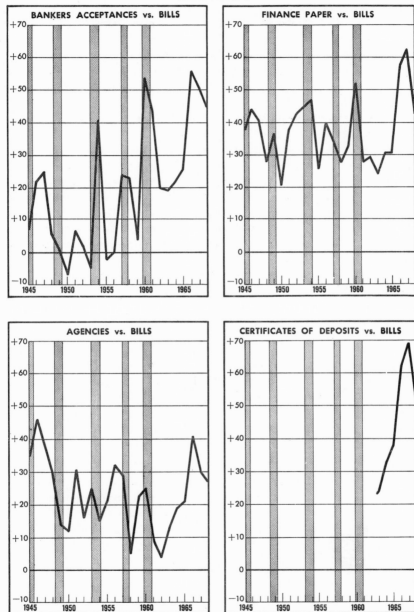

Shaded areas denote NBER Reference Cycles.
DATA: SALOMON BROTHERS & HUTZLER, An Analytical Record of Yields and Yield Spreads.

levels involved. In other words, it was the basis-point bonus that seemed to determine preferences, not the percentage bonus.*

No one type of short-term instrument always yielded the most or the least. In Table VII the annual averages of the yields of each type of instrument are ranked; i.e.: 1 = highest yield; 2 = second-highest, etc. There were some important shifts in rank over these years, as follows:

Finance paper and agencies alternated for highest yield in the immediate postwar years, but in the 1950's finance paper always yielded the most. However, in the 1960's, when CD's began to be traded, CD's soon yielded the most; and finance paper, which grew in popularity, occupied second, and finally third rank.

Agencies in the early postwar years often yielded more than any of the other instruments, but as time passed they grew in popularity and lost rank, finally yielding very little more than Treasury bills.

Acceptances in the early years occupied a low rank, yielding very little more than Treasury bills, and often less. In the 1950's, however, there were several years when acceptance yields were higher than most other yields, and they ended this period yielding more than finance paper.

CD's, after they appeared, almost always yielded more than all other instruments.

3-Month Treasury Bills vs. the Discount Rate

Before examining the specific yield spreads of these market instruments over Treasury bills, it may be useful to analyze the yields of bills themselves in relation to the discount rate. Chart XV shows that the discount rate has generally been above the bill rate. However, the positive spread in favor of the discount rate has usually been less than 50 basis points and often has been nominal. The chart also shows that in the three recessions of the Eisenhower administration, bill rates were allowed to decline unusually far below the discount rate, providing a

---

* Most of the yield-spread charts and tables in this book are expressed in basis points. A valid alternative method of presenting the history of a spread is in percentages of the base yield (see Chart XXV and Table XXI). If percentage calculations were employed, they would tend to enlarge the peak spreads of the 1950's relative to 1966–68 spreads, because the earlier spreads were on a lower yield base. We have employed the basis-point technique here (except for municipals) partly because it is simpler, but more importantly because it seems to present a truer picture of the meaning of these spreads to investors. The spread is an inducement for downgrading quality, or incurring call risk, or any other disability. Therefore, it is an absolute amount related to principal; there is no convincing reason why it must rise and fall with the level of interest rates.

Table VII

Relative Rank of Short Yields
(Annual averages)

3 Months	'46	'47	'48	'49	'50	'51	'52	'53	'54	'55	'56	'57	'58	'59	'60	'61	'62	'63	'64	'65	'66	'67	'68
CD's	–	–	–	–	–	–	–	–	–	–	–	–	–	–	–	–	–	2	1	1	1	1	1
Finan. Paper	2	1	2	1	1	1	1	1	1	1	1	1	1	1	1	2	1	1	2	2	2	2	3
Agencies	1	2	1	2	2	2	2	2	3	2	2	2	3	2	3	3	3	4	4	4	4	3	4
Acceptances	3	3	3	3	4	3	3	4	2	3	3	3	2	3	2	1	2	3	3	3	3	4	2
Bills	4	4	4	4	3	4	4	3	4	3	4	4	4	4	4	4	4	5	5	5	5	5	5

Data from Appendix.

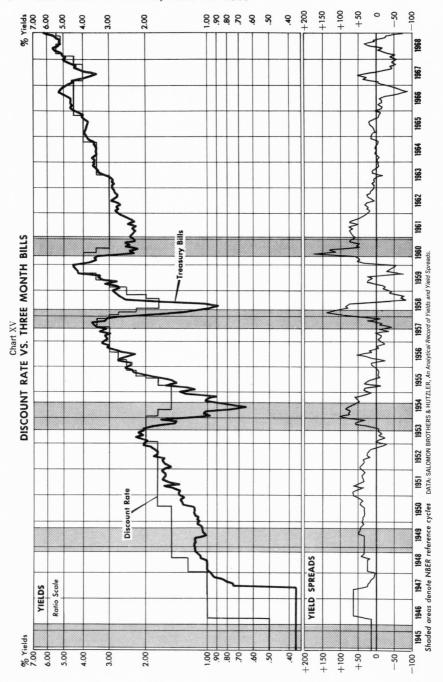

Chart XV

DISCOUNT RATE VS. THREE MONTH BILLS

YIELDS
Ratio Scale

Treasury Bills

Discount Rate

YIELD SPREADS

DATA: SALOMON BROTHERS & HUTZLER, An Analytical Record of Yields and Yield Spreads.

Shaded areas denote NBER reference cycles

positive spread of as much as 100 to 173 basis points in favor of the discount rate. In contrast, toward the end of recovery periods in the 1950's, the bill rate tended to rise above the discount rate, resulting in a negative yield spread of as much as 80 basis points. In boom periods, in 1966 and again in 1968, the bill rate also rose far above the discount rate.

Chart XV also shows that there were three distinct patterns for this spread, and these coincide with the three time periods chosen for analysis in Chapter VII. During the first period, 1945–53, the discount rate was normally kept at least 25 basis points above the rising bill rate. During the second period, from 1953 to 1961, there were great zigzag fluctuations in the spread; from +173 basis points to −80 basis points. From 1961 until 1966, the discount rate was usually kept close to the rising bill rate. Since late 1965, however, there have been wide swings again, and periods of large negative spreads when the bill rate was far above the discount rate.

3-Month Federal Agencies vs. 3-Month Treasury Bills

The yield spreads of agencies over bills have fluctuated within a moderate range, usually from 0 to +40 basis points and occasionally +50 basis points or a little higher, as shown in Chart XVI. The extreme wide positive spreads came most often in the mid-part of recovery periods, and the spreads tended to decline and indeed to vanish in recessions. This positive cyclical correlation is the opposite to that of most other yield spreads against bills.

In periods of sharply declining bill rates, which were usually recessions, the rates on most other short-term instruments declined less than bills. Agencies, however, followed closely the rate movements of bills during these periods, and often agency rates declined even faster. Similarly, when bill rates were rising, agency rates often rose even faster.

With the approach of the 1966 crunch period, the positive agency–bill spreads widened sharply, as did most other spreads. The heavy volume of agency flotations during this period, no doubt, contributed to the widening of this spread. In 1968, even though bill yields were higher on average than they were in 1966, the relatively heavier volume of bills as opposed to less agencies reduced the spread.

3-Month Bankers Acceptances vs. 3-Month Treasury Bills

The yield spreads of bankers' acceptances from Treasury bills have fluctuated considerably more widely than the agency–bill yield spreads

Chart XVI

AGENCIES VS. THREE MONTH BILLS

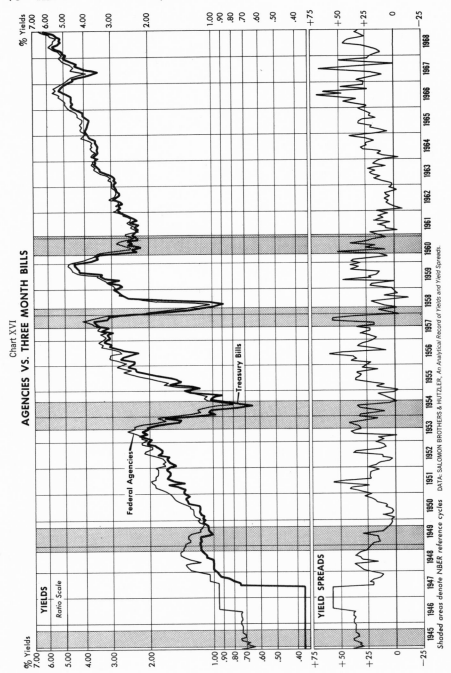

YIELDS

Ratio Scale

Federal Agencies

Treasury Bills

YIELD SPREADS

DATA: SALOMON BROTHERS & HUTZLER, An Analytical Record of Yields and Yield Spreads.

Shaded areas denote NBER reference cycles

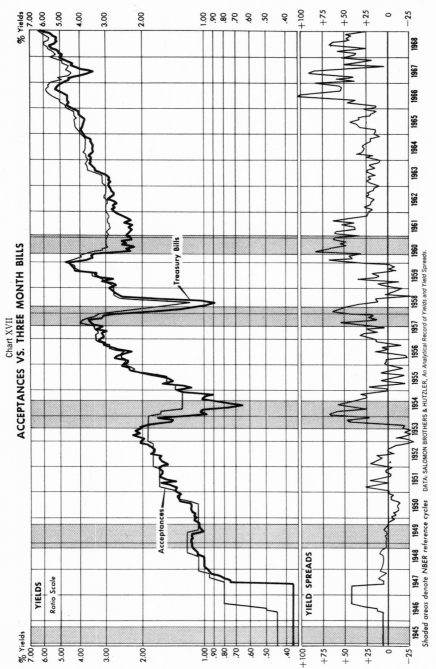

Chart XVII
ACCEPTANCES VS. THREE MONTH BILLS

YIELDS
Ratio Scale

Treasury Bills

Acceptances

YIELD SPREADS

Shaded areas denote NBER reference cycles   DATA: SALOMON BROTHERS & HUTZLER, An Analytical Record of Yields and Yield Spreads.

just discussed. In the 1950's the acceptance yield spreads shown in Chart XVII were in prosperous times typically to be found in the −25 to +25 basis-point range. During the economic recovery periods, the rise in bankers' acceptance rates often lagged behind the rise in bill rates, causing the yield spreads to become negative. In contrast, during recessions, the bill rates tended to drop more precipitously than rates on bankers' acceptances, and the spread in favor of acceptances tended to widen dramatically.

The pattern of these spreads changed in the 1960's, and positive spreads were the rule. The marked widening of the yield spread in 1966–67 occurred at a time when the economy was expanding vigorously. Pressures in the private sector of the money market were intense, sending rates on all private credit instruments sharply above the yields of all treasuries. Treasury-bill rates, in particular, lagged and consequently the yield spread widened sharply. There was some narrowing in late 1966, and again in late 1967.

The higher-than-average spreads that have prevailed in recent years were probably caused by the sharp growth in the volume of short-term private credit instruments. Also, money managers became much more flexible and, in the presence of a large array of outlets, were able to insist on a good positive spread from bills.

3-Month Finance Paper vs. 3-Month Treasury Bills

The yield spreads of finance-paper rates over Treasury-bill rates fluctuated with greater frequency than bankers'-acceptance spreads and at a higher positive average level. There were fewer negative spreads.

Chart XVIII shows that the positive finance-paper spreads widened markedly not only in recession periods, but also for brief periods in prosperous years, such as in 1951, 1956, 1959, and 1966. While a faint suggestion of this same pattern was also discernible in bankers' acceptance spreads, the mid-recovery widenings were much more pronounced for finance paper.

In the first part of the recovery periods in the 1950's there was a tendency for finance-paper rates to rise at first much more slowly than bill rates, but later to rise much faster than bill rates. This pattern resulted first in narrowing the yield spread to about zero, and then in widening it. In the last half of these recovery periods, bill rates once again tended to advance faster than finance-paper rates, and this resulted in another narrowing of spreads.

At the beginnings of recession periods, bill rates turned down earlier and more sharply than finance-paper rates and, hence, the spreads

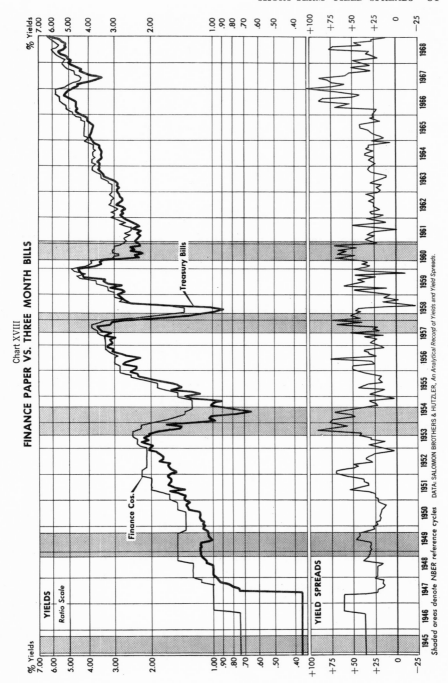

Chart XVIII
FINANCE PAPER VS. THREE MONTH BILLS

YIELDS
Ratio Scale

Treasury Bills

Finance Cos.

YIELD SPREADS

Shaded areas denote NBER reference cycles   DATA: SALOMON BROTHERS & HUTZLER, *An Analytical Record of Yields and Yield Spreads.*

widened significantly. Thus, in each cycle there tended to be two periods of widening and two periods of narrowing spreads, with the narrowest spreads generally coming at the start of the recovery, and the widest spreads appearing early in the recession.

In the years of gradually rising short-term rates from 1961 to late 1965, the finance-paper spread remained unusually stable at about 25 basis points. With the approach of the credit crunch in 1966, however, finance-paper rates rose at a much faster pace than bill rates and, consequently, their spreads widened to 75 and even 100 basis points.

During early 1967, finance-paper rates declined more than bill rates and, thus their spreads declined. Moreover, in the fall of 1967, bill rates recovered faster than finance-paper rates, and the yield spread narrowed further.

During early 1968, the finance-paper spread widened at mid-year, when short-term rates peaked and finance rates ran up faster than bill rates. Six months later at year-end, when bill rates set new post-1920 record highs, finance rates lagged and the yield spread narrowed sharply.

3-Month Certificates of Deposit vs. 3-month Treasury Bills

The relatively brief history of the yield spreads of secondary market prime certificates of deposit over Treasury bills, as shown in Chart XIX, has been highly dynamic. Within a very few years, it ranged from +25 basis points up to +100 and back to +25 basis points. The tremendous growth in the amount of outstanding CD's since the early 1960's, and their great importance to the commercial banking system as a source of funds have made CD rates and their spreads from other short-term instruments one of the most carefully watched indicators in the money market.

When CD's were initially offered in the early 1960's, they yielded about the same as finance paper. Hence, the yield spreads in Chart XIX closely paralleled the spreads in Chart XVIII during 1962, 1963, and early 1964. However, as the supply of CD's grew, they began to yield more than finance paper. CD rates, however, were more volatile, and they declined more than finance-paper rates in periods of lower rates during 1967 and 1968; consequently, at such times, finance paper yielded more than CD's.

In the first half of 1966, bill rates benefited by a strong seasonal position, while other short-term rates, including CD's, advanced rapidly. As a result, the yield spreads of secondary market prime CD's over bills widened sharply at mid-year, 1966; in the second half, bill rates soared and the spread narrowed. During early 1967, this spread widened once

Chart XIX

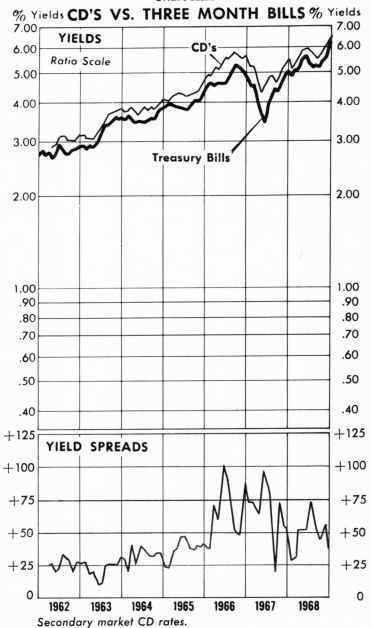

% Yields **CD'S VS. THREE MONTH BILLS** % Yields

Secondary market CD rates.

DATA: SALOMON BROTHERS & HUTZLER, *An Analytical Record of Yields and Yield Spreads.*

again for seasonal reasons. In the fall of 1967, when bill rates rose by 100 basis points in three months, the CD spread narrowed dramatically. In 1968 the spread again rose at mid-year, but at the close the spread declined; it was narrow by recent standards, but still a considerably wider spread than offered by competing private instruments.

The rates used here are for prime CD's in the secondary market, not in the new-issue market. At times when the level of market rates was above the maximum rates allowed by law on new CD's, such as in late 1966, and again in early 1968 and at the close of 1968, there were few, if any, new CD's being issued. This probably restrained the rise in yields and also the rise in spreads.

Long-Term Bond Yields

The large rise in long-term bond yields in the United States since 1946 has much more historical significance than the simultaneous rise in short-term interest rates described in Chapter VII. This is in part because American short-term interest rates before 1930 were sometimes higher than the peak rates achieved recently, while recent long-term prime bond yields were far above earlier peaks of this century, as Chart I showed. In fact, bond yields have risen to levels rarely seen before in the history of this country, and then only during crises such as the Civil War and the War of 1812. Furthermore, since long-term bond yields represent a charge over a long period of years, they have much more long-range economic significance than short rates, which may be effective only for a few weeks or months.

In order to put the bear bond market of 1946–69 into historical context, Table VIII below measures the five great secular fluctuations in the bond market since the days of Alexander Hamilton. These were pictured in Chart I. It will be seen that the rise in yields from 1946 into 1969 was much larger than that which occurred in any of the preceding bear bond markets; it amounted to 480 basis points for prime seasoned corporate bonds, which means that yields went up by 196% of the low starting yield. Furthermore, the rise in yields from 1946 into 1969 substantially exceeded the preceding decline in yields which began in 1920 and culminated in 1946. Table VIII also shows that the duration of this bear market to date was not exceptional, having been almost matched twice before. In fact, its duration was exceeded by both of the two preceding bull bond markets. The table also shows conclusively that the alternation of bull and bear bond markets in the United

Table VIII

Secular Trends of High-Grade Bond Yields

	Annual Average Yields			Change		Dura-tion in Years
	Peak, %	Trough, %	Peak, %	In Basis Points	In %	
Governments						
1798	7.56					
1810		5.82		−174	−23	12
1814			7.64	+182	+31	4
				+8		16
1814	7.64					
1824		4.25		−339	−44	10
1842			6.07	+182	+43	18
				−157		28
1842	6.07					
1853		4.02		−205	−34	11
1861			6.45	+243	+61	8
				+38		19
1861	6.45					
Corporates:						
1899		3.20		−325	−49	38
1920			5.27	+207	+65	21
				−118		59
1920	5.27					
1946		2.45		−282	−54	26
1969?			7.25	+480	+196	23
				+198		49

Source: *A History of Interest Rates,* seasoned prime corporates.

States has never been rhythmical in the sense of repetitive similar time spans or repetitive similar sizes of fluctuation.

The Environment

The economic and political environment during the 1946–69 bear bond market was far different from that of all earlier postwar periods. It was different partly because of the Cold War, with its occasional heating, partly because of the aftereffects of the techniques used to finance World

War II, partly because of technological and social change, and partly because of the new role of leadership the United States played in a nearer, smaller world.

No traditional postwar depression occurred, although one was widely expected at least until 1955. There were four small recessions, which began in 1948, 1953, 1957, and 1960, and in each case they were promptly and effectively cushioned by monetary and fiscal policy and by underlying growth trends. After 1961 there was sustained economic growth, and then an ominous inflationary boom. Economic growth and prosperity featured the entire postwar period, both in America and in the majority of European countries.

Some students of bond yields will be content to attribute their sustained rise during these twenty-three years merely to economic growth and prosperity. Others, however, will recall that on a number of occasions in the past sustained peacetime growth and prosperity occurred without any significant rise in bond yields; these observers may tend to ascribe the recent periods of sharp yield increase to frequent bouts with inflation usually associated with wars, to the sustained inflationary effect of the Cold War, and perhaps to the policy of maximum economic growth and social expenditure that developed during the early 1960's. In any event, bond yields after 1946 did two things: they recovered in the 1950's from the abnormally low yields of the depression and the war; and they rose much further in the 1960's to abnormally, indeed dangerously, high levels. In this chapter, we shall divide the period under review into the same three segments that were used in earlier chapters. These segments, which roughly coincided with political changes, are as follows:

(1) *The Democratic period from 1946 to 1953* was characterized by a sustained rise in long-term yields, which suffered only one cyclical interruption. These years included the great postwar inflation of 1946–48, when price controls were removed; the Korean War, with its brief sharp revival of inflation; and the first few months of the Eisenhower administration, with its return to monetary and fiscal orthodoxy. During this period, long-term government bond yields rose from a low of about 2.17% to a closing high of about 3.32%, almost, but not quite, back to their levels of the late 1920's.

(2) *The Republican period from 1953 to early 1961* was marked by a series of sharp fluctuations in bond yields in both directions, superimposed on a continued trend toward higher yields. During this span of eight years, neither short-term nor long-term interest rates advanced net by very much, but they both swung widely. During these years, monetary policy intervened quickly and frequently to offset threatened booms and recessions. Internationally, it was a period of comparative

stability. Long governments, which opened the period around 3.32%, closed it at around 3.75%.

3. *The Democratic period from 1961 to 1969* was characterized by four years of stable or declining yields, followed by four years of erratically escalating yields which, toward the end, were carried up to extraordinarily high levels. The sharp cyclical swings of the Eisenhower years were absent. The entire period was one of substantial economic growth. It was a period of stable commodity prices until 1964 but thereafter, inflation was resumed for the first time in six years, and in the course of the Vietnam War it gathered dangerous momentum. During this period, long-term government bond yields rose from 3¾% to over 6%.

1946–53

Chart XX shows that in early 1946 there was a brief decline in most bond yields. As a result, in April, 1946, the market established its all-time peak prices and low yields. Later in 1946, when the Congress forced President Truman to relax price and wage controls, yields rose.

The municipal market during World War II had been subject to extraordinarily bullish wartime influences, which included not only high taxes but an actual decline in outstanding muncipal debt. As a result, long prime municipals had enjoyed an exaggerated bull market all their own. Yields had declined to a level below 1%, where long municipals attracted only a very few high-bracket private investors. When peace returned, municipalities found that they could not float new issues at this nominal level of yields. As a result, market yields on municipals rose rapidly in 1946 and 1947 and had doubled by early 1948. At these higher yields, i.e., around 2%, the municipal market was able to attract sufficient funds to finance sizable new bonus issues.

In contrast, the yield rise for other departments of the bond market in 1946 and 1947 was much smaller. Corporations floated a modest volume of new issues, and the Treasury stopped the issuance of long-term bonds entirely. New-issue corporate bond yields crept up to 3%, while long government 2½'s were officially supported at small premiums. During the years 1946, 1947, and 1948, there was sustained rapid inflation. (See Chart XXI.) Short-term rates were rising, but were still at very low levels, below 1½%. On Christmas Eve of 1947, the Federal Reserve dropped its peg on long Treasury 2½'s from 100½ to 100 and, as a result, market confidence was shaken severely and liquidation became heavy. Nevertheless, support at par continued for three more years.

In late 1948, with the surprise re-election of President Truman, a

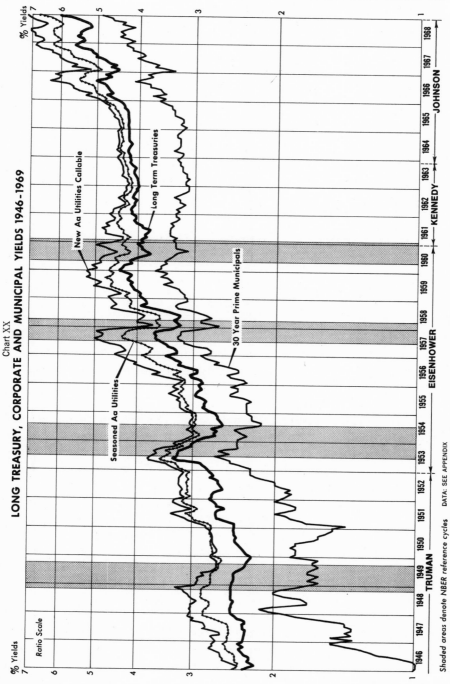

Chart XX

LONG TREASURY, CORPORATE AND MUNICIPAL YIELDS 1946-1969

% Yields

Ratio Scale

New Aa Utilities Callable

Long Term Treasuries

Seasoned Aa Utilities

30 Year Prime Municipals

TRUMAN   EISENHOWER   KENNEDY   JOHNSON

Shaded areas denote NBER reference cycles   DATA: SEE APPENDIX

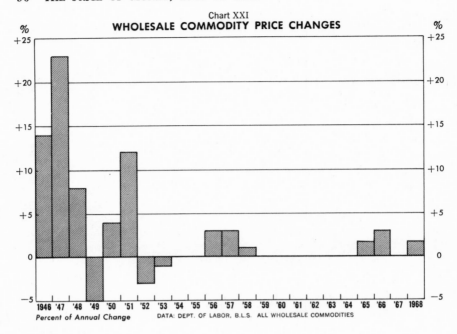

Chart XXI
WHOLESALE COMMODITY PRICE CHANGES

Percent of Annual Change   DATA: DEPT. OF LABOR, B.L.S.   ALL WHOLESALE COMMODITIES

small business recession began: commodity prices declined and bond prices rose. These cyclical fluctuations are set forth in detail in Table IX, which analyzes the 1946–69 bond market according to its five cyclical fluctuations.

By late 1949, Treasury 2½'s were selling freely at a premium of 4 points to yield 2.25%, and corporations could again finance at 2¾% or less. During this small cyclical bull market, municipal-bond fluctuations were again more substantial than those of other departments of the bond market, and a good volume of financing was done below 1¾%.

In early 1950, there was a business revival and a small rise in most yields. Then came the Korean War, with renewed inflation, higher taxes, and controls. It did not, however, lift long yields immediately. This was partly because of the fact that the Treasury 2½'s were still supported at par, in spite of heavy liquidation and in the face of the fact that commodity prices had started to rise again.

The Korean War had a curious effect on the municipal market: in late 1950 and early 1951, municipal prices soared and yields dropped to below 1½%. This was on the theory that wartime controls would again prohibit municipal financing, and that higher taxes would insure higher municipal prices. This rally proved abortive and was soon reversed.

Table IX

Cyclical High and Low Yields, Yield Changes, and Price Changes, 1946–69

Years	Yields at Turning Points			Yield Changes (Basis Points)		% Change in Price Index Years	De-cline	Recov-ery
PRIME SEASONED CORPORATE BONDS								
46-48-50	2.37%	2.87%	2.57%	+50	−30	46-48-50	−10	+7
50-53-54	2.57	3.43	2.91	+86	−52	50-53-54	−16	+11
54-57-58	2.91	4.23	3.59	+132	−64	54-57-58	−24	+12
58-59-63	3.59	4.65	4.16	+106	−49	58-59-63	−18	+8
63-69	4.16	7.25?		+309		63-69	−38	
NEW CORPORATE BONDS (Aa UTILITY, CALLABLE)								
46-48-49	2.51%	3.28%	2.58%	+77	−70			
49-53-54	2.58	3.78	2.90	+120	−88			
54-57-58	2.90	5.00	3.70	+210	−130			
58-59-63	3.70	5.25 *	4.19	+155	−106			
63-69	4.19	8.00?		+381				
LONG-TERM GOVERNMENTS								
46-48-50	2.17%	2.48%	2.24%	+31	−24	46-48-50	−7	+5
50-53-54	2.24	3.32	2.59	+108	−73	50-53-54	−20	+16
54-57-58	2.59	3.66	3.20	+107	−46	54-57-58	−20	+11
58-60-61	3.20	4.46	3.75	+126	−71	58-60-61	−21	+14
61-69	3.75	6.36?		+261		61-69	−35	
30-YEAR PRIME MUNICIPALS								
46-48-51	1.00%	2.30%	1.40%	+130	−90	46-48-51	−28	+25
51-53-54	1.40	2.75	2.15	+135	−60	51-53-54	−28	+15
54-57-58	2.15	3.30	2.65	+115	−65	54-57-58	−22	+15
58-59-63	2.65	3.65	3.10	+100	−55	58-59-63	−18	+11
63-69	3.10	6.00?		+290		63-69	−40	

* One eccentric issue sold to yield 5.62%.

% Price fluctuations do not add because each is calculated from its own starting price.

Intermonth highs and lows do not always agree with first of month data in the Appendix.

In early 1951, with inflation gaining momentum, there was a massive liquidation of long governments by institutions to meet the soaring credit demands of the economy. In March, 1951, the "Accord" was reached between the Treasury and the Federal Reserve, which had the effect of ending the Federal Reserve's commitment to buy long governments at par; bondholders were offered the privilege of switching their holdings at par into nonmarketable Treasury 2¾'s, and many did so. As a net result, there was in the next few months only a moderate 2 point drop in government-bond prices, a corresponding increase in government bond yields, and a much larger increase in corporate bond yields. Corporate new issues by late 1951 began to come out at 3¼% or higher. The municipal market reacted to the "Accord" far more vigorously, and yields rose back to 2%.

The prosperous year of 1952 was one of pause in most departments of the bond market. The Korean War went on, but at a declining pace; the inflation stopped, but the boom continued. While municipal yields rose, other long-term bond yields were virtually unchanged, in spite of a further rise in Treasury-bill rates and some other short-term rates. However, with a substantial rate of credit expansion, and a booming economy, and with the election of a Republican President, the stage was set for a further sharp rise in yields in 1953.

The new Eisenhower administration promised hard money and orthodox finance, and in early 1953 it delivered. Long-term Treasury financing was revived with an issue of 3¼% bonds (the Humphrey's). Monetary policy tightened, short rates rose, and bond yields soared. The new Treasury 3¼'s fell to a 1½ point discount. Toward mid-year there was a money-market crisis when it seemed difficult at one point to cover the Treasury-bill tender. Interest rates were still low by historic standards, with most short rates under 2½% and long rates well under 4%, so that the jarring effect of the tighter credit policy arose largely from its novelty: no credit stringency at all had been experienced for more than two decades. At just about the time in mid-1953 when the bond market reached its peak yields, the Korean War, which had been almost dormant for some time, ended, and the 1953–54 business recession began. This was the beginning of a series of bond market zigzags that characterized the Eisenhower years.

1953–61

The recession of 1953–54 brought with it a return to extreme ease in the money market and an important bull market in bonds. Bond prices rose by 11% to 16%. This brought long government yields down from 3.32% to 2.59%. Indeed, the wartime issues of long Treasury 2½% sold up without official support from 1953 lows of 89¾ (3.20%) to 1954 highs of 100⅞ (2.45%), and the new 3¼'s of 1983–78 sold up from a 1953 low of 98½ (3.32%) to a 1954 high of 112 (2.59%). Thus, long government bond prices, although not officially supported, were now above their level at the time of the "Accord."

In the 1953–54 recession, new-issue corporate bond yields came down from about 3¾% to about 2⅞%. Long municipal yields declined from 2¾% to about 2⅛%. Simultaneously, short-term rates declined to levels below 1%.

In the summer of 1954 the recession ended, and the bond market almost simultaneously bottomed out. Business sentiment had turned optimistic following the end of the excess-profits tax and under the stimulation of a strong stock market. Nevertheless, commodity prices remained stable in both 1954 and 1955.

In late 1954 there was a negligible rise in bond yields, but in January of 1955 another major cyclical bear bond market got under way and continued for the better part of three years, that is, until late 1957. Short-term rates rose sharply in late 1954 and all of 1955, and rose much more gradually in 1956 and 1957. Conversely long-term bond yields rose only moderately in 1955, and much more steeply in 1956 and the first ten months of 1957. During 1956, a great capital-goods boom began, which broke all precedents. Commodity prices, which had been stable or declining from 1952 through 1955, rose significantly in both 1956 and 1957.

This cyclical rise in yields from mid-1954 to late 1957 was led throughout by the yields on new issues of corporate bonds, which flooded the market. New-issue yields rose from 2.90% in early 1954 to 3.40% in late 1955, to 4½% in late 1956, to 5% at the 1957 peak, a total rise of 210 basis points. This was as large a rise percentage-wise in new-issue corporate bond yields as occurred in the 1965–68 bear market. In contrast, seasoned corporate bond yields rose only 143 basis points to 4.33%, and long government yields rose only 107 basis points to 3.66%. This meant, however, that Treasury 3¼'s of 1983–78 declined from 112 in 1954 to 104 in 1955, to 96¼ in 1956 and, finally, to a low of 92⅜ in 1957, an aggregate loss of 19⅝ points or 17%.

From 1954 low yields to 1957 high yields, long municipal yields rose from 2.15% to 3.30%, which equated to an average price decline of 22%. In fact, at these 1957 high yields, a long municipal price index which started in 1946 at 100 was down to 51¾, a loss of almost one-half. Because of the extraordinarily high price level of municipals at the end of World War II, their price decline during the first half of the postwar period was far more severe than the simultaneous price declines in all other departments of the market. After 1957, municipals tended to fluctuate more in line with the ups and downs of corporate bonds and government bonds.

November of 1957 saw a dramatic cyclical upturn in bond prices. During the first fortnight of November, prices continued their three-year fall, a new 5% Telephone issue failed to sell, and market pessimism was nearly universal. However, it turned out from slow statistics that the boom had been quietly cooling since summer. On the 15th of November, in the face of high market interest rates, the Federal Reserve lowered the discount rate from 3½% to 3%. The market's response was spectacular. Bond prices soared 8 points in a few weeks, and then soon rose another 3 or 4 points in early 1958.

The cyclical bull bond market of 1957–58 was sharp and very brief. In six months or so, seasoned corporate bonds rose an average of 12% in price, governments 11%, and municipals 15%. New-issue corporate bond yields declined from 5% to 3.70%; at this level, however, they were only back to the peak yields of 1953.

The recession of 1957–58 was also sharp and brief, and so was the business recovery of 1958–59. During this entire aborted business cycle, the traditional time span of cyclical market fluctuations was telescoped. In 1958 inflationary expectation reached a new postwar high just as the 1956–58 inflation ended and a new seven-year period of stable commodity prices began. In 1958 there was, in fact, a real flight from the dollar both into equities and into foreign currencies. This again brought on another abrupt swing to stringency by the Federal Reserve. The discount rates had been lowered in January, in March, and in April, 1958 but, by July, short-term market rates were permitted by open-market operations to rise, and in September the discount rate was raised. Thus, the 1957–58 bull bond market, although sizable, lasted only seven or eight months and ended in May, 1958.

The bear bond market of May, 1958, to January, 1960, was also severe and brief. Usually the start of a cyclical business recovery was followed by months or years of bond-market stability, or at worst of gentle decline; real cyclical bear bond markets usually waited until the later boom phase of a business recovery. Not so, however, in 1958. In July, only three months after the recession bottomed, a major bond-market decline began. Its initial severity resulted from a wave of public speculation in government bonds that had built up during the first half of 1958. Profits of 5 points or more had repeatedly been made by margin speculators in a succession of new Treasury issues. Finally in July, 1958, a new issue of 2⅝'s of 1965 was offered by the Treasury and was vastly oversubscribed by speculators, usually by amateur speculators, who put up little or no margin. By August, these 2⅝% bonds (subsequently nicknamed the Idiot's Delights) were down to 97½; by September to 94; by year-end to 92½; and in 1959 they declined to a low of 89⅛.

During this 1958–60 bear bond market, long government bonds declined an average of 21%. This was almost exactly the same size of decline that they had suffered in the cyclical declines of 1950–53 and again of 1954–57. It carried their yields up from 3.20% to 4.46%. Simultaneously, both long, seasoned corporate bonds and long municipals declined 18% in the market. Yields on new issues of prime corporate bonds rose from 3.70% in 1958 to 5.25% in 1959 (one eccentric issue came out at 5.62% in October of 1959). Throughout this 1958–60 bear bond market, monetary policy had become increasingly restrictive; the discount rate was raised three times in 1959, and short market rates climbed even more sharply, reaching the neighborhood of 5% by December of 1959.

This bear bond market climaxed between October, 1959 (corporates), and January, 1960 (governments and municipals). So restrictive was monetary policy, in spite of stable commodity prices, and so high were short and long rates by the end of 1959, that for six years thereafter most market commentators looked back to late 1959 as a freak period of stringency and high yields that was unlikely to be equalled again. For years most students of the bond market, even though bearish, would qualify their bearish forecasts with some such *caveat* as, "Of course, yields will not go up to 1959 peaks." This judgment was right for six years, and then spectacularly wrong.

The timing of the 1959–60 turning point toward lower yields was unusual. Corporate bond yields peaked in October, 1959, and municipal and government yields peaked in January of 1960; but the economy did not turn down until May of 1960, and the discount rate was not lowered until June of 1960. In January of 1960, bond-market opinion was intensely bearish: a steel strike had just been settled and six months of inventory restocking was guaranteed, with boom overtones; short-term rates had just risen above 5% for the first time in thirty years, and it seemed that the 4% discount rate must come up. Nevertheless, in January, 1960, in the face of such bearish expectations, the 3-month-bill rate in fact declined 80 basis points, and government bond yields started a large cyclical decline. At first the rally was considered technical, but in June the discount rate declined and the bull market was confirmed.

The cyclical bull bond market which began between October, 1959, and January, 1960, was a large one in long governments (+14%) and more moderate in municipals (+11%) and in seasoned corporates (+8%). The simultaneous decline in short rates, as we have seen, was not as large as in the previous recessions and did not carry them down to the usual nominal levels.

Most of the price advances in this bull bond market occurred in a few months in 1960 and early 1961. Thereafter, there was a series of small zigzags and then a long plateau. Long governments actually reached peak prices for the cycle in late 1960 and touched the same peaks again in mid-1961; municipals and corporates did not quite peak until 1963, but their 1961–63 peaks bettered 1960 peaks by very small amounts. This cyclical bull bond market thus could really be called the "1960 bull bond market." It was the last of the cyclical bull markets, at least until 1969, and it marked the end of the last of the postwar small business cycles. With the assumption of office by President Kennedy and the Democrats, a long period began when cyclical trends were muted in our economy and a policy of sustained economic growth was adopted.

1961–69

From early 1961 until mid-1965 the American bond market lacked a recognizable sustained price trend for the first time since the war. After a few false starts up and down it settled into an unprecedented groove that lasted for several years. Temporary technical forces prevailed, and yields in some departments of the market drifted down, while others simultaneously drifted up.

At first there were the Kennedy years, characterized by large unused resources and an official policy of stimulation aimed at producing faster economic growth. It was a period of alarm about our persistent gold losses and, as a result, monetary and fiscal policy brought about a steady rise in short-term interest rates. For a short time monetary policy simultaneously exerted itself to hold down long-term bond yields (Operation Twist), but actually very little intervention in the long market occurred because very little was needed: the economic environment favored stable to declining long yields.

During the years 1961 to 1965, there were many fiscal innovations. Massive advance refundings corrected the over-short maturity structure of the national debt, while our gold losses were reduced by the issuance of Roosa bonds to foreign central banks. Most important, however, was the growing ascendancy of the so-called "New Economics" (Keynesianism), which sponsored tax reductions as a means both of stimulating economic growth and of balancing the budget. Unused resources at home and peace abroad led to seven years (1958–64) of stable commodity prices; the BLS wholesale price index in 1964 was, in fact, a trifle below its peak of 1958. This period of prosperous stability has been called "the best of all possible worlds," but its sponsors did not think so. They sought faster growth and they got it.

In mid-1961 the bond market made a brief false start toward a new bear market. Business statistics had signaled the end of the 1960–61 recession and, with memories of 1958 still fresh, corporations rushed to sell bonds, and new-issue yields rose as much as $\frac{1}{2}\%$. It was a false start, and in late 1961 corporate and municipal yields turned down again, while government bond yields, influenced by advance refundings, rose a bit and stabilized. During the next two years, mid-1961 through mid-1963, corporate- and municipal-bond yields tended to decline gently, while government bond yields held up with the help of frequent new issues. There were vast flows of public savings into institutions, which were hard put to it to find adequate outlets. Avid institutional buying brought down the yields of all types of higher-yielding investments such as mortgages and medium-grade bonds and, therefore, as we shall see in Chapter X, yield spreads from governments came down to very low levels. Very few new corporate bonds were floated, but new long governments were offered in unprecedented peacetime volume and the mortgage market boomed.

Between mid-1961 and mid-1963 new-issue yields on prime corporate bonds came down from 4.85% to 4.25%, while long government yields tended to stay in a range of 4% to 4.12%. In 1964, there was a small yield increase in most departments of the market and another in early 1965, but until mid-1965 the persistent rise in short-term rates, which had been going on steadily since mid-1961, had little effect on long yields.

After the Kennedy assassination, Johnson put through the tax reduction, the first part of which became effective in 1964. Soon thereafter, he proposed in swift succession a series of massive measures of further economic stimulation. Most important probably was the Great Society program of January, 1965, which promised an end to the business cycle. No recessions at all would be permitted ever. Business believed, and took off on an unprecedented program of expansion. Commodity prices started to rise after seven years of stability. Then, at mid-year 1965, came the Vietnam War under the slogan "guns and butter."

The effect on the bond market of both the economic program and the war was swift and decisive. In early 1965 municipal and corporate yields started to rise. At mid-year they were joined by long government yields. In early 1966, the rise in yields gathered momentum. By that time it was evident that credit demands in 1966 would overwhelm the market. However, the government seemed to have little control over the situation and, therefore, a credit crunch was visibly in the offing. The Administration, however, was still talking growth and prosperity. Commodity prices continued to rise. A restrictive Federal Reserve policy, begun in December of 1965, had by mid-1966 pushed up short yields to a point where savings deposits and CD's were liquidating as depositors sought higher market yields, a process called by the ungainly term: "disintermediation."

In late August of 1966, the credit crunch was officially recognized by a series of fiscal measures to relieve market pressure. By that time, long governments had dropped 12% in price from mid-1965, corporate bonds 16%, and municipals 18%. All yields were well above their 1957 and 1959 cyclical peaks. A large increase in the volume of corporate financing had pushed up prime-corporate-new-issue yields to over 6%. Since long government yields did not rise much above 5%, yield spreads became very wide (see Chapter X).

The 1965–68 bond-market decline was in fact interrupted by two rallies as shown in Table X, i.e., from September, 1966 (the crunch), to February, 1967; and from November, 1967 (British devaluation), to August, 1968. Although both rallies were sizable (rises of 8 to 14 points in price), neither was a typical cyclical rally such as occurred three times in the 1950's, since they were too brief and not accompanied by business recessions. Both were corrections from periods of excessively rapid yield increase (June, 1965, to September, 1966; and February, 1967, to November, 1967), and both were stimulated by market hopes that high yields would exert a traditionally corrective influence on the economy, or at least on the fiscal and monetary managers. But market demands proved largely inelastic to high interest rates, and the managers kept on hoping that market forces would prove self-correcting.

The rally from September, 1966, to February, 1967, was almost as large as most postwar cyclical rallies. As Table X shows, municipals advanced 13 points and governments advanced 9 points, thus winning back three-fourths of their 1965–66 decline. Inflation and the growth rate of GNP slowed down, and there was talk of stability or even recession. But, instead, by early 1967 a huge Treasury deficit loomed in the offing and the Congress turned a deaf ear to the President's request for higher taxes. At the same time, the status of the pound sterling, and with it the dollar, began to seem precarious.

The decline in bond prices from February, 1967, to November, 1967, was again very large ($17\frac{1}{2}$ points for governments, 16 points for corporates, $15\frac{1}{2}$ points for municipals). It was in these months that the historically high yield records were broken back to the time of the Civil War. From February to May, 1967, there was the rare phenomenon of short rates declining substantially while long rates rose substantially. This was because the Federal Reserve's easy-money policy of November, 1966, to November, 1967, depressed short rates, but altogether failed to prevent long yields from simultaneously escalating.

Inflation threatened in 1967, and the attack on sterling and the dollar became irresistible. President Johnson belatedly (by one and one-half years) pressed for a large measure of fiscal restraint; conservatives in the Congress pressed for a larger package; nothing was done, and the Treasury's deficit soared. Finally, in November of 1967, sterling was de-

Table X

Price Fluctuations in Points of High-Grade Long-Term Bond Price Indices, 1965–68

	Long Govts.	Long High-Grade Municipals	Seasoned Corporate Discounts	New Corporates Callable*	Average
June, 1965–Sept., 1966............	−12	−18	−16	−25	−18
Sept., 1966–Feb., 1967	+9	+13	+8	+14	+11
Feb., 1967–1967 Lows	−17½	−15½	−16	−19½	−17
1967 Lows–Aug., 1968	+8	+4³/₈	+4½	+4½	+5⅝
Aug., 1968–June, 1969 †	−13³/₈	−20	−12	−13³/₈	−14⅝
Total Points Change............	−25⅞	−36½	−31½	−39⅜	−33¼

*New issue Aa utility yields capitalized throughout as 30-year 4¼'s.
† These point fluctuations at large discounts are less than similar fluctuations in percentages.

valued and the American bond market simultaneously bottomed out and started on another rally.

The bond-market rally of November, 1967, to August, 1968, was again technical and not cyclical. Bond prices rose 4 points to 8 points, or considerably less than in the 1966–67 rally. Oddly enough, during the first six months of this nine-month rally the Federal Reserve was vigorously moving to raise short-term interest rates; it raised the discount rate three times. This was the period of the gold crisis of March, 1968, when dollars lost their last market convertibility into gold. In June of 1968 the surtax was passed, and optimism rose that somehow automatically inflation and the economic boom would slow down. The Federal Reserve eased credit in June, and the bond-market rally accelerated briefly, reaching its peak in August of 1968.

From August of 1968 to June 1969 when this history ends, there was another major bond-market decline, the third in the series that began in 1965. Governments lost $13\frac{3}{8}$ points and corporates lost 12 points. It carried all departments of the market down to new lows where long governments sold to yield 6.36%, seasoned prime corporates to yield 7.25%, new-issue callable corporates to yield over 8%, and long prime municipals to yield 6.00%. Federal Reserve policy, which had permitted a record credit expansion during most of 1968, turned sharply restrictive in mid-December, and short rates soared to new highs as the market began preparing itself for another credit crunch.

During 1968 there were several developments that had favorable implications for the bond market: (1) the passage of the surtax; (2) the start of peace negotiations for Vietnam; (3) the withdrawal of Lyndon Johnson from the presidency and the victory of the Republicans; (4) the end for the time being, at least, of gold losses, and better balance-of-payments statistics; (5) a sharply improved Treasury position and the seeming end of large deficit financing.

Nevertheless, the market in 1968 and early 1969 tended to ignore these bullish influences in favor of some imposing bearish influences: (1) the economy had failed to respond to the surtax and to high interest rates, and the overheated boom continued unabated; (2) the inflation was accelerating; (3) expectations were nearly unanimous that at worst there would be a mild slowdown in 1969 to be followed by more boom and more inflation; it was thought by optimists that no recession would ever again be countenanced by either political party; (4) as a natural result of boom and inflation, there was a dangerous trend away from all fixed-income investments and toward equities.

In early 1969, as the market touched new lows, expectations became mixed: Some (including the authors) expected that there would be a real credit crisis in 1969 which would bring even higher interest rates for a period, but would cool the inflationary boom, and thus lead to lower interest rates later on; others expected that the Federal Reserve and the new Administration would side-step really effective restraint and be content with hoping that higher rates alone would curb the boom; these generally expected more inflation and higher interest rates for the indefinite future. Attention was thus focused on the near-term money-market policies of the Federal Reserve and on the budgetary policies to be followed by the new Administration. Bond-market psychology was at an all time low, as were bond-market prices.

Long-Term Yield Spreads

Although all American bond yields rose dynamically most of the time from 1946 into 1969, the rates at which yields increased within the various departments of the market were far from uniform. As the charts and tables in Chapter IX show, municipal bond yields at times were rising or falling much faster than taxable bond yields; at other times corporate yields were rising or falling much faster than other yields, and occasionally government yields rose or fell the most. Furthermore, within each of these three broad departments of the market, there were big shifts in yield relationships: for example, in the corporate sector the yields of new issues usually rose and fell more and faster than the yields of seasoned corporate bonds.

As a result of these changed internal relationships, certain kinds of bonds became relatively undervalued from time to time, while other kinds of bonds became relatively overvalued. In a few months or a year or two, these relationships were often reversed. One important tool for measuring undervaluation or overvaluation is a study of these yield differentials or spreads in a historic context.

Short-term yield spreads, which were discussed in Chapter VIII, only measure the differences in yield provided by various types of short-term credit instruments. They simply direct the investor to the highest high-grade yield among suitable instruments. In contrast, long-term yield spreads, which are discussed in this chapter, have a double significance: they reflect price movements, past and future, as well as yield differentials. Here is a theoretical example:

If government Bond A, a 30-year $4\frac{1}{4}\%$ bond, has moved from a

4.25% yield to a 5% yield, its price has declined 11%. Suppose simultaneously corporate Bond B, a 30-year 4½% bond, moved from a 4.50% yield to a 6% yield; if so, its price declined 21%. At the start, the yield spread was +25 basis points in favor of Bond B. The spread increase of 75 basis points meant that Bond B declined 10% in price more than Bond A. If in the future the spread returns to +25 basis points, either in a bull or bear market, the price action of B must be 10% better than the price action of A. The lower-yielding Bond A behaved much better during the assumed bear market because the spread against it at the start was presumably abnormally narrow, or in any event was liable to increase.

Thus, future changes in yield spreads will determine relative future price movements. An abnormally wide spread today not only measures higher yield, but could also suggest better future price action.

This chapter will start with an analysis of the yield spreads between long government bonds and seasoned long high-grade discount corporate bonds. Secondly, it will analyze the yield spreads between these same

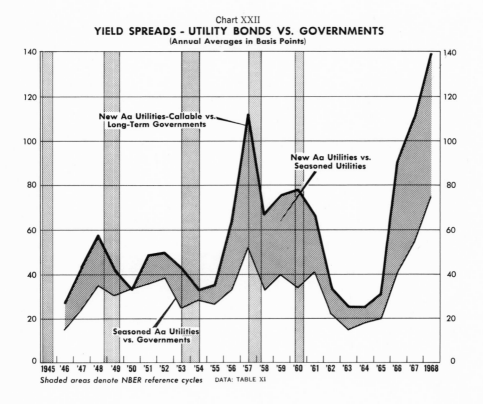

Chart XXII
YIELD SPREADS - UTILITY BONDS VS. GOVERNMENTS
(Annual Averages in Basis Points)

New Aa Utilities-Callable vs. Long-Term Governments

New Aa Utilities vs. Seasoned Utilities

Seasoned Aa Utilities vs. Governments

Shaded areas denote NBER reference cycles   DATA: TABLE XI seasoned discount corporate bonds and new issues of similar corporate bonds with no call protection. Thirdly, it will combine the above two spreads and thus analyze the spreads between the new-issue corporate bond yields and the long-government-bond yields.

These corporate-bond spreads are based throughout on the yields of Aa public utility bonds because there is such an abundance of new Aa utility issues and of seasoned Aa utility issues, and they are very uniform in market acceptance. Thus, they lend themselves to precise averaging.

Chart XXII and Table XI summarize these three spreads based on annual averages. They reveal several important long-term trends. First, the two component spreads have tended to widen or narrow concurrently. Second, there have been two extended periods of wide spreads and two periods of narrow spreads. Third, the spreads have tended to widen most in periods of sharply advancing interest rates, and decline in periods of stable or falling interest rates. Fourth, the aggregate new issue spreads from governments have fluctuated both ways considerably more than seasoned-issue spreads from governments.

Table XI

Yield Spreads–New Aa Utilities vs. Seasoned Aa Utilities vs. Governments
(Annual averages)

	Deep-Dis-count Utils. vs. Govts.	New-Issue vs. Deep-Dis-count Utils.	New-Issue Utils. vs. Govts.		Deep-Dis-count Utils. vs. Govts.	New-Issue vs. Deep-Dis-count Utils.	New-Issue Utils. vs. Govts.
1946	+15	+12	+27	1958	+33	+34	+67
47	+24	+19	+43	59	+40	+36	+76
48	+35	+23	+58	60	+34	+44	+78
49	+31	+11	+42	61	+41	+25	+66
50	+34	−1	+33	62	+22	+11	+33
51	+36	+13	+49	63	+15	+10	+25
52	+38	+12	+50	64	+18	+7	+25
53	+24	+18	+42	65	+20	+11	+31
54	+28	+5	+33	66	+41	+50	+91
55	+26	+9	+35	67	+55	+56	+111
56	+33	+31	+64	68	+74	+63	+139
57	+52	+61	+113				

Source: Appendix.

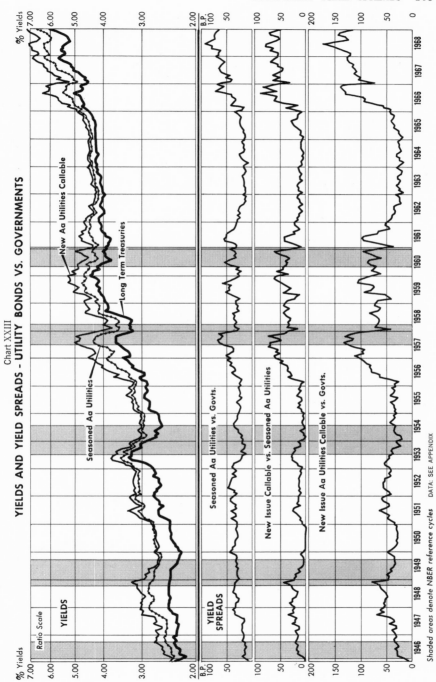

YIELDS AND YIELD SPREADS - UTILITY BONDS VS. GOVERNMENTS
Chart XXIII

YIELDS

New Aa Utilities Callable

Long Term Treasuries

Seasoned Aa Utilities

YIELD SPREADS

Seasoned Aa Utilities vs. Govts.

New Issue Callable vs. Seasoned Aa Utilities

New Issue Aa Utilities Callable vs. Govts.

Shaded areas denote NBER reference cycles   DATA: SEE APPENDIX

Seasoned-Utility Yields vs. Long Government Yields

Chart XXIII, which pictures all of these spreads in terms of monthly data, shows that the spreads of seasoned low-coupon Aa utility bond yields over the yields of governments have, throughout this period, usually fluctuated within a band of +10 to +50 basis points in favor of the utilities. Only in 1957, 1966, 1967, and 1968 has this range been significantly exceeded. This spread showed no clear-cut cyclical trend. However, in periods of rising or high yield since 1953 this spread has tended to rise.

This spread is probably responsive to shifts in the volume of new financing. Thus, from 1946 to 1952 when there was no new long-government financing the spread widened, but it declined in early 1953 when new long-term Treasury financing resumed. It rose with the flood of corporate-bond financing in 1956–57, and dropped in 1958, when corporate-bond financing declined and government new issues were fre-

Table XII

Peaks and Troughs of the Yield Spread Between Seasoned-Aa-Discount Utilities and Governments
(In basis points)

	Trough	Peak
Jan., 1946	+5	
Jan., 1950		+46
Aug., 1953	+11	
Aug., 1954		+38
Apr., 1956	+19	
Sept., 1957		+69
Feb., 1958	+26	
Oct., 1959		+59
Mar., 1960	+21	
June, 1961		+56
Dec., 1962	+10	
Oct., 1966		+73
Mar., 1967	+40	
July, 1968		+94
Average Trough & Peak	+19	+62
Average Jan., 1946–June, 1953	+30	
Average July, 1953–Apr., 1961	+34	
Average May, 1961–Dec., 1968	+36	
Average 1946–68	+35	

quent. It rose again in 1959 and in 1960–61, when there was a good volume of corporate-bond financing, but became very narrow in 1962, 1963, and 1964 and early 1965, when heavy Treasury advance refundings came out at a time when there was a subnormal volume of corporate-bond financing. Finally, this spread rose rapidly in 1966, stayed high in 1967, and rose again in 1968 when three things happened: all yields rose, long-Treasury financing ceased altogether, and the volume of corporate-bond financing soared to new high levels.

It is also probable that this spread of seasoned discount corporate-bond yields above government bond yields was primarily influenced by the spread of the yields of new issues of corporate bonds over government bond yields. Really dynamic yield and spread shifts probably originated in the market for new issues of corporate bonds and only gradually influenced the yields and spreads of seasoned discount corporate bonds.

The principal peaks and troughs of this spread were as shown on the facing page.

The difference between the average trough and the average peak in the table opposite is 43 basis points. For a 30-year bond this change in spread equates to about 7 points in price for each swing. The range from lowest to highest spread is 89 basis points, which equates to about 15 points in price.

Callable New-Issue Utility Yields vs. Seasoned Discount Utility Yields

The history of this new-issue–seasoned-issue spread since 1946 shows a very clear contrast between long periods of narrow spreads and long periods of wide spreads. This was partly because of the effect of heavy corporate new-issue volume. It was also the result of the difference in coupon between the new and seasoned issues.

During the years of relatively light volume of new corporate bond issues, such as between 1946 and 1955 and between 1962 and 1965, the spread of the yields of new issues of utility bonds over the yields of seasoned discount utility bonds usually remained within a narrow range of from +5 to +25 basis points. When corporate new-issue volume picked up, as it did in 1956 and 1957; and in 1959; and in 1966 and 1967 this spread rose sharply to a range of +40 to +80 basis points.

The pattern of yield spreads during the periods from 1956 to 1961 and from 1966 to 1968 illustrates the tendency for yields on seasoned utilities to catch up with movements in new-issue yields with a lag. During both intervals, the widest spreads occurred at the beginning of the period, followed by a trend toward narrower spreads in spite of progressively higher yield levels.

Table XIII

Peaks and Troughs of the Yield Spread Between Aa New-Issue and Seasoned Discount Utilities
(In basis points)

	Trough	Peak
Jan., 1946	−2	
Dec., 1948		+46
Apr., 1950	−5	
July, 1951		+25
Mar., 1953	+15	
July, 1953		+27
Mar., 1954	−1	
June, 1957		+75
Feb., 1958	+15	
Sept., 1958		+46
May, 1959	+10	
Dec., 1959		+62
Feb., 1961	+6	
June, 1961		+43
June, 1962	+4	
Sept., 1966		+89
Feb., 1967	+30	
June, 1968		+80
Average Trough & Peak	+8	+55
Average Jan., 1946–June, 1953	+15	
Average July, 1953–Apr., 1961	+30	
Average May, 1961–Dec., 1968	+30	
Average 1946–68	+25	

The chart further shows that during each of the four recession periods this spread has tended to decline. This was no doubt partly because of a decline in new-issue volume during such periods, which caused new-issue yields to decline more than seasoned-issue yields. Also when yields decline, the more sensitive new-issue yields usually decline faster and sooner.

The difference between the average trough and peak in the period since 1946 was 47 basis points, or the equivalent of about 8 points in price. Between the extreme wide and narrow spreads during this period, however, it was 94 basis points or about 16 points in price.

The deeply depressed prices of seasoned low- or medium-coupon utilities in recent years have rendered these issues virtually noncallable. As a result, their yield spread from new issues can be interpreted as reflecting the cost, in basis points, of complete call protection. In mid-1962, for instance, the investor could have bought complete call protection for a cost, or give-up, of only 4 basis points in yield, whereas during the crunch of 1966 this protection would for a brief period have cost him almost 90 basis points. In recent years, it has not been obtainable below 30 basis points.

Callable New-Issue Utility Yields vs. Long Government Yields

This yield spread is a composite of the two previously discussed yield spreads. It shows the widest swings, because the constituent spreads often tended to widen or narrow together. During the postwar period

Table XIV

Peaks and Troughs of the Yield Spread Between Callable Aa New-Issue Utilities and Governments
(In basis points)

	Trough		Peak
Jan., 1946	+5		
Dec., 1948			+79
Aug., 1950	+28		
July, 1951			+67
Feb., 1954	+19		
Sept., 1954			+44
Mar., 1956	+25		
Aug., 1957			+135
Feb., 1958	+41		
Sept., 1958			+85
Mar., 1959	+41		
Oct., 1959			+108
Feb., 1961	+37		
June, 1961			+99
Mar., 1964	+15		
Dec., 1966			+140
Feb., 1967	+73		
July, 1968			+173
Average Trough & Peak	+32		+103
Average Jan., 1946–June, 1953		+45	
Average July, 1953–Apr., 1961		+64	
Average May, 1961–Dec., 1968		+66	
Average 1946–68		+60	

this spread has fluctuated over a range of 168 basis points, with the widest spreads coinciding with periods of heavy corporate-bond volume, and with narrow spreads in periods of low corporate volume or when government financing increased.

A comparison of the yield spreads in the chart shows that periods of small spread-changes in the two component spreads often added up to moderately wide swings in new-issue–government yield spreads. Table XIV above shows that during one such period, from 1946 to 1955, there were several good opportunities for profitable selection between

Table XV

Per Cent of Total New-Issue-Government Spread Accounted for by the Seasoned-Issue–Government Spread
(Annual averages)

	Total Spread New-Issue Utils. vs. Govt. – B.P.	Seasoned-Util. vs. Govt. Spread as a % of Total Spread
1946	+27	56%
47	+43	56
48	+58	60
49	+42	74
50	+33	100
51	+49	73
52	+50	76
53	+42	57
54	+33	85
55	+35	74
56	+64	52
57	+113	46
58	+67	49
59	+76	53
60	+78	44
61	+66	62
62	+33	67
63	+25	60
64	+25	72
65	+31	65
66	+91	45
67	+111	55
68	+139	54
	1946–55	Avg. 71%
	1956–61	51
	1962–65	66
	1966–68	51

new corporates and governments. New-issue utilities, for instance, yielded as little as 5 basis points, and as much as 79 basis points more than governments; this was a change equal to a swing of about 12 points in price. The 71-basis-point difference between the average trough and peak since 1946 was equivalent to 12 points in price; whereas the over-all postwar range of this spread was 168 basis points, which equates to about 27 points in price.

Table XV on page 110 shows the extent to which the seasoned utility vs. government spreads accounted for the composite new-issue–government spreads. As might be expected, during periods of market pressure and wide spreads, such as from 1956 to 1960 and from 1966 to 1968, the seasoned-issue–government spread accounted for only about a half of the total spread; whereas in narrower-spread periods (1946–55 and 1962–65) it made up a major part, usually 60–80%, of the total spread, and the new-issue–seasoned-issue spread was small.

Callable vs. Deferred-Call New Utilities

Prior to the high yields of 1957, all new corporate issues were sold without call protection. With the higher yields, however, interest developed in a type of issue that offered a limited period of call protection (usually five years in the case of utilities and five to ten years in the case of industrials), in exchange for a lower yield. The cost of five year call protection, as measured by the yield spread, has fluctuated within a band of 0 to 30 basis points and most of the time between 0 and 20 basis points.

Table XVI reveals that the cost of 5-year-call protection tended to increase when yield levels advanced. When yield levels decreased, as in the early 1960's, the cost of the protection diminished to nothing. In 1968, however, although new-utility yields rose to levels about 100 basis points above the previous crunch highs of 1966, the cost of call protection remained below the 1966 high of +30 basis points. Perhaps investors were not as fearful of future call in 1968 at 7% as they were in 1966 at 6%. While heavy new-issue volume has tended to push new-issue yields up and make call protection generally more attractive, the volume of deferred-call as opposed to callable new issues has increased, and this has tended to reduce the spread.

Low-Coupon Corporate Bonds vs. High-Coupon Corporate Bonds

One consequence of the great bear bond market during the postwar years is that there are now outstanding in the market, bonds with a wide

Table XVI

Peaks and Troughs of the Yield Spread Between Callable and Deferred-Call New Aa Utility Issues
(In basis points)

	Trough	Peak
July, 1957		+15
Oct., 1957	0	
Mar., 1958		+13
Mar., 1959	+2	
Nov., 1959		+25
Jan., 1963	0	
Nov., 1966		+30
Jan., 1967	+15	
Nov., 1967		+25
Oct., 1968	+15	
Average Trough and Peak	+6	+22
Average July, 1957–Apr., 1961	+9	
Average May, 1961–Dec., 1968	+8	
Average 1958–68	+8	

Source: Salomon Brothers & Hutzler, *An Analytical Record of Yields and Yield Spreads.*

variety of coupons all the way from $2\frac{5}{8}\%$ to $8\frac{1}{8}\%$ on issues of the same high quality. The lowest-coupon issues naturally sell at deep discounts, while the highest-coupon issues usually sell at par or higher. Ever since the mid-1950's, when this wide diversity of coupons began to appear, there often have existed large yield differentials based solely on coupon. The rule has been that the higher the coupon, the higher the yield, even though maturity, quality, and other characteristics were identical. Thus, there is not one market or yield average for seasoned Aa utility bonds, but instead there is a wide variety of markets according to coupon. Furthermore, these various markets do not fluctuate by the same amounts, and occasionally they even move in opposite directions.

Table XVII on page 113 shows the average annual yields since 1957 of the lowest coupon and of the highest-coupon seasoned Aa utilities, and the yield spreads by which the highest-coupon yields exceeded the lowest-coupon yields. This spread has varied from +24 basis points to +79 basis points. It will be seen from the table that between 1957 and 1958 and again between 1959 and 1960 the yield of the lowest-coupon average declined, while the yield of the highest-coupon average advanced. Usually these yield averages fluctuated in the same direction, but by widely differing amounts. If a similar but more detailed schedule

Table XVII

Aa Seasoned-Utility Bond Yields by Coupon

	Annual Average Yields		Spread High Coupon vs. Low Coupon
	Lowest Coupon	Highest Coupon	
1957	4.00%	4.43%	+43
1958	3.80	4.59	+79
1959	4.48	4.76	+28
1960	4.41	4.87	+46
1961	4.35	4.70	+35
1962	4.28	4.64	+36
1963	4.23	4.63	+40
1964	4.39	4.64	+25
1965	4.46	4.70	+24
1966	5.13	5.42	+29
1967	5.49	5.94	+45
1968	6.15	6.48	+33

Source: Salomon Brothers & Hutzler, *An Analytical Record of Yields and Yield Spreads.*

were drawn up showing the yields for all the various coupons,* it would show that at any one point in time, yields usually advanced progressively as coupon increased, but with the biggest yield-jumps occurring between the two or three highest-coupon categories.

One reason for this progression in yield according to coupon is that very high-coupon issues are inhibited by nearness to call price and, thus, when market prices advance they cannot advance as much as low-coupon issues. Again, high-coupon issues compete directly with new issues, which are constantly coming to market, while low-coupon issues are often in small supply. Again, the deep-discount low-coupon issues have a potential tax advantage, in that some part of their yield is subject to capital-gains tax. In sharply advancing markets, like those of 1958 and 1960, the spread according to coupon is apt to become very wide because the highest-coupon issues are heavily restrained by call. This tendency of low-coupon issues to yield less than high-coupon issues accounts for a good part of the "new-issue–seasoned-issue" spread discussed earlier in this chapter and pictured in Chart XXIII.

One result of these differences of yield change according to coupon

* For such a schedule, see Salomon Brothers & Hutzler's *An Analytical Record of Yields and Yield Spreads.*

Table XVIII

Price and Yield Changes According to Coupon
(Aa seasoned utility bond yields)

Coupon	Yields and Yield Changes			Prices and Price Changes		
Bull Market: Sept., 1957–Feb., 1958						
2¾'s	4.33% to 3.55%	−78		72⅜ to 84¾	+17%	
4¼'s	4.43 to 4.02	−41		96⅞ to 104⅛	+7	
5's	4.76 to 4.50	−26		104 to 108⅜	+4	
Bear Market: Feb., 1958–Oct., 1959						
2¾'s	3.55% to 4.76%	+121		84¾ to 67⅝	−20	
4¼'s	4.02 to 4.77	+75		104⅛ to 91⅝	−12	
5's	4.50 to 4.89	+39		108⅜ to 101¾	−6	
Bull Market: Oct., 1959–Sept., 1960						
2¾'s	4.76% to 4.17%	−59		67⅝ to 75⅞	+12	
4¼'s	4.77 to 4.30	−47		91⅝ to 99⅛	+8	
5's	4.89 to 4.80	−9		101¾ to 103⅛	+1	
Bear Market: Sept., 1960–Sept., 1961						
2¾'s	4.17% to 4.50%	+33		75⅞ to 71¾	−5	
4¼'s	4.30 to 4.52	+22		99⅛ to 95⅝	−4	
5's	4.80 to 4.79	−1		103⅛ to 103¼	0	
Bull Market: Sept., 1961–Dec., 1962						
2¾'s	4.50% to 4.13%	−37		71¾ to 77⅝	+8	
4¼'s	4.52 to 4.20	−32		95⅝ to 100¾	+5	
5's	4.79 to 4.60	−19		103¼ to 106⅛	+3	
Bear Market: Dec., 1962–Sept., 1966						
2¾'s	4.13% to 5.46%	+133		77⅝ to 64	−18	
4¼'s	4.20 to 5.51	+131		100¾ to 83⅜	−17	
5's	4.60 to 5.57	+97		106⅛ to 92½	−13	

is that in sustained rallies low-coupon issues are apt to move up in the market much more than very high-coupon issues, partly because the latter are restrained by call; whereas in bear bond markets high-coupon issues are apt to decline much less than low-coupon issues because they start with a large yield advantage, which will be reduced if the market declines sufficiently.

Table XVIII above illustrates the variety of price fluctuations according to coupon that occurred during the various bull and bear bond market phases from late 1957 to 1967. It shows striking contrasts. For example, in the bull market of 1957–58 low-coupon issues advanced 17%, while highest-coupon issues advanced only 4%. In the succeeding bear bond market of 1958–59, low-coupon issues declined 20%, while highest-coupon issues declined only 6%. This relationship between low and high coupon applies equally well to other types of taxable bonds, such as industrial bonds and finance bonds.

New Industrial Bonds vs. New Utility Bonds

Industrial-bond financing in the postwar period has often taken the form of private placements; only occasionally, such as in 1957, 1958, 1961, 1966, and 1967, has there been a large number of public offerings of straight industrials. Therefore, data on industrial new-issue yields are inadequate for accurate monthly or annual averaging, such as has been done for utilities, which usually finance publicly. Nevertheless, the table below provides a rough idea of the yield spreads that have prevailed between Aa new industrial-bond issues and Aa new utility-bond issues. It will be seen that the industrials were almost always offered to yield less than the utilities. This negative spread was, in part, the result of sinking funds and the scarcity of industrial offerings and, in later years, partly the result of the fact that many new industrial bond issues enjoyed 10-year call protection, whereas public-utility issues at most enjoyed 5-year call protection. It will be seen that the spreads in favor of new utilities became very wide in 1956, 1957, and 1959 and again in 1966–68, that is to say, in periods of rising yields and heavy

Table XIX

Yield Spreads of New Aa Industrial Bonds vs. New Aa Utility Bonds
(Important issues only)

	Average	Maximum		Average	Maximum
1951	−5	−7	1960	−2	−11
1952	−5	−19	1961	−7	−15
1953	+3	−5	1962	0	−4
1954	−7	−8	1963	−3	−4
1955	−	−	1964	−	−
1956	−28	−44	1965	−4	−4
1957	−42	−58	1966	−15	−42
1958	−3	−16	1967	−12	−21
1959	−22	−31	1968	−15	−20

bond financing; whereas at other times the spreads were small or nominal.

Substantial sinking funds are provided for most new industrial issues, but not for most new public-utility bond issues. In declining bond markets, such as those of the postwar period, sinking funds often importantly support the markets for discount industrials, thus preventing them from declining to a level where their yields are competitive. Therefore, yield averages of lower-coupon industrial discount bonds do not have market significance, and do not permit meaningful comparisons of discount industrial yields with other corporate yields. This is why the corporate bond yield relationships systematically analyzed earlier in this chapter are confined largely to utility bonds.

Table XX

Yields and Yield Spreads by Quality — Annual Averages — Moody's

Year	Utilities Aaa	Utilities Baa	Industrials Aaa	Industrials Baa	Baa vs. Aaa Utils.	Baa vs. Aaa Inds.
1946	2.51	3.03	2.44	2.84	+52	+40
1947	2.59	3.08	2.53	2.92	+49	+39
1948	2.81	3.36	2.71	3.13	+55	+41
1949	2.67	3.28	2.58	3.02	+61	+44
1950	2.62	3.18	2.55	2.86	+56	+31
1951	2.88	3.39	2.78	3.04	+51	+26
1952	2.99	3.53	2.88	3.20	+54	+32
1953	3.24	3.73	3.12	3.55	+49	+43
1954	2.93	3.51	2.82	3.40	+58	+58
1955	3.09	3.43	3.00	3.47	+34	+47
1956	3.39	3.78	3.30	3.84	+39	+54
1957	3.96	4.46	3.76	4.79	+50	+103
1958	3.87	4.43	3.61	4.59	+56	+98
1959	4.49	4.96	4.27	4.91	+47	+64
1960	4.47	4.97	4.28	5.11	+50	+83
1961	4.37	4.83	4.21	5.10	+46	+89
1962	4.35	4.75	4.18	4.98	+40	+80
1963	4.27	4.67	4.14	4.90	+40	+76
1964	4.42	4.74	4.32	4.87	+32	+55
1965	4.50	4.78	4.45	4.92	+28	+47
1966	5.19	5.60	5.12	5.68	+41	+56
1967	5.58	6.15	5.49	6.21	+57	+72
1968	6.22	6.87	6.12	6.90	+65	+78

High-Quality vs. Lower-Quality Bonds

Almost all the yields analyzed in this book are yields on high-grade credit instruments.   There is also, of course, at all times a wide spectrum of higher yields.   These are usually associated with some degree of credit risk.   Precise measurement of risk yield spreads is difficult, however, because degree of risk does not lend itself to precise measurement and, in fact, is largely subjective.   A rough idea of changing quality spreads, however, is conveyed by comparing yield averages according to ratings. Table XX and Chart XXIV compare Moody's annual averages of Baa industrial- and utility-bond yields with Moody's annual averages of Aaa industrial- and utility-bond yields.

This spread was very wide in the 1930's, running up to 250 basis points in favor of the lower-rated issues.   During the period under review, however, this annual average spread for industrials fluctuated between a low of 26 basis points and a high of 103 basis points and, for utilities, between a low of 28 basis points and a high of 65 basis points.

The chart shows that these spreads did not always follow a cyclical pattern based on risk considerations; this would be to widen in recessions and narrow in good times.   The spreads were, in fact, wider in most postwar recessions, and they did come down in the early recovery periods.   However, there was also a tendency for the spreads to widen again in periods of boom, when all interest rates were rising.

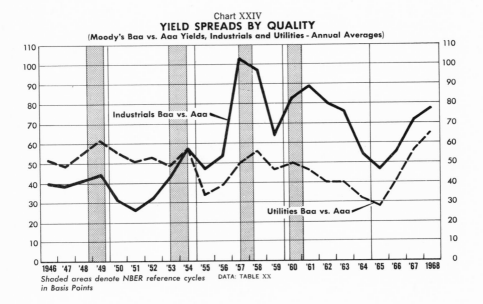

Chart XXIV
YIELD SPREADS BY QUALITY
(Moody's Baa vs. Aaa Yields, Industrials and Utilities - Annual Averages)

Shaded areas denote NBER reference cycles   DATA: TABLE XX
in Basis Points

Minimum spreads usually occurred in intermediate cyclical periods, such as 1951, 1955, and 1965. It seems probable, therefore, that factors other than the fluctuations in business optimism were involved in creating these spreads. For example, when institutions were starved for outlets and were scrambling for yield, the spread narrowed. On the other hand, at times when prime bonds gave unexpectedly good yields the spread widened, perhaps because there was less pressure on institutions to pick up extra yield by downgrading.

The long recovery period starting in 1961 was characterized by two major swings in this spread. Until mid-1965, prime yields were unusually stable at moderate levels, and institutions were flooded with funds, which were hard to invest. Therefore, quality standards were progressively liberalized and the quality spreads came down year by year. After 1965, when prime yields rose spectacularly during three successive years, quality spreads grew progressively larger. These wider spreads presumably did not reflect growing conservatism in the investment community or upward appraisal of risk, but rather the availability of surprisingly high yields from prime credits. This widening of the quality spreads probably also led many companies with lower credit to employ convertible bonds for their new-money financing.

Municipal Bond Yields vs. Government and Corporate Bond Yields

The relationship of municipal-bond yields to the yields of taxable bonds of similar quality and maturity is, of course, influenced by the level of taxes. However, many other factors, such as volume of municipal financing and money-flows into specific types of institutions, are more important. Indeed, during the postwar period, the percentage of municipal yields to taxable yields has apparently been very little influenced by changes in tax rates.

Table XXI below shows the percentage of the yields of 30-year prime municipals to the yields of long governments and also to the yields of new Aa callable utilities; the table is based on annual averages. These percentages are plotted in Chart XXV, and the chart also shows the inverse of the effective federal income tax rate both for large corporations and for top-bracket private investors. Therefore if, on the chart, a municipal-yield percentage exactly coincides with an inverted tax rate, it means that net income to that tax bracket is exactly the same from either the exempt or the taxable bonds in question. Thus, for example, if the investor were in the 48% bracket, and municipal yields were exactly 52% of corporate yields, it would be a matter of indifference

Table XXI

Municipal Yields as a Percentage of Government and Utility Yields
(Annual averages)

	30-Yr. Prime Municipal Ylds. as a % of			30-Yr. Prime Municipal Ylds. as a % of	
	Long Govts.	New Aa Utils.— Callable		Long Govts.	New Aa Utils.— Callable
1946	49%	43%	1958	85%	68%
1947	63	53	1959	82	69
1948	77	63	1960	83	70
1949	70	59	1961	85	73
1950	71	63	1962	79	73
1951	69	59	1963	79	74
1952	75	63	1964	78	73
1953	84	70	1965	74	72
1954	83	76	1966	80	67
1955	80	73	1967	79	64
1956	82	69	1968	82	65
1957	90	66			

from the point of view of income whether the investor held the exempt or the taxable bonds. To the extent that a municipal percentage is higher than an inverted tax rate, there is an advantage in the yield from municipals.

The chart shows that at the end of World War II, municipal yields were only 43% of corporate yields and less than 50% of government yields. These ratios made municipals highly unattractive to regular corporate taxpayers and to all institutions, but still attractive (in terms of yield only) to high-bracket private investors. During World War II, there was almost no new municipal financing and, in fact, municipal debt was being retired; therefore, municipal yields were extraordinarily low. With peace, however, there was a rush to sell bonus issues and to finance new municipal projects. Therefore, it was necessary to price new issues to attract medium-bracket investors. The percentage rose sharply in 1947 and 1948, reaching a point of indifference with corporate yields. Thereafter, taxes were increased, but municipal yields did not decline accordingly. After 1951 the percentages again rose sharply; the percentage to corporate yields, in fact, reached its high in 1954. This was a period when new municipals came out in volume,

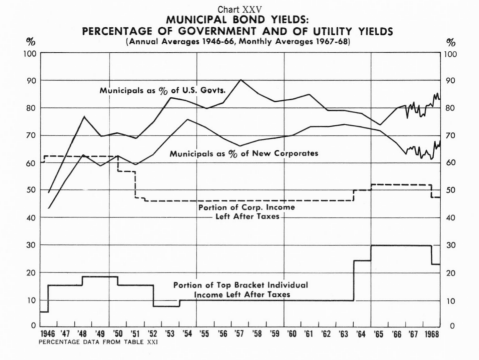

Chart XXV
MUNICIPAL BOND YIELDS:
PERCENTAGE OF GOVERNMENT AND OF UTILITY YIELDS
(Annual Averages 1946-66, Monthly Averages 1967-68)

PERCENTAGE DATA FROM TABLE XXI

and it was necessary to bid for the funds of institutions like life insurance companies whose tax rates were far below the corporate rate.

In 1954 the peak of 76% of corporate yields meant that the point of indifference was at an effective tax rate of 24%. This illustrates the bonanza that municipals then provided to corporate and other higher-bracket investors. In fact, municipals have had to provide a very large inducement ever since in order to float a growing volume of tax-exempt financing.

The municipal–corporate percentage declined a bit between 1954 and 1957 and then rose again, almost reaching a peak in 1963. This meant that municipal yields did not rise as rapidly as corporate yields between 1954 and 1957, but rose more rapidly between 1957 and 1963. During these years, the behavior of the municipal–government percentage was almost the opposite, since government yields rose less than others in the 1956–57 periods and somewhat more thereafter. Again, the tax reductions in 1964 and 1965 seem to have had little effect on the municipal percentage, and the same can be said of the surtax in 1968.

Over recent years the commercial banks have become the dominant factor in the municipal market, sometimes buying 80% of the total of new municipal financing. As the chart shows, municipals in the last five years have continued to offer bonanza spreads over both corporate and government bonds for corporate taxpayers. The municipal–government percentage is at the present time much the more significant of the two, since commercial banks are the dominant factors in the municipal market, and their investment is heavy in governments and negligible in corporate bonds. The municipal–government percentage has been rising since 1965 and in 1968 rose to 82%. This wide ratio not only reflected the pressure of extremely heavy municipal financing, but also the present restrictive monetary policy, which is curtailing bank purchases of municipals. Another factor in the high percentage is the absence of new long-term-government financing.

The Yield Curve

During recent decades we have become used to thinking in terms of a smooth progression of yields, according to maturity, along "a yield curve," which is either positive (yields rising with maturity), or negative, or flat, or humped. Before 1930 these curves were usually flat or negative (long yields lower than short yields), but since 1930 these curves have usually been positive. Since the mid-1950's, however, during periods of sharply rising rates, the curves have often become negative or humped, with the highest yields in the short or medium maturities.

There is a danger that when we think of the bond market in terms of rational smooth yield curves we may drop into the habit of thinking that by means of these progressions like is linked to like. It looks that way on the charts. Where does "short" end and "long" begin? Every answer is arbitrary. It is a little like a Zeno paradox. The short-term money-market credit instruments at one end of the curve are so drastically different from the long-term bonds at the other end, in purpose, in contract, in behavior, in mathematical content, and even in historic origin, that it can be misleading to link them together in this way. The fact is that we are looking at two distinct types of investment, short loans and long bonds, that are as different from each other as stocks are from bonds, or more so. Medium-maturity bonds, which partake of some of the qualities of both shorts and longs, seem to serve as a link, but this should not be allowed to obscure the basic differences between the extremes.

The purchase of a long-term bond is really not so much a loan of money as it is a purchase of income. This is so because, to the debtor and the creditor alike, the payment or receipt of the interest is more important than the ultimate repayment of the principal.   On the other hand, in the case of a short-term loan, repayment of principal far outweighs the payment of interest as a concern of both debtor and creditor.

The mathematics tell the story. First, take a $1,000 3-month note at a high interest rate of 12%. The debtor owes $1,030, of which only $30 is interest. Present value at a 12% discount rate is as follows:

Interest of $30	$ 29
Principal of $1,000	971
Total Present Value	$1,000

In contrast, take a $1,000 30-year bond at a rate of 5%. The debtor must ultimately pay $2,500, of which $1,500 is interest and $1,000 is principal. However, the relative significance of the interest is even greater because it is payable much sooner. Present value at a 5% discount rate is as follows:

Interest of $1,500	$ 773
Principal of $1,000	227
Total Present Value	$1,000

The short-term money market and the long-term bond market should be regarded as two entirely separate and only very loosely related markets. These markets seem by an optical illusion to be linked together by a chain of medium maturities, which sometimes are dominated more by the short end and sometimes more by the long end. Because a chain of medium maturities does exist, the yield curve is a fact to be reckoned with. However, the curve should not be expected to behave traditionally or logically, as though the rates were linked together by a mathematical formula.

Both markets, that for short paper and that for long bonds, are, of course, simultaneously influenced by the same economic environment. Therefore, short rates and long rates are apt to rise or fall together. Also, short rates have usually fluctuated much more vigorously than long rates. However, there have been occasions when long rates have fluctuated more than short rates, and a few occasions when they have moved in opposite directions.

Short-term rates of interest are heavily influenced, or even controlled, by government monetary policy. Government policy usually reinforces and hastens natural short-term interest-rate trends, but sometimes tries to change them. Long-term rates of interest, on the other hand, are in peacetime largely created by the free decisions of thousands of investors. Long-term rates, therefore, tend to discount expected future events which will ordinarily not be reflected in present short-term rates. Prospective inflation or deflation, prosperity or stagnation can have an important effect on long-term rates long before these conditions develop. This, of course, is because the long-term bonds will still be outstanding when these future events occur, whereas short-term loan contracts will have expired. At all times a basic influence affecting present long-term rates is expectation of future long-term rates.

Cyclical Changes in Treasury Yield Curves

Table XXII lists the gross yields of U.S. Treasury securities for all maturities at all of the major cyclical turning points since 1946. The turning points are the dates when long-term yields reached their cyclical highs or lows. These dates did not always coincide with the cyclical highs and lows of the short- or medium-term rates. At the bottom of the table is a supplement breaking down the long 1961–69 cyclical bear bond market into its five phases: two rallies and three declines. The table also shows at each of these dates four maturity yield spreads: (1) the spread between the longest yield and the one-year yield; (2) the spread between the one-year yield and the 3-month yield; (3) the total spread between the longest yield and the 3-month yield; and (4) the spread between the longest yield and the highest yield of any maturity.

The curves from Table XXII are all plotted in Chart XXVI as cyclical couplets: each little chart contains, in its lower part, the curve at the time of a yield trough for the long rate (dashed line), and in its upper part the curve at the time of the next cyclical peak for the long rate (solid line). Again, the long 1961–69 cycle is broken down into its three component phases.

At a glance these curves tell a story of important secular as well as cyclical changes in the maturity structure of the bond market, that is to say, in the relationship of long-term yields to short- and medium-term yields. The chart shows that in the two bear cycles, 1946–48 and 1950–53, the yield curves remained positive at both peaks and troughs, but in 1957 and 1960 negative or humped curves appeared whenever long yields rose to peaks; positive curves returned whenever yields declined. However, the 1961–69 breakdown reveals some important deviations from this pattern. In the following analysis a distinction will be made between the "short curve," i.e., 1 year to 3 months (sometimes called the bill curve) and the "long curve," i.e., 30 years to 1 year.

The 1946–48 Price Decline

The total curve at both cyclical extremes was sharply positive throughout (+163 and +143 basis points), and parabolic. The only important

Table XXII

Treasury Yields by Maturity at Cyclical Peaks and Troughs

First of Month	3 Mos.*	Years								Spreads in Basis Points			
		1	2	3	4	5	10	20	30	Longest to 1 Year	1 Year to 3 Mos.	Longest to 3 Mos.	Longest to Highest Yld.
Apr., 1946	0.37	0.59	0.92	1.18	1.36	1.43	1.68	2.00		+141	+22	+163	0
Aug., 1948	1.00	1.29	1.47	1.58	1.69	1.78	2.18	2.43		+114	+29	+143	0
Jan., 1950	1.08	1.14	1.21	1.25	1.32	1.38	1.93	2.26		+112	+6	+118	0
June, 1953	2.26	2.56	2.73	2.84	2.97	3.03	3.20	3.18	3.31	+75	+30	+105	0
Aug., 1954	0.88	0.94	1.13	1.37	1.63	1.82	2.37	2.50	2.64	+170	+6	+176	0
Oct., 1957	3.70	3.98	4.08	4.10	4.10	4.05	3.88	3.75	3.63	-35	+28	-7	-47
June, 1958	0.87	1.04	1.45	2.07	2.22	2.35	2.94	3.19	3.20	+216	+17	+233	0
Jan., 1960	4.43	4.91	4.98	4.98	4.91	4.84	4.67	4.55	4.41	-50	+48	-2	-57
June, 1961	2.37	2.94	3.30	3.49	3.58	3.66	3.80	3.80	3.80	+86	+57	+143	0
Feb., 1969	6.33	6.30	6.23	6.17	6.11	6.07	6.00	6.00	6.00	-30	-3	-33	-33
Breakdown of the 1961-69 Bear Phase													
July, 1965	3.87	3.89	3.95	4.00	4.03	4.10	4.19	4.18	4.17	+28	+2	+30	-2
Oct., 1966	5.44	5.53	5.48	5.40	5.32	5.24	4.85	4.76	4.74	-79	+9	-70	-79
Feb., 1967	4.60	4.62	4.61	4.61	4.61	4.60	4.50	4.44	4.42	-20	+2	-18	-20
Dec., 1967	5.05	5.58	5.62	5.66	5.68	5.70	5.70	5.60	5.56	-2	+53	+51	-14
Aug., 1968	5.26	5.31	5.30	5.30	5.30	5.30	5.21	5.12	5.10	-21	+5	-16	-21
Feb., 1969	6.33	6.30	6.23	6.17	6.11	6.07	6.00	6.00	6.00	-30	-3	-33	-33

*Bond yield equivalent.
High yield is underlined.

Source: Salomon Brothers & Hutzler, *An Analytical Record of Yields and Yield Spreads.*

Chart XXVI
TREASURY YIELD CURVES

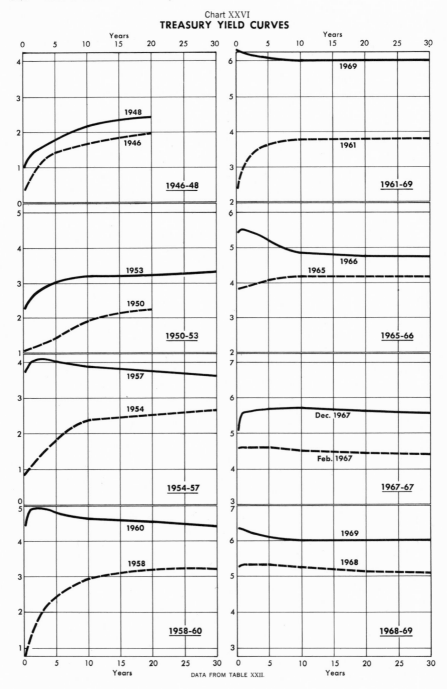

DATA FROM TABLE XXII.

shift in the structure of the curve was the result of the larger rise in all yields out to 2 years. The short curve became more positive, whereas the long curve declined in slope.

Yield Changes — Apr., 1946–Aug., 1948

3-Month Bills	+63 Basis Points
1-Year	+70 " "
5-Year	+35 " "
20-Year	+43 " "

The 1948–50 Rally and the 1950–53 Price Decline

At the 1950 yield trough the total curve was less steep (+118 basis points), and had lost the earlier parabolic pattern. This was because during the 1948–50 period of moderately declining long yields, bill yields actually rose a little further. Thus, the short curve actually flattened, but the slope of the long curve changed very little.

The 1953 peak yield curve was still positive (+105 basis points) and again parabolic, being almost flat from 10 years out. All yields rose very sharply from 1950 to 1953, but the largest rise was in 4–5 years, the smallest in 20 years, and the next smallest in 3 months. This then was a hidden step toward the humped curves which were not noticed until 1957. The short curve became much steeper and the long curve became more moderate.

Yield Changes: 1948 to 1950 to 1953

	1948–50	1950–53
3-Month Bills	+8 Basis Pts.	+118 Basis Pts.
1-Year	−15 " "	+142 " "
5-Year	−40 " "	+165 " "
20-Year	−17 " "	+92 " "

The 1953–54 Rally and the 1954–57 Price Decline

At the 1954 yield trough the total curve was more sharply positive (+176 basis points), largely because of the precipitous decline in all short yields. The short curve almost vanished, while the long curve was steep even beyond 10 years.

In dramatic contrast, the 1957 curve at the peak of yields was the first of the negative curves that ever since have characterized most periods of tight money. From tip to tip, it was almost flat (−7 basis points), but the yields at 3- and 4-year maturity were actually 47 basis points higher than the longest yields. Since the 4¼% legal ceiling on government bonds was not yet a restraining factor, this episode suggests that the legal ceiling was not the sole cause of the humped curves that returned later on when the ceiling was effective. The 1957 curve was created by very large increases in yields out to 5 years, accompanied by progressively much smaller increases in longer yields. During this bear phase, the short curve increased from +6 basis points to +28 basis points, whereas the "long curve" declined from +170 basis points to −35 basis points.

Yield Changes: 1953 to 1954 to 1957

	1953–54	1954–57
3-Month Bills	−138 Basis Pts.	+282 Basis Pts.
1-Year	−162 " "	+304 " "
5-Year	−121 " "	+223 " "
30-Year	−67 " "	+99 " "

The 1957–58 Rally and the 1958–60 Price Decline

In a few short months of falling yields, the negative-humped 1957 curve was transformed into the sharpest positive curve on this record (+233 basis points). Nevertheless, at the 1958 yield trough, the short curve was flatter, and the increased slope was all in the long curve. The chief factor was a collapse of short yields back to below their 1948 level, while long yields declined much less.

In the 1958–60 bear market the reverse occurred: short yields rose three times as much as long yields, and the curve again became flat and humped very much like that of 1957, but at higher yield levels. Again, the short curve became sharply positive at +48 basis points, and the long curve became negative at −50 basis points (−57 basis points from 3-year maturity to 30-year maturity).

Yield Changes: 1957 to 1958 to 1960

	1957–58	1958–60
3-Month Bills	−283 Basis Pts.	+356 Basis Pts.
1-Year	−294 " "	+387 " "
5-Year	−170 " "	+249 " "
10-Year	−94 " "	+173 " "
30-Year	−43 " "	+121 " "

The 1960–61 Rally and the 1961–69 Price Decline

Again, the slightly negative humped curve of early 1960 was quickly transformed by 1961 into another conventional positive curve (+143 basis points), this time parabolic and flat from ten years out. Differing from the patterns of earlier periods of easy money, the short curve stayed sharply positive at +57 basis points, little changed from 1960, and the long curve swung from −50 basis points in 1960 to +86 basis points in 1961. The total slope was less than those of the easy-money periods of 1954 and 1958, because short rates were not allowed to fall to nominal levels, no doubt because of balance-of-payments problems. This was the last conventional sharply positive recession curve on this record.

During the latter part of the long bear phase from 1961 to 1969 many interim shifts in the curve occurred with dynamic shifts in the environment, but the net was that by early 1969 a purely negative parabolic curve had developed (−33 basis points) with no hump and, therefore, quite unlike the 1957 and the 1960 tight-money curves. In 1969, for the first time, the short curve became slightly negative (−3 basis points). The huge rise in long yields was the feature of this bear market. It would be logical to expect a much steeper negative slope.

Yield Changes: 1960 to 1961 to 1969

	1960–61	1961–69
3-Month Bills	−206 Basis Pts.	+396 Basis Pts.
1-Year	−197 " "	+336 " "
5-Year	−118 " "	+241 " "
10-Year	−87 " "	+220 " "
30-Year	−61 " "	+220 " "

Interim Curves 1965; 1966; February 1967; December 1967; 1968; 1969

There were highly dynamic shifts in the yield curve in the course of the three sharp market breaks in 1966, 1967, and 1968 and the two intervening rallies. The chart shows that by mid-1965 the curve was still positive (+30 basis points), but dramatically less so than in the easy-money period of 1961 (+143 basis points). By the time of the 1966 crunch, the total curve had become sharply negative (−70 basis points), all in the long curve, the steepest negative curve on this record. Because of the force of a restrictive monetary policy, short rates had soared three times as fast as long rates.

At the peak of the rally in February, 1967, the curve was still negative, but very slightly so (−18 basis points). It did not resemble at all the positive easy-money curves of earlier years.

During the extraordinarily large 1967 bear bond market, monetary policy was strangely easy most of the time and, therefore, short rates rose remarkably little; whereas long rates soared, largely because of volume and inflationary and currency fears. Therefore, by the time the long market had reached its 1967 yield peak at the eve of the sterling devaluation, the curve was strangely positive (+51 basis points entirely in the short curve), and was humped, with maximum yields in 5 to 10 years. During the first four months of this bear phase, there was the unusual phenomenon of short rates declining substantially while, simultaneously, long rates rose substantially. Later, in 1967, both rose together.

The rally from December 1967, to August 1968, oddly enough restored a negative curve (−16 basis points entirely in the long curve). This was another most unusual period, since short rates rose and simultaneously long rates declined. The very ambiguity of the August, 1968, curve indicates the conflicting forces of monetary ease and inflationary boom that then prevailed.

Finally, between August, 1968, and February, 1969, virtually all yields from 1 year out rose by about the same amount, thus shifting the moderately negative curve upward. However, 3-month yields rose more than others, and the over-all negative slope of the long curve increased.

Yield Changes: 1961–69

	1961–65	1965–66	1966–67	Feb. 1967 to Dec. 1967	1967–68	1968–69
3-Month Bills	+150	+157	−84	+45	+21	+107
1-Year	+95	+164	−91	+96	−27	+99
5-Year	+44	+114	−64	+110	−40	+77
10-Year	+39	+66	−35	+120	−49	+79
30-Year	+37	+57	−32	+114	−46	+90

It is remarkable that in the bear phase in 1967 long yields rose more than short yields and that in the bear phase of 1968–69 long yields rose almost as much as short yields. Probably the monetary policy that held short yields down served to accentuate the upward pressure on long yields.

The Short-Term and the Long-Term Yield Curves

Chart XXVII traces the two component parts of the total Treasury yield curve derived from Table XXII; the short curve from 1 year to 3 months (sometimes called the bill curve); and the long curve from longest to 1 year. From 1950 to 1960, the chart shows, the cyclical fluctuations of these two curves usually moved in opposite directions. Thus, when yields rose (1950–53, 1954–57, 1958–60, 1961–69), the long curve always flattened, and often became negative; whereas when yields declined (1953–54, 1957–58, 1960–61) the long curve always rose, and often became sharply positive. However, until 1961 the short curve did just the opposite, becoming sharply positive in high-yield periods and flat in low-yield periods. It was this conflicting trend that helped create the humped curves; the effect of the shape of the short curve, no doubt, often extended beyond the arbitrary one-year limit that we have used.

However, from 1960 on, the short curve stopped moving opposite to the long curve and tended to move with the long curve. The detailed panel seems to suggest that in the crunch of 1966 and the subsequent recovery, the short curve did indeed move slightly counter to the long curve, but from February, 1967, on, it moved with the long curve, thus eliminating the hump.

Chart XXVII
TREASURY MATURITY SPREADS AT PEAKS AND TROUGHS:
Longest to 1 Year; 1 Year to 3 Months. In Basis Points

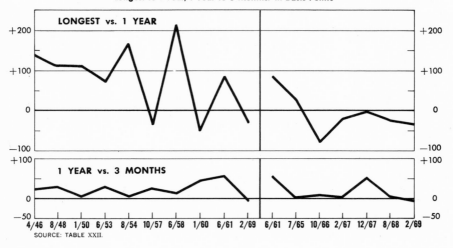

SOURCE: TABLE XXII.

Corporate and Municipal Yield Curves

Table XXIII presents the extremes of the total corporate yield curve by comparing very short-term and very long-term corporate yields in terms of annual averages of 3-months' prime finance paper, and long-term (generally 30 years) Aa seasoned discount utility bonds. No satisfactory data are available showing a complete corporate yield curve with a variety of maturities. Table XXIV presents prime-municipal yield curves derived from the Salomon Brothers & Hutzler municipal yields by maturity; it is also computed in terms of annual averages and it shows two spreads, i.e., 10 years to 1 year, and 30 years to 1 year. Table XXV presents the Treasury yield curves in terms of annual averages for all principal maturities; it records the yield spreads for 1 year vs. 3 months, 30 years vs. 1 year, and 30 years vs. 3 months. Since all three of these tables show annual averages, they miss the monthly extreme curves such as were recorded in Table XXII above. Chart XXVIII pictures the yield spreads between longest and shortest Treasuries, corporates, and municipals from 1950 to 1969 as listed in Tables XXIII, XXIV, and XXV.

The chart shows that all three of these maturity spreads usually fluctuated similarly. This was because with a few exceptions the

Table XXIII

Long-Term Corporate Bonds vs. 3-Month Finance Paper
(Annual averages)

	3-Month Prime Finance Paper	Long-Term Aa Util. Bonds (Seasoned Discounts)	Spread Long vs. Short in Basis Points		3-Month Prime Finance Paper	Long-Term Aa Util. Bonds (Seasoned Discounts)	Spread Long vs. Short in Basis Points
1950	1.42%	2.72%	+130	1960	3.47%	4.41%	+94
1951	1.91	2.96	+105	1961	2.66	4.35	+169
1952	2.16	3.07	+91	1962	3.09	4.28	+119
1953	2.37	3.31	+94	1963	3.41	4.23	+82
1954	1.43	2.98	+155	1964	3.85	4.39	+54
1955	2.00	3.13	+113	1965	4.24	4.46	+22
1956	3.07	3.40	+33	1966	5.39	5.13	−26
1957	3.57	4.00	+43	1967	4.93	5.49	+56
1958	2.14	3.80	+166	1968	5.70	6.15	+45
1959	3.79	4.48	+69				

Source: Appendix.

Table XXIV

Municipal Yield Scales and Spreads
(Annual averages)

| | Prime Yields Maturity in Years | | | | | | Spreads in Basis Points | |
	1	2	5	10	20	30	10 to 1 Year	30 to 1 Year
1950	0.75	0.80	1.00	1.20	1.55	1.70	+45	+95
1951	1.00	1.05	1.20	1.40	1.60	1.80	+40	+80
1952	1.00	1.05	1.20	1.45	1.75	2.00	+45	+100
1953	1.30	1.35	1.55	1.80	2.25	2.45	+50	+115
1954	0.75	0.90	1.15	1.50	2.00	2.30	+75	+155
1955	1.15	1.30	1.55	1.80	2.15	2.35	+65	+120
1956	1.70	1.90	2.10	2.25	2.40	2.55	+55	+85
1957	2.15	2.30	2.55	2.75	2.95	3.05	+60	+90
1958	1.30	1.50	2.00	2.40	2.80	2.95	+110	+165
1959	2.20	2.35	2.65	2.95	3.20	3.35	+75	+115
1960	2.05	2.30	2.60	2.90	3.20	3.40	+85	+135
1961	1.50	1.75	2.25	2.75	3.15	3.35	+125	+185
1962	1.60	1.75	2.15	2.55	3.00	3.20	+95	+160
1963	1.75	1.90	2.25	2.60	3.00	3.20	+85	+145
1964	2.10	2.25	2.55	2.80	3.05	3.25	+70	+115
1965	2.35	2.50	2.75	2.90	3.10	3.30	+55	+95
1966	3.40	3.45	3.50	3.55	3.65	3.75	+15	+35
1967	3.00	3.13	3.38	3.55	3.75	3.88	+55	+88
1968	3.30	3.47	3.73	3.93	4.18	4.36	+63	+106

Source: Salomon Brothers & Hutzler, *An Analytical Record of Yields and Yield Spreads.*

maturity spreads tended to decline (that is to say the positive curves tended to flatten or turn negative) in periods of rising yields such as 1953, 1956–57, 1958–59, and 1966; and the spreads tended to turn positive and widen substantially in easy-money periods such as 1954, 1958, and 1961.

Comparison of the corporate maturity spreads with the Treasury maturity spreads shows that the trends were almost always in the same direction and that the positive corporate spreads tended most of the time to be somewhat smaller than the positive Treasury spreads. There was no sustained trend in the relationship between these two spreads, although there were occasional aberrations.

The municipal maturity spreads, while usually following a similar pattern to those of the Treasury and corporate maturity spreads, were

Table XXV

Treasury Yields by Maturity

(Annual averages)

	3-Month Bills	Years								Spreads in Basis Points		
		1	2	3	4	5	10	20	30	Long-est to 1 Yr.	1 Yr. to 3 Mos.	Long-est to 3 Mos.
1950	1.18	1.28	1.37	1.42	1.47	1.54	2.11	2.39	—	+111	+10	+121
1951	1.49	1.70	1.83	1.90	1.96	2.03	2.41	2.60	—	+90	+21	+111
1952	1.70	1.87	2.03	2.14	2.22	2.26	2.47	2.68	—	+81	+17	+98
1953	1.90	2.13	2.32	2.42	2.50	2.57	2.78	2.92	—	+79	+23	+102
1954	0.92	1.03	1.24	1.46	1.70	1.89	2.43	2.57	2.76	+173	+11	+184
1955	1.70	1.97	2.27	2.42	2.51	2.58	2.72	2.83	2.95	+98	+27	+125
1956	2.64	2.89	3.03	3.10	3.12	3.13	3.08	3.07	3.10	+21	+25	+46
1957	3.17	3.48	3.58	3.63	3.64	3.63	3.54	3.45	3.44	−4	+31	+27
1958	1.81	2.17	2.50	2.75	2.89	2.98	3.27	3.45	3.48	+131	+36	+167
1959	3.26	3.90	4.10	4.21	4.26	4.26	4.18	4.12	4.08	+18	+64	+82
1960	2.88	3.55	3.78	3.97	4.08	4.13	4.13	4.13	4.12	+57	+67	+124
1961	2.30	2.89	3.23	3.46	3.61	3.69	3.84	3.90	3.94	+105	+59	+164
1962	2.73	3.05	3.28	3.47	3.61	3.71	3.96	4.02	4.06	+101	+32	+133
1963	3.10	3.29	3.45	3.61	3.72	3.80	3.98	4.04	4.07	+78	+19	+97
1964	3.51	3.80	3.94	4.01	4.05	4.08	4.17	4.18	4.19	+39	+29	+68
1965	3.98	4.07	4.11	4.15	4.17	4.20	4.25	4.23	4.22	+15	+9	+24
1966	4.91	5.12	5.19	5.20	5.18	5.14	4.86	4.72	4.69	−43	+21	−22
1967	4.36	4.77	4.87	4.94	4.98	5.00	4.97	4.93	4.90	+13	+41	+54
1968	5.37	5.54	5.56	5.57	5.57	5.56	5.48	5.40	5.35	−19	+17	−2

Source: Salomon Brothers & Hutzler, *An Analytical Record of Yields and Yield Spreads.*
These yields are read from curves and, thus, differ slightly from U.S. Treasury yields tabulated in Appendix.

Chart XXVIII
TREASURY, CORPORATE AND MUNICIPAL MATURITY SPREADS
(Annual Averages in Basis Points)

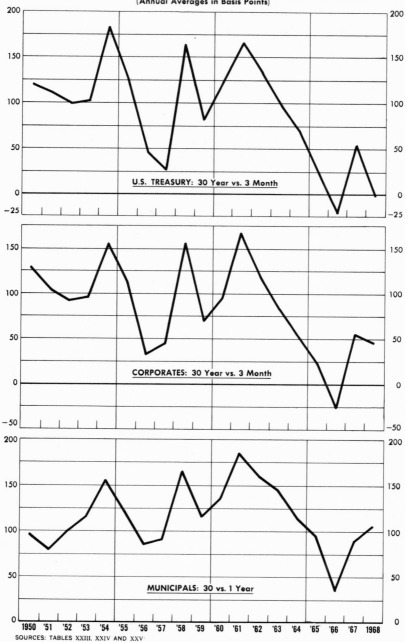

SOURCES: TABLES XXIII, XXIV AND XXV

usually more positive. Only once did they even approach zero, and they never were negative. Recently, in fact, when the government maturity spread was negative, the municipal maturity spread was positive by as much as 100 basis points. Furthermore, the positive municipal spreads tended to widen in the 1950's, whereas the government spread did not. During the period 1967–68, the positive municipal spreads widened while both other spreads declined.

This built-in tendency for the municipal yield curve to stay substantially positive even in tight-money periods is probably partly the result of the fact that commercial banks have been the chief investors in municipals, and for operational reasons they tend to favor shorter maturities. In addition, corporate operating funds are frequently invested in municipals where the rates after taxes are very attractive, but such funds rarely buy longer maturities. Municipals are also frequently used by high-bracket private investors as a temporary refuge, and this also favors short maturities. Over the years there has been a distinct shortage of funds for investment in longer-term municipals; the municipal market lacks a clientele of long-term institutional investors like life insurance companies, pension funds, and retirement funds, which are the mainstays of the corporate-bond market.

Looking Ahead

As this book goes to press in June, 1969, bonds are still in a bear market. Long prime discount corporate bonds are selling to yield around 7¼%— the highest yield since the Civil War. If in the next year or two yields rise further to, say, 9¼% (unprecedentedly high), there will be a capital loss from present prices of around 19%. If, on the other hand, yields return to 5¼% (the level of early 1967), there will be a capital gain of about 32%—provided the bonds retain their quality status and are not impeded by call. It is evident, therefore, that in bond investment the stakes today are high, very high. The difference between these two plausible projections adds up to over 50% of the principal invested. In terms of past performance, the odds have never been so favorable to bonds.

The stakes, however, are much higher than this calculation of capital values suggests. If yields trend up in a sustained way to an 8%–10% range, the political, economic, and social environment is bound to be dramatically worse than it will be if yields trend down to a 5%–6% range. This is not because higher or lower yields themselves will necessarily have a decisive influence on the future environment, but rather because prevailing yields will as usual signal either a return to peace, poise, and stability, or a further degeneration into war, inflation, factionalism, and frustration. It is pertinent here to paraphrase and amplify an observation quoted in the introductory chapter of this book from *A History of Interest Rates:*

> The record of prime bond yields over long periods of time in any modern industrial nation has provided a fever chart of the economic and political health of that nation. Extremely high or extremely low yields have invariably

marked periods of political or economic calamity. War and inflation are associated with every historic period of extremely high yields. Depression and deflation are associated with periods of extremely low yields. Moderate yields, neither very high nor very low, have signified health and prosperity.

If this observation is valid, and we think it is, it follows that the bond-portfolio manager, seeking in 1969 or 1970 to formulate an opinion on the longer-term outlook for bond prices, will not be able to rely solely on economic and technical analysis—such factors as the business outlook for a year or so, or the size of credit demands, or the probabilities for monetary and fiscal policy. Such factors will be important, but he must also make assumptions on political trends at home and abroad and their sociological corollaries. Above all, he must consider the likelihood of more war or more peace, which may be another way of saying more or less inflation.

Inferences from Postwar Market History

The massive decline in the bond market since World War II has provided a laboratory test for a number of economic theories and for much market dogma. It has refuted many firm convictions and has created new rules of the game. Here are some reasonable inferences from the behavior of the market over the last few years:

(1) The traditional band of long-term bond yields in the United States and the United Kingdom, which has prevailed over the past two or three centuries, is no longer limiting. Bond yields in both countries have recently risen well above the high limits of that band. However, short-term interest rates, which have historically fluctuated in a much wider band than long-term yields, though rising to high levels, have remained well within their historic ranges. This is probably because short-term rates in most countries are closely controlled by monetary authorities, whereas long-term bond yields in all free economies are determined by the independent decisions of thousands of investors.

(2) In an inflationary boom, high interest rates are not by themselves deflationary over the medium term and, therefore, they are not self-reversing. This is because they are not an effective restraint on many forms of economic activity if strong inflationary expectations prevail. Some traditional theory would have assumed that the high interest rates of 1966–67 must have dampened down the boom, at least with a lag, and led to lower interest rates, but in fact they were ineffective on both counts. Therefore, the market will no longer assume that rate trends, up or down, will lead to automatic reversals.

(3) Nevertheless, in periods free from inflationary expectations, it may well be that sharply rising interest rates will, in fact, prove effec-

tive in helping check overexpansion and, thus, be self-correcting. Something of this sort may have happened in 1957 and again in 1959.

(4) Rising interest rates have not been demonstrably effective in encouraging savings in either the United States or the United Kingdom. Furthermore, the rapid sustained rise in bond yields in both countries has probably gone beyond the point of optimum attraction of new saving. It has led to such severe capital losses as finally to divert needed funds away from bond investment into nonproductive media such as gold, land, foreign currencies, and competitive bidding for equities. (Equities have been nonproductive in the sense that few or no net new equities were being issued by corporations and, therefore, funds so invested were not directly financing public or private capital expenditures.)

(5) In periods of credit shortage, such as 1966 and early 1969, certain credit demanders in the United States were almost immune from credit rationing, but others were vulnerable. Demanders may be ranked as follows:

(a) The U.S. Treasury can always fill its credit requirements.
(b) Large corporations have such a diversity of credit sources that they can almost always find necessary funds and, with a few exceptions, are able and willing to pay a high price.
(c) Some small and marginal corporations are apt to be denied credit.
(d) Some finance companies are apt to be denied credit.
(e) Some municipalities may be forced to postpone projects, or to borrow short-term at banks instead of selling bonds.
(f) Home mortgages are the weakest credit demanders in a time of credit scarcity, because of their dependence on local institutions which, in turn, are dependent on time deposits. The earnings of mortgage institutions are tied to the rates paid by past mortgage acquisitions and, hence, the rates they can afford to pay to depositors do not move up with the going rates on new mortgages, or with the going rates available in the securities markets. Again, because of the fixed rate on policy loans, life insurance investment can be restrained at times of high interest rates, and this helps to starve the mortgage market.

(6) Interest rates alone are not a major determinant of surplus or deficit in a nation's balance of payments. Countries with relatively low interest rates, like Switzerland, have done well on balance of payments, but countries like the United Kingdom have found that extremely high interest rates have not been effective. This is probably because in recent years confidence has been low and because neither high nor low

interest rates have had their textbook effect on the internal levels of economic activity.

(7) The English-speaking countries, the United States, the United Kingdom, and Canada, have all suffered an extraordinary rise in interest rates since the late 1940's, which has recently brought unprecedentedly high rates.   This has not been true of France, Germany, Switzerland, and others.   In part, this was because the United States and the United Kingdom bore the major financial burden of World War II and necessarily shifted a good part of their vast wartime credit burdens into the postwar period.   On the other hand, Germany extinguished most of her war debts by a postwar "currency reform" (near cancellation), as did Russia and many other belligerents; and France did much the same, even though she participated only briefly in the war.   Furthermore, the English-speaking nations assumed most of the burden of financing a world-wide postwar recovery and also of helping keep the peace.   Finally, both the pound sterling and especially the dollar were reserve currencies and, therefore, subject to turbulent international pressures that did not directly affect national currencies.   Their interest rates, therefore, had to be high enough to attract or hold large foreign balances in a world of gold scarcity and convertible currencies; whereas in the 1940's and earlier, as refuges and largely because of their high credit standing, they could hold large foreign balances in spite of low interest rates.

The Future of Bond Investment

So disastrous has been the price history of bonds since World War II and so favorable has been the price history of equities since 1950, that the question is now being raised whether, in broad terms, bonds have any future.   Many traditional bond investors have turned to equities in the last decade and today this diversion of investment funds is continuing.   Will this trend, in the next five years, make bonds "obsolete" and, if so, how will this affect our capital markets?

It will, of course, be immediately noticed that this investment preference for equities is precisely the reverse of the investment preferences of twenty years ago.   Then price experience with equities had been so bad for two decades (down 57%), and experience with high-grade bonds had been so good (up 45%), that many institutional investors preferred bonds at 3% to blue-chip equities at 6% plus.   Both then and now these market preferences were, of course, based on extrapolations of market experience going back two decades.   In 1949 we heard much about a chronic shortage of equity capital, and today we hear of a shortage of funds for bond investment. In 1949 many asked, "Have stocks any future?"

This bit of history, of course, does not tell us that there will soon (or ever) be another reversal of sentiment or of market experience. But if, in fact, American institutions are going to avoid fixed-income securities, the effect will be much wider than a mere change in prices in our capital markets.

Our economy today is financed primarily in two ways: (1) By the retained earnings of business enterprises, and (2), more importantly, by a huge flow of private savings into fixed-income investments, either directly through the bond markets, or indirectly through institutions that buy bonds or mortgages, or make loans. This reliance on credit has been true since the days of Alexander Hamilton, and has been true in almost all advanced European countries since the seventeenth century. In recent years large American corporations have rarely financed themselves by new stock issues. Indeed, the entire corporate sector in 1968 retired more stock than it issued. Over the last decade American corporations raised an annual average of $17.0 billion net through the issuance of debt instruments and only $1.0 billion net through the issuance of equities (including the conversion of convertible bonds).

It would seem that corporate growth depends upon the willingness of individuals and institutions to buy debt instruments. Furthermore, our states, municipalities, and federal government depend entirely on their ability to sell debt. All told, in 1968 new debt instruments of all sorts provided $84 billion for economic growth, while net new equities provided nothing, and retained earnings provided $20 billion. What happens then if American capitalists and institutions continue to turn away from fixed-income investment?

Up to now this dual trend of business to rely for its growth on new debt, and of investors to prefer equities, has resulted merely in a progressive rise in bond yields, and a rise in equity prices based on acute scarcity. In fact, more bonds than ever before were sold in 1968 and, therefore, economic growth continued. But what if, as some suggest, these new trends and preferences accelerate and bonds "go out of style"?

One answer sometimes heard is that all bonds will be convertible bonds or bonds with warrants. If such a trend goes far enough, it would end the scarcity of equities, heavily dilute present shares, and no doubt tarnish the popularity of equities. But even so, such a solution applies to only the $13 billion corporate-bond sector of the capital markets out of a total 1968 credit expansion of $84 billion. States and municipalities cannot issue equities or convertible bonds, nor can Uncle

Sam. Home-owners cannot spice up their mortgage loans with equity participation, nor can short-term borrowers. Thus, regardless of investor preference, we will still be dependent on a massive flow of savings into fixed-income investment. If it is not forthcoming, our economic growth must stop. This is just one way that inflation inhibits growth.

This observation, of course, does not remove the threat or solve the problem, but it does suggest that the threatened hiatus between the preferences of savers and of investors is a basic threat to our economy and not merely a localized factor of change in the structure of our capital markets, or merely a threat to the price of bonds. If we rule out revolutionary changes in the structure of our economy, such as an end to free markets, programs of forced saving, etc., we know that a large and growing volume of bond investment will have to continue indefinitely, in order to meet our massive national needs. No doubt the relative popularity of stocks and bonds will change from time to time in response to the economic and political environment, but bond investment will necessarily continue to provide most of the new capital needed by our economy.

The Future of Interest Rates

Market experience over a long period of years suggests that inflation is the chief cause of high interest rates. By inflation we mean the kind of upward price trend that influences economic expectations and business plans. This is not the steady 1% upcreep of the cost of living index, which has been almost a built-in feature of our economic statistics for decades. By inflation we mean the erratic sharp rises in wholesale commodity prices, which have come in spurts and then subsided. Chart XXI shows how erratic inflation so defined has been. It has not been a permanent way of life. Inflation has almost always coincided with rising interest rates, and interest rates have rarely risen significantly without inflation.

Again, inflation in the United States has almost always coincided with wars. Therefore, those who are attempting a long-range forecast of interest rates probably should ask themselves first of all: "Is the outlook for more war or for more peace?" If the answer is "more war," then more inflation and high interest rates seem inevitable until we reach the point of wartime controls. If the answer is "more peace," then less inflation, and stable-to-lower interest rates seem likely.

Finally, of course, peacetime social expenditures accompanied by faulty fiscal and monetary policies could lead to a novelty in our history: peacetime inflation. This, too, no doubt, would bring high interest rates. We can console ourselves, however, that never in our history have we suffered these inflationary pressures in times of real peace. Somehow the great peacetime expansions of the late nineteenth century, and of the 1920's, and of parts of the 1950's and 1960's were achieved without inflation and without rising interest rates. In fact, during those very prosperous years, interest rates usually fell. There seems to be something about peacetime capital expenditures that is self-financing, or that creates the savings required to finance them.

In the introduction to this book, it was said that no attempt would be made to verify or refute economic theories on the causes and effects of high or low interest rates. Therefore, these speculations, which seem to follow logically from the market history recited in this book, are in the nature of suggestions rather than conclusions.

As this book goes to press, there seems to be under way a confrontation between a massive destructive inflationary boom and the forces of fiscal and monetary restraint. Our readers will know more about the outcome than we do now. It is our hope, perhaps more than a hope, that our new political leadership will persist in restraint with the co-operation of the Federal Reserve System, so that by the time this book is published this dangerous inflationary boom will have been checked. If not, then it is easy to predict that an even more destructive confrontation will be in the offing. This is because the inflation will surely accelerate or subside. It must be dealt with sooner or later. A stable unchanging rate of inflation is an economist's pipe dream. The future of American interest rates will depend for many years to come on the outcome of monetary and fiscal restraint in 1969.

Finally, one more generality seems pertinent. Many good citizens who are devoted to programs of federal or state expenditure for social improvement believe that somehow fiscal prudence clashes with their social objectives, since an economy-minded government may ignore or pare down the appropriations that they want. In the long run this is the reverse of the truth. In fact, social expenditures are the first to suffer from inflation. We have seen just that happen in 1967 and 1968. Sound money is a *sine qua non* of progressive programs of social expenditure.

By analogy, when a rich and philanthropic family suddenly becomes poorer, large cuts, rightly or wrongly, will probably be made in its philanthropies. Just so, nations with affluence and with strong currencies are most apt to venture into new social expenditures. Nations which are fighting desperately to maintain their currency and their credit can give little heed to new benefits. The social programs of President Kennedy, and later of President Johnson, were made possible by the surplus resources and price stability that we enjoyed four to eight years ago. They could never have been funded in today's inflationary environment.

Therefore, it is hoped that the lessons of the great bear bond market will influence those who feel an urgent need for new and costly national programs. Since there is a strict limit each year to the volume of real savings available to finance government and the private economy, priorities are needed. This means that at a time of full employment large new programs requiring credit must usually be matched by the cancellation of old programs. Sound and receptive credit markets are essential to prosperity, to rapid economic growth, and to social betterment.

Appendix

Monthly Yields and Yield Spreads

	1	2	3	4	5	6	7	8	9	10	11	12
		Aa Utility, Per Cent		Yield Spread (B.P.)		Prime Munici-pals, Per Cent		Short-Term Rates—3-Month, Per Cent				
First of Month	Long U.S. Govts., Per Cent	Low Cou-pon	New Call-able	2 vs. 1	3 vs. 1	1 Yr.	30 Yr.	U.S. Bills	Bank-ers' Ac-cept-ances	Fed. Agcs.	Fi-nance Paper	CD's
1946						.						
Jan.	2.41	2.46	2.44	+5	+3		1.00	0.37	0.44	0.75	0.75	
Feb.	2.29	2.39	2.39	+10	+10		0.95	0.37	0.44	0.75	0.75	
Mar.	2.20	2.38	2.39	+18	+19		0.90	0.37	0.44	0.74	0.75	
Apr.	2.17	2.37	2.47	+20	+30		0.90	0.37	0.44	0.74	0.75	
May	2.28	2.41	2.57	+13	+29		1.00	0.37	0.44	0.75	0.75	
June	2.26	2.41	2.55	+15	+29		1.05	0.37	0.50	0.75	0.75	
July	2.26	2.41	2.59	+15	+33		1.10	0.37	0.50	0.74	0.75	
Aug.	2.32	2.43	2.59	+11	+27		1.20	0.37	0.69	0.95	0.75	
Sept.	2.35	2.50	2.65	+15	+30		1.25	0.37	0.81	0.95	0.75	
Oct.	2.38	2.53	2.74	+15	+36		1.30	0.37	0.81	0.95	1.00	
Nov.	2.33	2.53	2.70	+20	+37		1.40	0.37	0.81	0.95	1.00	
Dec.	2.39	2.56	2.70	+17	+31		1.50	0.37	0.81	0.95	1.00	
Avg.	2.30	2.45	2.57	+15	+27		1.12	0.37	0.59	0.83	0.81	
1947												
Jan.	2.32	2.50	2.64	+18	+32		1.50	0.37	0.81	0.95	1.00	
Feb.	2.32	2.51	2.68	+19	+36		1.35	0.37	0.81	0.95	1.00	
Mar.	2.31	2.52	2.72	+21	+41		1.50	0.37	0.81	0.95	1.00	
Apr.	2.30	2.49	2.60	+19	+30		1.35	0.37	0.81	0.95	1.00	
May	2.30	2.49	2.60	+19	+30		1.40	0.37	0.81	0.95	1.00	
June	2.29	2.49	2.76	+20	+47		1.35	0.37	0.81	0.95	1.00	
July	2.33	2.50	2.69	+17	+36		1.35	0.75	0.81	0.95	1.00	
Aug.	2.33	2.50	2.70	+17	+37		1.40	0.75	0.81	0.95	1.00	
Sept.	2.31	2.56	2.74	+25	+43		1.40	0.81	0.94	1.05	1.00	
Oct.	2.31	2.66	3.00	+35	+69		1.50	0.85	0.94	1.05	1.00	
Nov.	2.40	2.74	2.96	+34	+56		1.65	0.93	0.94	1.05	1.13	
Dec.	2.43	2.82	3.06	+39	+63		1.80	0.95	1.06	1.05	1.13	
Avg.	2.33	2.57	2.76	+24	+43		1.46	0.61	0.86	0.98	1.02	
1948												
Jan.	2.48	2.82	3.03	+34	+55		1.90	0.97	1.06	1.20	1.25	
Feb.	2.48	2.82	3.00	+34	+52		2.05	1.00	1.06	1.30	1.25	
Mar.	2.48	2.81	3.03	+33	+55		2.15	1.00	1.06	1.32	1.25	
Apr.	2.47	2.75	3.00	+28	+53		2.00	1.00	1.06	1.35	1.25	
May	2.47	2.74	3.00	+27	+53		1.70	1.00	1.06	1.38	1.25	
June	2.43	2.75	2.92	+32	+49		1.70	1.00	1.06	1.15	1.25	
July	2.48	2.82	2.98	+34	+50		1.75	1.00	1.06	1.30	1.25	
Aug.	2.48	2.87	3.03	+39	+55		1.90	1.09	1.19	1.40	1.25	
Sept.	2.48	2.85	3.07	+37	+59		2.00	1.09	1.19	1.45	1.50	
Oct.	2.48	2.85	3.11	+37	+63		2.00	1.12	1.19	1.45	1.50	
Nov.	2.48	2.85	3.13	+37	+65		1.95	1.15	1.19	1.40	1.50	
Dec.	2.48	2.81	3.27	+33	+79		1.80	1.16	1.19	1.40	1.50	
Avg.	2.47	2.82	3.05	+35	+58		1.91	1.05	1.11	1.34	1.33	

Monthly Yields and Yield Spreads (continued)

	1	2	3	4	5	6	7	8	9	10	11	12
								Short-Term Rates—3-Month, Per Cent				
First of Month	Long U.S. Govts., Per Cent	Aa Utility, Per Cent		Yield Spread (B.P.)		Prime Munici- pals, Per Cent		U.S. Bills	Bank- ers' Ac- cept- ances	Fed. Agcs.	Fi- nance Paper	CD's
		Low Cou- pon	New Call- able	2 vs. 1	3 vs. 1	1 Yr.	30 Yr.					
1949												
Jan.	2.47	2.74	2.95	+27	+48		1.70	1.16	1.19	1.38	1.50	
Feb.	2.45	2.73	2.93	+28	+48		1.60	1.17	1.19	1.38	1.50	
Mar.	2.43	2.72	2.90	+29	+47		1.70	1.17	1.19	1.30	1.50	
Apr.	2.43	2.73	2.93	+30	+50		1.65	1.16	1.19	1.30	1.50	
May	2.43	2.73	2.83	+30	+40		1.60	1.17	1.19	1.32	1.50	
June	2.44	2.72	2.87	+28	+43		1.70	1.17	1.19	1.32	1.50	
July	2.36	2.68	2.73	+32	+37		1.70	1.00	1.06	1.30	1.50	
Aug.	2.33	2.63	2.66	+30	+33		1.65	1.04	1.06	1.15	1.50	
Sept.	2.29	2.62	2.65	+33	+36		1.60	1.06	1.06	1.15	1.50	
Oct.	2.29	2.62	2.65	+33	+36		1.65	1.06	1.06	1.12	1.50	
Nov.	2.28	2.59	2.64	+31	+36		1.65	1.06	1.06	1.10	1.38	
Dec.	2.26	2.59	2.68	+33	+42		1.60	1.12	1.06	1.15	1.38	
Avg.	2.37	2.68	2.79	+31	+42		1.65	1.11	1.12	1.25	1.48	
1950												
Jan.	2.24	2.70	2.74	+46	+50	0.65	1.85	1.10	1.06	1.18	1.38	
Feb.	2.29	2.69	2.70	+40	+41	0.65	1.80	1.14	1.06	1.15	1.38	
Mar.	2.31	2.70	2.65	+39	+34	0.70	1.80	1.12	1.06	1.23	1.38	
Apr.	2.35	2.70	2.65	+35	+30	0.70	1.80	1.17	1.06	1.25	1.38	
May	2.38	2.72	2.67	+34	+29	0.75	1.85	1.18	1.06	1.25	1.38	
June	2.39	2.74	2.70	+35	+31	0.80	1.80	1.17	1.06	1.25	1.38	
July	2.42	2.74	2.72	+32	+30	0.80	1.80	1.17	1.06	1.30	1.38	
Aug.	2.43	2.71	2.71	+28	+28	0.75	1.65	1.18	1.06	1.30	1.38	
Sept.	2.41	2.70	2.70	+29	+29	0.75	1.60	1.32	1.31	1.45	1.50	
Oct.	2.44	2.74	2.73	+30	+29	0.75	1.60	1.33	1.31	1.50	1.50	
Nov.	2.44	2.76	2.75	+32	+31	0.80	1.55	1.36	1.31	1.55	1.50	
Dec.	2.45	2.74	2.75	+29	+30	0.85	1.50	1.30	1.31	1.58	1.50	
Avg.	2.38	2.72	2.71	+34	+33	0.75	1.70	1.21	1.14	1.33	1.42	
1951												
Jan.	2.44	2.74	2.80	+30	+36	0.95	1.50	1.39	1.38	1.60	1.63	
Feb.	2.44	2.74	2.80	+30	+36	0.90	1.40	1.39	1.50	1.70	1.63	
Mar.	2.44	2.79	2.90	+35	+46	0.90	1.70	1.36	1.63	1.78	1.63	
Apr.	2.55	2.97	3.05	+42	+50	1.05	1.75	1.49	1.63	1.88	1.75	
May	2.66	2.99	3.10	+33	+44	1.05	1.85	1.65	1.63	1.88	2.00	
June	2.68	3.02	3.20	+34	+52	1.10	1.90	1.38	1.63	1.95	2.00	
July	2.68	3.10	3.35	+42	+67	1.15	2.00	1.54	1.63	1.98	2.00	
Aug.	2.67	2.98	3.20	+31	+53	1.05	1.90	1.66	1.63	1.88	2.00	
Sept.	2.56	2.92	3.01	+36	+45	1.00	1.80	1.65	1.63	1.88	2.00	
Oct.	2.66	2.98	3.14	+32	+48	1.00	1.80	1.60	1.63	1.83	2.00	
Nov.	2.66	3.10	3.23	+44	+57	1.00	1.85	1.60	1.63	1.83	2.00	
Dec.	2.70	3.16	3.30	+46	+60	1.00	2.00	1.69	1.63	1.83	2.25	
Avg.	2.60	2.96	3.09	+36	+49	1.00	1.80	1.53	1.60	1.84	1.91	

Monthly Yields and Yield Spreads (continued)

	1	2	3	4	5	6	7	8	9	10	11	12
		Aa Utility, Per Cent		Yield Spread (B.P.)		Prime Municipals, Per Cent		Short-Term Rates — 3-Month, Per Cent				
First of Month	Long U.S. Govts., Per Cent	Low Coupon	New Callable	2 vs. 1	3 vs. 1	1 Yr.	30 Yr.	U.S. Bills	Bankers' Acceptances	Fed. Agcs.	Finance Paper	CD's
1952												
Jan.	2.76	3.14	3.28	+38	+52	1.00	1.95	1.63	1.75	1.88	2.25	
Feb.	2.72	3.02	3.13	+30	+41	1.00	1.90	1.51	1.75	1.68	2.25	
Mar.	2.73	3.10	3.18	+37	+45	0.95	1.85	1.59	1.75	1.73	2.25	
Apr.	2.69	3.05	3.19	+36	+50	0.95	1.90	1.63	1.75	1.68	2.13	
May	2.58	3.07	3.15	+49	+57	0.90	1.85	1.68	1.75	1.70	2.13	
June	2.61	3.07	3.19	+46	+58	0.90	1.95	1.62	1.75	1.73	2.13	
July	2.63	3.08	3.21	+45	+58	0.95	2.00	1.84	1.75	1.95	2.13	
Aug.	2.66	3.09	3.21	+43	+55	1.05	2.00	1.75	1.75	2.13	2.13	
Sept.	2.66	3.06	3.20	+40	+54	1.05	2.10	1.75	1.75	2.10	2.13	
Oct.	2.77	3.09	3.19	+32	+42	1.05	2.20	1.80	1.75	1.93	2.13	
Nov.	2.70	3.09	3.17	+39	+47	1.05	2.25	1.86	1.75	1.93	2.13	
Dec.	2.72	3.03	3.13	+31	+41	1.05	2.25	2.09	1.75	2.18	2.13	
Avg.	2.69	3.07	3.19	+38	+50	1.00	2.00	1.73	1.75	1.89	2.16	
1953												
Jan.	2.77	3.12	3.19	+35	+42	1.05	2.25	2.02	1.75	2.20	2.13	
Feb.	2.79	3.20	3.26	+41	+47	1.05	2.25	1.94	1.88	2.03	2.25	
Mar.	2.87	3.25	3.40	+38	+53	1.10	2.40	2.03	1.88	2.18	2.38	
Apr.	2.91	3.28	3.45	+37	+54	1.20	2.50	2.25	1.88	2.23	2.38	
May	3.25	3.49	3.75	+24	+50	1.25	2.50	2.06	1.88	2.43	2.38	
June	3.32	3.52	3.78	+20	+46	1.35	2.60	2.18	1.88	2.58	2.50	
July	3.26	3.46	3.73	+20	+47	1.65	2.70	2.05	1.88	2.35	2.50	
Aug.	3.24	3.35	3.60	+11	+36	1.60	2.50	2.09	1.88	2.40	2.50	
Sept.	3.23	3.46	3.65	+23	+42	1.55	2.65	1.87	1.88	2.23	2.50	
Oct.	3.11	3.28	3.50	+17	+39	1.40	2.40	1.43	1.88	1.85	2.38	
Nov.	3.01	3.14	3.22	+13	+21	1.25	2.40	1.41	1.88	1.68	2.25	
Dec.	3.02	3.22	3.30	+20	+28	1.20	2.40	1.70	1.88	1.85	2.25	
Avg.	3.07	3.31	3.49	+24	+42	1.30	2.45	1.92	1.87	2.17	2.37	
1954												
Jan.	2.91	3.10	3.23	+19	+32	1.10	2.40	1.21	1.88	1.53	2.00	
Feb.	2.86	3.04	3.05	+18	+19	1.00	2.40	0.97	1.63	1.28	1.75	
Mar.	2.69	2.91	2.90	+22	+21	0.75	2.30	1.04	1.63	1.13	1.63	
Apr.	2.71	2.90	2.93	+19	+22	0.75	2.35	1.02	1.25	1.18	1.50	
May	2.68	2.96	3.00	+28	+32	0.75	2.40	0.79	1.25	1.10	1.38	
June	2.74	3.01	3.10	+27	+36	0.75	2.45	0.64	1.25	0.98	1.38	
July	2.65	2.99	3.00	+34	+35	0.70	2.25	0.75	1.25	0.80	1.25	
Aug.	2.59	2.97	3.00	+38	+41	0.60	2.15	0.90	1.25	0.88	1.25	
Sept.	2.61	2.99	3.05	+38	+44	0.60	2.15	1.02	1.25	1.05	1.25	
Oct.	2.64	2.97	3.03	+33	+39	0.60	2.25	1.00	1.25	1.08	1.25	
Nov.	2.66	2.96	3.00	+30	+34	0.65	2.25	0.90	1.25	1.05	1.25	
Dec.	2.66	2.96	3.02	+30	+36	0.70	2.25	1.24	1.25	1.25	1.25	
Avg.	2.70	2.98	3.03	+28	+33	0.75	2.30	0.96	1.37	1.11	1.43	

Monthly Yields and Yield Spreads (continued)

	1	2	3	4	5	6	7	8	9	10	11	12
								Short-Term Rates — 3-Month, Per Cent				
First of Month	Long U.S. Govts., Per Cent	Aa Utility, Per Cent		Yield Spread (B.P.)		Prime Munici- pals, Per Cent		U.S. Bills	Bank- ers' Ac- cept- ances	Fed. Agcs.	Fi- nance Paper	CD's
		Low Cou- pon	New Call- able	2 vs. 1	3 vs. 1	1 Yr.	30 Yr.					
1955												
Jan.	2.69	2.96	3.00	+27	+31	0.70	2.30	1.38	1.38	1.30	1.50	
Feb.	2.81	3.06	3.14	+25	+33	0.75	2.30	1.14	1.38	1.18	1.50	
Mar.	2.88	3.12	3.20	+24	+32	0.85	2.30	1.27	1.38	1.45	1.50	
Apr.	2.85	3.07	3.20	+22	+35	1.00	2.30	1.61	1.38	1.70	1.75	
May	2.85	3.10	3.20	+25	+35	1.05	2.30	1.41	1.50	1.62	1.88	
June	2.82	3.13	3.25	+31	+43	1.10	2.25	1.48	1.50	1.83	1.88	
July	2.88	3.14	3.20	+26	+32	1.25	2.35	1.57	1.50	1.92	1.88	
Aug.	2.98	3.18	3.25	+20	+27	1.35	2.50	1.84	1.63	2.14	2.00	
Sept.	2.97	3.23	3.40	+26	+43	1.35	2.50	2.03	2.13	2.32	2.25	
Oct.	2.94	3.18	3.30	+24	+36	1.40	2.40	2.30	2.25	2.64	2.50	
Nov.	2.88	3.14	3.22	+26	+34	1.50	2.40	2.32	2.13	2.45	2.50	
Dec.	2.91	3.19	3.32	+28	+41	1.60	2.50	2.55	2.50	2.85	2.88	
Avg.	2.87	3.13	3.22	+26	+35	1.15	2.35	1.74	1.72	1.95	2.00	
1956												
Jan.	2.93	3.16	3.25	+23	+32	1.60	2.40	2.46	2.50	2.73	2.88	
Feb.	2.87	3.12	3.20	+25	+33	1.50	2.30	2.37	2.38	2.59	2.88	
Mar.	2.90	3.12	3.15	+22	+25	1.45	2.35	2.37	2.38	2.77	2.88	
Apr.	3.03	3.22	3.45	+19	+42	1.60	2.50	2.75	2.50	3.08	3.00	
May	3.07	3.33	3.70	+26	+63	1.65	2.55	2.70	2.50	3.07	3.00	
June	2.94	3.29	3.57	+35	+63	1.65	2.40	2.48	2.50	3.07	3.00	
July	2.94	3.34	3.73	+40	+79	1.65	2.40	2.22	2.38	2.70	3.00	
Aug.	3.11	3.43	3.90	+32	+79	1.65	2.50	2.65	2.63	2.72	2.88	
Sept.	3.25	3.62	4.07	+37	+82	1.85	2.70	2.80	2.88	2.98	3.13	
Oct.	3.20	3.64	4.01	+44	+81	1.85	2.65	3.04	2.88	3.38	3.38	
Nov.	3.29	3.70	4.20	+41	+91	1.90	2.75	3.00	3.13	3.31	3.38	
Dec.	3.34	3.83	4.30	+49	+96	1.95	2.85	3.25	3.38	3.49	3.38	
Avg.	3.07	3.40	3.71	+33	+64	1.70	2.55	2.67	2.67	2.99	3.07	
1957												
Jan.	3.48	3.90	4.50	+42	+102	2.10	2.90	3.15	3.38	3.33	3.38	
Feb.	3.27	3.78	4.40	+51	+113	2.00	2.75	3.04	3.38	3.20	3.38	
Mar.	3.27	3.71	4.22	+44	+95	1.90	2.75	3.10	3.38	3.32	3.38	
Apr.	3.31	3.69	4.29	+38	+98	1.95	2.80	3.14	3.25	3.45	3.38	
May	3.43	3.80	4.35	+37	+92	1.95	3.00	2.98	3.25	3.20	3.38	
June	3.48	3.87	4.62	+39	+114	2.00	3.15	3.35	3.38	3.57	3.50	
July	3.58	4.15	4.85	+57	+127	2.15	3.15	3.08	3.38	3.42	3.63	
Aug.	3.65	4.31	5.00	+66	+135	2.25	3.25	3.44	4.00	3.62	3.63	
Sept.	3.64	4.33	4.81	+69	+117	2.35	3.25	3.59	3.88	3.77	3.88	
Oct.	3.63	4.24	4.78	+61	+115	2.45	3.20	3.65	3.75	4.21	3.88	
Nov.	3.66	4.23	4.97	+57	+131	2.45	3.20	3.15	3.38	3.71	3.88	
Dec.	3.36	4.04	4.47	+68	+111	2.25	2.90	3.10	3.25	3.39	3.50	
Avg.	3.48	4.00	4.61	+52	+113	2.15	3.05	3.23	3.47	3.52	3.57	

Monthly Yields and Yield Spreads (continued)

	1	2	3	4	5	6	7	8	9	10	11	12
		Aa Utility, Per Cent		Yield Spread (B.P.)		Prime Munici-pals, Per Cent		Short-Term Rates—3-Month, Per Cent				
First of Month	Long U.S. Govts., Per Cent	Low Cou-pon	New Call-able	2 vs. 1	3 vs. 1	1 Yr.	30 Yr.	U.S. Bills	Bank-ers' Ac-cept-ances	Fed. Agcs.	Fi-nance Paper	CD's
1958												
Jan.	3.20	3.59	3.94	+39	+74	2.10	2.75	2.60	3.13	2.57	3.38	
Feb.	3.29	3.55	3.70	+26	+41	1.45	2.65	1.73	2.38	1.77	2.13	
Mar.	3.27	3.62	4.00	+35	+73	1.25	2.90	1.33	1.88	1.47	1.88	
Apr.	3.31	3.67	4.00	+36	+69	0.80	2.90	1.14	1.63	1.12	1.63	
May	3.24	3.55	3.90	+31	+66	0.75	2.75	0.98	1.38	1.07	1.38	
June	3.21	3.56	3.85	+35	+64	0.65	2.80	0.89	1.13	1.03	1.38	
July	3.29	3.66	3.95	+37	+66	0.70	2.90	1.02	1.13	1.23	1.38	
Aug.	3.51	3.86	4.25	+35	+74	0.75	3.00	1.74	1.88	1.83	1.50	
Sept.	3.75	4.14	4.60	+39	+85	1.25	3.25	2.55	2.25	2.41	2.38	
Oct.	3.92	4.18	4.57	+26	+65	2.00	3.30	2.70	2.75	2.78	2.88	
Nov.	3.81	4.11	4.42	+30	+61	1.90	3.25	2.78	2.75	2.74	2.75	
Dec.	3.82	4.10	4.55	+28	+73	1.80	3.10	2.84	2.75	2.84	3.00	
Avg.	3.47	3.80	4.14	+33	+67	1.30	2.95	1.86	2.09	1.91	2.14	
1959												
Jan.	3.88	4.19	4.60	+31	+72	1.75	3.10	2.93	2.75	2.95	3.00	
Feb.	3.97	4.28	4.65	+31	+68	1.80	3.15	2.68	2.75	2.90	3.00	
Mar.	3.96	4.18	4.37	+22	+41	1.75	3.15	2.74	2.88	2.94	3.25	
Apr.	3.99	4.29	4.47	+30	+48	1.85	3.20	3.14	3.00	3.14	3.25	
May	4.07	4.49	4.59	+42	+52	2.15	3.25	2.75	3.13	3.21	3.38	
June	4.10	4.61	5.05	+51	+95	2.20	3.40	3.26	3.38	3.47	3.75	
July	4.14	4.60	4.95	+46	+81	2.30	3.50	3.40	3.50	3.62	3.75	
Aug.	4.10	4.57	4.85	+47	+75	2.35	3.35	3.28	3.50	3.42	3.75	
Sept.	4.23	4.63	5.00	+40	+77	2.40	3.40	4.25	4.13	4.37	4.50	
Oct.	4.17	4.76	5.25	+59	+108	2.70	3.55	4.25	4.25	4.65	4.75	
Nov.	4.11	4.59	5.15	+48	+104	2.65	3.40	4.35	4.25	4.67	4.25	
Dec.	4.20	4.53	5.15	+33	+95	2.70	3.45	4.50	4.50	4.90	4.88	
Avg.	4.08	4.48	4.84	+40	+76	2.20	3.35	3.46	3.50	3.69	3.79	
1960												
Jan.	4.42	4.66	5.25	+24	+83	2.85	3.65	4.52	4.88	4.82	5.00	
Feb.	4.34	4.63	4.95	+29	+61	2.75	3.55	3.70	4.38	4.09	4.00	
Mar.	4.31	4.52	5.10	+21	+79	2.45	3.55	3.47	3.88	3.83	3.88	
Apr.	4.10	4.42	4.85	+32	+75	2.40	3.45	3.55	4.00	3.60	3.88	
May	4.18	4.45	4.88	+27	+70	2.25	3.50	3.45	3.75	3.57	3.88	
June	4.08	4.53	4.90	+45	+82	2.20	3.40	2.27	3.13	2.79	3.00	
July	3.92	4.45	4.80	+53	+88	1.85	3.35	2.40	3.13	2.47	2.88	
Aug.	3.75	4.21	4.60	+46	+85	1.70	3.30	2.19	2.88	2.45	2.88	
Sept.	3.86	4.17	4.47	+31	+61	1.45	3.10	2.54	3.00	2.69	3.13	
Oct.	3.92	4.28	4.65	+36	+73	1.60	3.30	2.45	3.00	2.85	3.13	
Nov.	3.94	4.25	4.75	+31	+81	1.60	3.30	2.55	3.00	2.78	3.00	
Dec.	4.03	4.37	5.00	+34	+97	1.60	3.30	2.25	2.88	2.42	3.00	
Avg.	4.07	4.41	4.85	+34	+78	2.05	3.40	2.95	3.49	3.20	3.47	

Monthly Yields and Yield Spreads (continued)

	1	2	3	4	5	6	7	8	9	10	11	12
								Short-Term Rates—3-Month, Per Cent				
	Long	Aa Utility, Per Cent		Yield Spread (B.P.)		Prime Munici-pals, Per Cent			Bank-ers'		Fi-	
First of Month	U.S. Govts., Per Cent	Low Cou-pon	New Call-able	2 vs. 1	3 vs. 1	1 Yr.	30 Yr.	U.S. Bills	Ac-cept-ances	Fed. Agcs.	nance Paper	CD's
1961												
Jan.	3.89	4.32	4.60	+43	+71	1.55	3.30	2.28	2.88	2.35	2.75	
Feb.	3.95	4.26	4.32	+31	+37	1.45	3.35	2.44	2.75	2.59	2.63	
Mar.	3.83	4.13	4.32	+30	+49	1.50	3.30	2.37	3.00	2.59	2.75	
Apr.	3.86	4.21	4.52	+35	+66	1.50	3.40	2.30	2.88	2.26	2.63	
May	3.79	4.33	4.75	+54	+96	1.40	3.40	2.25	2.63	2.32	2.50	
June	3.76	4.32	4.75	+56	+99	1.45	3.40	2.38	2.75	2.45	2.75	
July	3.92	4.42	4.85	+50	+93	1.50	3.40	2.22	2.75	2.36	2.50	
Aug.	3.95	4.45	4.65	+50	+70	1.55	3.35	2.50	2.88	2.53	2.50	
Sept.	4.07	4.50	4.75	+43	+68	1.65	3.40	2.25	2.88	2.43	2.50	
Oct.	4.09	4.45	4.55	+36	+46	1.60	3.30	2.35	2.75	2.43	2.88	
Nov.	4.05	4.38	4.52	+33	+47	1.50	3.25	2.52	2.75	2.66	2.63	
Dec.	4.08	4.40	4.60	+32	+52	1.50	3.30	2.64	2.88	2.68	2.88	
Avg.	3.94	4.35	4.60	+41	+66	1.50	3.35	2.38	2.82	2.47	2.66	
1962												
Jan.	4.14	4.45	4.65	+31	+51	1.75	3.30	2.76	3.00	2.91	3.13	
Feb.	4.13	4.42	4.55	+29	+42	1.70	3.25	2.84	3.00	2.76	3.00	
Mar.	4.16	4.40	4.55	+24	+39	1.65	3.30	2.73	3.00	2.74	3.00	
Apr.	4.01	4.30	4.40	+29	+39	1.60	3.20	2.80	3.00	2.83	3.13	
May	3.97	4.20	4.29	+23	+32	1.55	3.15	2.68	2.88	2.75	2.88	2.94
June	3.97	4.25	4.29	+28	+32	1.55	3.25	2.72	2.88	2.76	3.00	2.99
July	4.03	4.30	4.39	+27	+36	1.60	3.25	2.98	3.13	3.06	3.25	3.19
Aug.	4.11	4.35	4.47	+24	+36	1.70	3.35	2.86	3.13	2.89	3.13	3.19
Sept.	4.09	4.25	4.30	+16	+21	1.65	3.25	2.78	3.00	2.84	3.13	3.09
Oct.	4.07	4.19	4.30	+12	+23	1.60	3.15	2.76	3.00	2.83	3.00	3.04
Nov.	4.02	4.15	4.26	+13	+24	1.50	3.10	2.85	3.00	2.81	3.13	3.04
Dec.	4.03	4.13	4.28	+10	+25	1.60	3.10	2.86	3.00	2.90	3.25	3.14
Avg.	4.06	4.28	4.39	+22	+33	1.60	3.20	2.80	3.00	2.84	3.09	
1963												
Jan.	3.97	4.15	4.28	+18	+31	1.60	3.10	2.92	3.00	2.94	3.13	3.19
Feb.	4.01	4.13	4.19	+12	+18	1.60	3.15	2.93	3.13	2.95	3.13	3.19
Mar.	4.01	4.14	4.27	+13	+26	1.60	3.15	2.88	3.13	2.98	3.13	3.16
Apr.	4.03	4.15	4.27	+12	+24	1.55	3.10	2.94	3.13	3.10	3.13	3.13
May	4.08	4.23	4.39	+15	+31	1.60	3.15	2.91	3.13	3.02	3.25	3.12
June	4.09	4.24	4.35	+15	+26	1.65	3.15	2.99	3.13	3.16	3.25	3.20
July	4.09	4.25	4.32	+16	+23	1.75	3.20	3.19	3.38	3.40	3.38	3.30
Aug.	4.07	4.25	4.35	+18	+28	1.90	3.20	3.38	3.63	3.53	3.50	3.50
Sept.	4.06	4.25	4.35	+19	+29	1.95	3.20	3.38	3.63	3.61	3.50	3.62
Oct.	4.17	4.30	4.38	+13	+21	2.00	3.25	3.49	3.63	3.55	3.75	3.75
Nov.	4.20	4.30	4.40	+10	+20	1.95	3.25	3.54	3.75	3.72	3.88	3.80
Dec.	4.19	4.31	4.43	+12	+24	2.00	3.30	3.53	3.63	3.68	3.88	3.80
Avg.	4.08	4.23	4.33	+15	+25	1.75	3.20	3.17	3.36	3.30	3.41	3.40

Monthly Yields and Yield Spreads (continued)

	1	2	3	4	5	6	7	8	9	10	11	12
		Aa Utility, Per Cent		Yield Spread (B.P.)		Prime Munici-pals, Per Cent		Short-Term Rates—3-Month, Per Cent				
First of Month	Long U.S. Govts., Per Cent	Low Cou-pon	New Call-able	2 vs. 1	3 vs. 1	1 Yr.	30 Yr.	U.S. Bills	Bank-ers' Ac-cept-ances	Fed. Agcs.	Fi-nance Paper	CD's
1964												
Jan.	4.21	4.38	4.50	+17	+29	2.05	3.25	3.54	3.63	3.65	3.88	3.88
Feb.	4.19	4.35	4.42	+16	+23	2.00	3.20	3.50	3.75	3.45	3.75	3.80
Mar.	4.24	4.32	4.39	+8	+15	2.00	3.20	3.59	3.75	3.68	3.88	3.80
Apr.	4.25	4.42	4.50	+17	+25	2.10	3.35	3.53	3.88	3.67	3.88	3.95
May	4.23	4.44	4.48	+21	+25	2.10	3.30	3.46	3.75	3.56	3.75	3.72
June	4.18	4.41	4.48	+23	+30	2.10	3.25	3.48	3.75	3.75	3.88	3.80
July	4.15	4.40	4.44	+25	+29	2.15	3.25	3.49	3.75	3.79	3.88	3.90
Aug.	4.21	4.37	4.42	+16	+21	2.15	3.25	3.47	3.75	3.70	3.75	3.85
Sept.	4.22	4.37	4.45	+15	+23	2.15	3.25	3.50	3.75	3.75	3.88	3.85
Oct.	4.22	4.39	4.47	+17	+25	2.20	3.30	3.56	3.75	3.72	3.88	3.88
Nov.	4.22	4.39	4.47	+17	+25	2.20	3.30	3.55	3.75	3.80	3.88	3.90
Dec.	4.22	4.42	4.50	+20	+28	2.20	3.25	3.81	3.88	4.21	3.88	4.15
Avg.	4.21	4.39	4.46	+18	+25	2.10	3.25	3.54	3.76	3.73	3.85	3.87
1965												
Jan.	4.24	4.38	4.45	+14	+21	2.25	3.20	3.83	4.00	4.03	4.13	4.17
Feb.	4.23	4.35	4.39	+12	+16	2.20	3.15	3.87	4.00	3.92	4.00	4.10
Mar.	4.24	4.37	4.47	+13	+23	2.25	3.25	4.00	4.13	4.11	4.25	4.25
Apr.	4.22	4.39	4.48	+17	+26	2.25	3.20	3.94	4.25	4.15	4.25	4.30
May	4.22	4.39	4.48	+17	+26	2.25	3.20	3.92	4.25	4.10	4.25	4.30
June	4.23	4.43	4.59	+20	+36	2.25	3.25	3.89	4.25	4.21	4.25	4.35
July	4.22	4.44	4.56	+22	+34	2.30	3.35	3.81	4.25	4.12	4.25	4.30
Aug.	4.23	4.46	4.60	+23	+37	2.30	3.35	3.80	4.13	4.07	4.25	4.28
Sept.	4.27	4.49	4.67	+22	+40	2.40	3.35	3.90	4.25	4.05	4.25	4.28
Oct.	4.33	4.55	4.70	+22	+37	2.50	3.40	4.05	4.25	4.27	4.25	4.42
Nov.	4.33	4.54	4.66	+21	+33	2.50	3.40	4.06	4.25	4.27	4.38	4.47
Dec.	4.40	4.68	4.80	+28	+40	2.60	3.50	4.12	4.25	4.39	4.38	4.50
Avg.	4.26	4.46	4.57	+20	+31	2.35	3.30	3.93	4.19	4.14	4.24	4.31
1966												
Jan.	4.48	4.83	4.90	+35	+42	2.90	3.60	4.47	4.75	4.79	4.75	4.90
Feb.	4.57	4.77	4.98	+20	+41	2.90	3.50	4.63	4.75	4.86	4.88	5.00
Mar.	4.76	4.91	5.30	+15	+54	3.15	3.75	4.64	4.88	4.95	4.88	5.00
Apr.	4.60	5.01	5.15	+41	+55	3.10	3.50	4.52	5.00	4.97	5.25	5.30
May	4.66	5.04	5.50	+38	+84	3.15	3.55	4.65	5.00	4.98	5.25	5.25
June	4.73	5.05	5.67	+32	+94	3.25	3.60	4.64	5.38	5.12	5.38	5.40
July	4.76	5.08	5.67	+32	+91	3.30	3.80	4.58	5.63	5.29	5.50	5.60
Aug.	4.80	5.20	5.77	+40	+97	3.70	3.80	4.76	5.75	5.25	5.63	5.65
Sept.	5.05	5.46	6.35	+41	+130	4.10	4.10	5.10	5.88	5.75	5.63	5.75
Oct.	4.76	5.49	6.05	+73	+129	3.90	3.90	5.34	5.88	5.58	5.75	5.85
Nov.	4.66	5.31	6.00	+65	+134	3.75	3.75	5.23	5.75	5.71	5.88	5.70
Dec.	4.80	5.35	6.20	+55	+140	3.65	3.85	5.17	5.75	5.44	5.88	5.75
Avg.	4.72	5.13	5.63	+41	+91	3.40	3.75	4.81	5.37	5.22	5.39	5.43

Monthly Yields and Yield Spreads (continued)

	1	2	3	4	5	6	7	8	9	10	11	12
		Aa Utility, Per Cent		Yield Spread (B.P.)		Prime Municipals, Per Cent		Short-Term Rates—3-Month, Per Cent				
First of Month	Long U.S. Govts., Per Cent	Low Coupon	New Callable	2 vs. 1	3 vs. 1	1 Yr.	30 Yr.	U.S. Bills	Bankers' Acceptances	Fed. Agcs.	Finance Paper	CD's
1967												
Jan.	4.53	5.22	5.85	+69	+132	3.50	3.65	4.81	5.63	5.07	5.88	5.70
Feb.	4.47	4.90	5.20	+43	+73	2.75	3.35	4.52	4.88	4.85	5.25	5.25
Mar.	4.65	5.05	5.70	+40	+105	2.90	3.70	4.52	5.13	4.72	5.13	5.25
Apr.	4.54	5.05	5.55	+51	+101	2.75	3.65	4.12	4.50	4.22	4.88	4.80
May	4.72	5.15	5.80	+43	+108	2.45	3.75	3.71	4.38	3.89	4.50	4.35
June	4.83	5.40	5.95	+57	+112	2.55	3.95	3.47	4.38	3.88	4.38	4.45
July	5.06	5.68	6.15	+62	+109	3.00	4.05	3.90	4.75	4.58	4.50	4.80
Aug.	5.04	5.70	6.15	+66	+111	3.15	3.90	4.20	4.63	4.55	4.75	5.00
Sept.	5.13	5.75	6.30	+62	+117	3.05	3.95	4.45	4.50	4.45	4.75	4.65
Oct.	5.16	5.75	6.30	+59	+114	3.15	4.15	4.39	4.88	4.70	4.75	4.88
Nov.	5.47	6.00	6.70	+53	+123	3.25	4.15	4.56	4.88	5.05	5.13	5.30
Dec.	5.64	6.27	6.90	+63	+126	3.55	4.30	4.96	5.13	5.20	5.25	5.50
Avg.	4.94	5.49	6.05	+55	+111	3.00	3.88	4.30	4.81	4.60	4.93	4.99
1968												
Jan.	5.54	6.25	6.80	+71	+126	3.55	4.30	5.09	5.63	5.30	5.50	5.65
Feb.	5.35	6.01	6.55	+66	+120	3.25	4.10	4.88	5.25	5.05	5.38	5.15
Mar.	5.40	6.06	6.60	+66	+120	3.35	4.30	5.03	5.38	5.13	5.25	5.35
Apr.	5.58	6.20	6.90	+62	+132	3.50	4.45	5.17	5.75	5.29	5.50	5.70
May	5.45	6.25	6.90	+80	+145	3.50	4.35	5.52	5.75	5.71	5.88	6.05
June	5.46	6.25	7.05	+79	+159	3.75	4.45	5.68	6.00	5.94	6.00	6.20
July	5.32	6.26	7.05	+94	+173	3.60	4.30	5.33	6.00	5.78	6.13	6.00
Aug.	5.15	6.00	6.65	+85	+150	3.05	4.10	5.15	5.75	5.59	5.88	5.90
Sept.	5.21	5.94	6.45	+73	+124	3.00	4.40	5.20	5.63	5.59	5.63	5.80
Oct.	5.29	6.03	6.60	+74	+131	2.90	4.35	5.16	5.63	5.41	5.63	5.60
Nov.	5.42	6.15	6.85	+73	+143	3.00	4.60	5.49	5.88	5.79	5.75	5.95
Dec.	5.64	6.34	7.05	+70	+141	3.15	4.65	5.52	6.00	5.88	5.88	6.10
Avg.	5.40	6.15	6.79	+74	+139	3.30	4.36	5.27	5.72	5.54	5.70	5.79
1969												
Jan.	6.05	6.70	7.20	+65	+115	3.70	4.90	6.25	6.50	6.56	6.38	6.65
Feb.	6.15	6.54	7.30	+39	+115	4.00	4.95	6.20	6.38	6.41	6.25	6.45
Mar.	6.16	6.69	7.40	+53	+124	4.00	5.10	6.20	6.63	6.44	6.38	6.65
Apr.	6.18	7.06	7.60	+88	+142	4.20	5.40	6.02	6.63	6.09	6.50	6.65
May	5.92	6.71	7.50	+79	+158	4.00	5.15	5.86	7.00	6.39	6.50	7.00
June	6.33	6.97	8.00	+64	+167	4.50	5.80	6.10	7.50	6.99	7.00	7.55
July	6.18	7.04	7.95	+86	+177	5.00	5.70	6.15	8.50	7.40	8.00	8.25
Aug.	6.19	7.09	8.05	+90	+186	5.00	5.80	7.07	8.13	7.76	8.25	8.50
Sept.												
Oct.												
Nov.												
Dec.												
Avg.												

Monthly Yields and Yield Spreads (continued)

	1	2	3	4	5	6	7	8	9	10	11	12
		Aa Utility, Per Cent		Yield Spread (B.P.)		Prime Munici-pals, Per Cent		Short-Term Rates — 3-Month, Per Cent				
First of Month	Long U.S. Govts., Per Cent	Low Cou-pon	New Call-able	2 vs. 1	3 vs. 1	1 Yr.	30 Yr.	U.S. Bills	Bank-ers' Ac-cept-ances	Fed. Agcs.	Fi-nance Paper	CD's
1970												
Jan.												
Feb.												
Mar.												
Apr.												
May												
June												
July												
Aug.												
Sept.												
Oct.												
Nov.												
Dec.												
Avg.												

Sources: These monthly yield and spread series are among those compiled and published by Salomon Brothers & Hutzler in a booklet entitled *An Analytical Record of Yields and Yield Spreads,* in which the nature of each series is discussed in detail. Briefly, (1) "Long U. S. Governments" is the yield of one representative long issue. The 30-year Treasury yields used in the yield curve tables in Chapter XI are a little different since they are derived from plotted curves. (2) Seasoned Aa utilities with low coupons; and (3) new-issue callable Aa utilities, are 2 of 12 series of long Aa utility-bond-yield averages according to coupon or issue status compiled by Salomon Brothers & Hutzler. (6) and (7) are from prime municipal scales compiled by Salomon Brothers & Hutzler weekly; (8), (9), (10), (11) and (12) are standard market quotations on short-term credit instruments as of mid-month through 1963; first of the month thereafter.

Changes in Discount Rates and Prime Rates

Rate in Effect	Discount Rate *	Prime Bank Rate	Rate in Effect	Discount Rate *	Prime Bank Rate
Jan. 1, 1945	½ & 1 †	1½	Nov. 7, 1958	2½	
Apr. 25, 1946	1		Mar. 6, 1959	3	
Dec. 1947		1¾	May 18, 1959		4½
Jan. 12, 1948	1¼		May 29, 1959	3½	
Aug. 1948		2	Sept. 1, 1959		5
Aug. 13, 1948	1½		Sept. 11, 1959	4	
Aug. 21, 1950	1¾		June 10, 1960	3½	
Sept. 1950		2¼	Aug. 12, 1960	3	
Jan. 1951		2½	Aug. 23, 1960		4½
Oct. 1951		2¾	July 16, 1963	3½	
Dec. 1951		3	Nov. 23, 1964	4	
Jan. 16, 1953	2		Dec. 6, 1965	4½	5
Apr. 27, 1953		3¼	Mar. 10, 1966		5½
Feb. 5, 1954	1¾		June 30, 1966		5¾
Mar. 18, 1954		3	Aug. 16, 1966		6
Apr. 16, 1954	1½		Jan. 26, 1967		5½–6
Apr. 15, 1955	1¾		Jan. 27, 1967		5½–¾
Aug. 3, 1955		3¼	Mar. 28, 1967		5½
Aug. 5, 1955	2		Apr. 7, 1967	4	
Sept. 9, 1955	2¼		Nov. 20, 1967	4½	5½–6
Oct. 14, 1955		3½	Nov. 21, 1967		6
Nov. 18, 1955	2½		Mar. 22, 1968	5	
Apr. 13, 1956	2¾	3¾	Apr. 19, 1968	5½	
Aug. 20, 1956		4	Apr. 22, 1968		6½
Aug. 24, 1956	3		Aug. 30, 1968	5¼	
Aug. 6, 1957		4½	Sept. 25, 1968		6–6½
Aug. 23, 1957	3½		Sept. 26, 1968		6–6¼
Nov. 15, 1957	3		Nov. 12, 1968		6¼
Jan. 22, 1958		4	Dec. 2, 1968		6½
Jan. 24, 1958	2¾		Dec. 18, 1968	5½	6¾
Mar. 7, 1958	2¼		Jan. 7, 1969		7
Apr. 18, 1958	1¾		Mar. 17, 1969		7½
Apr. 22, 1958		3½	Apr. 4, 1969	6	
Sept. 12, 1958	2	4	June 9, 1969		8½

* New York Federal Reserve Bank.
† ½% on Government securities due or callable within one year, 1% on eligible paper.